)RTURE
The Grand Conspiracy

Malise Ruthven

TORTURE
The Grand Conspiracy

WEIDENFELD AND NICOLSON LONDON

FOR DEREK AND PAMELA COOPER

Contents

Acknowledgments

I am especially grateful to Professor William Twining of Warwick University for his encouragement and guidance and for drawing my attention to errors and omissions in the drafts of the early chapters before it was too late to put them right. Needless to say, he is in no way responsible for any which remain. I wish to thank Dr J. L. Sturgis of Birkbeck College, London, for looking through Chapter 8. He too must be exonerated from any errors of fact or interpretation.

I would also like to thank two good friends, Roy Foster and Colin Thubron who have taken more than a polite interest in my efforts and patiently read through many pages of manuscript offering useful suggestions and encouragement.

I am grateful to Oxford University Press for permission to reproduce passages from E.E. Evans-Pritchard's *Witchcraft, Oracles and Magic among the Azande*; to Macmillan for Merle Fainsod's *Smolensk under Soviet Rule* and Robert Conquest's *The Great Terror*; and to Stanford University Press for H. C. Erik Midelfort's *Witch hunting in South Western Germany 1562–1684*.

Above all, I wish to express my gratitude to those members of my family who supported me morally and materially during the gestation of this book; and especially to my wife Tiggy, for whom the many months of delay and uncertainty were a kind of torture.

London
July 1977   *Malise Ruthven*

PART 1

Torture according to law

ONE

The abolitionists

In the small hours of a summer morning in 1630, when the plague was raging through Milan, a woman looked out from her window near the Porta Ticinese and saw a man dressed in cloak and hat apparently writing something on the wall of a nearby house. At once she became suspicious. A rumour had been circulating that a secret society of evil men was deliberately spreading the plague by smearing an infectious unguent on the walls of people's houses.

She was not the only person to see the stranger that morning, and to jump to the same conclusion. One of her neighbours watched as he turned the corner and casually greeted a passer-by. The latter turned out to be an acquaintance. The two neighbours conferred and asked the passer-by the name of the man they had seen him greet. He could not recall his name, but thought he was one of the commissioners of the *Sanità*, the state security department. Others joined in the conversation, and rumour soon gelled to certainty. The stranger must be one of the notorious *untori*, the secret society of daubers who were deliberately infecting the population with their devilish unguents. People began to inspect the walls of their houses and, sure enough, to discern suspicious smears among the centuries of grime. As panic spread they started piling loose straw against the walls and firing it to burn the poison away. Soon the smoke, and the general commotion, reached the offices of the chief of police.

The inquiries, gossip and rumour all pointed to one man, Guglielmo Piazza, commissioner of the *Sanità* and the son-in-law of a well-known local midwife. Within twenty-four hours he had been arrested oblivious, apparently, of the danger threatening him, for he was picked up outside the house of his chief, the president of the *Sanità*. Rigorous interrogation and a thorough search of his house yielded nothing suspicious. But the mob, already convinced of his guilt, was clamouring. The examining magistrates found two of his answers 'implausible' and this entitled them, according to the laws of the city, to have him put to the question.

Piazza was given the treatment known as the 'rope' or *strappado*, the traditional method of torture under rules framed by the inquisition and adopted by the secular law. His hands were tied behind his back and the rope attached to a pulley or beam which hoisted him into the air, painfully wrenching his arms and dislocating his shoulders. He persisted in denying any knowledge of the alleged smearings to the point where he became totally incoherent. The examining magistrates, seeing he was past giving any further answers, ordered him to be let down and returned to his cell. A report of the interrogation was sent to the senate, which decreed that Piazza be 'shaved, given a purgative, dressed in clothes provided by the court and then tortured again'. This time the rope was tied in such a way as to dislocate his hands as well as his arms, a very painful addition. The results were equally barren.

Still the authorities were not satisfied. In accordance with the rule that a prisoner should not be informed of the charges against him until after the torture (a precaution against false confessions), Piazza was still in bewildered ignorance. But from the following day's proceedings it appears that one of the magistrates privately took steps to remedy this deficiency. Having obtained from the governor a promise of immunity for Piazza should the latter reveal the names of his accomplices, he made the offer in private, with no clerk to record the details. It is reasonable to suppose that he also informed him of the charges, and suggested the outline of his 'confession'.

A simple episode from Piazza's life, plus a few sinister details, provided the authorities with the plot they were seeking. A few days before his arrest, Piazza had visited a barber named Mora who, like most of his competitors, claimed to have invented a uniquely potent remedy against the plague. Mora had been out of stock when Piazza called, but promised to have the medicine within a few days. It so happened that Mora contacted his customer just as he was being interviewed prior to his arrest, so the authorities were aware of the connection between the two men. Few extra details were required to convert this innocuous transaction into a plot to destroy the state, as revealed by Piazza during his next examination. The ointment became the deadly yellow paste which Piazza, in return for a substantial sum of money, had undertaken to spread about the city. (The fact that there was no circumstantial evidence that Piazza had actually received the deadly substance was, like so many other details in this case, conveniently forgotten.)

Next day the examining magistrates arrived with a posse of gendarmes at the barber Mora's shop, where they found their second culprit innocently ensconced with his son. After turning the place upside down and examining the contents of every jar, they found two things to 'arouse their suspicion': a brass cooking-pot containing a 'sticky yellowish-white substance' and two jars filled with human excrement. The barber insisted that both had innocent explanations. The sticky white substance was the residue of some lye left by his wife after her last laundry-day (this was corroborated by the woman herself). The jars were full of excrement because, for reasons of hygiene during the plague, he had avoided sharing the upstairs privy with his family. Unfortunately for Mora, forensic examination by two doctors and three washerwomen failed to confirm that the 'sticky yellow-white substance' was lye; while his explanation about the excrement, unchallenged at first, was to prove equally damaging in the end. However, it was a third suspicious circumstance that gave the magistrates their initial pretext for torturing Mora. During the search of his shop the auditor (one of the magistrates) found a scrap of paper which he handed to the barber, demanding an explanation. Mora, assuming it was the recipe of his precious remedy and afraid of losing his secret, snatched it from the auditor's hand and tore it to bits. The judges interpreted this gesture as demonstrating that Mora really did have something to hide.

Before he was put to the question a confrontation was arranged between Mora and Piazza who, in order to gain his immunity, persisted in his accusation. He had already been tortured twice to 'prove the truth' of his confession, and the judges, sensing further 'implausibilities' in his replies (the official pretext for torture), threatened to withdraw their offer of immunity. This induced Piazza to name two 'witnesses' to his transaction with Mora. The latter, duly tortured, corroborated this. Under torture, Mora proved much less robust than Piazza. He instantly confessed to all the accusations implied by the gist of the judges' questions. He admitted to manufacturing the deadly concoction that had caused the plague. It was made from lye, mixed with human excrement and – for good measure, just to give a further touch of plausibility – with the saliva taken from fresh corpses supplied by the commissioner. The motive for this monstrous crime was nothing more than puny financial gain: as the plague spread through the city, increasing its toll of human life, more and more would buy the barber's patent remedy. He and the commissioner would amass a fortune out of the sufferings of their fellow-citizens. Mora and Piazza were both put on trial, the latter's immunity being withdrawn on the grounds that there were still some inconsistencies in his statements. Both were found guilty and sentenced to the severest penalty known to law.

However, the matter did not end there. A few days before he was due to be executed, either out of spite or perhaps in the hope of securing a postponement, Piazza announced that he had some important new disclosures to make and requested a private audience with the auditor. The principal party in the plot, he revealed, was none other than the son of the Spanish governor of Milan Castle, Don Juan Padilla. Rather than let the matter lie there (which would have saved a great deal of trouble) the auditor took Piazza's deposition and presented it to the governor (whose reactions are not recorded). Piazza's new confession was then ratified, and another confrontation arranged between him and Mora. This proved to be a relatively simple affair. Piazza was merely asked, in Mora's presence, if it were true that the governor's son had been behind the plot. The unfortunate barber's expressions of incredulity were taken as evidence of deceit, and he was once more put to the torture (this time 'without prejudice' to whatever had been confessed, so there would be no danger of any new bricks causing the whole slender edifice of fabrication to collapse). Mora duly confessed, adding a few more names to the list of accomplices, including that of a prominent banker and another, fictitious, Spanish officer. Piazza's confirmatory deposition also named a banker, but a different one from Mora's – which was awkward. But rather than go through the tedious ritual of a further confrontation between the two men, the judges arrested both bankers, together with various subordinates and associates, and had the whole lot of them tortured.

The new investigations, however, did not postpone the sentences already passed on Piazza and Mora. Before the preliminaries of the Padilla case had been completed, both of them suffered a horrible death, even by the gruesome standards of those times. In accordance with the sentences passed upon them, they were taken in a cart to the place of execution, being torn with red-hot pincers on the way. In front of Mora's shop their right hands were cut off, and their bodies broken on the wheel. While still alive, they were then twisted into the wheel and lifted off the ground. After six hours – just in case a thread of life survived – their throats were cut, their corpses burned and the ashes scattered in the river. Mora's house was then demolished (his family now rendered homeless as well as destitute, for all his goods had been confiscated) and a monument erected on the spot, it being decreed that no one should ever build upon the site again. The 'Column of Infamy' remained an object of curiosity to travellers until its demolition in the nineteenth century.[1]

*   *   *

The evils of torture depicted in this story of the Milanese *untori* had parallels in almost every other country where torture was part of the legal procedure – and until the beginning of the nineteenth century that included the majority of European states; all of those, in fact, with legal systems deriving from the Roman law. (Only England and Sweden forbade the use of torture under their domestic laws.) But it was no more than one of the thousands of historical examples which might have been used to demonstrate how torture could become the basis of a nexus of false accusations in which perfectly innocent people were forced into denouncing themselves and others for crimes which had never been committed and which were indeed impossible. The story of the *untori* played a part in the campaign for the abolition of torture and other legal reforms. It forms part of a fierce polemic against torture written by Pietro Verri, a Milanese aristocrat and intellectual, at the time when the city's senate was debating the abolition of torture. Verri, with his brother Alessandro, was the leader of a group of radical reformers, admirers of Montesquieu and the French encyclopaedists. They had a powerful ally in Baron Sonnenfels, professor of law at Vienna and councillor to the Empress Maria Theresa. Sonnenfels and the empress were personally in favour of abolishing torture, although it was prescribed in exacting detail in dozens of provisions of the official code of the Habsburg empire, the *Theresiana*, published in 1764. Against the personal wishes of the monarch, how-

ever, stood the dead weight of the Roman law and the jealous conservatism of the local authorities who resented any interference with
their privileges and their right to administer the law in accordance
with time-honoured tradition. Verri's father was a member of the
senate, and it seems to have been out of deference to his father's views
that he decided not to publish this discreditable account from the
city's past. It was published eventually after Verri's death in 1803.

There were other outlets, however, for Verri and his radical friends.
Together with his brother Alessandro, he founded *Il Caffè*, a literary-
political journal modelled on the English *Spectator*. *Il Caffè* had considerable influence on the higher councils of state – in Vienna. At
home it was liable to cause offence, and the editors decided to publish
in Brescia, outside the jurisdiction of the Milanese city fathers. One
of the contributors to the magazine was a young marquis, Verri's
friend and protégé, Cesare Beccaria. He was, by most accounts, a lan-
guid and melancholy youth, given to fits of depression. Although he
had a brilliant mathematical mind he was far from being industrious,
unlike Verri and his brother, both of whom were engaged in writing
weighty historical and economic treatises. Verri evidently found Beccaria's lassitude irritating, and it was to keep him occupied that he
originally suggested that Beccaria should write a treatise on the criminal law. Alessandro, who was a prison governor, would provide him
with up-to-date information. For the rest, Verri would act as his
amanuensis or 'supervisor'; and, as the ideas and perceptions began
to appear rather fitfully from Beccaria's pen, Verri would gather them
up and impose some order on them. Within a year (in 1763) the work,
in its brevity, was finished and ready for publication. It was entitled
simply *Dei delitti e delle pene* – 'On crimes and punishments'. Its author
was only twenty-five; it must have been rather galling for Pietro Verri
when it turned out to be the most famous and influential treatise on
criminal law ever written. And it contains what is still after more
than two centuries the classic denunciation of torture.

Beccaria's book instantly became a bestseller. It was translated
into many languages. Voltaire wrote the commentary for the first
French and English editions. The author was publicly fêted in Paris.
In Russia the Empress Catherine read it and tried, unsuccessfully,
to incorporate its wisdom into the criminal code – and invited the
author to Moscow. Beccaria was asked to advise on the framing of
a new penal code for Tuscany. And in England the greatest of all

legal reformers, Jeremy Bentham, acknowledged his debt to Beccaria in extravagant terms: 'O my master, first evangelist of Reason, you who have raised your Italy so far above England ... You who have made so many useful excursions into the path of utility, what is there left for us to do? – Never to turn aside from that path'.[2] Few books as short, by so young an author, have ever had such a powerful impact.[3]

Bentham's words are well chosen. Beccaria's tract has all the pure fervour of the evangelist who has nothing to say for a past corrupt beyond redemption, whose demand is for a society of the future to be universally governed according to a few elementary principles.

What punishment is best suited to a given crime? Is death a punishment which is really *useful* and *necessary* for the security and good order of society? Are torture and instruments of torture *just*, and do they attain the *ends* propounded by law? Are the same penalties always equally useful? What influence do they have on social custom? These are the problems that ought to be solved with a precision so geometric that it cannot be overcome by mists of sophistry, seductive eloquence, or timidity and doubt.[4]

Beccaria's penchant for 'geometric' precision sometimes led him to formulate some rather curious theorems, such as 'the likelihood of crimes is in inverse ratio to their atrocity',[5] while some of his interpretations of utility seem perverse – at least in the light of contemporary experience. For instance, he attacks on grounds of 'false utility' laws forbidding the carrying of weapons 'because they disarm only those who are neither inclined to crimes nor determined upon them'.[6] But in other respects many of his ideas have a distinctly modern sound. His attack on capital punishment is cogent, and far from sentimental. (He argues that a life-sentence of hard labour is preferable to the death penalty because the prolongation of the prisoner's suffering serves as a reminder to other would-be criminals long after his execution would have been forgotten.) Like many modern criminologists he argues that certainty of detection is a better deterrent than a heavy sentence, and that those convicted of robbery should be made to pay compensation to their victims. He pioneered the idea that criminals have a 'debt' to society, and that punishments should be fixed strictly in proportion to the seriousness of the crime. Many of the changes he proposed are now law in civilized countries, the most important being 'the certainty of the law, the respect for the principle *nulla poena sine lege*, the adoption of clear and simple rules of procedure' and 'the very notion of punishment as a measure of safety and prevention, not expiation and revenge'.[7]

Beccaria's attack on torture, then, deserves special examination, because it embodies most of the arguments implied in the ban on torture imposed by nearly every modern state and international convention. If there are flaws in his arguments (as Jeremy Bentham believed), then these flaws will, perhaps, account for the failure of the abolitionists to eradicate torture permanently through legislation. For, as Beccaria would have been the first to admit, legislation can only succeed which takes full account of rational principles.

Beccaria discerns five reasons or motives behind judicial torture:

> The torture of an accused man while the case against him is being prepared is a cruelty consecrated by long usage among the majority of nations, its purpose being to make him confess to the crime, or clarify his contradictory statements, or discover his accomplices, or purge him in some metaphysical and incomprehensible way of infamy, or finally bring to light other crimes which he may have committed but of which he is not accused.[8]

None of these reasons, he argues, stands up to rational analysis. First, there is no juridical reason why an accused man should be required to confess. Either his guilt is certain, or it is not. If certain, he should be punished according to law, and it is unjust to inflict torture, a form of punishment, on him. No purpose is served by extracting a confession which adds nothing to the prosecution evidence. According to Beccaria, the effect of this need for a confession by the accused, a requirement of the law in cases of serious crime, is merely to confuse guilt with innocence;[9] it is simply 'a matter of temperament and of calculation' which varies with each man according to his physical strength and response to pain. It is a problem better solved by a mathematician than a judge: 'Given the strength of muscles and the sensibility of nerves of an innocent man, find the amount of pain required to make him confess that he has committed a given crime.'[10] The injustice is such that the innocent necessarily suffer *more* than the guilty:

> Both are tortured, but the former has every chance stacked against him: if he confesses to the crime, he is condemned; if he is declared innocent, he has suffered an undeserved punishment. But the guilty man's situation is in his favour. If he stands up firmly to torture, he is acquitted as if he were

innocent, and he will have undergone a lesser punishment instead of a greater one. So the innocent man always loses by torture, while the guilty man stands to gain.[11]

The other arguments for torture are despatched more briefly. The idea that torture clarifies contradictory statements (for instance the 'implausibilities' noted in connection with the examinations of Piazza and Mora) is quite unreasonable. There are always contradictions when people give evidence: '... as if the fear of punishment, the uncertainty of the verdict, the pomp and majesty of the judge, and the ignorant state of guilty and innocent alike, were not enough to make it probable that the innocent as well as the guilty would fall into contradiction ... '[12] Another reason – to discover if a man is guilty of further crimes – barely merits argument; while the notion that torture will compel a man to reveal his accomplices is demonstrably false, since 'torture is a bad method of discovering the truth',[13] and a man cannot therefore be expected honestly to reveal their names. The final reason, that torture purges a man 'in some metaphysical and incomprehensible way' of infamy is manifestly contradictory: for what is torture itself but the worst kind of infamy? How can one infamy purge another?[14]

For Beccaria, torture is not only cruel, but irrational. The cruelty, he believes, is the result of its barbarian origins:

This infamous crucible of truth is an enduring monument of that ancient and barbarous system of law which held that ordeal by fire and boiling water, and the uncertain outcome of trial by combat were the 'judgements of God' ... the only difference [being] ... that the issue of the one seems to depend upon the will of the accused, and of the other on a purely physical and irrelevant fact: but this difference is apparent, not real ... .[15]

while the 'irrational' requirement that the accused must confess in cases of capital crime even where there is enough evidence to convict him, is the result of

... the religious and spiritual motives which exert so much influence on human thought in all countries and in all ages ... an infallible dogma assures us that the blemishes due to human frailty, which have not deserved the everlasting wrath of the Supreme Being, must be purged by an incomprehensible fire ... I believe that the confession of an accused man, which some courts insist upon as necessary to condemnation, originated in a not dissimilar way,

seeing that in the mysterious tribunal of penance a necessary part of the sacrament is the confession of those who have sinned.[16]

The anti-religious sentiment was enough to get Beccaria's book placed
on the papal index – which helps to account, no doubt, for its success
in France.

Like many bestsellers, Beccaria's book succeeded less on account
of the originality or force of his arguments, than because they conformed to the expectations of an influential body of public opinion.
The ground had been well prepared – not only by the work of the
French encyclopaedists and *philosophes*, but by the social organisms
such as the salons and masonic lodges that flourished all over Europe
during the eighteenth century, which enabled the upper ranks of
society to receive those ideas. Beccaria was not a lone prophet crying
in the wilderness. Many eighteenth-century writers considered it self-
evident that torture was a horrible relic of barbarism, compounded
of tyranny and superstition, and with the progress of reason and enlightenment destined to disappear from the face of the earth. The great
Montesquieu, for example, had evidently considered the subject beneath consideration:

> The wickedness of mankind makes it necessary for the law to suppose them
> better than they really are. Hence the deposition of two witnesses is sufficient
> in the punishment of all crimes. The law believes them, as if they spoke by
> the mouth of truth. Thus we judge that every child conceived in wedlock
> is legitimate; the law having confidence in the mother as if she were chastity
> itself. But the use of the rack against criminals cannot be defended on a like
> plea of necessity . . . So many men of learning and genius have written against
> the custom of torturing criminals, that after them I dare not presume to
> meddle with the subject. I was going to say that it might be suitable for
> despotic states, where whatever inspires fear is the fittest motor of government.
> I was going to say that among the Greeks and Romans, slaves . . . – but I
> hear the voice of nature crying out and asserting her rights.[17]

It was Voltaire who pointed out that torture was, among other
things, the consequence of the irrational system of 'legal proofs' that
Montesquieu found necessary in view of the 'wickedness of mankind'.

> It is in vain [says Mr Ramsay in the *History of Elizabeth Canning*] that
> the law requires two witnesses against an accused. If the Chancellor and the
> Archbishop of Canterbury both testify that they saw me murder my father
> and mother and then proceed to eat them for supper in a quarter of an hour,

the Chancellor and the Archbishop should be locked up in Bedlam rather
than that I should be burnt on their testimony![18]

The *question préparatoire* by which it was necessary for an accused person charged with a capital crime to confess before he could be condemned was a similar absurdity.

All mankind, being exposed to the attempts of violence or perfidy, detest
the crimes of which they may possibly be the victims: all desire that the principal offender and his accomplices may be punished; nevertheless, there is
a natural compassion in the human heart, which makes all men detest the
cruelty of torturing the accused in order to extort confession. The law has
not condemned them, and yet, though uncertain of their crime, you inflict
a punishment more horrible than that which they are to suffer when their
guilt is confirmed. 'Possibly thou mayst be innocent; but I will torture thee
that I may be satisfied: not that I intend to make thee any recompense for
the thousand deaths which I have made thee suffer, in lieu of that which
is preparing for thee'.[19]

Voltaire's campaign against torture achieved concrete results. As
early as 1740 his friend Frederick the Great had abolished ordinary
torture in Prussia, and himself wrote a dissertation against a 'custom
shameful to Christians and civilized peoples and, I dare say, as cruel
as it is useless'.[20] In France, Voltaire's polemics on the Calas case
helped to bring about the retrial and posthumous pardon of an elderly
Protestant from Toulouse who had been burnt, on a forced confession,
for murdering his son who wished to become a Catholic. And following the triumph of rational principles in 1789, the last traces of torture
were removed from the statute books not only in France, but throughout Europe.

So what Beccaria had to say in 1763 was already well on the way
to becoming the 'conventional wisdom' of the leaders of eighteenth-
century society. What distinguished his essay was the sustained
passion of its polemical vigour and the systematic way he attacked,
in so short a space, the ancient citadel of the Roman law. As he informed his friend and translator, the Abbé Morelet, 'I must confess
that while writing, the examples of Machiavelli, Galileo, Giannone
were there before my eyes. I heard the noise of chains being rattled
by superstition and fanaticism, stifling the fragile tremblings of
truth'.[21]

It was the young Italian's sensibility, not his arguments (of which most thinking people were already convinced) that conquered Europe. As W.E.H.Lecky was to write during the following century:

> The movement that destroyed torture represented much less a discovery of reason than an increased intensity of sympathy. If we asked what positive arguments could be adduced on the subject, it would be difficult to cite any that was not perfectly familiar to all classes at every period of the Middle Ages. That brave criminals sometimes escaped, and that timid persons sometimes falsely declared themselves guilty, that the guiltless frequently underwent a horrible punishment and that the moral influence of legal decisions was sometimes seriously weakened.[22]

In fact, as we shall see, the arguments against torture, or its too ready application, were almost as old as the institution itself. The fact that neither Verri nor Beccaria took account of them cannot be put down to mere lack of erudition. The omission appears to have been deliberate – and in Verri's case amounted to a serious misrepresentation of the efforts of the writers on law to limit the use of torture and circumscribe the conditions of its application. For Verri held that it was the doctors of law themselves who were primarily responsible for the survival of the system:

> Ignorant and brutal men, indifferent to those questions of principle without a firm grasp of which it is impossible to frame a system of laws in harmony with Nature and Reason and conducive to the good of society; men who never thought of asking themselves whence comes the right to punish crime, or what is the purpose of punishment, or whether a man may ever be forced to surrender his right to self-defence. Men of no standing in society, mere private individuals, they took on themselves to elaborate with ignoble subtlety a system for inflicting the maximum pain on their fellow-men, and then solemnly to publish their conclusions with all the impassivity of physicians recommending remedies for a disease. And such men were set up as authorities, nay legislators. And the books in which they give careful instructions as to how to dislocate living bodies and how precisely to prolong its agonies and add pain to pain, these inhuman writings found a welcome in all legal libraries and were seriously and calmly studied.

If, said Verri, attacking jurists for writing in Latin with a view to hiding 'their hideous prescriptions', they had

> expressed their inhuman principles in plain language, and their careful descriptions of nicely calculated torments in a style less insufferably barbarous to any sensitive and civilized reader, [they] could hardly have escaped that

abhorrence and contempt with which we regard the tortures themselves. What is horrible [he concluded] is not merely the suffering caused by torture ... but also the teaching of the jurists on the circumstances attending its application.[23]

Though there was an element of truth in the accusation, the spirit was manifestly unfair. The doctors of law were not, for the most part, legislators. The 'inhuman writings' most certainly existed, but these were the work of jurists commissioned by the secular rulers to codify existing rules into laws. No doubt Verri had in mind the authors of the *Theresiana*, the huge encodification of the laws of the Habsburg empire which was published in 1769, and which contained the most minute and detailed prescriptions of torture ever written. But even the *Theresiana*, hideous though it seemed to an enlightened sensibility, represented an advance on what had gone before. It had been found necessary to establish strict procedural rules governing the application of torture because the dangers of arbitrary use had come to be universally recognized. In fact, the very publication of the *Theresiana* so offended public opinion in Vienna that the sections on torture had to be withdrawn from circulation; and the ensuing scandal gave an immeasurable boost to the movement for abolition which triumphed in the Austrian empire in 1780.[24]

In mounting their attack on torture both Verri and Beccaria failed to observe the distinction between its use and its abuse. The point, no doubt, would have struck them as an academic one. However strictly controlled, however minute the regulations governing its application, torture was an affront to their most cherished notions of civilization. But there was a lack of candour in their failure to examine the qualifications and arguments of the legal writers which, in retrospect, fatally weakened their case. The jurists had not for the most part been 'ignorant and brutal' men, but, in the context of the time, learned and humane men who had themselves attacked the ignorance and brutality of the administrators of the law. Above all, the rules they laid down governing the application of torture were, within certain limitations, perfectly rational. The whole of Beccaria's and Verri's argument depended on the assumption that torture was irrational as well as cruel. In consequence it did not occur to them that there might be contingencies when torture might be defended on rational grounds, according to the principle of utility.

Two writers at least were aware of the weaknesses in the abolitionist case. One was the Italian novelist, Alessandro Manzoni, author of *I Promessi Sposi* and, incidentally, the grandson of Beccaria. In his research for his famous historical novel, which was set in Milan, Manzoni came across the transcripts of the trial of the *untori* and this, in turn, led him to re-examine Verri's essay. In *The Column of Infamy* he published a rather laboured critique of Verri, pointing out that by basing his case for abolition on this particular story, Verri had in fact chosen the worst possible target. For far from illustrating the horrors of the ancient system with its arcane rules, the story of Piazza and Mora demonstrated exactly the opposite – that if only the rules governing torture had been observed, the whole disastrous situation would never have come about.

As Manzoni pointed out, the grotesque catalogue of injustices ensuing from Piazza's arrest was not the result of the blind workings of the system – as Verri sought to demonstrate – but rather of the deliberate attempts of a group of corrupt judges to subvert, for their own political ends, the course of justice. The legal writers, so fiercely castigated by Verri, who had framed the innumerable rules governing the use of torture, had done so with the specific intention of minimizing the opportunities for error, injustice and arbitrary cruelty. If only the judges had obeyed the rules, with which they were perfectly familiar, neither Piazza nor anyone else would have been convicted for a crime that was 'morally and physically impossible'. Manzoni went on to detail a number of instances in the story where 'in order to suppress the truth ... the judges had continually to exercise the utmost ingenuity and have recourse again and again to expedients of whose injustice they could not have been ignorant'.[25]

Behind Manzoni's critique of Verri there was an important philosophical difference. Was evil the result of the 'system', the automatic workings of bad human institutions, or was it really the consequence of individual human wickedness? In the heyday of the Enlightenment, before the collapse of the hopes raised by the French revolution, men such as Verri and Beccaria believed that it only needed a radical change in the system to ensure that henceforth man's social relations would be governed by reason and light. For Verri, the story of the *untori* was symbolic of the fear and superstition in which men lived before the dawn of the Enlightenment. Faced with the 'public disaster' of the plague, 'human weakness [was] led to suspect extravagant causes, instead of seeing in them the result of the natural course of physical laws'.[26] With the advent of laws based on reason and a system of universal education – so they imagined – such things could never happen again. The fault had been with the age.

Manzoni, living two generations later, after three decades of revolution, war and counter-revolution, saw things very differently. There may have been contradictions and irrationalities in the ancient laws – the old system might even have been completely unworkable. But no attack on the system should ignore the role of individual moral responsibility. In lumping the bad Milanese judges together with the writers and doctors of law who had tried to rid the system of its worst barbarities, Verri had been guilty of a serious distortion of the truth. For in this episode, at least, the evils lay less in the system than with the irresponsible and culpable actions of the men in authority. The judges had not been compelled to act in the way they had done; they had exercised their freedom to choose an evil course in the full knowledge of its consequences.

Such was the moral and ethical aspect of a dialogue on torture spanning three generations. But there remained a yet more fundamental question to be disposed of. For by failing to draw the distinction between the use of torture under the old system and its abuse by unscrupulous judges who broke the rules, neither Verri nor Beccaria had disposed of the utilitarian aspect of the problem. Throughout his essay Beccaria based his arguments on the assumption that torture was a bad means of arrival at the truth – a matter he seems to have considered self-evident, for at no point did he go beyond the familiar argument that the innocent might lie to avoid the pain while the guilty, but strong, might succeed in holding out. This was not the same as saying that torture was necessarily a bad means of discovering the truth – nor, for that matter a good one. The crux of the matter, as argued by every leading authority from Aristotle onwards, was that no valid generalization could be made about torture: *everything depended upon circumstances.*

It was this unresolved aspect of the problem that engaged another, more powerful, mind than Beccaria's – that of his acknowledged disciple, Jeremy Bentham.

Bentham's thoughts are contained in two recently published manuscripts written between 1775 and 1780.[27] Both are sketchy and incomplete and not entirely consistent. Nevertheless his arguments do identify an area where torture may, under certain circumstances, contribute to utility, and therefore deserve consideration. From the start Bentham makes it clear that he is not defending torture as it was used on the European continent. If he had to choose between retaining it in its present form, or total abolition, he would not hesitate to choose the latter. He 'admit[s] the justice' of Beccaria's 'observations almost without exception'. At first, he had fully shared the Italian's views himself: 'If a few years ago any one had foretold me that in any case I should be in the least disposed to approve of any thing to which the name of Torture could with any sort of propriety be applied, I should have thought he had done me a great Injustice.' However, 'scrupulous examination' and 'very attentive consideration' had led him to the conclusion that there were 'a very few cases in which for a very particular purpose, Torture might be made use of with advantage'.[28]

For Bentham, torture involves the infliction of pain for the purpose of compulsion: that is to say, the pain is applied under circumstances in which the victim has it within his power to stop the torture by complying with the wishes of his torturers: 'Torture, as I understand it, is where a person is made to suffer any violent pain of body in order to compel him to do something or desist from doing something which done or desisted from the penal application is immediately made to cease.'[29]

Torture therefore differs from punishment in respect of its purpose (coercion) rather than by virtue of the intensity of the pain involved. Elsewhere Bentham clarifies this distinction:

> The notion of torture is not included in a punishment attached to an act of disobedience, of which no remission is allowed; but suppose the same lot of pain attached to the same offence, with power to remit any part of it in case of, and immediately on compliance with, the requisition of the law, and here the punishment comes under the notion of torture.[30]

Thus punishment, in the normal sense of the word, is a reward for wrongdoing, and is 'past-directed' in the sense that it relates to an act or crime which has already been committed. Torture, by contrast, is 'future-directed' in that it is designed to compel the patient to do or say something against his will.

With this distinction in mind, Bentham argues that in some circumstances it is easier to justify torture than corporal punishment because the amount of pain may be more easily controlled. Torture might also be a form of punishment applied to a person who refused to plead, give evidence or answer questions as required by the law. In such cases, it might be more humane than imprisonment for contempt of court:

A man may have been lingering in prison for a month or two before he would make answer to a question which at the worst with one stroke of the rack and therefore almost always with only knowing that he might be made to suffer the rack, he would have answered in a moment; just as a man will linger on a month with the Toothach which he might have saved himself from at the expence of a pang.[31]

In this sense, each moment of pain was simply a punishment for each moment's refusal to comply with the law. But it was more humane than normal punishment, for once the offender desisted the pain would instantly stop.

The danger, as Bentham recognized, was that the innocent might suffer wrongfully or that torture might be used unnecessarily. He proposed therefore that it should only be used in cases where it was certain that the victim had it in his power to stop the torture by doing what was required of him. The amount of proof needed to torture a man must be as much as would normally be needed to punish him. If his ability to comply were less than absolutely certain, torture should only be allowed if the public interest in what he had to reveal were greater than the danger of an innocent man suffering. Bentham does not suggest how these imponderables should be quantified, though he hints that where proof is less than certain, torture should only be used 'where the safety of the whole state may be endangered'.[32] Torture should only be used in cases of extreme urgency; it must be subject to prescribed limits; and generous compensation must be given if victims are subsequently proved innocent.

As an illustration of a case which satisfied these requirements, Bentham suggested the following: Two men are caught setting fire to a house. One of them escapes. His re-arrest becomes a matter of urgency for there are grounds for suspecting that he may set fire to another house. The captured arsonist refuses to name his accomplice. What is to be done? The prisoner cannot be threatened with punishment, for (as this is the eighteenth century) he is already liable to the utmost penalty of the law. There are only two options: either he must be bribed to reveal his accomplice in return for commuting the death-sentence (which, from a sense of honour, he still might not accept) or, says Bentham, he must be subjected to instant pain. Even if he were to accept the bribe, the public interest would scarcely benefit – for in order that the second arsonist be apprehended, the eventual release of the first must be conceded. Torture is therefore the preferable alternative on utilitarian grounds.

Beccaria argued that the use of torture to compel criminals to reveal the names of their accomplices was irrational because torture was a bad way of discovering the truth. Bentham disagrees with this, though he does not state his reasons. In fact he argues that in cases of grave public danger, it is because torture may be the only available means of obtaining vital information that it may be used – provided there are stringent safeguards.

Thus the essential difference between Beccaria and Bentham was a question of opinion rather than fact. Did people tell the truth under torture, or did they not? According to Bentham, Beccaria overstated his case. By rehearsing the familiar and logical argument, he had pointed out that torture was a bad method of obtaining the truth. And he drew from that the conclusion that it could not therefore be justified on rational, or utilitarian, grounds. Bentham, while agreeing with Beccaria that in most of the instances where torture was permitted under the Roman law it added nothing to proof, and was therefore contrary to utility, nevertheless believed that there were exceptions, when the evidence required could be obtained in no other way. Bentham did not agree with Beccaria that torture was invariably a bad method of obtaining the truth. But even had he done so, this would not necessarily invalidate his argument. In an emergency, a bad method of obtaining information might be better than no method at all.

Bentham should not be misunderstood. Unlike Beccaria, he was not a polemicist seeking to abolish a prevalent and anachronistic evil. His argument was a purely theoretical one. He did not develop it in a final form, and as with most of his work he did not write it for publication. Above all, he was fully aware of the dangers attendant on permitting torture, the greatest objection to which, he believed, was its efficacy.

This efficacy is so great, that by the help of it a few weak lights will commonly be sufficient to enable the magistrate of himself to unravel the most intricate and fine-spun thread of delinquency, whether consummated or projected. Armed with this he can extort information from the person who for a certainty is able to afford it; without this, he is forced to go a-begging for it at a venture among persons who let them be ever so well disposed to yield it, may or may not have it in their power. Thus armed he has power enough within himself to punish every act which the law has pronounced to be punishable... '[33]

This very efficacy, however, brings Bentham by a kind of paradox to an unexpected conclusion. If torture were used, the magistrate would in effect be able to dispense with the cooperation of the public in detecting crime, and to enforce the law without reference to the wishes of the people, who might be disposed for a variety of reasons to prevent his attempts to do so.

It appears therefore that while so much of the chance the magistrate has of executing the law depends upon the concurrence of the people, the people have a kind of negative upon the law; and although they should have no direct share in the enacting of it, they have a material share in the execution of it, without which its enactment can be of no effect.

The danger is then that the magistrate when armed with such effectual powers may in spite of the people give execution to laws repugnant to the interest as well as to the affections of the people; that the magistrate, in short, may find the same facility [in] the establishment of tyranny or usurpation as in the maintenance of a beneficent and rightful government.[34]

In the light of other instances of torture that will be examined later in this book the solution Bentham proposed is interesting. Torture – he argued – should only be allowed in cases of individual, not political crimes.

The danger will always be great that torture, if allowed in these cases, may be made subservient to the establishment of usurpation, or which comes to the same thing of a government repugnant to the interests and affections of the great body of the people. Those whom it is found necessary to proscribe under the names of rebels, libellers, or sowers of sedition, may in fact be the best friends and defenders of the people: against these the hand of the government may be too strong. But incendiaries, assassins, highwaymen and housebreakers are under every government, be the government what it may, the standing enemies of the people: against these the hand of government can never be too strong.[35]

In an age of civil violence and 'urban guerrillas', the distinction between rebels and incendiaries, 'sowers of sedition', and highwaymen (or hijackers) is difficult to maintain. Not the least of the objections to

Bentham's thesis is the difficulty entailed in distinguishing between torturable and non-torturable categories. Who decides, and on what basis, that a particular crime constitutes an act of rebellion? Nor did Bentham succeed in refuting the important abolitionist argument that the use of torture is inseparable from its abuse, although he states this to be one of his objectives. For the safeguards he proposed were little different from those provided for under the continental system. They were found universally to be unworkable, which in practice left complete discretion in the hands of the judges. Bentham himself admitted that no magistrate should have such power at his disposal.

Nevertheless, Bentham's views on torture are interesting, less for what he proposes than for the attitudes he reveals. His thoughts are more subtle and complex than Beccaria's, and they lead, as Beccaria's did not, into a paradox. On the one hand, torture is a weapon of inestimable power which can be employed to enforce the laws for the good of society. On the other, this very power is a source of danger, since it means that the law can be enforced against the wishes of a recalcitrant population, and this may open the way to tyranny. We shall have many occasions to respect the force of this conclusion in the course of this book.

TWO

Torture in the ancient world

Torture appears to have been known to all the societies of the ancient world with the possible exception of the Hebrews. In fact, the Christian opposition to torture which contributed to the abolitionist case clearly reflected the Judaic tradition which regarded the practice as contrary to the 'law of God'. Probably the first recorded reference to torture is that of an Egyptian poet who described how Ramses II learned the dispositions of his enemies by torturing some Hittite prisoners.[1] This is not likely to have been an isolated case. Prisoners of war in the ancient world were either massacred outright or taken into slavery, and slaves, almost by definition, meant those who could be tortured.[2]

In Ancient Greece prisoners of war were also liable to be tortured. Thucydides records how during the Peloponesian war the Corinthians and Syracusans put the captured Athenian commander Demosthenes to death for fear that he might reveal to their Spartan allies – under torture – their treasonable dealing with the Athenians.[3] In domestic law, however, the torture of citizens was unknown, except among the Rhodians. Torture was restricted to slaves and strangers or foreigners – all members of groups lying outside the *polis* and therefore without standing in society. In legal proceedings it was customary to offer one's slaves for torture or to demand the right to torture those of an opponent. In Athens, as in Rome, torture was usually conducted in public, and litigants had the right to administer it themselves. Alternatively, they could employ the services of the *basanistes*, often himself a former slave, since free men considered the work degrading.[4] In matters of public concern, however, the State could demand slaves for torture. The manner in which Athenian slaves were tortured was satirized by Aristophanes in *Frogs*. Xanthus, servant of Bacchus, accompanies his master to the underworld in the guise of Heracles, with Bacchus disguised as his slave. Arriving in Hades, they are challenged by Aecus, and Xanthus offers his 'slave' for torture:

'How am I to torture him?' [asks Aecus]
'In every way' [replies Xanthus], 'by tying him to a ladder, by suspending him, by scourging him with a whip, by cudgelling him, by racking him and further, by pouring vinegar into his nostrils, by heaping bricks on him and every other way ... '[5]

A number of specific instances in which slaves were offered or demanded for torture survive in the writings of the Athenian orators. Examples from two of them, Lycurgus and Antiphon, make it clear that, while the testimony of slaves was only admissible if given under torture, its evidential value was not rated very highly. It all depended, as Aristotle pointed out, on which side one was on: 'If it is in our favour, we can exaggerate its importance by asserting that it is the only true kind of evidence; but if it is against us and in favour of our opponents, we can destroy its value by telling the truth about all kinds of torture generally ... '[6] In one case, Lycurgus, acting for the prosecutor, denounces the defendant Leocrates for refusing to accept his challenge to torture the accusers' slaves:

By the very act of refusing to accept this [challenge] Leocrates condemned himself as a traitor to his country. For whoever refuses to allow the testimony of those who share his secrets has confirmed that the charges of the indictment are true.[7]

Lycurgus' contemporary, Antiphon, scored a similar rhetorical point by showing up the refusal of the accuser, Philocrates, to take up the challenge of the defendants who offered their own slaves for torture:

Let him [Philocrates] question the free men as befitting free men. For their own sakes and in the interests of justice, they would give a faithful account of what had occurred. As to the slaves, if he considered that they were answering his questions truthfully, well and good. If he did not. I was ready to place all my own at his disposal for examination under torture, and should he demand any that did not belong to me, I agreed to obtain the consent of their owner and hand them over to him to be examined as he liked.[8]

But in another case, where he was defending a man on a murder charge, Antiphon took the opposite line. The family of Herodes, who had disappeared on a journey from Mytilene, had purchased a slave who had been with Herodes on the voyage, and under torture the slave had accused the missing man's companion, Euxitheus, of murder. Antiphon told the jury that the charge was false, since there were no other witnesses and the slave had been forced, under torture, to accuse his client:

> You have listened to evidence for the length of delay before the man's examination under torture; now notice the actual character of that examination. The slave was doubtless promised his freedom: it was certainly to the prosecution alone that he could look for release from his sufferings. Probably both of these considerations induced him to make false charges against me, which he did. He hoped to gain his freedom, and his one wish was to end the torture. I need not remind you, I think, that witnesses under torture are biassed in favour of those who do most of the torturing. They will say anything likely to gratify them.[9]

The torture of slaves, then, may have been largely a tactical device for calling the bluff of one's opponent in court. According to one modern scholar, demands were made in such a way as to ensure refusal, in order to compromise the opposing party. There is no surviving instance of a challenge being accepted – a fact that permits more than one interpretation. A plausible suggestion is that the torture of slaves was really an alternative species of trial, rather than a regular part of normal procedure: in this case, the torture would have been a form of trial by ordeal, with slaves as 'proxies' for their masters, and therefore a way of determining judgement rather than a mode of examination.[10] In medieval Europe the replacement by torture of trial by ordeal resulted in some cases from changes in criminal procedure, rather than changes in the mode of applying pain. It is therefore possible to envisage a transitional stage between the trial by ordeal and investigative torture, which shares some of the features of both. The criminal process in fifth-century Attica, from which most of our evidence comes, may well have reached such a stage.

Cicero was almost certainly wrong in stating that the Athenians, like the Rhodians, tortured free citizens – at least during the classical period.[11] As in Rome, tyrannical rulers in all parts of the Greek world were notorious for using torture against anyone they suspected of treason, but whether this was done according to customary law is difficult to establish. The torture in about 520 BC of the Athenian Aristogeiton, who was involved in a plot to assassinate the sons of the tyrant Peisistratus, cannot have established a legal precedent.[12] The Roman writer Valerius Maximus narrates, with macabre relish, a number of torture stories involving Greek tyrants. One famous victim was the philosopher Zeno of Elea who was tortured to reveal his accomplices in a plot to overthrow the tyrant Niarchos. Unable to endure the pain, he intimated that his secret was so important that it could only be imparted to the tyrant in private. When Niarchos bent down to hear the whispered message, Zeno bit his ear so hard that by the time the guards arrived to kill him he had severed it completely. Another of Valerius' anecdotes concerned the 'virtuous Theodore' who endured whips, cords, the *eculeus* and red-hot irons without revealing the names of his co-conspirators against the tyrant Hieronymos. He did even better than Zeno by finally naming the tyrant's most trusty henchman – whom Hieronymos killed in a fit of rage before realizing he had been duped.[13]

If anything these and similar stories, whether true or fabled, show how scandalized most Greek and Roman writers were at the torture of free citizens, at least until the later years of the Roman empire. The Athenians, especially, are notable for resisting a demand for the introduction of torture in the case of a national atrocity: the episode, involving the equivalent of high treason, sacrilege and national emergency, is worth recording, since it shows the lengths the Athenians were prepared to go to in safeguarding traditional liberties in circumstances where most other peoples, ancient and modern, would have felt the need to sacrifice them.

The occasion was in 415 BC when an Athenian expeditionary force was about to set sail for Sicily during a war against the Syracusans. One morning, shortly before the fleet was due to leave, it was found that nearly all of the statues of Hermes, the god of travellers, had been mutilated during the night. This was – to put it mildly – a bad omen for the coming expedition; but, to make matters worse, further acts of sacrilege were soon reported. A number of young men were denounced in the council for having lampooned the Mysteries of Eleusis, the most sacred rite in the Athenian calendar. They were said to include Alcibiades, none other than the commander of the expeditionary force. Public indignation, already roused, was fanned to fury by demagogic orators, led by Alcibiades' most bitter rivals, Peisander and Androcles. Alcibiades demanded an immediate public trial in order to clear his name. His enemies, however, adopted delaying tactics, fearing that no Athenian court would indict a popular commander on the eve of a military campaign. The trial was postponed; the fleet set sail, and with it Alcibiades. Later, after further denunciations, he was condemned to death in his absence.

Meanwhile in Athens a resident foreigner named Teucer supplied the council with the names of the rest of those suspected of taking part in the Eleusinian parody, and those who did not succeed in fleeing abroad were quickly tried and executed. He also supplied eighteen names of those whom he claimed were responsible for mutilating the statues of Hermes, and most of them were duly arrested. Soon afterwards, however, a second informer, one Diocleides, came forward. He claimed to have actually watched the party mutilating the statues: at least three hundred people had been involved. As a preliminary, he supplied the names of forty-two of them.

At once alarm in the city turned to panic. A vast conspiracy was suspected, led by the old oligarchic families who were dissatisfied with the city's democratic government and intended to return to power. Arrests continued at a prodigious rate: many of them of members of the old aristocracy. Finally, one of the arrested, Andocides, turned approver, and in exchange for immunity from prosecution made a confession in which some – but not by any means all – of those arrested were implicated. The people heaved a sigh of relief, and public anxiety subsided. Although Andocides could not be prosecuted, he had admitted being guilty of sacrilege, and the public execration he had to endure eventually drove him into exile. The degree of Andocides' guilt is still the subject of scholarly controversy. A recent authority suggests that while he probably took part in the profanation of the Mysteries, and denounced the others in exchange for immunity, he was in fact innocent of the mutilations.[14]

It was during the proceedings in council that the question of torture was raised. Peisander, Alcibiades' political enemy, demanded that all those accused by Diocleides should be put to the torture to reveal the names of their two hundred and fifty-odd accomplices: he urged that the Decree of Skamandrios (date unknown), which forbade the use of torture against citizens, should be repealed. Whatever truth lay behind Teucer's denunciations regarding the parodying of the Mysteries (and most scholars seem agreed that there was some truth in them) the allegations of Diocleides were highly suspect. For instance, under cross-examination he claimed to have watched the mutilations by the light of the moon, when the event was recorded as having taken place at the beginning of the lunar month. The fact that it was Peisander himself who made the demand for reintroducing torture lends weight to the suspicion that much, if not all, of the hysteria had been deliberately whipped up by him for political purposes. The actions themselves – whether true or false – could be seen as amounting to treason, since they had clearly been calculated to cause offence to the gods.

In cases of sacrilege it was believed that, unless the offenders were promptly punished, the gods would wreak their vengeance on the whole community. To provoke them thus on the eve of a military campaign was tantamount to sabotage. It was not unreasonable to suspect the oligarchs, or members of the old aristocracy: as the wealthiest class of Athenians, they stood to lose most by a costly war. The charge against Alcibiades suggests crude smear-tactics: as commander of the expedition and leader of the war-party, he was far from being a natural ally of the oligarchs.

While the final details of the mystery may never be solved, the probability is that some if not all of the accusations were fabrications. Peisander may perhaps even have been responsible for the mutilations himself, in order to discredit his enemies and create a climate of panic suitable to his designs. Alternatively, he may have been a brilliant opportunist, who engineered a political crisis out of what had been no more than a series of drunken orgies. In either event, he revealed his true political colours four years later, in 411, when he put himself at the head of the despotism of the Four Hundred. If he did fabricate the case, he would not have been the last Greek dictator to raise the spectre of one revolution in order to perpetrate another, and try to use torture as his instrument. However, his demands were avoided when two of the accused opted for public trial instead of torture – another indication that even where treason was concerned torture was seen as a substitute for, not a part of, normal legal procedure.

In Rome, as in Greece, torture was originally restricted to slaves and foreigners, that is to say, persons in the first instance without rights. Both were outside the political community and were therefore originally regarded as enemies. The word *hostis* originally meant a stranger. As foreign peoples came into treaty relations with Rome and therefore came under Roman protection, the meaning was narrowed to designate those not covered by such treaties, who were considered to be in a state of war with Rome, regardless of whether or not hostilities were in progress.[15] There was no concept of a 'family of nations': war was the primal condition of mankind, and the status of slaves derived ultimately from their original condition – or that of their forebears – as captives or prisoners of war. Nor were slaves only foreigners in this fundamental, legalistic, sense. The vast majority of them were of non-Roman origin, as the supply of slaves was periodically replenished by the conquest of neighbouring peoples or warfare between them, piracy or plunder. Only in times of general peace, when captives were in short supply, did slaves begin to acquire embryonic political rights.[16]

In the course of time, however, a more complex social structure developed which eroded the distinction between the free Roman citizen and the enslaved foreigner. The practice of manumitting slaves created a large intermediate class of freedmen who were no longer slaves in the formal sense, yet who did not qualify for citizenship. The old citizen–slave distinction gave way to a new division between the privileged classes, known as the *honestiores*, who by and large enjoyed the rights and benefits originally reserved for citizens, and the underprivileged classes, the *humiliores* who, though nominally free, continued to suffer from many of the disabilities of foreigners and slaves, including, in some circumstances, torture and cruel punishments.[17]

The Emperor Augustus is on record as sanctioning the use of torture against slaves where there seemed no other way of discovering the truth:

> The question – in my judgement – must not always be ordered in every case and for all kinds of person. But when the more serious and capital crimes cannot be investigated except by the torture of slaves, then I believe it to be the most effective way of discovering the truth, and resolve that it should be used.[18]

Most of the Roman law on torture, as preserved in the forty-eighth book of the Digest, is concerned with regulating the conditions under which slaves may be tortured. Augustus himself is cited in the preface to chapter eighteen (*De Quaestionibus*) – the work, presumably, of Justinian's compilers – as laying down that 'One must not begin with torture . . . [and] must not trust it completely'.[19] A rescript of Hadrian, cited by Ulpian, is even more explicit: 'One must come to the torture of slaves at the end when the accused is already suspect, and when other proofs come near to being demonstrated, so that all that seems to be lacking is the confession of slaves'.[20]

It seems probable that the evidence of slaves was inadmissible except under torture, although the Roman jurists, like their Greek counterparts, seem to have been fully aware of its shortcomings as a means of discovering the truth. Thus Ulpian, for example, records a judgement that the evidence of a solitary tortured slave must not be believed without other proof.[21] Paulus, generally less cautious in his pronouncements on torture, cites the decision of one of the emperors which went even further by laying down that a slave could not be tortured on the evidence of a single witness.[22] Even a slave's self-accusation was invalid without other proofs.[23]

In contrast to Attic law, Roman slaves were normally forbidden to testify either for or against their masters. As a witness, the slave was considered irremediably biased: if he was for his master, he might be inspired by the promise of freedom; if against him he might be motivated by spite. Moreover, as Paulus is quoted in the Digest, to allow the slave to testify against his master would be to undermine the institution of slavery: 'A slave who confesses something against his master must not be believed, for it would not do for the lives of masters to be put away at the discretion of their slaves'.[24] Such evidence was inadmissible even if given without torture, or acquired incidentally in the course of other investigations.[25] The rule applied even when slaves were accused of complicity in their masters' crimes; and though Trajan tried to revise this by allowing slaves to incriminate their masters when they themselves were under accusation, this rescript, according to Ulpian, was not adhered to by later emperors. The main exceptions to this general rule, apart from treason, were adultery and incest – crimes committed within the family very difficult to prove without the testimony of slaves and almost impossible to commit without their knowledge.*

---

* The principle that the evidence of slaves should not be used against their masters created a number of difficulties, and many of the rules were concerned with preventing abuses and tightening loopholes. Thus a slave freed expressly to save him from torture could be tortured, provided it was not against his former master; a slave bought by a defendant after proceedings had begun *could* be tortured against him; it was illegal to buy another's slave to torture him against his former master. A slave who had

The attitude of the jurists towards evidence obtained under torture was extremely cautious, and may be summarized by Ulpian's famous dictum:

The constitutions declare that torture is not always to be trusted, nor is it always to be disbelieved: it is a delicate, dangerous and deceptive thing. For many persons have such strength of body and soul that they heed pain very little, so that there is no means of obtaining the truth from them; while others are so susceptible to pain that they will tell any lie rather than suffer it.[27]

The rhetoricians were equally circumspect. According to Cicero, 'investigations by torture are governed by fear, ruled by the arbitrary whim of the investigator, corrupted by false hopes and undermined by intimidation – so that in the last resort, little room is left for truth'.[28] Quintilian, in his famous system of rhetoric, essentially repeated Aristotle's argument that one's attitude towards torture depended on which side one was on:

... one party will style it an infallible method of discovering the truth, while the other will allege that it often results in false confessions ... What more needs to be said on the subject? Ancient and Modern writers have said everything. If the question of the application of torture arises, everything will depend on who demands it, who offers it, who is subjected to it, against whom the evidence sought will tell, and what is the motive behind the demand ... Such questions are as varied as the number of individual cases.[29]

In fact the consensus which emerges from nearly all ancient writings on the subject of torture is that valid generalizations about its value as a source of evidence cannot be made. In consequence a great deal of discretion was left in the hands of the judges which no doubt suited the inquisitorial style of procedure as it was being developed for the lower ranks of society.

In the later years of the empire the earlier restrictions on torture were gradually abandoned. Antoninus Pius ruled that torture could be employed on slaves in pecuniary cases (such as those involving the payment of fines or damages) though these did not fall within the

---

recently changed hands could not be tortured against his former master, if the latter had owned him for some time. Slaves co-owned by several masters could not be tortured against any one of them. Slaves in a bequest subject to litigation could not be tortured against any of the interested parties. A slave who served a master in good faith could not be tortured against him, even if the master turned out not to be the legal owner.[26]

category of 'capital and atrocious' crimes as defined by Augustus.[30] More ominously, a judgement by Callistratus early in the third century states that 'it is not right to torture a free man when his evidence does not waver' – the implication being that free men could be tortured if they vacillated in their testimony. A clause in one of Paulus' sentences states that prisoners must not be tortured without charge – indicating what may have become a widespread abuse.[31] Finally, by the end of the third century or thereabouts, it had become normal procedure for free men up to the rank of decurion (who were, of course, *honestiores*) to be tortured in cases of *falsum* – a crime that included forgery, certain kinds of bribery and bearing false witness.[32]

The erosion of the traditional privileges exempting free men from torture is also clear from its application as a punishment. Under the Romans it was never exclusively, or even primarily, a mode of examination. It was often an aggravation of the death penalty, though the texts usually make clear the distinction between punitive and interrogative torture. From about the second century, 'servile' punishments such as crucifixion, previously restricted like torture to slaves or aliens, were applied to the *humiliores* in general. The latter were subject to the jurisdiction of courts employing an inquisitorial mode of procedure in which the judges had very wide discretionary powers in awarding sentences. Thus *humiliores* would normally suffer the death penalty for crimes for which the penalty for *honestiores* was only exile overseas.[33] Not surprisingly, investigative torture was also resorted to by these courts.

There was one crime for which members of all classes were sometimes tortured, either as a punishment or as a mode of investigation. This was the *crimen majestatis*, normally translated into English as high treason, into French as *lèse-majesté*. According to Mommsen,[34] the *crimen majestatis* of imperial times arose from the fusion of two originally distinct ideas, the *perduellio* and the *crimen majestatis imminutae*. Both involved the conception of crimes against the state. *Perduellio* originated with military desertion, and came to be applied to a number of acts involving neglect or abuse of civil or military duties, including desertion and unlawful dealings with the enemy, cowardice on the battlefield, the surrender of a city to the enemy, and the abuse of official powers by magistrates and other authorities. *Majestas* entailed the notion of dignity, originally the dignity or respect demanded by the Roman people in their dealings with other nations. In domestic terms it came to mean the respect owing to the tribunes or magistrates representing the people. The *crimen majestatis imminutae* was therefore applied to acts tending to diminish the prestige or to deny the competence of public officials. Ironically, the *crimen majestatis* which was to become the main legal instrument of imperial tyranny was originally designed to protect the prestige of the *plebs*, the lower classes in Roman society. However, the merging of the *plebs* in the greater entity of the state, and the fusion of the state with the person of the emperor, created a situation in which no distinction could be maintained between crimes against the state and crimes against the emperor as an individual.[35]

There is little if any evidence that free citizens were tortured according to law for treason under the republic. During the crisis of 63 BC Cicero argued that Catiline and his fellow-conspirators had put themselves beyond the pale of citizenship and had become enemies of the state.[36] No one in the senate, however, suggested that they should be tortured. During the next two centuries the torture of free men and citizens in treason cases is relatively well documented, though it is not always clear whether they were tortured as witnesses or suspects, and to what extent the emperors concerned were acting above the law. The torture of the praetor Gallius, whom Augustus suspected of plotting against him, shocked both Suetonius and Tacitus – though there were other comparable episodes during the civil wars of the first century.[37] After the discovery of the plot of Sejanus, according to Suetonius, the Emperor Tiberius abandoned himself so completely to the use of torture that he mistakenly had a friend who arrived on a social call put to death on the rack; and he goes on to describe in lurid detail the emperor's atrocities in Capri.[38] The cruelty of Tiberius' successor, Caligula, is proverbial. His favourite entertainment was watching prisoners being tortured to death while feasting.[39] On succeeding Caligula Claudius took an oath never to torture a free man; but he made an exception of conspirators and would-be assassins. According to Cassius Dio, men of high birth, both aliens and citizens, were tortured in the second year of his reign,[40] while Tacitus mentions the case of an Equestrian who was tortured for wearing a sword when greeting the emperor. It was hoped he would reveal his 'accomplices'.[41] Similarly, the use of torture is recorded in connection with the conspiracy of Messalina, Claudius' wife,[42] and with that of Piso during the reign of Nero. In the latter case, however, it was not the principals who suffered most, as Tacitus caustically points out when contrasting with the cowardice of her more illustrious confederates the heroism of the free woman Epicharis, who held out against a whole day of torture before hanging herself with her bodice rather than give away any names.[43]

Despite these facts, it is difficult to establish the extent to which the torture of the more privileged classes was sanctioned by law, even in cases of high treason. The law of *majestas* was itself confused during the early years of the empire, its interpretation and enforcement being left largely to the discretion of individual emperors themselves. Although the emperor derived his authority from the senate, the latter body was too weak or 'constitutionally illiterate' to prescribe formal limits to his power or carefully to define its own privileges, such as exemption from the death penalty or torture.[44] And although rescripts of Hadrian and Antoninus Pius formally reiterated the ban on torture against freedmen,[45] by the end of the third century Arcadius Charisius was able to state categorically that the torture of all classes was permissible in cases of treason: 'Any person without distinction in cases of the crime of High Treason which concerns the prince's person, if his evidence is needed, where circumstances require it, may be put to the question.'[46] By the fourth century, then, torture had become firmly established as an instrument of imperial prerogative – a fact which was to have important consequences for Christianity, both in its revolutionary period and after it had become the state religion.

Before it became the state religion, the profession of Christianity was treasonable under Roman law because the Christians refused to acknowledge the state gods and the emperor's dignity as high priest of the state religion; and this, of course, entailed refusal to participate in those public ceremonies, such as sacrificing to the emperor's genius, which Roman citizens were obliged to perform.[47] Thus Christians were liable to fall into the crime of *perduellio* whether or not they were Roman citizens, and to be treated as public enemies. They were persecuted, in the first instance, as Christians – and only secondarily as common-law criminals guilty of anti-social crimes (such as debauchery, magic, possession of forbidden books) of which they were also accused – in consequence, no doubt, of hostile propaganda. Nero, as is well known, sought to divert from himself responsibility for the burning of Rome by blaming the Christians and Jews, and no doubt the tortures to which they were subjected sometimes produced confessions substantiating these allegations.[48] This, however, was many years before much was known about Christian beliefs and practices. By early in the third century, Christians were being tortured not primarily to make them confess to the heinous offences of which they were often accused, but in order to force them to deny Christ and affirm the sovereignty of the emperor. As Tertullian berated the Romans in a famous passage in the *Apologeticus*:

> ... you do not deal with us in accordance with your normal criminal procedure. If other criminals plead 'not guilty' you torture them to make them confess. The Christians alone you torture to make them deny [their faith] ... Yet if it were something evil, we should deny our guilt – and you would then use torture to force us to confess it ... You assume that we are criminals from the fact that we confess the Name [i.e. Christ]; and under torture you try to force us to renounce our confession, so that in effect we are really forced to deny the crimes which you presumed we were guilty of in the first place ... [49]

With his sharp legal mind, Tertullian in fact points out a contradiction which is present wherever torture is employed as a weapon of religious or ideological persecution. Is the purpose of torture to force the victim to renounce his allegiance to a belief which he openly professes? Or is he being forced to admit to criminal acts which, without torture, he would insist on denying? Logically speaking, these two aims are mutually incompatible, as Tertullian makes clear in contrasting the treatment of Christians with that of ordinary criminals. Yet as will be seen from subsequent chapters, these two contradictory aims are often present simultaneously where torture is widespread. Ultimately, this contradiction derives from contradictions inherent in the notion of treason itself, between the original ideas of *perduellio* and *laesae majestatis*. The former is a crime of commission, the hostile act or conspiracy against which the state requires protection. Within certain limits, as defined by successive emperors and jurists, the use of torture in investigating such crimes or conspiracies was rational, if inhuman. *Laesae majestatis*, on the other hand, is in one sense a crime of omission: the failure to accord the Roman people or their representatives, including the emperor, the dignity they considered their due.[50] Thus the offender could in the latter case be described as being in 'contempt of sovereignty' – a condition he may purge by acquiescing in the demands of his torturers. In either case it becomes difficult, if not impossible, to maintain a clear distinction between the use of torture as a means of coercion or as a punishment. The Christian vic-tim might be coerced into renouncing his allegiance to Christ and into acknowledging the divinity of the emperor; or he might alterna-tively be punished for his act of disobedience.* Whether the purpose of torture was compulsive or retributive would not necessarily be known for certain to the torturer, especially if he was operating outside a strict procedural framework. All that was necessary for the torturer to know was that the Christian, or the man accused of treason, had set himself against the state, and was therefore beyond the boundaries of its laws. He had become literally an outlaw, whose juridical condi-tion was identical to slavery – in fact, the two terms, slave and foreigner, were virtually interchangeable.[51]

With the triumph of Christianity, the situation was dramatically reversed. The penalties for treason were attached to pagans – and more especially to heretics, as 'traitors against God's Majesty'. Another development of the law in later Roman times, particularly significant in view of the persecutions of later European history, was the assimilation of magic, in addition to religious heresy, to the laws of treason. In fact, by the beginning of the fourth century AD these terms were almost synonymous.

From the earliest times certain forms of magic had been prohibited, and may have been regarded as treasonable since they challenged the official monopoly of the priests in manipulating the forces of des-tiny in the interests of state or emperor. According to Appollonius of Tyana in the first century AD: 'Sorcerers claim to be able to alter the course of destiny by having recourse either to the torture of lost spirits or to barbaric sacrifices, or to certain incantations or anoint-ings'. Of particular concern were consultations about the death of a reigning emperor or member of his family: such oracles, of course, could be manipulated with far-ranging political consequences. Thus, before he became emperor, Septimus Severus was indicted for making forbidden inquiries – though he was acquitted, to see his brilliant horoscope fulfilled. Once he became emperor, he took no chances, and in at least one instance torture was used against a provincial gov-ernor suspected of plotting against him by occult means.[52]

Such consultations with astrologers and other diviners were con-sidered *prima facie* evidence of treason from about the first century

* cf. Bentham's argument that a person who is tortured is being punished for the 'crime' of silence. (See W. L. and P. E. Twining, 'Bentham on Torture', *Northern Ireland Legal Quarterly* (1973), 24, 3, pp. 312, 353.)

AD. Under Claudius and Nero there were several cases of occult practices underlying the charge of treason. Nero's mother Agrippina seems
to have made a speciality of using such charges to rid herself of her
enemies,[53] while two of the Pisonian conspirators were accused of
using occult means in their plot against Nero.[54] Not that all forms
of magical practice and divination were illegal. Ulpian allowed the
study of astrology, provided it was purely theoretical;[55] while, even
after Christianity became the state religion, the Theodosian code
made a distinction between harmful magic, which was punishable,
and traditional rural rites such as those designed to protect crops
against hailstones.[56] The same code, however, contains an edict dated
357 which foreshadows the language of papal pronouncements on
witchcraft a thousand years later.

> Many have dared by means of magical arts to disturb the course of nature
> and do not hesitate to ruin the lives of innocent people. They even dare to
> summon the shades of the dead and disquiet them, so that they may destroy
> their enemies by their wicked arts. Since these magicians are nature's outlaws,
> let a deadly plague destroy them![57]

More ominously still, with the later centuries of witch persecution
in mind, a decree the following year states that there is to be no exemption from torture on grounds of social status for magicians found at
the imperial court, for they are to be considered 'enemies of the human
race': ' ... if he be found guilty, and by denial still resist those who
investigate his crime, let him be delivered to the rack [eculeus], let
his body be torn with hooks, so that he may endure the punishment
befitting his own peculiar crime'.[58]

This growing fear of the activities of magicians cannot be attributed
solely to the superstition of emperors or to the fanaticism of a militant
new Christianity. A text dating from about 302, twenty years before
the conversion of Constantine, reveals the extent to which magical
practices had already become associated with religious heresy, even
to pagan emperors. In this the threat came not from Christianity,
as might have been expected, but from the rival religion of the Manichees; the text attacks the

> Manicheans who oppose new and unheard-of sects to the old-time religions,
> in order that in accordance with their own perverse judgement they may
> drive out those doctrines which were formerly granted to us by the gods. Now
> as to these Manicheans [. . .] we learn that they quite recently, like strange

and unexpected portents, have moved forward or sprung up in this world of ours from the race of Persians, our enemies, and that they are everywhere committing many crimes. For reports say that they are throwing peaceful peoples into commotion and that they are subtly introducing harm into the cities. So that it is to be feared that ... they may attempt through their accursed customs and the ... laws of the Persians to infect, as with their own malevolent poison [*venenis*] men of a more innocent nature, the Romans, a modest and peaceful race, as well as our entire world. And because in the report on your religion which you disclose, you decide that there are to be found all sorts of most evidently malicious magic [*maleficia*], sought out and invented and falsely denied: for these reasons we decree that they shall suffer the pains and penalties which they so richly deserve.[59]

As this document makes clear, this and the subsequent attacks on magicians cannot be fully understood except in the context of the long struggle with Persia that clouded the later years of the Roman empire. 'Magic' was a Persian word: in the context of the time, its practice came to be seen as unpatriotic and treacherous, regardless of whether or not it was specifically directed against the person of the emperor or his family. Even before the triumph of Christianity in 324, Manicheism was seen as a threat, emanating from the East, to the established religion. During the next two centuries or so, it would be singled out for mention in the texts on heresy – so much so, in fact, that with the development of popular religious dissent in the Middle Ages, 'Manicheism' would become synonymous with heresy, just as in a more recent period, political or social dissent in the United States was designated *a priori* as 'communist'. This early association between magic and Manicheism makes it the less surprising that when Dominican inquisitors active in the persecution of heretics in the fourteenth century came across old women practising traditional sorcery in remote country districts, they should have taken them for members of an organized sect. Several more centuries, however, were to elapse before the dark skies of Europe would be lit with the glow of *autos-da-fé* and witch-burnings. In the meantime the Roman law, with its strictures on treason, heresy and magic, would fall into a long eclipse.

*　　　*　　　*

What, then, was the function of torture in the ancient world? This is not a simple question: but some answer to it must be attempted if we are to gain insights into its use after the revival of Roman law late in the Middle Ages and its more recent eruption in the modern world. It is a truism of sociological thinking that 'the voluntary character of a practice or institution should never be assumed beforehand'.[60] Slavery was integral to the social and psychological milieu of the Greeks and Romans, as to that of all ancient peoples. This is a fact which needs to be taken as certain. As a modern historian, M.I.Finley, points out: 'our sources do not permit us to go back to a stage in Greek history when [slavery] did not exist'.[61]

Since physical punishment was integral to the institution of slavery, it is important to avoid attributing to it rational purposes, beyond those which relate directly to slavery. The arguments that seem to have been advanced to justify torture were *post hoc* rationalizations of a practice whose existence was taken for granted. Only thus can the apparent contradictions between torture as punishment, torture as coercion and torture as investigation be understood.

It is often assumed that torture was primarily a mode of examination, employed against slaves, from which citizens were exempt as a species of privilege. Statements by classical authors are cited to prove that the ancients genuinely believed that slaves mechanically repeated the truth under torture – the implied assumption being that citizens would react in the same way if deprived of their privilege. Where high matters of state were involved, the privilege was lifted – hence the employment of torture against citizens in cases of treason, when torture was needed to unravel the threads of conspiracy.

The argument is attractive, in that it has a certain consistency. Unfortunately, there are several drawbacks. As we have seen, the foremost authorities on the law, from Aristotle to Ulpian, expressed far more scepticism about the value of evidence obtained under torture than one would expect if they had really believed that people on the rack mechanically repeated the truth, whether slaves or free men. Another difficulty is that where treason was involved torture seems to have been directed towards one of two mutually incompatible purposes. On the one hand, it could be used to unravel conspiracies, real or imagined, against the emperor or state, as in the Pisonian conspiracy against Nero. On the other hand it could be used, as Tertullian pointed out in the case of the Christian martyrs, as a means of compelling political or religious dissenters to renounce their faith and obey the law. In the former case, torture is directed to revealing a hidden crime by forcing the suspect to give information. It seeks an affirmative reply to the questioning: 'Yes, I do have the information you want, and will give it to you if you stop the pain'. In the latter case, torture confronts open dissent: the victim is not a suspect, but a self-proclaimed rebel. The torture seeks to elicit a denial: 'No! I am not a Christian (or a communist)! I denounce Jesus Christ (or the party)! I will obey the Emperor (or the Führer – or the King of Greece)!' Of course, under certain circumstances, the two aims may be present simultaneously: the self-proclaimed rebel may be constrained to denounce his confederates, or reveal their hiding places. Nevertheless, in terms of his own predicament, the two aims are incompatible: a man cannot simultaneously be a secret conspirator and an open dissident. In the former case he may resist torture in order to conceal his knowledge; in the latter, in order to persist in proclaiming his belief. Only in the former case can torture be described as a mode of investigation. In the latter it has the simultaneous character of coercion (to force a renunciation of the victim's allegiance) and punishment (for his original act of disobedience), thereby blurring the distinction between them.

There is little in ancient literature, apart from Tertullian's perspicacious comment, to suggest that the lawyers and jurists were fully aware of this contradiction. Their business, after all, was to interpret the law, not to challenge its basic premises. When the Roman law was rediscovered and reinterpreted during the later Middle Ages, the same confusion was apparent. The heretic, as 'traitor against God's Majesty' was originally an 'open' dissident who publicly proclaimed his dissatisfaction with the Church and usually urged a return to primitive Christian principles. The pressures and tortures to which he was submitted were designed, in the first instance, to make him recant. This was cruel, but quite logical. However, no sooner was 'open' heresy suppressed than the Church became obsessed with the 'secret' heretics, those 'robbers and assassins of souls' (in the language of Innocent IV) who concealed their dissent behind a deceptive veil of orthodoxy.[62] What would have satisfied the torturer in the first instance – a public profession of orthodoxy – merely whetted his appetite in the second, where an admission of guilt, not a proclamation of innocence, was demanded. Thus it emerges that what in the first instance is a means of coercion and retribution becomes, in its more complex evolution, a mode of examination. It is this, above all, which accounts for the contradiction noted earlier: that several ancient writers, including Aristotle, simultaneously held the view that slaves mechanically repeated the truth under torture and questioned its value as a source of evidence.

Since slavery originated in warfare, the 'primary torture situation' (if one may so describe it) was between the prisoner of war and his captor. For the captive, who expected to be put to the sword, his enslavement was at first an act of mercy; however, once his rebellious instinct asserted itself, he had to be continually forced to do his master's bidding and acknowledge his sovereignty. In Greek literature, the flogging of slaves is a perennial theme: for example, the pseudo-Aristotelian *Œconomica* dating from around the turn of the fourth and third centuries BC sums up the life of the slave as consisting of three elements – work, punishment and food.[63] Corporal punishment, of course, is the only kind possible for slaves, since they possess no property and cannot be fined, while imprisonment or exile would be to the detriment of their masters. So long as it is administered continuously, physical ill-treatment does not encourage rebellious instincts. On the contrary, the worse treated the slave, the less inclined he is to rebel. As Frederick Douglass, an ex-slave, wrote in 1855:

Beat and cuff your slave, keep him hungry and spiritless, and he will follow the chain of his master like a dog; but feed and clothe him well – work him moderately, surround him with physical comfort – and dreams of freedom intrude. Give him a *bad* master, and he aspires to a *good* master; give him a good master and he wishes to become his *own* master.[64]

For the slavemaster, then, torture was primarily a form of coercive violence, necessary to goad the slave into doing the work assigned to him. Its introduction into the criminal process was a secondary development. Even under Attic law in the classical period, its function was not solely, or even primarily, investigative. The slave witnesses were tortured in the course of a contest between rival masters, in what amounted to a form of trial by ordeal with the slaves as proxies. As the procedure became formalized, a form of contract or challenge (the *proklesis*) was devised, binding both parties to accept the decision of the *basanos* (enquiry) as final.[65] For the sake of the contest it was assumed that the slave who confessed under torture could not lie. This was a statement of legal etiquette, not a scientific truth, a device necessary to determine judgement, similar to the rule that the jury's verdict is final, and therefore cannot be wrong.[66] The frequent reiteration of this maxim has led some modern writers into supposing that the ancient authors accepted slave testimony at face value.

Although there are no traces of an ordeal-like process in the earliest Roman texts, torture developed in a similar evolution from slavery. When he was on trial the free citizen had sureties to stand guarantee for him, and his character would have been generally known to his peers. The slave, on the other hand, was of 'infamous' character, whose testimony had to be tested in circumstances when it would seem to have been against his interest to lie, that is to say, under stress of physical pain, the only 'payment' of which a slave was capable.[67] Similarly, the judicial procedures to which the *humiliores* of a later period were subject developed from the institutions of slavery. The head of a household had always been entitled to torture or administer corporal punishment to his slaves in cases of wrongdoing.[68] (Even in civil suits where their evidence was required he was entitled to administer the torture himself.) A slave-owner's private inquiry would obviously have an administrative, rather than quasi-judicial character. No doubt the procedures to which the *humiliores* were subject grew out of these household inquisitions.

If it seems strange, then, that the idea of dispensing with torture never seems to have occurred to the ancient writers, given that they appear to have been aware that the disadvantages were equal to, if not greater than, the advantages, it must be remembered that slavery was so rooted in their social consciousness, that no thinker, however free-ranging his outlook, ever called it into question – at least not before the coming of Christianity. The furthest the Greeks ever went was to try to abolish slavery among themselves, on grounds of their spiritual and intellectual superiority to the barbarians, who were 'naturally' suited to slavery.[69] When philosophers and men of letters took slavery for granted, as part of the natural order of things, it is hardly surprising that writers on law, whose focus was directed to a narrower area of human concern, should have taken torture equally for granted. Not till the coming of Christianity, with its subversive message of universal equality, were slavery and its corollary, torture, called into question.

THREE

The inquisitorial process

The triumph of Christianity created for the first time in history a disposition to challenge the institution of slavery; and this fundamental change of outlook was reflected in the hostility of Church leaders towards torture. As early as AD 384, the synod of Rome declared that no Christian might exercise secular power without sinning since he would be obliged to order torture in judicial pleadings.[1] St Augustine, though he never went so far as wholly to condemn torture, which he saw as the inevitable consequence of the need for man to pass judgement on his fellow-men in a sinful world, nevertheless considered it a 'hateful mark of human wretchedness'; and he lamented the fact that judges, through their ignorance of men's consciences, were often 'compelled to seek the truth by torturing innocent witnesses'.[2] By the sixth century, St Gregory was stating categorically that confessions extorted by hunger or imprisonment were worthless.[3]

In 866, Pope Nicholas I, in a letter to Prince Boris of Bulgaria who was at that time flirting with the idea of joining the Latin Church, warned him that the practice of torturing confessions from criminals in his country was sanctioned by neither divine nor human laws:

A confession must be spontaneous, not extracted by force. Will you not be ashamed if no proof emerges from the torture? Do you not recognize how iniquitous your procedure is? If the victim who has not the strength to resist confesses himself guilty without being so, who is then the criminal – if not the one who has forced him to make a lying confession?[4]

The attitudes of the early fathers had a decisive influence on canon law which, with the general disintegration of secular power, profoundly affected all judicial practice during the Middle Ages. Thus the most influential of the canonists, Gratian, whose *Decretum* was compiled about 1140, stated that while confession was the best kind of proof, it must always be spontaneous.[5] This was to remain the official teaching of the Church until the mid-thirteenth century, when Innocent IV authorized the use of torture against heretics.

There was more to the Church's opposition to torture than a purely humanitarian aversion to cruelty. Despite the disintegration of the western empire into 'an infinity of tiny pieces', most of which were in a state of continuous warfare verging on anarchy, a new moral order had been created, the *Civitas Christiana*, whose members all belonged to a single nation.[6] The former distinction between Roman and foreigner, citizen and slave, was superseded by a new division between Christian and non-Christian. Within the walls of Christendom, warfare was conducted under certain moral constraints. In particular, Christian captives could no longer be enslaved by their fellow-Christians. And while the Church never went so far as to condemn slavery outright (how could it when bishops and abbots were themselves often large slave-owners?) manumissions were encouraged. Many a slave-owner, having enjoyed the benefits of slavery in this world, was able to earn some credit in the next by freeing his slaves at the approach of death. The supply of foreign captives gradually dwindled while the remaining Christian slaves eventually acquired those rights which were to convert them into semi-free tenants or bondsmen.[7]

Another consequence of the collapse of imperial power was the disruption of the legal system caused by the barbarian invasions. Though the conquered peoples continued to live under the old Roman laws, the Germanic invaders brought with them tribal laws in which torture had no place. The Burgundian and Salic laws and the laws of the Visigoths, assimilating Roman tradition, still made provision for the torture of slaves.[8] But torture, as it had been practised under Roman law, was out of place in proceedings which were mainly open, oral or based on private accusation.

The influence of Roman law first made itself felt in the development of a formal accusatory procedure, a symptom of an emerging consciousness of the difference between private litigation and public welfare. The idea that prosecution was a social function had yet to appear: every criminal still required an accuser, the judge being merely an arbiter between two parties. If the accused confessed, the summary procedure presented no difficulties. The problem arose if he denied his guilt. It was then that he had to prove his innocence by taking an oath, supported by a number of 'oath-helpers' or compurgators whose number was fixed according to the gravity of the offence. Until the beginning of the thirteenth century the compurgators swore, not to their knowledge of the facts, but as partakers in the oath of denial. Obviously the system was biassed in favour of the feudal classes who would have had less difficulty in bribing or finding compurgators from among their families and dependants than the poor and landless. The system depended on a naïve belief in the direct and immediate retribution of God in cases of perjury: and there are many examples in pious medieval literature of perjurers suffering instant catastrophe. The system was retained in ecclesiastical law until the rise of the inquisition.[9]

It gradually became apparent, however, that the Almighty did not exercise such a direct and immediate control over human affairs and that punishment for perjury was, likely as not, to be deferred to the next world. In secular law the various trials by ordeal generally replaced compurgation as a means of determining guilt in criminal prosecutions. Broadly speaking they were of two kinds: the bilateral ordeals, in which the contending parties submitted themselves to a form of contest such as the judicial duel or the ordeal of the cross (in which they had to stand with uplifted arms before the crucifix while masses were said, victory going to whoever kept up this position for longest); and the unilateral ordeals, such as the hot iron or boiling water, in which God was expected to indicate his judgement directly, by preventing injury to the innocent. Another, milder group of unilateral ordeals resembled the modern polygraph or lie-detector in their psychological efficacy: in these ordeals God was expected to indicate his judgement by preventing the guilty from performing an otherwise normal function, such as swallowing a piece of consecrated bread or cheese, or the Eucharist, or taking an oath upon a sacred relic.[10]

The painful ordeals as practised in Europe had pagan origins, and in fact are almost universal, in that identical or similar judicial practices survive in most pre-literate societies. The earliest recorded example is in the code of Hammurabi, the eighteenth century BC Babylonian text, which prescribes the swimming ordeal for those accused of sorcery (though it was applied in the opposite way to its use against witches in Europe).[11] The earliest Roman texts are exceptional in that they appear to show no traces of the ordeals, which is probably why the Roman-influenced canon lawyers ignored them during the early Middle Ages. With the general rationalization and extension of Roman–Canon law in the twelfth century, influenced by the great school of Bologna, the ordeals came under increasing attack – not just from lawyers but from theologians. The most influential critic was Peter the Chanter (d. 1197) who pointed out that the ordeals, by demanding miracles, violated the scriptural injunction 'Thou shalt not tempt the Lord thy God'.[12] (Had not Christ himself, on the Mount of Temptation, refused to perform miracles upon demand?). Peter recorded many instances of innocent people being condemned after failing the ordeals. These, in any case, were widely open to abuse. People could train themselves to pass the swimming ordeal by exhaling when they were thrown in the water, causing them to sink; while it was no accident – or proof of innocence – that the last of three suspects using the same hot iron was the most likely to survive the test.[13]

Peter the Chanter was especially opposed to the use of the hot iron ordeal in cases of suspected heresy; he deplored the practice of princes and prelates who demanded this test, taking no notice of professions of orthodoxy. Medieval literature, of course, abounded in accounts of heretics being worsted in trials of faith, involving the ordeals of fire or boiling water, in which the Catholic was invariably the winner.[14] There was a Biblical precedent in the story of Shadrack, Meshak and Abednego and the fiery furnace – as there was to be a curious survival of it in the *Sperimento del Fuoco* between the rival champions of Savonarola and the Franciscans in Florence in 1498. In 1144 the Bishop of Soissons, encouraged by St Bernard, convicted a number of heretics by applying the cold water ordeal.[15] In 1157 the council of Rheims prescribed the red-hot iron for all those suspected of being Manicheans.[16] In 1172 a clerk named Robert was burned for failing this ordeal after an argument with a knight on the vexing problem as to whether the Eucharist retained its holiness on evacuation from the body.[17] In 1210, after Peter the Chanter's death, Bishop Henry of Strasbourg condemned about a hundred obdurate heretics to the hot iron ordeal. The appeal of one of them was upheld by Innocent III, who had evidently been influenced by Peter the Chanter's views. He removed the Church's sanction from all the ordeals and the ban, which was to have momentous consequences, was inscribed in the canons of the fourth lateran council in 1215.[18]

Although the ordeals were primarily ways of determining judgement, there is evidence that they were sometimes used to procure confessions. A suspect might confess rather than face the ordeal: from there it was but a short step to applying the test, not as a way of determining judgement, but in order to procure the confession. The likelihood of the painful methods, such as hot iron or water, being used in this way increased once the procedure of trial by ordeal fell under the papal ban. What followed was not, in the first instance, so much the *introduction* of torture as the continuation of the ordeals under a new mode of procedure.

Until the early 1400s, when torture was fully institutionalized, there had been some confusion of terminology. Thus between 866 and 869 Pope Stephen v had imposed an earlier ban on the ordeals in cases of infanticide, thinking them to be the means of torture to produce confession.[19] Two texts from the Assises of Jerusalem dating from the thirteenth century suggest that the ordeal and torture were interchangeable, as does another twelfth-century text, the *Très-ancienne Coûtume de Bretagne*. In the case of a suspected murderer, according to the latter,

If he deny the deed, and be taken red-handed or in pursuit or the deed be notorious among the people of the parish, it is proper that he submit to the inquiry and the 'garantie' [proof by witnesses] ... and if it cannot be completely proved and common report or strong presumptions are found against him, he should have ordeal or torture three times. And if he can endure the torture or the ordeal without confessing he shall have saved himself (and it will be evident that God performed miracles for him) and he should go unscathed concerning the deed and it should be adjudged that he be acquitted and released.[20]

The continuity between the ordeal of red-hot iron and the subsequent application of torture in Brittany is further emphasized by the fact that until the eighteenth century the local manner of judicial torture was by 'the approach of fire'.[21]

There was thus in some areas a natural affinity between the older ordeals and subsequent methods of torture. The decisive changes, however, were in the field of criminal procedure generally: especially in the transition from the mainly oral accusatory procedure to the mainly written inquisitorial process in which the confession, usually induced under torture, became the most certain form of proof.

As early as the ninth century the canon law had taken a step in the direction of the inquisition by admitting a limited right of accusation to the judge in cases where a suspect was thought, by common report, to have committed a crime. At first, the judge did not have the right to summon witnesses, and the accused person, known as the *infamatus*, was merely obliged to exculpate himself by canonical purgation. The canon law still clearly forbade the magistrate from being both judge and prosecutor – the essence of the inquisitorial system. However, early in the thirteenth century, an ingenious theory was devised which overcame this difficulty: the notoriety, or *infamia* in which the subject was held by public opinion was deemed equivalent to a formal accusation. Then, in a further evolution, the judge was permitted to initiate a prosecution on the basis of a denunciation by a private individual. This struck at the root of the accusatorial system: for the denouncer was no longer subject to the *lex talionis*, hitherto a powerful deterrent against idle or malicious accusations. Although the penalties inflicted at first under this system were milder than those of the accusatorial process, the accused was deprived of the right of defence and was entirely at the mercy of the judge-prosecutor. It seems ironic that this accretion of arbitrary power into the hands of the clerical judges was not originally directed against heresy (though the new procedures were sometimes used against members of the clergy suspected of heretical tendencies) but against corruption among the clergy and in the monasteries. In attempting to limit the clerical abuses that did so much to foster the spirit of heresy during the high Middle Ages, the bishops or their commissioners usually faced considerable resistance from the objects of their reforms and local vested interests, and needed the wider discretionary powers to deal with them. Only after the suppression of the Albigensians in the twelfth century were special inquisitors, usually members of the mendicant orders, given commissions by the pope to root out and extirpate heresy.[22]

Parallel developments occurred in the secular law. At the beginning of the ninth century, Charlemagne appointed special officials to travel all over his empire with the task of enquiring into the causes of disorder, crime and injustice with jurisdiction over both clerks and laymen, regardless of rank. Their procedure, styled *per inquisitionem*, was more rational and less arcane than the traditional forms of trial entailing the ordeal, the judicial duel or compurgation. On arriving in a district the royal commissioners summoned the notables before them, in the name of the king, and took on oath their declarations on the matters in dispute, and having evaluated the evidence pronounced sentence according to their opinion. The procedure, a function of the royal prerogative, lasted so long as Charlemagne's successors were able to assert their power, and was revived towards the end of the tenth century by the Capets.[23] It survived in a later French code, the *Livre de Jostice et de Plet* which contains an important chapter on 'What Matters Should Be Dealt With By Inquest'. They include nearly all matters in which the king had a personal interest, including royal claims to heritable or moveable property, the maltreatment of royal officials, armed robberies or raids of destruction. The procedure was also extended to certain categories of ordinary crime, excepting those involving capital or corporal punishment.[24]

By the time Innocent III issued the order removing the sanction of the Church from the ordeals, the inquisitorial process was already available to provide an alternative. In fact the fourth lateran council, which banned the ordeal, prescribed the *inquisitio* as a mode of criminal procedure alongside older ones. The influence of Roman canon law was most apparent in the shift from mainly oral to written proofs. The banning of the ordeals had been part of a general tendency towards rationalization, not only of criminal procedure, but of government in general. At first, this rationalization was mainly a result of clerical influence. Until about the middle of the twelfth century, the study of law had been largely in the hands of clerics since the Church had effectively monopolized education. At a time when a good many knights and feudal lords were barely literate, the educated clerks with their superior knowledge of Roman law gave the ecclesiastical courts a decisive advantage over the primitive rusticity of feudal courts. Not surprisingly, the more efficient proceedings of the ecclesiastical courts were soon imitated by monarchs eager to extend the royal jurisdiction over feudal territories. The shift from the accusatory and oral to the inquisitorial and written procedures is exemplified in France by a law of Louis IX (*c.* 1260) replacing the aristocratic wager of battle with the more egalitarian *processus per inquisitionem*. The change was initially popular with the peasants and townsfolk who traditionally looked to the king to protect them from the exactions of feudal barons.[25]

It is sometimes suggested that the reintroduction of torture was an inevitable consequence of the revival of Roman law during the twelfth century. For example, a modern authority, Walter Ullmann, states that the acceptance of Roman law necessarily entailed the adoption of torture, since Roman law came to be 'axiomatically held to be the perfection of everything legal'.[26] Similarly, the French writer, Alec Mellor, describes chapter eighteen of the forty-eighth book of the Digest as the 'poisoned fruit' by which torture entered the European legal system.[27]

Yet there is little evidence that Roman law was directly responsible. Most of the Roman law of torture, as we have seen, was concerned with regulating its use against slaves. During the thirteenth century, at the very time when torture was becoming institutionalized, the lay clerks and canon lawyers, who were becoming increasingly familiar with the Roman texts, were dropping the word *servus* from their terminology because they recognized that the Latin word for 'slave' was quite inappropriate to describe the status of the 'serfs' with whom they were familiar. Thus a bull of Urban iv, dated 1262 (only ten years after the formal authorization of torture by Innocent iv) expressly rules that the ancient canon laws regarding the *servi* are no longer applicable to serfs. With the word *servus* banished from the legal vocabulary, it cannot have escaped the attention of the clerks that much of the Roman law on torture was inapplicable.[28]

Actually, the early commentators, both secular and canonist, were selective in their borrowings from Roman texts. The *Livre de Justice et de Plet* (about 1260) which generally follows the order of the Digest, abandons Roman law completely for 'the purest and most archaic customary law' in the section which should correspond to the *De Quaestionibus*.[29] Similarly, another contemporary French text, the *Conseil* of Pierre de Fontaines (*c.* 1260) contains no reference to torture, despite its familiarity with Roman law.[30] A reference to torture in an ordinance of 1254 for the 'reform of the customs of the Languedoc and Languedoeil' was omitted when the document was officially adopted by the Council of Béziers the following year, suggesting that despite the continuity of Roman law in southern France, torture was still considered extra-legal.[31] On the other hand, a charter for the town of Auzon in the Auvergne, dated 1260, suggests a widespread use of torture in the area, for one of the privileges granted its citizens is exemption from torture in all trials, however serious the crime.[32] Moreover, it seems clear that in German-speaking areas torture arose more or less spontaneously, without direct influence of the Roman law, once the changes in criminal procedure had taken place which put emphasis on obtaining confession rather than determining judgement through archaic means. Thus a criminal procedure ordinance from Tyrol as late as 1499 gives detailed instructions for torture which, according to a recent authority, are 'untouched by Roman–Canon learning'.[33]

The reintroduction of torture, then, was less the direct consequence of the revival of Roman law than the result of much wider changes in criminal procedure, in particular the decline of the ordeals and the change from oral to written proofs. In the latter case the Roman law was a decisive influence. By the thirteenth century the canon law, and increasingly the secular law, were placing emphasis on the need for written instruments and witnesses as the best kind of proof. In the nature of things, the Roman requirement that two witnesses were necessary in the case of serious crime must often have been hard to satisfy.[34] In earlier times, confession had always been an alternative to the archaic forms of proof – in fact some of the ordeals, such as the holy morsel were, whether consciously or not, designed to elicit it. There was also a strong tradition in canon law, deriving no doubt from the practice of sacramental confession, that a confession was final and incontrovertible – the 'proof of proofs' or 'queen of proofs' as it was known to lawyers. Confession could, therefore, under the new and more difficult rules, obviate the requirement for 'legal proof' in the form of at least two witnesses. While these changes were happening, the painful ordeals though banned, were still in recent memory. It is hardly surprising, therefore, that judges and lawyers should have found torture a convenient substitute for the old ordeals, ideally suited to the requirements of the new procedure.[35]

It would, however, be misleading to suggest that torture returned to the legal system for purely procedural reasons. The major impulse behind its institutionalization was the campaign against heresy. The inquisitorial process was particularly well-suited to the discovery of this impalpable, in a sense, unprovable crime, whose locus was in the human brain and whose very existence could only be inferred by placing a particular construction upon an assortment of often innocent-seeming acts. Above all, this crime was virtually unprovable *without* confession – although the purpose of the confession had about it the same ambiguity as its ancestor, the Roman law of treason. These matters will be discussed in greater detail in the next chapter. Here it need only be pointed out that the heretic, as member of a recognized 'outgroup', was with the Jew the first to bear the brunt of the new procedures.

From the thirteenth century the inquisitorial process gradually gained ground, not only in southern France and northern Italy, where most of the heretics were concentrated, but also in Germany, where the sources reveal a steady increase in torture-induced confessions. Significantly, a large number of confessions was extracted from Jews between 1348 and 1349, who were accused of spreading the Black Death by secret poisoning. Although this case too was exceptional, in that the Jews as a typical outgroup were blamed for the sufferings of the whole community, the procedures to which they were subjected had all the features of what was eventually to become the inquisitorial process – as used against the witches. The principal legal historian of the period writes of these sources:

> One sees before oneself the whole of the *Inquisitionsprozess*: examination conducted in the torture chamber by personnel of the municipal council; questioning of the accused about all the details; repetition of examination following the intervening arrest of accomplices; extraction of confessions with torture, in case the accused was not prepared without the application of force to admit the facts which it was desired to hear from him.[36]

In introducing the new procedures, against the resistance of local custom and authority, it became necessary to use them first against recognized outgroups, such as Jews or heretics. In the words of a modern legal historian, 'resistance to procedural innovation is diminished when its objects are conceived as standing apart from the community; such lines blur, once the new institutions have been allowed to arise'.[37] A similar process has been observed with the introduction of the inquisitorial process in the north Italian city states, where it came to be used, first in the political struggles of the cities against the territorial nobility, and later of the urban aristocracy against its own expanding proletariat.[38]

In France and southern Italy the new procedures rapidly became the instrument of royal absolutism. The new class of professional jurists needed to administer it helped to develop the doctrine that the king – who had originally dispensed justice in his own territories in the manner of any other feudal baron or 'lord justiciar' – was the 'keeper of the kingdom' and therefore the sole fount of justice throughout the realm.[39] Everywhere the royal jurisdiction began to extend beyond the limits of the king's own feudal territories, at the expense of the feudal and ecclesiastical jurisdictions; and in the best tradition of the Roman emperors, the kings used the flexible and hard-to-define charge of *lèse-majesté* to attack the privileges and exemptions enjoyed by nobility and clergy.[40]

Except in Germany, where the process was delayed for more than a century, feudal lords were powerless to resist these encroachments. The Church of course resented them equally, but the secular rulers, posing as zealous defenders of the faith, used the Church's particular weapon, the laws against heresy and the inquisitorial procedure that developed with them, to their own advantage. By invoking the secular power against heretics and urging the rulers to persecute them in their kingdoms, the popes in fact presented their rivals with a source of tremendous power. This emerged clearly after the Albigensian crusade, in which it was the French monarchy, rather than the Church, that emerged triumphant, as it did in its campaign against the Templars. But it is also evident, for example, from the way in which the *secular* laws against heresy were used by the Emperor Frederick II to consolidate his own royal power in Italy.

Frederick was a German, born and raised in Italy, a polyglot who bestrode several cultures, reputedly one of the finest intellects of his age. Even if the famous remark attributed to him – that Moses, Jesus and Muhammad were 'Three Impostors' – is apocryphal, his reputation as a free thinker, if not an atheist, is well deserved. Nevertheless the laws enacted by him against heretics were unprecedented in their savagery and would have satisfied the most sanguinary and fanatical of popes. The reason was neither fear of excommunication – which when pronounced on him in 1227 appears to have caused him no loss of sleep – nor any desire to appease the popes whom he treated with varying degrees of disdain: but rather because he understood how useful the anti-heresy laws could be in extending royal power and dealing with potentially rebellious subjects. Thus in Naples and Sicily, where he was determined to prevent the pope from exercising power directly, he entrusted the business of seeking out heretics to his own royal functionaries, before handing them over to the Church for examination.[41]

Such, in brief, was the background against which torture began to reappear after centuries of eclipse in the West. Everywhere the primitive, but relatively open and public, customs introduced by the barbarian invaders after the fall of the Roman empire were giving way before a double assault. On one side the Church was increasing its own internal discipline by extending a procedure that facilitated the power of prosecution at the expense of the traditional rights of the accused. On another, the secular rulers found in the new procedures a useful way of extending their jurisdiction over the divergent and pluralistic society that had grown up in the ruins of the Carlovingian empire, a society where ancient and arcane customs had reinforced the power of petty chieftains at the expense of central government. As with the similar expansion of imperialism in the nineteenth century, the process was accelerated by competition, in this case the rivalry between the papacy and the new monarchies. It would be wrong, therefore, to lay the blame for the reintroduction of torture with its direful consequences at the door of either Church or state, since the responsibility clearly belongs to both.

*　　　　*　　　　*

The general rules governing the administration of torture were laid down by the inquisition during the fourteenth century and were basically the same for the ecclesiastical and the secular law, although it was another century or more before the torture system was fully integrated in the latter. The foremost authority was Nicholas Eymeric (Eymericus), the papal inquisitor of Aragon during the latter half of the fourteenth century, whose *Directorium Inquisitorum* was continuously reprinted, with copious notes and commentaries by subsequent authorities. It was a maxim inherited from Roman law that 'one must not begin with torture'. In theory at least, torture was intended to verify uncertainties and was not to be used on insufficient grounds, or where guilt was certain; it was an aid to, not a substitute for, other proofs:

> One must not resort to the question till other means of discovering the truth have been exhausted. Good manners, subtlety, the exhortations of well-intentioned persons, even frequent meditation and the discomforts of prison are often sufficient to induce the guilty ones to confess.[42]

The following categories of suspect could be sentenced to torture:
  i Those who vacillated in their replies during interrogation;

ii   Those with a general reputation for heresy, against whom one witness could be found to testify having seen them do, or heard them say, something contrary to the Faith;

iii Where there were no witnesses, those against whom there were several other *indicia* of heresy; or

iv   Where there was no general reputation of notoriety, those against whom there was at least one witness and one or more vehement *indicia*.[43]

The *indicia* or proofs required for torture or conviction were of course different according to the type of crime or heresy of which the accused was suspected. For the Cathars or Albigensians, it was enough to show that the accused had 'venerated' one of the leaders of the sect, or 'perfecti' as they were known, or to have attended the death-bed 'heretication' of a dying apostate. These, and the *indicia* relating to witchcraft, will be dealt with more fully in the next chapter. They were divided into three grades remote, vehement and violent; in the secular law, they evolved into the fractions of legal proofs (half-proofs, quarter-proofs etc) against which Voltaire vented his invective. Josse de Damhouder, a Flemish jurisconsult, described them in terms of the criminal law during the sixteenth century, showing they had changed little in the course of two centuries. In a case of murder, notoriety (i.e. a general reputation as a murderer) constituted a remote indication, insufficient by itself to justify torture; a nearer or proximate indication (equivalent to 'vehement' suspicion in cases of heresy) would be proof that the accused was an enemy of the deceased, that he had threatened to fight him and that he was known to carry out his threats; an 'infallible' indication would be the testimony of two reliable witnesses who saw the accused leaving the wood where the body was found, carrying a bloody stick. In a case of adultery, a remote indication would be the suspicion that the couple were in love; a proximate indication when the couple were seen talking on the woman's balcony in the absence of her husband; an infallible one when the two of them are found together in bed.[44]

It was up to the inquisitors and judges to establish when the *indicia* for torture were sufficient, and it is evident from the often vague and contradictory nature of these rules that everything, ultimately, depended on their discretion. There is no obvious way, for example, in which one may distinguish from Damhouder's text, between the infallible *indicia* or proofs just mentioned, which rendered torture virtually certain, and the 'ordinary means' by which conviction could be reached without it. In both cases, the strongest *indicium* – the bloody knife carried by the accused, the discovery of the couple in bed – should logically have been enough to secure convictions without recourse to torture, by 'ordinary means'. In fact, there was a widespread belief among jurists that in all crimes involving capital or corporal punishment (and this included the cases mentioned above) it was necessary to secure the confession of the accused. This apparently flowed from a misconceived attempt to safeguard the accused against wrongful conviction;[45] it also had the added convenience of protecting the judge who could always rightly claim that the accused's conviction came from his own mouth. Damhouder is at pains to point out 'this is entirely against the advice and teaching of the doctors and lawyers'.[46]

In Flanders the grand council only had to take note of the culprit if he had been convicted on sufficient proof, comprising the 'clear testimony of two reliable witnesses who saw the accused commit the crime': this, according to Damhouder, was the *probationem plenissimam*, and was stronger than all other proofs. Yet from the earlier passage it is clear that such a degree of proof constituted an 'infallible' *indicium* for torture. A similar contradiction persists in the writings of many other jurists. Partly it may have been inherent in the law taken over from the inquisition, in which no very clear distinction seems to have been made between the *indicia* necessary for torture and those adequate for conviction without it. But it was emphasized, paradoxically, by the very humaneness of the legal writers who, like Damhouder, were anxious to curb the irresponsible use of torture by cruel and unscrupulous judges. They placed a high assessment on the minimal amount of evidence needed for torture, but in so doing they permitted it to stray into areas in which, under a strict interpretation of the rules, it should have been unnecessary.[47]

These *indicia*, or proofs, were fundamental to a judicial system that made little distinction between examination and punishment. At no time was the accused considered an innocent person under investigation. The degrees of his guilt were assessed according to an ascending scale measured in equivalent degrees of pain. The three grades of 'suspicion', substantiated by the various *indicia*, were themselves considered crimes or punishable offences. The objection that the innocent might suffer torture therefore did not arise, at least in theory, since so long as the rules were observed no one could be tortured unless there was a degree of proof equivalent to the severity of the torture against him. Should he fail to confess under torture, he was not presumed innocent or considered to have suffered wrongfully. Instead he was released as having purged the *indicia* against him. In effect, he had been subjected to corporal punishment for the 'crime' of having aroused suspicion. In theory, no one could be subject to torture a second time without new *indicia*.[48]

Viewed as a punishment for heresy, torture was actually considered milder than compurgation and abjuration, which may seem odd since the latter merely involved solemn oaths entailing no bodily suffering. However those who were sentenced to abjure their heresy received no second chance should they relapse, and upon a second conviction were automatically 'relaxed' to the secular arm for burning. Those who confessed under torture, if their crimes were considered serious enough, might still be required to abjure; but since the *indicia* for torture were less rigorous than those required for abjuration, they might still receive a milder sentence or be freed altogether, having sufficiently 'purged' the evidence against them.[49]

The prisoner was put to the torture according to an interlocutory sentence pronounced by the judge:

We, by the Grace of God, N ..., Inquisitor of ..., having carefully considered the proceedings against you, and seeing that you vacillate in your replies and that there is nevertheless much evidence [*indicia multa*] against you, sufficient to expose you to torture and torment [*quaestionibus et tormentis*]; in order that the truth may be had from your mouth and that you should cease to offend the ears of the judges declare, judge and sentence you by an interlocutory order at such-and-such a time and day, to undergo torment and torture...[50]

The formula was slightly misleading, for as Eymeric makes clear, the culprit could be tortured even if he did not vacillate in his replies, provided there were enough *indicia* against him. After the sentence had been pronounced, more efforts had to be made to make the prisoner confess without torture. The executioners would strip the prisoner, after which he was again taken aside and urged to confess. He could be promised his life, provided he was not a lapsed heretic or guilty of any other crime carrying the death penalty. He was then tortured, beginning with the mildest methods, and interrogated on the least serious points of which he was suspected, the assumption being that he was most likely to confess to the lightest offences. After this, he was shown the more severe instruments of torture and told he must pass through all of them unless he told the truth.[51]

Eymeric has little to say about the actual methods of torture but there were other commentators able to fill the gap. Damhouder states that the only methods permitted by law in the Spanish territories are those employing the use of ropes, which he describes from his experience as a councillor at Bruges:

> The victim is stripped naked and laid on a straight bench, his hands tied behind his back, his belly in the air. His pudenda are covered with a linen cloth. He is tied down to the bench under his armpits and round his diaphragm to prevent his falling off. His two big toes are tied to a cord which stretches his body by means of a wheel, stick or similar instrument. Afterwards another cord may be tied above the knee round his thighs which can be tightened, more or less, at the discretion of the judge ... Sometimes a loop made of knotted rope, known as a *paternoster* is tied round the head and forehead, tightened with two sticks or bones, according to the judge's discretion. Then the executioner may place a clean cloth over the patient's eyes, and forcing his nostrils closed with it, pours a jar over his diaphragm, calves, toes and elsewhere and then forcing open his mouth with a small bridle pours in cold water till he swells up to the point where the judge and his council consider he can no longer endure it without the greatest peril.[52]

In Italy the classic method of torture employed by the inquisition and widely used under the secular law was the *strappado*, in which the victim was tied with ropes and suspended from a pulley or beam. An account of it by Paulus Grillandus, a Florentine lawyer, closely follows Eymeric's ascending order of proofs, and may be taken as the definitive instructions for torture in their original form.

According to Grillandus, there were five grades or degrees of torture, increasing in severity according to the gravity of the charges and the completeness of the proofs. The *first* consisted merely in stripping the culprit and tying his hands as if he were really going to be tortured. This might be done in the absence of the *indicia* necessary for torture proper, since no physical pain was inflicted. Grillandus stated from his own experience that it was a very efficacious way of obtaining confessions from weak or timorous persons; he considered it 'mental' torture. With the *second* degree, the victim was tied and

hoisted for a short period – for the space of an Ave Maria, a Pater-
noster or one Miserere; but no shaking or pulling at the ropes was
allowed. Grillandus described this as 'light' torture, to be used where
the culprit was under 'grave' suspicion, but where the *indicia* were
insufficient for 'full' torture. With the *third* degree, the suspension was
prolonged for the space of one or two Misereres, but without jerking.
This was to be used where the *indicia* were adequate for full torture,
but where the crime was less than 'atrocious': for example, where
the object stolen was only moderately valuable, or the wound inflicted
less than fatal, or for other non-capital offences. It was also to be used
in cases of serious crime where the suspect was of noble birth or of
previous good character.

The *fourth* degree introduced the jerking or shaking of the ropes.
The suspect was hoisted once more and the ropes were given one or
more jerks, causing severe pain, according to the strength of the evidence and the gravity of the crime. This was prescribed for serious
crimes such as sacrilege or murder. The *fifth* and last grade, in which
weights were attached to the victim's feet to amplify the effects of
the jerks, was to be reserved for the most heinous of crimes when the
suspect had hitherto persisted in his denials. These included heresy,
treason, attempts to overthrow the government and the murder of
high dignitaries such as cardinals and princes. This was the most
severe torture known to the law and it was a terrible one: it shattered
the victim's bones and tore his limbs, often wrenching them completely
from his body.[53]

Many of the legal writers were agreed that the judges rarely stuck
to these rules. Hippolytus of Marseilles, one of the most influential
authorities, gives a grim catalogue of some of the extra-legal methods
in use early in the sixteenth century. They include the infusion of lime
mixed with water in the victim's nostrils; the placing of scratching
insects on his navel; interspersing small pieces of wood between the
fingers and binding them; tying the victim on a table covered with
hawthorn twigs; and the famous torture of the Goat's Tongue, in
which the victim's feet were washed in brine and given to a goat to
lick. The rasping motion of the goat's tongue caused the most exquisite
agony without doing any bodily damage. Hippolytus must also be
one of the first writers to mention the sexual tortures that have become
such a feature of our own era, though in his day they appear to have
been restricted to men.[54]

Some of the more lurid methods, however, may have derived from literary sources. The Goat's Tongue, for example is mentioned in the writings of classical authors, as is the *tormentum cum scarabaeo*, also mentioned by Hippolytus. One cannot be certain of the extent to which, when they referred to unapproved methods, the legal writers spoke from personal experience. Many of them, like Damhouder and Hippolytus, were humane by the standards of their day, and were campaigning to prevent abuses. Hippolytus himself went so far as to state that victims who murdered their judges after being tortured on insufficient *indicia* were not guilty of homicide and should not be sentenced to death.[55] Jean de Grèves (Grevius), writing a century after Hippolytus, produces an almost identical catalogue of horrors.[56]

There can be no doubt, however, that the system which placed so much power in the hands of the judges was widely abused, as much through ignorance as wilful cruelty. It was in order to restrict these abuses that legislators found themselves faced with the problem of standardizing procedures. In France, for example, a curious dialogue preceded the drafting of the ordinance of 1670, which finally encoded the torture system in the laws of the *ancien régime*. The president of the drafting committee, Lamoignon, recommended complete uniformity in the methods of applying torture, in order to put to an end the arbitrary action of the judges: 'It is to be wished', he said, 'that the method of administering the torture be uniform throughout the whole kingdom, because in certain places it is administered so harshly that he who suffers it is unfitted for work and often remains a cripple for the rest of his life'.[57] But his view was opposed by one of the members of the committee, M. Pussort, who stated that 'it would be difficult to make torture uniform ... The description which it would be necessary to make of it *would be indecent* in an Ordinance...'[58]

Pussort's view prevailed, and the procedures were never standardized, despite a twenty-page memorandum issued by the *parlement* of Paris in 1707 which laid them down in precise detail, and was subsequently adopted by other jurisdictions. Until the abolition of torture in France, the methods varied according to local custom. In Paris the principal methods were by water and the 'boot' (an iron clamp for constricting the lower part of the leg which was sometimes lined with spikes); in Brittany it was by approach of fire (a relic, presumably, of the older ordeals); in Besançon, by the *strappado* (with metal weights added for the 'extraordinary' torture in cases of severe or political crimes); in Autun with the use of boiling oil, and so forth.[59] Most of these methods were recommended by the various *parlements* after the attempted murder of Louis xv in 1757: an indication that, where the crime of *lèse-majesté* was concerned the absence of distinction between interrogative and retributive torture, noted earlier in connection with the Roman law, was still evident.

Similarly in Germany complaints resulting from the widespread abuses of the torture system created demands for reforms in which torture would be regulated and standardized along the lines of the rules originally laid down by the inquisition. The first of these reforms, the Wormser reformation, dates from 1498.[60] Similar rules were encodified in the *Bambergensis* (1507) most of which were to be expanded and included in the Constitutions of Charles v known as the *Carolina* (1532). This great compilation, which runs to hundreds of articles, represents the inquisitorial system in its most characteristic form. Translated into French, Dutch, Polish and Russian, its influence was enormous; in parts of Germany courts were basing their decisions on its provisions as late as 1870.[61] Many of its provisions, including those on torture, were included in the reformed code of the Empress Maria Theresa, the *Theresiana*, in 1769.

The *Carolina*'s preconditions for torture are very similar to those of the inquisition, and the extent to which torture was generally abused in Germany may be gathered from the added note of caution regarding its provisions for examination under torture. Article 20, for instance, contains an exclusion clause:

When legally insufficient indication of the crime which it is desired to investigate has not been produced and proven beforehand, then no one shall be examined; and should, however, the crime be confessed under torture, it shall not be believed nor shall anyone be condemned upon that basis.[62]

Many of the provisions are designed to minimize the possibility of a false confession: thus when he has confessed, the culprit is to be subsequently questioned, on points of detail, without torture, to maximize the possibility of verification. Moreover, not only does the '*Carolina* distrust its tortured confession': it contains a clear warning that innocent people might inculpate themselves through ignorance of criminal procedure:

When ... the accused denies the crime under consideration, then it shall be assiduously inquired of him whether he can show that he is innocent of the alleged crime, and the prisoner shall in particular be asked to remember whether he can prove and establish that at the time the crime under consideration was committed he was with people or at a place or location whereby it can be recognized that he cannot have done the crime of which he is suspected. *And such exhortation is thus needed because many a person out of simpleness or fright, even when he is quite innocent, does not know how he should proceed to exculpate himself of the thing.* (emphasis added)[63]

The efficacy of such warnings, and of the humane procedure of the *Carolina* in general, may be judged from the German witch panics which will be considered in a following chapter. It may be argued, of course, that witchcraft was an exceptional crime and that the functioning of normal criminal procedure cannot therefore be judged by reference to it. Unfortunately, since the inquisitorial process in the first instance owed its introduction, complete with torture, to the 'exceptional crime' of heresy, this argument cannot be sustained. It was through the operations of the inquisitorial process, and above all by means of torture, that the continental witch-hunts maintained an impetus which would have been impossible under the common-law system. It is under conditions of stress that human institutions, like all other organisms, must ultimately be judged.

The *Carolina* contained no provisions regulating the modes of torture, which were left to the discretion of individual judges. Its only disposition is a prescription under Article 59 that when 'the accused has serious wounds or other injury to his body, examination under torture against him shall be conducted so that he is as little as possible hurt in these wounds or injury'.[64] Other surviving documents, however, yield insight into the manner in which torture was applied in some German towns. For example, a protocol from Leipzig dated 1754 gives precise instructions to executioners on how to tighten and twist the cords in ascending degrees of severity:

i   There must be no jerks, but a gradual tightening and release of the ropes, and blows with the rope, first on one arm and then the other, are permitted;

ii Each turn [of the ropes] must be three fingers more than the previous one, for each arm in turn;

iii The rope must be tied round the two arms together;

iv The knot must not pass [above] the elbow and the jerks must be applied in such a way as to prevent the knots from loosening;

v   Penetration of the rope to the bone must not be achieved by the jerks, but by the sliding motion of the rope;*

vi   Since the blows frequently rupture the skin, it is a good idea to use this method, which increases the pain according to how hard one strikes the rope;

vii When the rope is released on one side, the tension must be maintained on the other;

* The sliding motion of the rope mentioned in subsection v above is achieved by the action of pulling and releasing the rope tied round the victim's arm as if the torturers were sawing. The effect of this torture is approximately similar to that of a saw, since the skin and muscles may, according to circumstances, be cut to the bone.[65]

In the event, no elaboration of the rules, however precise, was likely to prevent the wholesale abuse of the system. In most countries there existed in theory an appeals procedure against sentence of torture, but it is unlikely that any but a few victims can have had any idea how to set it in motion. The burden of torture fell most heavily on the poor and uneducated, for the law had inherited from the Romans a list of exempted social categories which, translated into medieval terms, included most members of noble families, higher clerics, doctors and, not surprisingly, the lawyers themselves. Only in Spain after the sixteenth century, does torture seem to have been administered in strict accordance with the inquisitorial rules. In its rigid centralization and direct subordination to the state, its standardized procedures and its army of bureaucrats, the Spanish inquisition represented three centuries of advance in literacy and efficiency over its medieval precursor. In consequence, torture was effectively reduced to the minimum necessary to sustain the inquisitorial mode of procedure, with all the assumptions that this implied. (A Survey of the Toledo district for the years 1575–1610 concludes that torture was used in about 30 per cent of prosecutions for heresy.[66])

Elsewhere, the inquisitorial process had become, in effect, a weapon in the rivalry between Church and state, and there existed no effective machinery for containing its excesses. The best that could be hoped for was a wise and humane attitude on the part of the judges, such as was continually urged by many of the legal writers. A sample of such well-intentioned moderation in the administration of torture is found in Damhouder, in his advice to the Good Judge:

The good judge is always compassionate, and must take into account the youth or age of his patient and the state of his health, to ensure that his office

be that of the good judge and not the bloodthirsty tyrant. He must start carefully and moderately, then rigorously, and finally very rigorously indeed,
according to the gravity of the crime and the degree of proof against the
accused, and the nature of his replies. He must take no notice of the screams,
cries, sighs, tremblings or pain of the accused; and all must be done with
such care and moderation that the patient be neither driven mad, wounded,
hurt nor unduly distressed. He must carefully watch and take note of the
countenance and manner of the prisoner on the bench, listen carefully to his
words and replies, to hear if he remains true to his [original] account. Above
all, the clerk must write everything down.

The questions and answers must be rapid, and of a general nature: for
example, where was he on Saturday evening? Who was he with? What was
he doing? In order that the details always come from the culprit, the judge
mustn't lead him on, nor suggest that he knows something against him, nor
threaten him with greater pain if he does not confess; but must always continue the torture coldly, just until it seems to him in reason and conscience
that the patient has had enough. He must *not* ask him about other crimes
or misdemeanours which he may have committed, only those for which he
has been accused and charged; for no one may be tortured without sufficient
evidence. Neither must he ask the victim about the crimes and misdemeanours of anyone else; or about their lives, their conversation or their
conduct, whether they be robbers, murderers, forgers and the like. But many
judges of this country do the complete opposite as a matter of course, which
is greatly to be reproved.[67]

The futility of such advice is evident from its very contradictoriness.
What kind of compassion was it that could render the magistrate indifferent to the 'screams, cries, sighs', of the accused? What meaning
could 'undue distress' have when the law authorized the wholesale
dislocation of limbs, the rupture of every tendon and membrane in
a man or woman's body? The ultimate cruelty of the system resided
not in the sadism of the judges or the barbarity of the instruments
of torture, but in the search for a final certainty that must forever
remain an elusive goal in human affairs, at the expense of probability
and the risk of occasional injustice. It was a classic example of the
ancient truism that the 'best is enemy of the good'.

The most ironic and tragic illustration of the way in which such
efforts at moderation were doomed to futility is to be found in the
methods of torturing witches. It was a universal belief, enshrined in all
the legal writings after Eymeric, that victims could protect themselves
from the effects of torture by sorcery. It is possible that some sorcerers

may have used analgesic drugs or rendered themselves insensible to pain by some form of hypnosis. The most widespread belief, however, was that sorcerers, and especially witches, could protect themselves by the use of magic charms written in strange characters on pieces of parchment (virgin parchment according to one authority) which they secreted about their persons. Damhouder recounts at length the case of a suspected witch at Bruges, who, having been hauled in for questioning after performing some miraculous cures in the district, twice resisted torture, apparently indifferent to the pain. On the second occasion, she was foolish enough to openly defy her judges who, recalling what they had heard about magic charms, ordered her to be thoroughly shaved and searched in the pubic area. The charm with its magic characters was discovered in the obvious place, and the witch was brought to confess without any more trouble.[68]

However it was that ingenious humanitarian, Hippolytus of Marseilles, who found what was to prove the most effective remedy against the sorceries of witches: the torture of sleeplessness. He considered it a humane method, since it caused no bodily injury, and it soon acquired great popularity among the respectable judges for that reason, and because of its efficacy. The method consisted simply in placing the victim on a bench between two guards who were changed at intervals, and keeping him awake by pricking or shaking, for forty hours or so. Hippolytus relates that he tried it successfully on two witches of Lugano who had proved impervious to every other kind of torture.[69] Grillandus, another humane judge, found it equally efficacious in the case of two obdurate monks.[70] Grevius mentions a horrible version of it in which the victim's nostrils were pierced with a thread soaked in pitch which could be periodically tweaked.[71] One of the most famous Italian jurists, Prosper Farinacius, claimed it was the most excellent of all tortures, 'for out of a hundred martyrs exposed to it not two could endure it without becoming confessors as well'.[72] It even spread to England, where other forms of torture were prohibited according to common law, and was used by Matthew Hopkins to obtain confessions from the Essex witches during the 1640s.[73]

By the beginning of the fifteenth century the torture system in Europe was already complete; it was to remain unchanged for nearly three centuries. The system was far from uniform and was rent with contradictions, most of which stemmed from the contradictory nature of torture itself. The result was that the strict rules of procedure laid down by the inquisition gave way to a variety of practices as the system became consolidated within the secular jurisdictions of the various European states. The progressive encodification of torture in which the rules were everywhere laid down in increasingly minute detail, and which Pietro Verri and Beccaria saw with such horror as evidence of the inhumanity of the judges, was really an attempt by lawyers and legislators to impose some restrictions on the reckless proliferation of the system. However most of these efforts were vitiated, not so much by ordinary human weaknesses or cruelty, but by the ideological and intellectual currents that will be described in the following chapter. Here, however, it will be sufficient to describe briefly the general direction of this evolution, which everywhere entailed a progressive abandonment of the restrictions derived from Roman law and a proportionate increase in the discretionary power of the judges.

The three areas in which torture was extended well beyond the confines of Roman law were in its duration and repetition, in its application to obtain the names of accomplices and its use against witnesses. Under the original rules of the inquisition, the careful designation of degrees of torture corresponding to the degrees of evidence and the seriousness of the crime maintained the retributive or 'purging' function of torture; to some extent, it operated in the interest of the accused, whose will might sustain him for a limited period in the knowledge that the pain would purge the evidence against him and clear him of suspicion. This idea of torture as a form of punishment for 'suspicion', however, militated against the whole tendency of the inquisitorial process which was entirely geared to the obtaining of confessions, even when these were not strictly required according to law. Once torture had become an established practice, the desire to obtain confessions regardless of legal necessity became irresistible. It was here that the tradition derived from canon law, requiring confession as indispensable to conviction, overrode the more logical and scrupulous legal doctrine that regarded confession – and therefore torture – as unnecessary when there were sufficient other proofs. The fusion of canonical and secular legal traditions in the inquisitorial process had, in fact, resulted in the adoption of the worst features of both. Gratian had insisted on confession, but no torture. The secular legislators had introduced torture, but without the absolute necessity for confession; and in the end, torture and confession became the normal requirements for conviction in all crimes meriting corporal or capital punishment. This, in practice, meant that any limitations on torture, restricting its duration and severity according to the amount of testimony against the accused, were bound to be discarded.

Inevitably, it was the campaign against heresy that provided a way out of the restriction limiting the duration of torture to the quantity of evidence available. Not only were the most severe forms of torture (for example, the *strappado* with weights) reserved for suspected heretics, but a pernicious semantic formula was devised by Eymeric to overcome the limitation that no one could be tortured more than once without new *indicia*. According to this formula, though torture could not be *repeated*, it could be *continued*, if necessary for the second and third *day* following its initial application.[74] This extension soon found its way into the ordinary criminal law.

Another relic of the canonical tradition was the doctrine that confessions extracted under torture were legally worthless. They therefore had to be ratified not less than twenty-four hours afterwards, in a place other than the torture chamber. In many cases, for example in southern France, the inquisition only recorded these subsequent ratifications which were considered voluntary confessions.[75] This tendency has led some historians to overestimate the extent to which people confessed *without* torture, especially during the great witch-hunts. Even where torture was not used, the threat of it was always there, as was recognized by those jurists who put confessions without torture on the same legal footing as those where it was used.[76]

The necessity for ratification, however, created the problem of retractions. What could be done about those prisoners who refused to ratify and withdrew their confessions as having been extracted under duress? In fact, the only references to torture in some of the records are in these relatively rare cases of brave or reckless individuals who dared to protest.[77] Here, judicial opinion was divided and the practice was evidently far from uniform. The sixteenth-century philosopher and demonologist, Jean Bodin, complained that some judges merely released those witches who subsequently retracted their confessions.[78] Damhouder, who usually gave the most humane interpretation to the rules, stated that the culprit should be tortured a second time to see if he persisted in his denial. Afterwards he should be released, as having purged the *indicia* against him. He condemned as acting contrary to law those judges who, he said, continued to work on him with hunger and thirst so that he may be brought to confess again without torture or new *indicia*.[79] Most authorities were agreed on the need for a second round of torture after retraction. The disagreements arose when the culprit made two or more retractions, like the rascal quoted by Hippolytus as saying – after repeated tortures and revocations – 'that he would rather be tortured a thousand times in the arm than once in the neck'.[80]

In dealing with bandits, some judges were in favour of continuing the process indefinitely, since it was known that some professional criminals practised torture on each other in secret, to loosen their muscles and increase their resistance. (The ancient Cappadocians, who lived by banditry, were said by the Romans to have immunized their children in this way.)[81] However, it was also recognized that this course was subject to the law of diminishing returns, since those who survived torture once or twice were likely to be able to continue to do so, at least where the officially approved methods were used. The inquisitor Eymeric was aware, no doubt from experience, that the distension of the muscles caused by the pulley was far more effective against novices than against those who had suffered it before.[82] While most authorities favoured a third round of torture, some of them urged release in case of a third retraction on the ground, as one of them said, 'that nature and justice alike abhorred infinity'.[83] Others advised release after a thorough scourging, or imprisonment where the *indicia* warranted it. The most humane procedure prevailed in parts of Germany, perhaps because the tradition of the ordeal was still fairly recent, where prisoners might still be released after one retraction, on the ground that the torture had already purged their testimony.[84] (This provision, of course, did not apply to the *crimen exceptum* of witchcraft.)

Gradually, however, an odious doctrine emerged, especially in France and Italy, whereby torture was administered 'under reservation of proofs'. Here, if the accused failed to confess or retracted, he was no longer deemed to have purged the evidence against him, but could be given a sentence less than death or corporal punishment, according to the gravity of the *indicia* against him.[85] Bodin mentions the case of a nobleman of Le Mans, sentenced to nine years in the galleys for 'violent suspicion' of murder.[86] He rejected as obsolete the principle that torture purged the incriminating evidence. The provision, embodied in the ordinance of 1670, survived until the abolition of torture in France. As late as 1740 a court at Orleans sentenced a man to the galleys for life for being 'strongly suspected' of premeditated murder.[87]

A further extension of the torture system beyond the boundaries established by Roman law was in the torture of witnesses. Under the Romans, torture had been a means of purging the testimony of slaves and other people of 'infamous character' – such as gladiators – whose condition was generally servile, whether they were witnesses or under accusation. The category was retained and extended after the revival of torture during the late Middle Ages to include all those of low social status or infamous character whose testimony was in any way considered doubtful. The torture of witnesses represented a further departure from the original inquisitorial principle of linking the severity of torture to the amount of evidence against the accused, since the witness's own guilt was not in question. However, its atavistic origins are evident, from the tradition going back to the ancient Greeks that 'unknown' or 'infamous' persons, unable to provide sureties or evidence of character, had to purge their testimony by torture. This was itself a relic of slavery, long after the formal institution had disappeared.

But the most pernicious – and dangerous – of all the departures from Roman law was the torture of those already convicted to obtain the names of possible accomplices. In France, where it was finally laid down by the *ordonnance* of 1670, this was known as the *question préalable* or preliminary torture, to be distinguished from the *question préparatoire*, the preparatory torture employed to obtain the suspect's own confession. It was applied in direct violation of the Roman law, which stated unequivocally that 'he who has confessed against himself cannot be put to the question against another'.[88] This limitation makes it clear that, so far as the criminal law was concerned, the worst of all the abuses to which torture was put cannot be blamed on the 'revival' of Roman law. The torture of criminals to obtain the names of accomplices was practised before the adoption of torture by the inquisition. The bull of Innocent IV authorizing the introduction of torture for heretics refers explicitly to its use against ordinary criminals to obtain denunciations, which suggests that the custom had grown up independently of the teachings of Roman law. From the start its purpose was to facilitate denunciations, for the inquisition was not prepared to consider any confession sincere, with or without torture, unless the heretic betrayed his associates. This, of course, might have been justified by reference to the laws of treason, since heretics were considered 'traitors against God's Majesty' and therefore subject to the Roman treason laws in which most of the restrictions on torture were lifted. But these laws would not have justified the *question préalable* in cases of ordinary crime. Yet it is clear from surviving records of the Châtelet of Paris (covering the years 1389–92) that the *question préalable* was applied not only to obtain the names of the possible accomplices of common criminals, but simply on the off-chance of obtaining revelations of other crimes the accused might at some time have committed.[89]

With the use of torture to discover accomplices, the inquisitorial process realized its full potential as an instrument of social terror. For once it came to be generally accepted that heresy and witchcraft were crimes that necessitated accomplices, it was inevitable that under torture each suspect would denounce others who, duly arrested and tortured, would make further denunciations. The system rapidly became self-fulfilling and self-extending, with nothing to check its expansion but pressure applied externally or a crisis of confidence on the part of the inquisitors. This was by far the worst of the abuses to which the system was open, and it did not happen everywhere. In Spain and the papal territories, for example, witchcraft and sorcery were not taken so seriously as they were in Europe north of the Alps; in dealing with these crimes the inquisition adhered more strictly to the Roman law and the use of torture to obtain the names of accomplices was forbidden. In consequence the witchcraft trials in those areas were conducted with moderation, as they were in England where the use of torture was ordinarily forbidden. The result was that these persecutions never acquired the impetus of the great witch-hunts in Germany, France and Switzerland.

The assumption underlying these persecutions, that there existed an organized conspiracy to destroy the Church, will be described in the following chapter, and forms the second subject of this book, the belief in the Grand Conspiracy which is both the result of and the justification for torture. The inquisitorial process, including the use of torture to obtain confessions and the names of accomplices, was the necessary precondition for the working out of this belief in social terror. Without the inquisitorial process and its corollary, torture, the belief would have remained a comparatively harmless superstition, dangerous to those unfortunate enough to fall victim to it, and indicative of a certain kind of stress within the social order. Allied to the inquisitorial process, the belief was transformed into something incomparably more threatening; it took on the garb of a hidden but palpable reality in which the inner fears that lurk beneath the superstructure of human consciousness were invested with the terrifying majesty of social and political power.

With the aid of the torture system the disparate manifestations of social stress were transformed and objectified in the minds of the authorities, appearing finally as works of the purest evil, emanating from a single source of corruption – the devil himself.

PART 2

The manufacture of heresy

FOUR

The Albigensian crusade

When in April 1207 Pierre de Castelnau, apostolic delegate and envoy plenipotentiary of Pope Innocent III, was stabbed to death by one of the retainers of Count Raymond VI of Toulouse, a train of events was set in motion that destroyed Europe's most brilliant civilization and inflicted a body blow on the Roman Catholic Church from which it was destined never to recover fully. No one, of course, could have foreseen the consequences, either of the murder or of Innocent's reaction to it; nor is it useful to speculate as to whether or not these events would have happened without it. But whether it is seen symbolically, as a solitary act of terrorism that signalled the centuries of terror that were to follow, or as one of those fateful accidents that occasionally tilt the finely-balanced probabilities of action into a new and irrevocable course, the events of that year marked a turning point in the history of the Church. In the struggle against religious dissent, the most powerful of the medieval popes finally abandoned persuasion and diplomacy and initiated a war of destruction. And since the object of his enmity was an idea or series of ideas, rather than the concrete and corporeal manifestations of military power, new and terrible weapons were needed in the campaign. The dazzling military victories initially won by papal arms were no more than the prelude to the battle for hearts and minds waged daily in the tribunals of the inquisition.[1]

For years the Church had been alarmed at the spread and tenacity of heresy in the count of Toulouse's dominions. As early as 1147 St Bernard of Clairvaux, the greatest preacher of his day, had visited Toulouse in order to counteract the dangerous doctrines of a monk called Henry from Lausanne, who had acquired a large following in the area. The situation in the Languedoc had filled St Bernard with despair:

How much evil has the heretic Henry done, and is still doing, to the Church of God! The Churches are without congregations, congregations without priests, priests without honour, and to sum it all up in one word, there are now only Christians without Christ.

The heresiarch, however, was no match for the saint. The latter challenged him to a public disputation, but Henry refused, either because he knew he would be outclassed by Bernard's renowned eloquence, or because he feared for his own safety. After that, most of Henry's supporters deserted him. He was captured the following year and brought to the bishops in chains, and is believed to have died in prison.[2]

Despite St Bernard's triumph, conditions in the Languedoc did not improve for the Church. In 1178 Count Raymond v appealed to the pope for another mission similar to that of St Bernard:

Heresy has penetrated everywhere. It has introduced discord into all families, dividing husband and wife, father and son, daughter-in-law and mother-in-law. The priests themselves have been affected. The churches are deserted and falling into ruin. I myself am doing all I can to stop this plague, but I feel that my powers are not equal to the task. The most important persons in my country have allowed themselves to be corrupted. The masses have followed their example, so that I neither dare nor am able to repress the evil.[3]

We need not suppose that the count was inspired by purely religious fervour in making this appeal to the Church. Although still virtually an independent ruler (he had the advantage of being a vassal of the kings of both England and France), his actual power had been declining. He had lost the contest for Provence to the king of Aragon, who also continued to press him on his western borders. He had backed the wrong side in the struggle between the Emperor Frederick Barbarossa and the pope. Above all, the citizens of Toulouse, his capital, were showing growing signs of independence under their elected consuls. So in seeking to re-establish his credit with the Church, Raymond hoped for support not only against his foreign enemies, but against the powerful burghers of Toulouse whose anti-clericalism and political insubordination sprang from the same source. He was too weak, as he admitted, to act on his own; but if the artillery of the Church could be brought in on his side, there would be worldly benefits as well as spiritual ones.

A mission, led by Cardinal Peter of Pavia and including St Bernard's successor, Abbot Henry of Clairvaux, was duly sent, and for three months established what was the first 'real inquisitorial tribunal' ever in Toulouse.[4] Among the first to appear before it was one of the city's richest merchants, described to the tribunal by informants as a 'prince' of the 'sect', who referred to himself as 'John the Evangelist'. According to the chronicler who described these events (he was an Englishman, Roger of Hovedene) he was 'examined and found to impugn all the articles of the Christian faith'.[5] In fact, the text of his confession has survived. At first he denied any heresy, but when he was asked to re-affirm his innocence on oath, he broke down and confessed that he had denied the reality of the Eucharist – his only error. Abjuring his heresy, he begged forgiveness and was sentenced to be flogged naked through the streets of the city and to undertake the pilgrimage to Jerusalem. Meanwhile, all his goods were confiscated.[6]

This ferocious example, we are told, brought many heretics back into the fold who confessed to the cardinal in secret and were treated with mercy. Information about the heretics began to pour in. It was now established, to the satisfaction of the prelates, that they were contending not with Arians (which is what St Bernard had supposed the followers of Henry to be), but Cathars or dualists in the Manichean-Gnostic tradition. Two Manichean 'bishops' who had fled to the territories of the viscount of Béziers were summoned to appear. They did so on prom-ise of safe conduct; and, before an impressive assembly of the cardinal, bishops and clergy, and the count of Toulouse and his barons, they were examined on the document they brought with them containing the articles of their faith. According to the chronicler

... on the articles of the Christian faith, the men answered on all points as soundly and prudently as though they were thoroughly Christian. But when the Count of Toulouse and others who had previously heard them preaching things contrary to the Christian faith heard this, they were struck with astonish-ment and kindled with zeal for the Christian faith. Rising to their feet, they proved to the very faces of the men that they had manifestly lied.

They asserted that they had heard from some of them [i.e. the heretics] that there were two gods, one good, the other evil; the good one had created only invisible things, those which could not be altered or corrupted; the evil one had formed the heavens, the earth, mankind and other visible things. Others affirmed that they had heard in their preaching that the body of Christ was not consecrated by the ministry of an unworthy priest or of one who was tramelled by any crime.[7]

The accused heretics denied all these charges, and several others, in-cluding the doctrine that men and women who had sexual intercourse could not achieve salvation, or that baptism had no effect on children.

They made a complete confession of orthodoxy, stating explicitly that a priest, however wicked, could consecrate the body and blood of Christ. But, says the chronicler, when the cardinal ordered them to swear on their confession ' ... verily, like men of twisted mind and warped purpose, they were still unwilling to abandon their heresy, in which the superficial meaning of any authority seemed to delight their gross and dull minds'.[8] They quoted the gospel against swearing; the historian, on weaker ground, cites the Old Testament to refute them. After being convicted by many witnesses, they were urged to repent and accept reconciliation according to the usage of the Church. Thereafter,

The Cardinal and bishops, in the presence of the whole people, together with the bishop of Poitiers and other religious men who were present ... denounced them as excommunicates and damned them, together with their sponsor the devil, and they commanded the faithful of Christ carefully to shun the aforesaid Bernard and Raymond and their accomplices as excommunicates and men given over to Satan.[9]

The two heretic 'bishops' evidently returned to the lands of the viscount of Béziers, for when in 1181 Abbot Henry (who by now had been promoted cardinal) raised a troop of horse and foot and captured the fortress of Lavaur, both were seized and converted back to the faith, and were rewarded by being made canons in two churches in Toulouse.[10]

These measures, however, were not enough to silence the dissidents. They still found protection in the courts of the seigneurs, among whom they are supposed to have made converts, they still walked unmolested through the streets and – to the scandal of the faith – debated openly with Catholics, and with each other. It was not till Innocent III mounted the papal throne in 1198 that a long-term strategy was undertaken. On the one hand the cooperation of the local nobility must be sought to prosecute the heretics in their areas. At the same time, since neglect was obviously the main cause of the trouble, the Church must be reformed, with the help of a sustained campaign of popular preaching of the kind that produced such results for St Bernard.

The second part of the strategy, the campaign of popular preaching spearheaded by the orders of Sts Francis and Dominic whose foundations were authorized by Innocent, was to produce long-term benefits for the Church in the second half of the thirteenth century when heresy notably declined. But in the short term the results were meagre.

Dominic himself, who began his ministry in Toulouse in 1204, is only known definitely to have made a single convert.[11] Similarly, a preaching order led by a converted heretic one Durand of Huesca, yielded very poor results at first.[12]

Meanwhile, the first part of the strategy, to obtain the cooperation of the local nobility, also ran into difficulties. Raymond v had died and was succeeded by his son Raymond vi, an altogether less reliable son of the Church. Although he continually professed his orthodoxy, he made no secret of his hostility to the plans of the papal legate, Pierre de Castelnau, who was seeking to form a league of Catholic barons from among his, Raymond's, vassals in order to wage war on those seigneurs who continued to protect the heretics. Raymond refused to join the league, suspecting rightly that the loyalist vassals would seek their own advantage at his expense. The papal legate responded by publicly excommunicating the count of Toulouse and placing his territories under interdict. Immediately afterwards he left for Rome, and was about to cross the Rhône the following morning when he was stabbed to death by one of the Count's retainers. Whether Raymond had given the order for the murder (which is most unlikely) was immaterial: everyone assumed he bore the responsibility. It was this act that finally hardened Innocent's resolution to deal with the situation by force.[13]

The war which followed has come to be known as the Albigensian crusade after one of the dioceses (Albi) in which the heretics had been established. At first the pope tried to involve the king of France, but without success. But he did find an ardent champion in Simon de Montfort, earl of Leicester, a devout Catholic and one of the foremost warriors of his time. The army consisted of knights tempted by the rich spoils of the south and the usual spiritual benefits, as well as a moratorium on any of their debts; and an infantry consisting mainly of *routiers* or mercenaries drawn from the toughest criminal elements and lured, no doubt, by the prospect of an unlimited orgy of looting, murder and rape at God's expense (that is to say, any sins incurred in the course of the campaign would not have to be paid for in the next world).[14]

The crusade was dominated throughout by secular interests. Count Raymond vacillated between support for the rebels and loyalty to the Church, uncertain of which side would better serve his interests. Accordingly, he lost out to both: the pope took advantage of his attempts to prove his fidelity by making him give up his best castles, which fatally weakened his capacity to resist. But his leading vassal, the viscount of Béziers, was exasperated, as were the counts of Foix and Comminges, for they correctly judged, as Raymond did not, the extent to which the campaign against heresy was merely the cloak for the worldly ambitions of the northern barons and ultimately, the king of France. The rebels were supported by a majority of the people of the towns and their leaders. Some of these were heretics or sympathizers; but most of them, including many of the Catholic clergy, resisted for purely secular reasons. The rich and varied culture of the south had seen the development of a municipal independence, similar to that which created the political mosaic of northern Italy about the same time. The Church's offensive represented a threat to the economic and commercial life of the greatest city of the region, Toulouse. As in other places at other times, religious and commercial liberty were inextricably bound together.[15]

So it was that Catholics and heretics fought shoulder to shoulder in the struggle. At Béziers the crusaders agreed to raise the siege in return for two hundred and twenty-two named heretics. The citizens indignantly refused – and when the Catholic army breached the city walls, most of them were massacred in consequence. Arnald-Amalric, abbot of Citaux and one of the papal envoys, is supposed to have uttered the famous exhortation: 'Kill them all! For God will know his own'. After the terror of Béziers, resistance in the region temporarily collapsed. Carcassonne surrendered; other cities – Lavaur, Minerve, Casser, Termes, were rapidly taken. The biggest holocaust was at Lavaur, where four hundred heretics were burned in a single day.[16] Toulouse and Narbonne refused to surrender their heretics, claiming disingenuously that they had none to hide. After the battle of Muret (1213) however, where King Peter of Aragon who supported the rebels was decisively beaten,[17] the council of Lateran (1215) stripped Count Raymond of all his territories west of the Rhône including Toulouse and Montaubon, and gave them to de Montfort. The decision was the signal for a spontaneous rebellion against the pope and the king of France, who was now receiving de Montfort, his vassal, in triumph. The issue of heresy had been pushed even more firmly into the background: it was now a war between two nations and two social systems – the southern Occitan, with its own distinctive language and culture, its self-governing city communes or loosely federated earldoms, against the rigid feudalism of the north, represented by Simon de Montfort and the king of France. When de Montfort arrived to claim his fiefdom, the gates were once more closed against him. He prepared to sit out a long seige. But while supervizing the construction of one of the engines used for scaling the walls, he was killed by a stone from a catapult.[18]

The war dragged on for a time under de Montfort's successor Amauri and Louis VIII of France. After the death of Raymond VI, his son Raymond VII realized that outright victory was impossible, and sought a compromise. He promised to extirpate heresy in his dominions, if only he could have them back. He assisted the Dominicans and welcomed the Franciscans in his territories. St Anthony of Padua preached in Toulouse, and created a storm of persecution against the heretics. Raymond was received back into the Church, and he undertook to persecute ruthlessly the heretics and all their followers; the same year, 1229, the inquisition was established at Toulouse.[19]

* * *

There were two principal heresies fought by the inquisition in France and Italy during the thirteenth century: the Cathars or Albigensians, and the followers of Peter Waldo, the Waldensians or Poor Folk of Lyons.[20] The latter, who merged with the followers of Arnold of Brescia in Italy, then quarrelled and separated again. The Italians became known as the Poor Folk of Lombardy.

The origins and development of the Cathars is still a controversial subject about which scholars disagree. Until recent years, most scholars assumed that the Cathars or Albigensian heretics were dualists in the Manichean tradition, whose ideas were imported from the East. The classic account was set forth by Steven Runciman in 1947: the heresy, he believed, derived ultimately from the gnostics and dualists of the early Christian era. The prophet Mani, who began his ministry in Mesopotamia in AD 242, had taught a complicated cosmogony compounded of Zoroastrian, Christian and Judaic elements. In the great cosmic struggle between good and evil, Adam had been created by the Prince of Darkness in order to hide in him a portion of the spirit he had stolen from the Prince of Light. The object of the good life was to free the imprisoned spirit from the coils of the mortal flesh which, like all created things, was the work of evil. This purpose could best be achieved by extreme asceticism, including abstinence from meat and all animal foods and from all sexual activity. After the death of Mani at the hands of a Zoroastrian ruler in 276, his doctrines spread throughout the

Middle East, north Africa and southern Europe, where they came into increasingly severe conflict both with the pagan Roman emperors and the early Christians. Diocletian persecuted the Manicheans even more severely than the Christians. St Augustine was for nine years a Manichean, and rounded on them violently after his conversion to Christianity, though he absorbed some of their assumptions about the powers of evil. In the West the Vandal invasion had cut off the Manichees from their ultimate source of inspiration in the East, and by the sixth century they had disappeared. But they survived in the East, where one of their offshoots, the Paulicians built a powerful military state on the upper Euphrates. Some of them settled in Bulgaria, where their doctrines spread among Slavic peasants oppressed by Bulgarian overlords. According to this thesis, Manichean heretics began to appear in the West during the tenth century.[21]

This traditional view of the development of Catharism conformed essentially to the Catholic version which sought to emphasize the alien, unchristian origins of the doctrine. Recent scholarship, however, has tested some of the links in the chain and found them very weak. It has now been established from the study of Armenian sources that the Paulicians were only faintly tinged with Manichean dualism during the latter phase of their development.[22] There is no positive evidence that eastern dualistic ideas appeared in the West before the second half of the twelfth century; the Church had been discovering 'Manicheans' for a century or more before that. Several scholars now suggest that dualistic ideas evolved independently in the West, as the theological by-product of a much wider movement of dissent and anti-clericalism arising wholly from within the framework of Catholicism.[23]

The anti-clericalism that became manifest during the eleventh and twelfth centuries in many parts of Europe generally expressed itself in the form of an exaggerated asceticism and piety – though there were other responses as well, as for example in the celebration of profane and adulterous love among the troubadours of the Languedoc. One of the most common charges levelled against heretic preachers was the donatist doctrine that the sacraments lost their efficacy in the hands of wicked and corrupt priests.[24] From the Church's point of view, this represented a systematic and deliberate attempt to destroy the authority of the priesthood, and it was natural that it should have responded by seeking to link such dangerous doctrines with the forbidden teachings of the Arians and Manichees which had been fought off and destroyed by the early fathers. In fact, there is no need to explain the appearance of medieval donatism by reference to any prior manifestation of this or any other heresy.[25] It was entirely in keeping with the practical wisdom of the age. The success of Christianity had depended as much on the universally held belief in personal immortality as on the appeal of a higher morality. The Church claimed to possess a monopoly of the means of salvation; and in an age when men were beginning to feel the first attractions of personal selfhood against the diffusion of identity experienced in a more primitive social environment, the question of individual salvation acquired an overwhelming importance. The wages of sin was death; the reward of virtue eternal life. Only the Church possessed the power to absolve from sin and administer the sacraments, those magical insurance premiums which had to be paid regularly to secure one's place in heaven. At the same time, the belief that poverty, piety and asceticism in this world were necessary for immortality in the next had been deeply implanted in Christianity, from the lives and teachings of Jesus and his apostles. So long as the Church had been poor and the priests virtuous, the people had confidence in the sacraments. But when bishops and abbots were seen to enjoy inordinate wealth, and the priests to be living in sin, genuine doubts arose. How, people asked themselves, could a wicked man intercede for them with God? Might not their immortal souls, through no fault of their own, be placed in jeopardy?

Nearly all the medieval heretics held donatist tenets,[26] the logical consequence of which, of course, was the establishment of a rival priesthood. In contrast to the ordination of priests by the Church, in which the bishop's hands transmitted a magical power that functioned automatically, regardless of the worthiness of the giver or the recipient, the heretic priest only acquired his intercessionary power by prolonged chastity, piety and abstinence. Indeed, so discredited had the idea of priesthood become that the dissidents eschewed the term altogether, referring to themselves simply as 'good men' or 'Christians'. The Catholics usually called them 'perfects' (or Cathars, using the Greek word), in imitation of the original gnostic or Manichean sectarians who adopted a similar organization. Similarly, the more radical among the heretics challenged the automatic efficacy of the sacraments, particularly those which contained a predominantly magical, as distinct from an ethical or moral element. Infant baptism and the 'miracle' of transubstantiation were both attacked as samples of the superstitiousness purveyed by the priests. They also objected very strongly to the taking of oaths, which depended on magical premises, and were in any case condemned in the Gospel.[27] In many of these things the dissidents anticipated the attitudes that would develop among the Protestant sectarians after the reformation.

Inevitably the inquisitors and Catholic polemicists put a greater emphasis on the theological errors of the heretics than on the positive aspects of their beliefs. The more honest inquisitors, like Bernard Gui, did testify to the piety of the sectarians – but implied that this was worthless because it was based on false doctrines.[28] The possibility that these doctrines were the consequence, rather than the origin, of the heretics' rebellion against the established organization and practice of the Church would hardly have occurred to those involved in prosecuting them. A similar assumption informs the descriptions of those modern historians who see in the doctrines of the Cathars the survival of an ancient dualist *tradition*.

The alternative view, which seems to be gaining ground among scholars,[29] accords better with what we now know of the evolution of the sects. Their doctrines varied considerably, and in any case evolved radically under the stimulus of persecution. What started as a movement of protest or reform became a rebellion and ultimately a revolution; and, as with the secular movements of modern times, the ideological superstructure was adjusted accordingly. The common ground among all the heretics, as we have seen, was the tendency to challenge the Church's monopoly over the sacraments, and accordingly to evolve a separate lay priesthood, based on poverty, piety and abstinence. The most successful of the heretical groups, the Waldensians or Poor Folk of Lyons, exemplifies this process.

The career of Peter Waldo,[30] whose ministry as a reformer began about 1175, closely resembled that of St Francis of Assisi, three decades later, except that instead of being canonized, he was excommunicated and his followers persecuted as heretics. Like Francis, he abandoned a life of luxury for holy poverty, giving most of his goods to the poor, and took to preaching the gospel and the sayings of the early fathers among the poorest sections of society. Although the pope approved the vows of poverty undertaken by Waldo and his followers, he only permitted them to preach with the permission of the local clergy – which effectively amounted to a ban, since the local bishop had previously excommunicated them. After further appeals to the pope had failed the heretics were anathematized and excommunicated, and subjected to increasingly severe persecution. From the 1190s they were the objects of the first medieval legislation against heretics, subjecting them to all the penalties of traitors and outlaws, with the additional horror of death by burning.[31] Yet until the middle of the thirteenth century, they remained touchingly loyal to the Church. Despite repression and persecution, for nearly forty years they continued to maintain the orthodox doctrine that only properly ordained priests could perform the essential sacraments; in order to receive these, they attended Church disguised as ordinary Catholics.

Eventually, under pressure of persecution, they adopted the same organization as the Cathars: a priesthood of 'perfects' who by arduous asceticism and piety acquired the right to preach and administer the sacraments, and a laity of followers who were required to live by less exacting standards. The latter were exempted from the ban on taking oaths, an aversion for which the Waldensians shared equally with the Cathars. But like their Cathar counterparts, the Waldensian perfects would die rather than submit to an oath. The inquisitors, of course, were perfectly aware of this. Bernard Gui, in his famous manual, preserved an account of the tortuous semantic wiles by which the suspected Cathar or Waldensian tried to avoid being trapped into openly refusing an oath.[32]

The Waldensians continued their ministry among the poor artisans and journeymen of the cities, where they enjoyed protection and relative obscurity. Their communication was mainly oral, consisting of memorized passages from the gospels and the 'sentences' of the early fathers, translated into the vernacular languages for the benefit of the illiterate. Attracting few followers from the educated classes, they never needed to develop a sophisticated theology or cosmogony in opposition to that of the Church – a factor which partly accounts for their survival, since the Church never felt they constituted a rival religion as the Cathars did. The inquisitors often made a distinction between 'heretics' and 'Waldensians' – a tacit acknowledgement that the doctrines of the latter, in the final analysis, fell short of the truly heretical.[33]

The history of the Waldensians should warn us against assuming too readily that the Church's objection to these heretics was that they maintained doctrines incompatible with Catholic teaching. Their real offence had been to challenge the vested interests of the ecclesiastical establishment by drawing attention to the abuses that arose inevitably from the Church's monopoly of the means of salvation. Yet, as we have seen, it was nearly half a century before the Waldensians were driven to challenging the theological basis of that monopoly, by assuming the right to administer the sacraments themselves. Their heretical doctrines arose from their alienation, and not vice versa.

A similar development occurred among the dualists, although it took a more radical form. From the accounts of the heretics who were persecuted in the Rhineland and Flanders during the 1150s and 1160s, historians have assumed that they were Manicheans, firstly because they were referred to as such by the ecclesiastical authorities and, more convincingly, because the practices and doctrines attributed to them were similar to those of both the ancient Manicheans and the Languedoc Cathars. In 1157, the Council of Rheims had expressed its exasperation with 'slippery Manicheans' who, they declared, 'hide among the innocent folk, especially the weavers who move from place to place and change their names'.[34] Until after the Albigensian wars, Catharism remained firmly established among journeymen weavers in the Languedoc. In 1163, Abbot Eckbert of Schonau referred in a polemical tract to a group of heretics burnt in Cologne that year as Cathars or Weavers, and gave a description of their practices and beliefs which for many scholars contained positive evidence of Manicheism.[35] He states that they reject all marriage, infant baptism and any baptism by water, that they refuse meat, spurn the Eucharist and deny purgatory. He adds that they claim that Christ only appeared to take on human flesh and that the souls of men are really apostate angels.[36] Eckbert's description, however, may well have been coloured by his knowledge of St Augustine's writings on the Manichees. Apart from the purely theological points, none of these practices or beliefs is specifically dualist. The rejection of baptism and the Eucharist is evidence of no more than radical anti-sacerdotalism. Hostility to marriage and all forms of sexual activity later became one of the hallmarks of Catharism in the eyes of the inquisition, as evidence of the dualistic belief that the flesh, like all created matter, was the work of the devil. But in fact, there is no need to postulate heretical dualism in accounting for the heretics' commitment to total sexual abstinence. The belief that virginity was a higher spiritual state than matrimony derived from St Paul, and had been fully and continuously endorsed by the Church's commitment to a celibate priesthood. Similarly, abstinence from meat and all other products of coition, another Catharist practice, could be related to their aversion both to sex and to the killing of animals, which they derived from the interpretation of certain passages in the Old Testament.[37] Hatred of the flesh poisoned Christian teaching long before the appearance of the Cathars, and would continue to do so for many centuries, among Catholics as among Protestants. It was very far from being confined to those holding explicitly dualistic ideas about the creation.

Accusations that the heretics' aversion to procreation resulted in sodomy and other abominations were made by Catholic polemicists for the same reasons that they were made against the early Christians, as part of a deliberate and systematic campaign of vilification.[38] They totally contradict the impressions of other more scrupulous contemporaries, including many of the inquisitors, who have left impressive testimonials to their piety and the purity of their morals.[39] Nor is there much evidence to support the claim that their practices, as distinct from their doctrines, tended to elevate chastity above all other virtues. There was, as in orthodox Christianity, a contradiction between the celebration of chastity (a subject on which Jesus himself was notably reticent) and the needs of biological existence. If every Christian had succeeded in emulating St Paul, that sect would also have ended in extinction. As it was, a compromise was reached; the priesthood (in the West) became celibate, and the laity permitted to marry. Among the Cathars there was a similar contradiction, but their aversion to the idea of a separate priesthood led to a different solution. They were unable to avoid what amounted to a division between clergy and laity (or 'perfects and believers', as the Cathars called them); but they continued to acknowledge their original republican principles by conferring the rite of *consolamentum* (by which the believer, after much fasting and abstinence, was admitted to the ranks of the perfected) on ordinary rank and file followers at the moment of death.[40]

This is the most likely explanation for their organization, on the basis of which a doctrinal superstructure developed as the movement began to flourish. Unlike the Waldensians, the Cathars attracted in the Languedoc a considerable number of followers from among the seigneurs and the urban bourgeoisie, people of learning who would not be content with simply repeated maxims like Peter Waldo's 'Sentences'. Moreover, protected as they were by the seigneurs of the Languedoc, the heretics were free to debate with the local clergy. Though we have no objective accounts of these colloquies, the Cathar preachers must have acquitted themselves formidably to have competed successfully with the trained minds of the clergy in what was still the liveliest culture in Europe.[41]

During the mid-twelfth century Bulgarian dualists are believed to have arrived in southern France to give advice on doctrine and organization, although the crucial document concerning this event has been challenged as a forgery.[42] What is clear is that from the last part of the twelfth century two theological tendencies become apparent among the Cathars: the absolute dualism of Eastern origin, which maintained the co-equality of the Good and Evil Principles, and the predominantly indigenous mitigated dualism (or monachism) which maintained that, though the Evil One had created the visible world, everything had been with God's permission.[43] These intellectual errors, however, lay primarily in the area of metaphysics, and it would be wrong to suppose that the Cathars incurred the Church's hostility mainly on account of them. The Averrhoists, whose philosophical materialism and toleration towards Islam and Judaism posed a far greater challenge to orthodoxy, barely produced two martyrs to the inquisition in as many centuries and they continued to flourish well into the sixteenth century. For unlike the Cathars, who seem to have borrowed some of their doctrines, the Averrhoists never constituted a serious threat to the social power of the clergy. They were not a populist sect, and were mainly confined to the universities.[44]

In fact, the metaphysical aspect of the Cathars' beliefs, although it provided the theological justification for persecution, was not the main concern of the inquisitors. References to dualism in the records are surprisingly rare. Although heresy was defined by the Church as a crime of belief, so that those who maintained an outward conformity could still be considered suspect, in practical terms the inquisitors inferred it from the observance of certain practices and rituals.[45] Their main concern was to smash what they took to be the heretics' organization. So while Manicheism was assumed to be the source of the Cathars' errors, it did not play an important part in the daily business of rooting them out.

Nor does an explicit dualism loom large in the practices of the Cathars themselves. A surviving thirteenth-century text of the *consolamentum* suggests a compromise with Catholic observance: 'Yet let none of you suppose that *this baptism* [i.e. the *consolamentum*] should lead you to despise the other baptism, or anything good or Christian said or done by you hitherto...'[46] Another text from the same period is replete with conventional references to Father, Son and Holy Ghost. Catholic persecutors and polemicists were aware of this ostensible orthodoxy, and attempted to explain it away. Bernard Gui, struck by the similarities with Christian observances, suspected a parody;[47] while Eckbert of Schonau believed that the perfects concealed their true doctrines from the followers for fear of betrayal.[48] All of them proceed from an *a priori* assumption of Manicheism which, one suspects, was more prominent in the minds of the Catholics than of the sectaries themselves.

Thus the charges of heresy normally resulted from the forbidden practices rather than the doctrines that were assumed to have engendered them. The most important of the Cathar rituals was the *consolamentum*, in Catholic terms the 'heretication', which combined the characteristics of the Catholic sacraments of baptism, ordination, confirmation and extreme unction. The ceremony was usually performed at the point of death in accordance with a covenant (*covenenza*) made earlier in the believer's life, to avoid persecution. The *covenenza* was really a device by which the weaker brethren were spared the rigours of celibacy and asceticism demanded of the perfects. But it also had the practical effect of creating a distinction between the clergy and laity of the order. Similarly hierarchical distinctions did develop between the perfects, out of the administrative needs that followed the rapid growth of the sect. The Cathars observed a simplified form of the mass in which bread was broken and the Lord's Prayer recited. Like the English puritans the Cathars seem to have been grave and solemn in their daily habits: they recited a prayer before every act of eating or drinking, and attended monthly assemblies for communal confession. When greeting one of the perfect, the ordinary believer would bow three times and utter the formal greeting 'Pray God make me a good Christian'.[49] Catholics took the bowing to be a form of ritual adoration and dubbed it the *melioramentum*, but it is doubtful if it had any sacramental significance.[50] Although it seems strange that such an apparently joyless religion should have taken root in the land of the troubadours, each was in its own, opposite, way a reaction against the organization and dogma of the Church.

*   *   *

Such were the actions with which, from the time they appeared in Toulouse, the inquisitors were obliged to concern themselves. Their procedure was nothing if not thorough, but from the beginning they faced enormous difficulties. The Albigensian war had created a rapprochement between all classes in the Languedoc in the face of French imperialism backed by the moral power of the papacy. The local clergy had divided loyalties, torn between their social ties with the heretics (many of them came from well-known Cathar families) and the demands of their ecclesiastical superiors. The local nobility and public authorities had protected the heretics during the war; many of them, moreover, had themselves become infected – less, perhaps, through the intrinsic attractions of Cathar austerities than because the cause of orthodoxy had come to be identified with the hated foreigner.

The first inquisition after the war was established by the Cardinal-Legate Romanus of St Angelo. Sitting in the council of Toulouse he issued a series of draconian decrees designed to destroy the enemies of Christ – measures which in most of northern Europe had worked well enough. Each parish priest, accompanied by two or three reliable Catholics, was ordered to visit all the houses and suspected hiding places such as barns and caves, where heretics might be found. Similar searches were to be conducted by the seigneurs in their districts, as well as in the towns. Whoever was convicted of allowing a heretic to live in his domain would forfeit it and be handed to his seigneur for summary justice. Bailiffs showing themselves negligent in the pursuit would forfeit their goods and posts. Furthermore, a register was to be made in each parish and everyone over the age of fourteen was required to swear on oath to the bishop or his deputy: anyone refusing the oath would be treated as suspect. The oath had to be renewed every three years, and each person having attained the age of reason had to make three annual sacramental confessions to the parish priest and make his communion at Christmas, Easter and Pentecost. Those who failed to attend Holy Communion incurred suspicion.[51]

Needless to say, without the backing of the local seigneurs, the clergy and the whole-hearted support of the count of Toulouse, the decree was unenforceable. One heretic was burned; another 'perfect' recanted in exchange for restoration of his civil rights, and denounced a number of ordinary believers who refused to confess and had to be tried outside the jurisdiction of Toulouse, in the French territory of Orange. Among the most notorious heretics denounced to the cardinal-legate were the three seigneurs of Niort, powerful vassals of the Count of Toulouse who had supported the viscount of Bézier's rebellion against the French. In

1230 they murdered a royal official, a crime which remained un-
punished, though they were formally accused, together with the count
of Toulouse. Emboldened by this in 1233 they attacked the archbishop
of Narbonne, injuring him and assaulting his servants and removing
the pallium, the symbol of his authority, before setting fire to the surrounding countryside. After frantic appeals by the archbishop to the
pope and the king of France, two of the seigneurs were arrested and an
inquisition held by the bishop of Toulouse. There were plenty of witnesses prepared to substantiate the charges which included harbouring
up to thirty perfects at one of their castles, and putting down a priest
in his own church so that a heretic could preach in his stead. But a large
number of witnesses also appeared for the defence – including unimpeachable Catholic dignitaries like the archbishop of Vielmore and
the preceptor of the Hospitallers at Puysegur, who swore that the chief
of the brothers, Bernard-Otho, had been such a zealous persecutor of
heretics that he had been responsible for the deaths of more than a thousand of them. With so many good Catholics prepared to perjure themselves, the case against the brothers collapsed, and it was only in 1235,
after the inquisition had been permanently established, that Bernard-
Otho and his brother Guillaume were once again brought to book.[52]

Some idea of the popular attitudes towards heresy at the time may
be gathered from the notorious case of Jean Tissière, a weaver of Toulouse who, like many of his fellows, found himself the object of the inquisitor's attention. Before his arrest, he ran through the streets of the
town shouting

> Listen to me, citizens! I am no heretic! I have a wife and sleep with her, and
> she has borne me sons. I eat meat, I tell lies and swear, and I am a good
> Christian. So don't believe it when they say I'm an atheist ... They'll very likely
> accuse you too, as they have me. These accursed villains want to put down
> honest folk and take the town away from its lawful master![53]

After this, the inquisitors arrested him and, since he persisted in maintaining his orthodoxy, he was 'relaxed' to the secular arm for burning.
His arrest caused riots in the streets and the Dominican convent was
attacked. But his supporters were soon disillusioned, for during his time
in prison he met some Cathar perfects who so impressed him that he
asked for the *consolamentum*, which they granted. Before his execution
he made an 'open confession' of his allegiance to the Cathar church –
much to the satisfaction of the inquisitors.[54]

The inquisition as it developed was constructed on three pillars: denunciation, interrogation and secrecy. When the inquisitors visited a district, they first encouraged denunciations by summoning everyone to come forward within a week or so and reveal, on oath, whatever they had heard or known about *anyone*, which might have led them to believe that he or she was a heretic, a defender of heretics, or in any way unusual or unconventional in his behaviour. Failure to heed the summons automatically incurred excommunication. At the same time, a 'period of grace', varying from fifteen days to a month, was announced, during which any heretics who came forward spontaneously and confessed, abjured their heresy and denounced their fellow sectaries would be treated with mercy. This usually meant that they would be exempted from 'relaxation', the heavier penances such as the pilgrimages to Compostella, Canterbury or Jerusalem, and the confiscation of their property.[55]

Thus, before beginning the interrogation of suspects (who were usually referred to formally as 'witnesses') the inquisitors had a substantial body of information before them. To protect the witnesses, the evidence was taken in secret, so that the suspect had little or no idea of the amount of evidence that had accumulated against him. In some districts, such as Narbonne and Béziers, the suspect was even deprived of his right to disqualify hostile witnesses on grounds of personal enmity, since the inquisitors were ordered not to disclose the names of witnesses in any manner whatsoever.[56] Similarly, the Roman prohibitions against witnesses of evil character, such as harlots, convicts and even former heretics, were abandoned;[57] while the Roman law debarring spouses and servants from testifying *against* the accused was entirely inverted: they were allowed to give evidence against him but not on his behalf.[58] Theoretically, the existence of two hostile witnesses was sufficient to have one condemned for heresy, but in practice, most inquisitors insisted on a confession. Even Nicholas Eymeric admitted that witnesses often conspired to ruin an innocent man.[59]

The interrogations were conducted under oath, and were both preceded and followed by abjuration. This, of course, automatically eliminated the true heretics, or *Perfecti*, among the Cathars and Waldensians, although some other sects deemed it lawful to swear falsely to the inquisition. From the start, therefore, the interrogations were directed at the two inferior categories designated by the inquisitors: the *credentes*, or believers, who might or might not have made the covenant to receive the *consolamentum* on their deathbeds, and the *fautores* (protectors) of heresy: those who were not themselves believers who might, in some way or other, have helped or protected them. Voluminous reports of these interrogations survive, but they are summaries, not verbatim records.[60] We do not therefore know exactly by what stages the inquisitors brought their victims to confession and what questions were asked, either before or after the formal introduction of torture. One striking feature, however, is the comparative absence of references to the beliefs of the heretics. Although heresy was an intellectual crime, the locus of which was in the human brain, the inquisitors were usually content to infer it from external acts, such as the breaking of bread, the 'adoration' of perfects, the *covenenza* and the *consolamentum*. In particular, they appear to have been more concerned with obtaining the names of those who attended or took part in these forbidden rites than with the personal guilt of the individual under examination. Before the penitent could expect mercy, it was essential for him to prove his genuineness by denouncing his fellow sectaries. In consequence the records are filled with monotonous catalogues of names, places and dates.[61]

The criteria of guilt were often extremely trivial. In 1244 the council of Narbonne stated that it was sufficient that the accused had shown by any word or sign that he considered the heretics 'good men'. Inordinate emphasis was placed on 'popular repute' and the most unreliable hearsay evidence.[62] In 1254 the council of Albi declared that entering the house of a heretic amounted to 'vehement suspicion'. According to Bernard Gui, some inquisitors held that visiting heretics, giving them alms or guiding them in their travels was enough for condemnation.[63] A Florentine merchant of unimpeachable orthodoxy found himself in serious trouble for bowing socially to a group of men who subsequently turned out to be heretics – his polite gesture having been taken as an act of 'adoration'.[64] A priest was once condemned for eating some pears in the company of a group of heretics he met in a vineyard.[65]

Most of these measures were designed to attack any form of intercourse between the heretics and the Catholic population, virtually all of whom might, according to the inquisitors' designation, fall into the category of fautors of heresy. The inquisitor of Tarragona, Raymond of Pennaforte, divided these into 'defenders', who knowingly defended heretics in words and deed; 'receivers' who knowingly welcomed them into their houses several times; 'concealers', who did not report heretics when they saw them; and 'secretors', who conspired to suppress such reports.[66] The operative principle in these as in many other similar offences was, of course, intention. In a society where heretics or heretic suspects might be one's next-door neighbours or even members of one's own family, it might be impossible to avoid an unwitting transgression. As Innocent III had reminded the authorities at a time when the heresy was at its height, even violent presumptions were not the same as proof.[67] The effect of any such scruples, however, was to ensure that the inquisitors extracted a confession.

Even before the formal introduction of torture in 1252, the inquisitors had at their disposal a number of expedients that were to become familiar once more during the twentieth century: prolonged solitary confinement in dark, festering cells, a starvation diet, the use of 'stool-pigeons' (fellow prisoners posing as heretic sympathizers), as well as the 'torture of delay' – the agonizingly drawn-out legal proceedings that sapped the morale by keeping the suspect in suspense for months, years or even decades.[68] It was not unusual for five or ten years to elapse between a prisoner's first audience and his final conviction.[69] In one case, a prisoner at Carcassonne was brought to confess after nearly thirty years.[70] The inquisition's vigil was ceaseless, its memory bank almost infinite; and since the concept of innocence did not enter into its scheme of things, there was no such thing as being 'cleared' of suspicion, of wiping the slate clean.[71] For all but those with the most determined religious convictions, the best course was to confess and ask for mercy – and then to keep firmly out of trouble, for the penalty for relapse was invariably 'relaxation'.

The introduction of torture was probably a gradual process and, as with the secular edicts of Frederic II, the bull *Ad Extirpanda* merely gave formal sanction to a practice that was already well established. Harsh prison conditions were consciously used to extract confessions. The '*durus carca et arcta vita*', consisting of starvation and chains in a narrow dungeon, satisfied all the criteria of torture, and it was fully understood that they weakened resistance. However the process was slow, and in southern France the prisons were already overflowing with penitents sentenced to perpetual imprisonment by the inquisitors. The adoption of the tortures employed by the secular law brought matters to a head much more quickly.[72]

The aim of torture, of course, was to induce denunciations as well as confessions. This is a fact of crucial importance that has surprisingly been overlooked by some scholars.[73] The relevant text from the bull *Ad Extirpanda* is quite explicit:

The podesta or ruler [of the city] is hereby ordered to force all captured heretics to confess and accuse their accomplices by torture which will not imperil life or injure limb, just as thieves and robbers are forced to accuse their accomplices and to confess their crimes, for these heretics are true thieves, murderers of souls and robbers of the sacraments of God.[74]

The introduction of torture led, within thirty years, to a new reign of terror such as the Languedoc had not seen since the days of the Albigensian crusade. Since every heretic suspect was obliged to denounce several others, eventually almost every member of the population found a place in the inquisitors' books. Moreover, zeal for the faith was far from being the only motive of the persecutors. Their own power and influence depended increasingly on the confiscation of heretic property they shared with the municipal authorities. Convents, even cathedrals like the great brick fortress of Albi, were built or enlarged at the expense of wealthy merchants or their descendants whom the inquisitors and their collaborators had every interest in convicting as heretics. Since the heirs of those posthumously condemned as heretics were automatically disinherited, no moderately prosperous family in the region could feel entirely safe, however firm its orthodoxy.[75]

In 1280 the citizens of Carcassonne and Albi protested to the king of France against the cruelty and greed of the inquisitors who they believed were using unspeakable tortures to extract confessions from wealthy but blameless Catholics. The appeal was dismissed for lack of evidence; and in their frustration and fear the consuls of Carcassonne, aided by some senior members of the clergy, may have tried to sabotage the inquisition's records.[76] An appeal to the pope was equally unsuccessful, and merely resulted in a reaffirmation of his support for the inquisitors whom he urged to punish severely all those who stood in their way. This naturally increased the arrogance of the inquisitors who now overreached themselves. When the citizens tried to make an appeal to the new king, Philip the Fair, the inquisitor of Carcassonne, Nicolas d'Abbeville, threw the notary who drew it up into prison. The citizens responded by sending a delegation to the king, and this time their appeal was heard. In 1291 Philip addressed a stern rebuke to the seneschal of Carcassonne condemning the newly invented system of torture by which the living and the dead were fraudulently convicted, and forbidding the royal officials from carrying out arrests for the inquisitors except where the culprits were notorious or confessed heretics. There may have been similar protests from Toulouse, for the following year he prohibited the magistrates from using torture on clerks under the jurisdiction of the bishop.[77]

These restrictions merely encouraged the hatred felt by the people for the inquisitors and the Dominicans, and in 1295 there took place what amounted to a rebellion in Carcassonne. The people took to the streets, Nicolas d'Abbeville was driven from his pulpit and the Dominicans and their supporters were assaulted wherever they dared to appear. The inquisition could not survive without the support of the secular authorities, and for a time, because relations between Philip and the pope were bad, its operations were suspended.[78] After a rapprochement in 1299, however, it was renewed with redoubled virulence. At Albi twenty-five of the wealthiest and most respected Catholic citizens were made to confess to heresy with torture and denounce their accomplices; again, it was widely believed that the victims had been selected entirely because of their wealth and that the extracted confessions had been false. Moreover the inquisitors were accused in some cases, it would seem with justice, of falsifying their own records in order to obtain confiscations.[79]

By 1300 the king had renewed his quarrel with the pope and, posing once more as the champion of his southern subjects, he ordered the fullest investigation into the abuses of the inquisition. After receiving a deputation in Paris, he took the unprecedented step of removing the inquisitor of Toulouse from his post and the bishop and seneschals were informed that among the inquisitor's manifold crimes was the habit of beginning his examinations with unspeakable tortures. His cruelty had threatened to provoke a popular rising among the king's loyal subjects.[80] As well as dismissing the inquisitor of Toulouse, the king introduced a number of reforms. The prisoners were put under the joint control of the bishops and the inquisitors, each of whom had to give their approval for arrests. 'We cannot,' the king declared, 'endure that the life and death of our subjects shall be abandoned at the discretion of a single individual who, even if not activated by cupidity, may be insufficiently informed.'[81]

The inquisition did not respond to this insult with Christian meekness. When the king's official removed the twenty-five prisoners of Albi from the jurisdiction of the inquisitor of Carcassonne, the latter promptly excommunicated him for impeding the work of Christ.

Nevertheless the king pressed ahead with the reforms. The prisoners were to be visited regularly by royal officials accompanied by the inquisitors. The prisons were to be safe, but not punitive; all inquisitorial trials were to be attended by the bishops as well as the inquisitors.[82] Whatever the immediate effects of the reforms, they do not appear to have lasted. In 1306 the citizens of Carcassonne, Albi and Cordes addressed an appeal to the new pope, Clement v, offering to prove that good Catholics had been forced to confess to heresy by torture and the other pressures of the inquisition. The pope ordered an investigation by two cardinals, during which torture and imprisonment were suspended. Most of the complaints were upheld. At Carcassonne, all but the chief jailer were dismissed, and their replacements were obliged to swear, among other things, not to steal the prisoners' food.[83] At Albi the cardinals ordered new, lighter cells to be built, and gave instructions that the chains which some prisoners had been wearing for up to five years should be removed. They decreed that in future torture should be conducted in the presence of the bishop as well as the inquisitors, in order to safeguard Catholic innocence. These reforms – which became known as the 'Clementines' – were incorporated into canon law at the council of Vienne in 1311.[84] They were bitterly resented by inquisitors like Bernard Gui, who argued that they would seriously cripple the efficiency of the inquisition; and they were either ignored or wilfully misrepresented by other inquisitors, or technical loopholes were found which made them nugatory.[85]

Thus in the half-century that torture had been institutionalized in the Languedoc, it had progressed from being an instrument of coercion for use against recalcitrant heretics and their protectors, to a weapon of mass intimidation. The rules of the inquisition had yet to be formalized; as with the later developments in the secular law, the establishment of fixed rules and procedures was prompted by the awareness on the part of the lawyers and inquisitors of the abuses to which the system was liable. As it then stood, the torture system was a weapon of inestimable power in the hands of popes or monarchs. In 1304 King Philip the Fair had found it expedient to attend to his southern subjects' grievances over the exactions of the inquisition. Within three years, however, the same monarch was adapting the system to his own ends in what is perhaps the most celebrated scandal of the Middle Ages, the Affair of the Templars.

FIVE

The purge of the Templars

The Knights Templars were an order of military monks established after the capture of Jerusalem in the First Crusade (1099) to protect the pilgrims visiting the Holy City from attacks by Saracens and ordinary bandits. They were founded about the same time as the Hospitallers who provided shelter and medical care for the thousands who arrived sick and exhausted from the journey; they took their name from the quarters they were granted near the Al Aqsa mosque on the site of Solomon's temple. As military pressure on the kingdoms of Outremer increased, the Hospitallers also took up arms, and between them the two military orders remained the principal defenders of Christian Palestine until its final evacuation after the fall of Acre in 1291. The prestige and fame acquired by both the military orders in the East led to a considerable accession of wealth in the West. Combining as they did the finest ideals of medieval chivalry with the rigorous asceticism of the monastic orders, they became the darlings of kings and popes alike. From early in the twelfth century, European rulers vied with each other in granting them privileges and making gifts of land for their Houses. King Alfonso I of Aragon even left them each a third of his kingdom, including most of Navarre and a large part of Castile. The will was challenged by his heirs and the knights decided not to involve themselves in a protracted legal struggle – a shrewdly magnanimous gesture that could only increase their prestige. With the general development of trade during the twelfth and thirteenth centuries, the value of their properties rose considerably. The king of France borrowed money from the Templars, and gradually this order took up banking on the grand scale, a function for which its international organization and reputation for probity made it ideally suited. It issued letters of credit to merchants throughout Europe, and managed to circumvent the Church's ban on usury by disguising the interest on the loans it issued as rent. Its houses became safe deposits for crown jewels and other royal valuables, and it was entrusted with the transfer of Church tithes to Rome as well as monies for the Holy Land.[1]

The military orders were entirely autonomous institutions, owing no allegiance other than to the pope himself. They paid no tithes or taxes and enjoyed all the immunities from civil law accorded to those in holy orders; at the same time, the bishops were forbidden to excommunicate them, and were ordered to refer even the local disputes in which they might become involved with them direct to Rome. Naturally these privileges made the Templars and Hospitallers the object of considerable resentment among the bishops and ordinary clergy. The policy of the popes oscillated between unconditional support for the orders and fierce castigations for their pride which, among the Templars especially, began to be notorious. In 1207 Innocent III delivered a stinging rebuke to the fighting élite of Christendom in a bull entitled *De Insolentia Templariorum*, in which, among other things, he accused them of apostasizing from God, scandalizing the Church, and employing doctrines worthy of demons. Although successive popes reconfirmed the orders in their privileges, this polemical attack by the most magnificent of all the princes of the medieval church would not be forgotten.[2] As the military situation in Palestine deteriorated, it was inevitable that the two orders should be blamed for the Christian losses. The charges were exacerbated by the growing rivalry between them. Rumours of treason and corruption began to circulate, fanned by the mutual antagonism. After the loss of the last Christian stronghold at Acre, the Hospitallers regained some of their prestige by conquering the island of Rhodes; the stock of the Templars, on the other hand, was further diminished by a pointless expedition in which they enriched themselves at the expense of the Latin Princes in Greece.[3]

Meanwhile, relations between the Templars and their two most powerful protectors, the pope and the king of France, came under increasing strain as a result of the refusal of the Grand Master of the order, Jacques de Molay, to agree to a merger with the Hospitallers. The idea had been mooted ever since the loss of Palestine, which had been widely attributed to the rivalry between the two orders. It was indispensable to the ambitious new crusade that Philip was planning to launch. This entailed not only the recovery of the Holy Land, but also the conversion of the Saracen by a special team of missionaries trained in Arabic who would follow in the wake of the new model army to be commanded by Philip himself.[4] De Molay's reluctance to go along with the king's wild design, coupled with his order's apparent inactivity and lack of Christian enthusiasm, would have been enough to arouse the irritation of both king and pope, without the additional annoyance of Philip's financial troubles. Like the Tudor monarchy in England, two centuries later, the French kingdom was rapidly outgrowing its financial resources. Philip had begun by taking over some of the Church's sources of income – a move which had drawn him into conflict with Boniface VIII; then he devalued the currency, provoking popular riots in Paris. Then, in 1306, he turned on the Jews, who were thrown into prison, their money stolen and their goods sold for the benefit of the exchequer. Finally, it was the turn of the Templars: it might have been the Hospitallers, who were just as wealthy, if not more so. But they were also more powerful, and, what was more important, they were more popular in France where they carried on their tradition of providing shelter for the poor. The Templars provided a softer and easier target.[5]

Since the inquisition was to be Philip's instrument for the destruction of the order, the charge he brought against them was heresy – though it was heresy of an obscure, and peculiarly abominable kind. The proclamation for the arrest of the knights has survived, and even in translation retains something of its original flavour:

... on the report of persons worthy of trust, we have been informed that the brothers of the military order of the Temple, hiding under the habit of the order as wolves in sheep's clothing, insulting miserably the religion of our faith, have once more crucified in our time our Lord Jesus Christ, already once crucified for the redemption of mankind, and inflicted on him worse injuries than he suffered on the Cross; when, on entering their order, they make their vows and are presented with His Image and by a sorrow – what shall I say, a miserable blindness, they deny Him thrice and by a horrible cruelty, spit thrice on His face; after which, divested of the clothes they wore in secular life they are taken naked into the presence of him whose task it is to receive them and there they are kissed by him, according to the odious rite of their order, first at the base of the spine, secondly on the navel, and finally on the mouth, to the shame of human dignity. And after they have offended against the Divine Law by equally abominable and detestable acts they oblige themselves, by an oath and fearless of the offence against human law, to deliver themselves one to another, without refusal – and from this time they are required by this vice to enter into an horrible concubinage; and that is why the wrath of God has fallen upon these sons of infidelity. . . . [6]

These odious rites and sodomies were not the only charges brought against the order. According to the detailed instructions given to the commissioners charged with the arrests, an even more sinister significance was attached to the belts the Templars wore over their tunics and which they were never supposed to take off for the whole or their lives. Although it was known only to the Grand Master and the elders of the order, each of these girdles had been secretly consecrated to a heathen idol in the form of the head of a bearded man, which was kissed and adored in each of the provincial chapters.[7] The proclamation was issued in September 1307 – though the actual arrests were not carried out for another month. The Templars seem to have had no inkling of the impending catastrophe. The secret was well kept and the *coup de main*, masterminded by Philip's chief minister Guillaume de Nogaret, well coordinated. At daybreak on 13 October, the Templars throughout France were arrested, and the inquisition at once began its work.

Theoretically, in the matter of heresy, the king was acting at the request of the ecclesiastical authorities. At this stage, Pope Clement v was not to be trusted to do Philip's bidding. However the latter had at his disposal his own confessor, Frère Guillaume, whom Philip had previously persuaded the pope to invest with plenipotentiary powers as inquisitor of France. The formalities caused few problems. There were plenty of witnesses happy to discredit the order, by testifying against them. Many of these were former Templars dismissed for misconduct, the chief one being Esquiu de Floyran, a knight of Béziers who had once been sentenced to death for murder. According to some accounts, Esquiu was the originator of the charges against the order – having claimed to have heard them from another ex-prisoner while both were awaiting death in prison. He had tried unsuccessfully to interest King James ii of Aragon in the affair, before finding a more willing listener in Guillaume de Nogaret. The story is not implausible, since Esquiu played a leading part in the interrogation and torture of the Templars, and was handsomely compensated for his trouble by being granted one of their properties as his personal estate. However, the ready acceptance of these allegations by the king, his ministers and hundreds of lay and clerical officials cannot be explained by reference to its origins.

We have already seen how the ground had been well prepared by Innocent iii. At least some of the charges listed in the proclamation could have been reached by giving a literal interpretation to the hyperbolical polemics of the bull *De Insolentia Templariorum*. There were other malicious rumours as well – such as the kiss on the posterior – which the Hospitallers took pleasure in circulating. There might even have once been a grain of truth in the suggestion. A kiss of peace, given on the mouth, was a common act of courtesy during the Middle Ages, and may have been part of the initiation ceremony.[8] It is possible that at some time or other the ritual kiss was parodied in the form of a 'kiss on the arse', either as a joke or in order to keep the growing number of non-combatant servants who were admitted into the order in their place.[9] The ritual of spitting on the cross may also have had some basis in reality. It might have been a test of constancy in case of capture by the Saracens: the initiate who spat on the cross on the orders of a superior would be unlikely to resist a similar demand from his Saracen captors.[10]

However, the most powerful and disastrous source of evil rumour was the elaborate and theatrical secrecy with which the Templars, unique among religious orders, shrouded their ritual. Its origins were doubtless in the need to create an *esprit de corps* among a polyglot collection of celibate knights who, unlike ordinary monks, were in daily contact with the sinful world. However the passion for secrecy eventually developed into a meaningless obsession. When the preceptor of Auvergne was asked the reason for it at his trial, he could only reply: 'Through folly'.[11] Such secrecy, however innocent its intentions, invariably invites suspicion, as is shown by the hostility, amounting at times to persecution, encountered by European freemasons, who during the eighteenth and nineteenth centuries borrowed some of the Templar nomenclature and organization in order to enhance the mystique of the Craft.[12]

It was perhaps inevitable that the emphasis on secrecy, combined with a celibacy fanatical even by monastic standards, would give credence to allegations of homosexuality. Many ordinary folk were under the impression that the order had some monstrous secret to hide – what more natural than sodomy, the obvious vice of a celibate community?[13] A similar scandal had led in 1292 to the resignation of several professors and theologians from the university of Paris.[14] Public opinion would have little difficulty in accepting the charges as true. As with the ritual kissing, they may have held a fraction of truth. According to the rules of the order which, of course, were a closely guarded secret, the knights were obliged to sleep two by two in bare cells; the lamp had to remain alight throughout the night and, whatever the heat, they were obliged to keep on their shirts and breeches, as well as their famous girdles. The object of this rule, copied from St Bernard's rigorous régime at Clairvaux, was almost certainly to discourage any form of sexual activity.[15] No doubt in the course of two centuries there were lapses which were fanned into rumours of systematic vice by renegades and malicious Hospitallers. The same allegations are often made, with some justice, by the former inmates of British public schools, and they have been employed, even in modern times, by Catholics against freemasons. There was however an unbridgeable gulf between occasional, or even frequent, lapses, and the charge that the rule of chastity had been completely inverted so that sodomy became obligatory. Significantly, while most of the Templars admitted the sacrilege of spitting on or near the cross, all but two or three denied having taken part in homosexual acts.

Popular rumour apart, there was a further reason why the charge of sodomy should have been credited. The order's manifest wealth had been at variance with the vows of poverty made by its members. Although the wealth was a corporate one, and not vested in individuals, the majority of simple people would have been unaware of the distinction. For them, the Templars had made the vow of poverty, yet lived in splendour. Might not a similar contradiction apply to the vow of chastity?[16] Sodomy was a serious crime in the Middle Ages, punishable by death by burning. But it was not enough to have the order condemned as a whole. For this it was necessary to substantiate the charge of heresy, not only against individuals, but against the whole order – to prove, in fact, that the order was the cover for a heretical sect. Here the denial of Christ and the vilification of the cross were important but insufficient indicators. Spitting on the cross, while a serious act of blasphemy, was not in itself heretical unless the perpetrators could be proved to be part of an organized cult. The worship of the bearded idol was therefore the lynchpin which connected all the other charges. Without the idol, there might be sodomy and blasphemy, crimes for which only individuals could be prosecuted. But only if these were ancillary to the worship of the idol could the charge of heresy be sustained and the order destroyed. It is significant, however, that the worship of the idol did not play a prominent part in the proclamation for the arrest of the Templars or in the initial interrogations. Its importance only emerged in the course of the episcopal inquisition which began in the spring of 1308, six months after the initial arrests.

The proclamation was evidently framed to arouse the maximum popular prejudice, and emphasis was given to those charges that had, at least, a basis of credibility in popular rumour. Sodomy and blasphemy, even sacrilege, were among these, but not heresy. The basis of this charge was known only to a handful of the leaders of the order, who were supposed to have used the ordinary corrupted members as unwitting tools. There is no mystery as to why the arrested Templars confessed to most of the charges. Although many of them denied under oath that they 'had mixed any falsehood in their depositions or . . . withheld the truth as a result of violence, fear of torture, imprisonment or any other reason',[17] this was no more than a form of words they were forced to sign to in accordance with the rules of canon law. The formula is virtually identical in most of the surviving depositions. Otherwise, the instructions to the royal commissioners who arrested the Templars are unusually explicit. After having ascertained, by secret enquiries, the number of the order's houses in each district, the commissioners are instructed to select a number of

. . . worthy and influential men, free from suspicion, knights, magistrates and councillors, and inform them secretly under oath of their task and of the information the King has received from the Pope and the Church;* and immediately they are to be sent to arrest the [said] persons in each place, to seize their goods and arrange for their custody . . . .

Then they will place the [arrested] person, separately under good and safe guard, and make preliminary inquiries of them; next they will summon the Inquisitors' commissioners and investigate the truth carefully, using torture if necessary. And if they confess the truth, they will consign their depositions to writing, having summoned witnesses, . . . [18]

An unusual feature of the procedure is the manner in which the royal commissioners, rather than the inquisition, are entrusted with the preliminary enquiries – although this can have had little bearing on the outcome since the inquisitor of France, Frère Guillaume, was so obviously the king's rather than the pope's man. In another, more significant departure from the rules of the inquisition and the whole tradition of Roman law, the suspects were to be given a clear indication of the gist of the charges – and consequently of the replies they could be expected to make if put to the torture.

Manner of making the enquiry.

Exhortations will be addressed to them relative to the articles of faith and they will be told of the information laid before the Pope and King by several

---

* This was a barefaced lie. It was, of course, the king who informed the pope of the charges.

reliable witnesses, members of the order, of the error and buggery of which they render themselves especially guilty on entering the order, and of their declaration; and they will be promised a free pardon if they confess the truth on returning to the Faith of Holy Church, or else they will be condemned to death. They will be asked under oath, carefully and judiciously, how they were received, what vow and what promises they made, and they will be questioned in general terms until the truth is extracted from them and they are prepared to persevere in it.[19]

With such unambiguous instructions it is hardly surprising that the examiners should have succeeded in obtaining most of the admissions they desired. In Paris, only four out of 138 refused to confess to any of the charges.[20] Elsewhere few of the records of this first inquisition survive, but the general picture was almost certainly the same. Torture is rarely mentioned explicitly: in many cases, perhaps, the stark alternative of death or recantation was enough. In any case, the threat of it was always there, as is shown by one example that survives from Caen:

Brother Guy Pesnée, resident in the Temple at Lourigny, was received and invested alone by Brother Richard de Villiers, late Commander of France, and has been in the order about five years, according to his twice-sworn testimony; he was diligently examined on the said articles, which he denied. Put to the torture on Saturday, he still refused to confess; but, re-examined and interrogated on the said articles the following day, he made an open and true confession of his errors in the same manner as the aforesaid (persons) mentioned above. .... [21]

It is significant that the clerk did not trouble to repeat the details of the confession – so similar were they to those already recorded. They included most of the charges in the proclamation except the adoration of the idol.

It does not seem a coincidence that the number of offences confessed to in the first inquisition correspond approximately in order of precedence, to the charges listed in the proclamation. Nearly all the Templars examined in Paris admitted denying Christ, and spitting on the cross at their reception – the first two charges in the proclamation. Three-quarters admitted to at least part of the next group of charges – the indecent kisses, though only a third mentioned the kiss at the base of the spine. Only half, however, admitted receiving instructions about sodomy, while only a very few admitted having seen the idol, whose existence was so essential to substantiate the charge of heresy.[22] One of those who did was the Visitor of France, Hugues de Pairaud, and this, at least, was consistent with the statement in the proclamation that the idol's existence was only known to the elders of the order[23] (its existence was also admitted, however, by a number of junior members and serving brethren).[24] In fact de Pairaud went a good deal further than the other brothers by admitting that he had instructed the novices to 'calm themselves' with each other if their 'natural warmth' forced them into incontinence. No one, however, claimed to have availed himself of the opportunity.[25]

A similar pattern emerges from the internal contradictions in this body of evidence. There was most agreement about the denial of Christ – the first item in the proclamation, although even here there are discrepancies, some stating that it was God whom they denied, others the cross. There were rather more discrepancies about the spitting, some admitting to having spat thrice, others stating they only did so once. The kisses produced a variety of contradictions as to number, degree of obscenity and above all as to whether they were given or received by the initiate. Finally, among the few who mentioned the idol, there were utterly conflicting versions.[26]

One thing that emerges fairly clearly from the discrepancies mentioned above is that in the majority of cases, the inquisitors were satisfied with confessions of the first two of three offences listed in the proclamation. Assuming they had the resources of the torture-chamber at their disposal, they did not demand a parrot-like acceptance of all of the charges in each and every case. What the bias of the questioning, as revealed by the answers, does indicate is this: the examiners were more interested in eliciting answers pointing to the guilt of the order as a whole rather than that of the individual under investigation. The emphasis was less on the crimes of individual knights than on the orders they had received to commit them. The denial of Christ and spitting on the cross, admitted by almost everyone, were enough to show that sacrilege had been institutionalized in the order. That was enough – so far as public opinion was concerned – to enable the rest of the charges to stick. Having admitted they had received *orders* to spit on the cross, commit buggery, and so forth, individuals were permitted within certain limits to exculpate themselves and earn the court's indulgence.

This is in line with the fact that the second most senior member of the order, Hugues de Pairaud, was required to make the most complete confession. As Visitor of France, he had a thorough knowledge of all the Temple's workings; and it was the institutional aspect of his confession that carried weight. He admitted *authorizing* the brothers to commit sodomy (whether they chose to do so or not was irrelevant) but he did this, like everything else he admitted doing, 'not with his heart but with his lips' – that is to say, purely automatically, *because it was the rule of the order*. The importance the inquisitors attached to Hugues' confession is shown from the records, for whereas at first he would only admit that he himself had received initiates according to the rites described in the proclamation, he subsequently admitted, after torture or pressure, that he believed it to be general practice throughout the order and 'rectified his deposition in order not to perjure himself'.[27] At least one other senior member of the order, Raymbaud de Caron, preceptor of Cyprus, appears to have been similarly tortured after failing to satisfy the inquisitors with his initial confession. At his first interrogation, he would only admit to having been told that he would have to renounce Christ on entering the order. After being removed and brought back later, he remembered that at his reception he had been forced to spit on the cross as well and had been told that buggery was permissible.[28]

Further evidence of direct pressure by the inquisitors comes from certain expressions or phrases that occur in the depositions. In describing the permission given for acts of sodomy, for example, several of the Paris group of depositions – including that of Raymbaud de Caron – follow Hugues de Pairaud who permitted initiates to 'calm themselves' with other brothers if their 'natural warmth' forced them into incontinence.[29] Yet a group of depositions taken at Cahors about the same time uses the phrase 'carnal union' or similar. Furthermore in the latter group another striking phrase occurs that does not occur elsewhere : in more than one of the statements the preceptor receives the posterior kiss on hands and knees 'like a quadruped' (though in other statements of this group and elsewhere, he is described more orthodoxly as merely bending down).[30] It is impossible to believe that these and other phrases that occur in similar sequences were not suggested to the deponents by the inquisitors. This does not, of course, mean that the latter were acting in bad faith or a cynical spirit. On the contrary, it could mean that they were so convinced of the order's guilt that, in order to hurry on the process of conviction, they abandoned the most elementary of the rules of the inquisition and Roman law, which was not to ask leading questions.

By far the most important of the contradictions in the internal evidence concerns the descriptions of the idol. The proclamation described it merely as 'the head of a bearded man' which was adored in the provincial chapters of the order and around which 'one hears it said' the Templars hung their girdles. This is the vaguest of all the charges in the proclamation, and the only one which is apparently self-contradictory. On the one hand, 'only the Grand Master and the elders' of the order are supposed to know about it. On the other, the 'head is kissed and adored in the provincial chapters' and the girdle which each knight wears day and night is supposed to have been consecrated to it by being hung around its neck. What is very obscure from the proclamation is the mechanics by which the ordinary knight obtains his girdle and has it consecrated, and how such an exclusive ceremony can remain a secret within the chapters. We can assume, therefore, that the inquisitors were unsure as to what answers to expect from their inquiries about the idol. If we suppose that they were acting throughout in good faith, a wide range of answers must have been acceptable.

Here again, the evidence is in line with both these assumptions. Among the acknowledged leaders of the order, only Hugues de Pairaud confessed to having seen and adored the idol. The inquisitors, uncertain as to how far down the hierarchy its knowing devotees extended, hesitated to torture other senior members of the order into admitting having seen it (whereas over the spitting, kissing and sodomy, there were no such doubts). On the other hand, Hugues' own testimony made it imperative to discover some other devotees, firstly to provide corroboration and secondly because he had admitted worshipping it at one of the provincial chapters, implying the company of others. In consequence, other brothers were found who confessed to the idol, but they were not from the senior ranks of the order. Brother Guillaume de Herblay[31] said he saw it in two of the chapters held by Hugues; other, junior, members who admitted seeing it were Raynier de Larchant, Jean du Tour[32] and Raoul de Gizy.[33] Since, however, the proclamation had been vague about the precise nature of the idol, beyond stating that it was possibly in the form of the head of a bearded man, the descriptions the inquisitors found acceptable varied considerably. That of Hugues de Pairaud suggested a sphinx-like statue, the head having four feet, two in front and two behind; Guillaume de Herblay said it was wooden, with a kind of beard, and covered with gold and silver; Jean du Tour said the head was merely painted on a piece of wood; while Raoul de Gizy in his description evidently got carried away: 'It was terrible – it seemed like the face of a demon, *d'un maufe*. Each time he looked at it, he was so terrified he had to avert his eyes, trembling in every limb!'[34]

The first group of confessions, all of them obtained within about six weeks of the arrest of the Templars, were the basis of all subsequent elaborations. Any germs of truth contained in the charges were in these depositions, most of which were made when the shock of arrest was still with the victims, before prolonged imprisonment and starvation had done their work. As has been suggested, the outlines of the confessions were laid down by the original proclamation. What was definite and clear in the proclamation was confessed with a fair amount of consistency; what was vague and undetailed produced a variety of contradictory answers. Had the inquisitor Eymeric's rules been strictly observed and those under interrogation given no hint of the charges against them, it would be fair to conclude that some of the charges were substantially true. But there is an abundance of evidence, from the orders in the proclamations to stylistic similarities and contrasts in the statements themselves, which proves that this was not the case. The Templars were interrogated according to a prepared list of articles so that they must have known at least the gist of whatever answers would satisfy their examiners. The same was true – to an even greater extent – of the episcopal inquisition, as will be shown in due course.

There was, however, an important exception. According to this analysis Jacques de Molay, Grand Master of the order, should have made the most detailed and serious confession. His position, however, was different from that of his deputy, Hugues de Pairaud. Together with the leaders of the order, he had already been informed of the charges at a meeting with the pope to which he was summoned in the spring of 1307. Confident of his innocence he had urged the pope to make a thorough investigation, and he had every reason to believe that the measures were in hand that would finally clear the name of the order from idle and malicious rumours. His fears were further allayed by Philip who, on 12 October, the eve of the arrests, had granted him the honour of being a pall-bearer at the funeral of Catherine of Valois. His sudden arrest the following day must have come as a terrible shock, and possibly broke his nerve. At any rate he confessed to some of the charges, with or without torture, within a fortnight. He admitted that on his entry into the order some thirty years previously he had been made to deny the name of Christ, but claimed to have avoided further sacrilege by spitting on the ground only once. But he denied that he had ever been ordered to commit sodomy with his brethren, or that he had ever done so.[35] This admission, though falling far short of the crimes mentioned in the proclamation, was evidently considered enough to give credence to the rest of the charges. It is possible that some kind of 'deal' was made: for although his personal admissions were not of the most serious kind, he agreed to do something far more destructive to the order by issuing a circular to all the brothers urging them to confess as he had done.[36] Perhaps he hoped that by admitting to the least serious part of the charges they might escape with heavy penances, and that the order itself could be saved.

The day after his arrest de Molay was made to repeat his confession publicly before an assembly of clerical and lay dignitaries. Thirty-two other brothers did likewise (in a ceremony that predated the Moscow show-trials by six hundred years or so). The scandal had been publicly proven, or so Philip hoped, sufficiently to convince his fellow princes in Europe, whom he urged to proceed against the order in their territories.

So far everything had gone as well as might have been expected. The pope had been caught off guard, and the clerical and lay establishment in France persuaded of the truth of the charges before the pope had managed to mount an investigation of his own. At first Clement expressed considerable annoyance at the usurpation of his inquisitorial prerogative by the king of France; but his irritation was allayed, conveniently enough for Philip and not, one imagines, by coincidence, when a Templar from his own entourage came forward and made a voluntary confession to the effect that he himself had denied Christ before a full assembly of the order under the Grand Master. Believing therefore that there was some truth in the charges, Clement issued a bull ordering all the kings and princes of Christendom to arrest the Templars in their territories and to confiscate their property pending a full inquiry by the Church.[37]

But then there came a snag in Philip's plans. Two cardinals sent by the pope to Paris returned with the news that some of the Templars they had interviewed in prison, including Hugues de Pairaud, and Jacques de Molay, had withdrawn their confessions. Clement hesitated and, conscious of the reluctance of foreign governments to move against the order without the strongest proofs, he suspended the inquisitors' commissions. Although the king of France had taken the initiative throughout the affair, he was powerless in the face of the pope's outright opposition, and the investigations were brought to a halt. There began a political struggle between the pope and the king to wrest jurisdiction from each other. The king mounted a propaganda campaign against the Templars and the pope. Already, the day after the arrests and even before the public confessions, Dominican friars had been sent all over France to explain to clergy and people the charges that had been 'proven' against the order. Now, to increase the general hysteria, Philip convoked the Estates General at Tours. France's leading polemicist, Philippe Dubois, launched a full-scale verbal attack on the pope, accusing him of nepotism (a charge to which he was justly sensitive) and containing the thinly-veiled threat that he himself would lay himself open to the charge of heresy if he did not allow the investigations to continue.[38] Another writer challenged the validity of the Grand Master's revocation:

It is quite scandalous that he who has confessed openly and publicly should invalidate his own testimony . . . His first confession before several good people was spontaneous; and, persevering in it for several days, he made a public avowal before the University of Paris . . . He sticks to it at the beginning of his trial, and then bewailing his human shame, he demands to be tortured so that his brothers cannot accuse him of voluntarily causing their ruin.[39]

Swayed by arguments such as these, the Estates General voted overwhelmingly for the execution of the Templars, and Philip, pressing his advantage, negotiated with the pope at Poitiers. Selected Templars were produced who reaffirmed their confessions. Eventually, after two months' hard bargaining, the pope compromised. The inquisitors' suspension was revoked, allowing the investigations to continue. But they were placed under the control of the bishop in each diocese. At the same time a separate papal commission of inquiry was to be set up to investigate the charges against the order as a whole, not only in France but throughout Europe. It was to report back to the council at Vienne to be convened in three years' time. The effect of this compromise was an immeasurable increase in the sufferings of the Templars. The papal commission – their best hope of defence – took more than a year to set up. Meanwhile they could expect no mercy from the episcopal inquisitors in France, where many of the bishops were effectively controlled by the king and where in any case the regular clergy, including the bishops, were among the Templars' most bitter enemies.

Some idea of the manner in which this second episcopal inquisition was conducted survives in the records of the papal commission. Confident that the pope's commissioners would protect them against the French king and his bishops, some five hundred Templars eventually

decided to defend the order. Many of those who had previously confessed before the royal or episcopal inquisitions now revoked their confessions, and in so doing described the treatment to which they had been
subjected. Thus Ponsard de Gisy:

> asked if he wished to defend the Order, replied that everything he had said
> about denying Christ, spitting on the Cross, being given permission to unite
> carnally with other brothers and the other enormities consequent thereon were
> false, and that everything he and other members of the Order had confessed
> before the bishop of Paris or elsewhere was false, and that they only confessed
> through danger and terror, because they had been tortured by Floryan de
> Béziers, the monk Guillaume Robert their enemies ... and through fear of
> death, because 36 of the brothers had died in Paris, as well as in many other
> places, following tortures and torments.[40]

Brother Ponsard was then asked to describe the treatment that had
forced him and his brethren to confess, and under which so many of
them had died:

> He replied that three months before he had made his confession to the Arch-
> bishop of Paris [*sic*] he was put in a dungeon, his hands tied behind his back so
> tightly that it caused the blood to run down his fingernails, and that he was left
> there, unable to stretch out full length ... [41]

In a macabre episode, Brother Bernard de Gué described his treatment
at the hands of the inquisitors of Albi: his feet had been burned so
severely that the bones of his heel fell out a day or so afterwards – and
he showed two of them to the commission in evidence.[42] Evidently conditions in the south had not improved since Philip's visit, and reforms,
a few years previously.

Having abandoned all the restraints of the inquisitorial rules, it is not
surprising that the episcopal inquisition brought forth an even richer
harvest of confessions than Guillaume de Paris and King Philip's
officials. Thirty-six of the brothers died of the tortures and depredations
in Paris, another twenty-five died at Sens.[43] Who knows how many un-
chronicled deaths there were in other dioceses?

It would be pointless to analyse this second crop of confessions. In
most cases, those interrogated by the bishops merely repeated their previous confessions – to refuse to do so rendered one liable to torture,
as was shown in the case of Brother Humbert de Corbou who now
denied what he had previously admitted, that he had been forced to
renounce the cross and had spat on the ground at his initiation. The

record states tersely 'et post fuit questionatus vi tormentorum' after which Humbert returned to his original story and stuck to it.[44]

However, the episcopal inquisition also produced a new and much richer diversity of material. After some ninety knights had been selected by their brothers to defend the order before the papal commission, a list of 127 articles was drawn up for them to answer, based on the confessions obtained by the episcopal inquisition. They contain an astounding, and contradictory, variety of admissions, far exceeding in credibility anything contained in the original proclamation. Not only do postulants deny Christ, but some renounce 'God', the Virgin and the saints as well. He is not the true God/he is a false prophet/he did not suffer for mankind, but for the crimes he committed. Postulants spat on the cross/the sign of the cross/a sculpted cross, or on Christ's image. Sometimes they stamped on the cross, sometimes they urinated on it, sometimes they desecrated it on Good Friday. Some committed buggery, and assembled for the purpose in Holy Week. Sometimes a cat appeared at this reunion which they worshipped. The kisses at the initiation are delivered on the mouth/the navel/the bare belly/the anus/the base of the spine/the penis. There were idols in each province which they adored, together or singly, especially at their great chapters and assemblies. The idols usually consisted of heads, but some had three faces, others one, others were human skulls. They were venerated like the Saviour as the equal of God – they could save their worshippers' souls, make them rich; they were responsible for all the wealth of the order, they made the trees flower, the earth bring forth its abundance...[45]

Some of the more fantastic admissions belong to a tradition of vilification going back to pre-Christian times, whose pedigree has been diligently traced by Norman Cohn. As early as AD 177, slaves of the Christians of Lyons had been tortured into denouncing their masters for cannibalism, incest and sexual promiscuity; in the eighth century the head of the Armenian Church, John of Ojun, had accused the Paulicians of ritual devil-worship in which the blood of the babies they sacrificed was mixed with flour to make the Eucharist. In the eleventh century, the Bogomils were accused by a leading Byzantine statesman and philosopher of holding sexual orgies, the offspring of which were sacrificed and similarly consecrated. Almost identical accusations were made against a group of heretics at Orleans in 1022 – who were also accused of worshipping the devil, who appeared sometimes as a black man, sometimes as an angel of light. Towards the end of the eleventh century these allegations were repeated by a monkish writer of Chartres with the difference that the devil appeared among the heretics 'in the guise of some animal or other'. The manuscript evidence, of course, only provides an occasional clue to the countless permutations such stories must have run into in popular belief.[46] Within a century, Norman Cohn suggests, 'it had become a commonplace that the Devil, or a subordinate demon, presided over the nocturnal orgies of heretics in the form of an animal, usually a cat'.[47]

A graphic account of one such diabolical conventicle is contained in the writings of the Welsh poet and ecclesiastic, Walter Map. Such stories became increasingly respectable.[48] The distinguished French philosopher, Alain de Lille, suggested the word 'Cathar' might derive from the Latin *cattus* (a cat) because this was the form in which Lucifer presided over their ceremonies; and the same version of heretic rituals is given by the bishop of Paris, Guillaume d'Auvergne, in the 1230s.[49] The final seal of orthodoxy was given in a bull of Pope Gregory IX in 1233, describing the initiation rites of the heretics. The devil appears in the form of a creature such as a goose, or a duck, or a toad; the initiate is received by a strange man with coal-black eyes whose skin is cold to the touch. Later, the usual obscene ritual takes place, presided over again by the devil, now in the form of a cat.[50]

It does not require, then, much conjecture to explain how the Templars were brought to confess to such an outlandish variety of offences in their second inquisition. The new inquisitors were no longer bound by the charges as listed in the proclamation. During the intervening months the Templars had been subjected to a systematic campaign of vilifying propaganda; the abominations of the sect were widely accepted. There remained only the necessity of providing details from the confessions: not surprisingly, there was even less conformity about these than there had been in the first batch of confessions. On the other hand, given the provenance of the tales about heresy just mentioned, it was to be expected that most of them would find their way into the depositions.

It is a moot point whether it was the inquisitors or their victims who first quarried into these rich seams of fantasy. One suspects it was the latter: for among the records of the inquisition of the Languedoc, there are very few hints that the inquisitors in that area, where heresy had been truly rife, either came across or believed in such stories. The ideas of devil-worship in general, as Norman Cohn has pointed out, were more likely to be held by amateur fanatics like Conrad of Marburg than seasoned professional inquisitors like Bernard Gui. On the other hand, it is clear that all professional restraints had been lifted in the case of the Templars, as they had been among the torturers of the south. The system, once admitted, was so open to abuse that it was impossible to restrict it without the strongest deterrents or incentives – and in the case of the Templars there were no deterrents at all since, in France at any rate, Church and state were united in demanding the order's destruction.

It might seem strange that the victims should gratuitously condemn themselves by confessing to more than the standard charges required. We have already mentioned how, in the first group of confessions, most of them tried, and were allowed, to minimize their individual responsibility. But in the first inquisition they were not tortured so severely (all the complaints of cruelty, so far as it is possible to judge, refer to the episcopal inquisition), nor had they been subjected to prolonged imprisonment and starvation (the documents published by Michelet end on 27 November, only five weeks after the arrests). It is impossible to overestimate the havoc prolonged debilitation, starvation and sleeplessness cause in the human mind. The victim hallucinates frequently, becoming increasingly divorced from a sense of reality. His brain, as several modern studies have shown, is liable to react in a paradoxical fashion to the intensity of his anxieties.[51] The torturer becomes his friend, his lover almost, whom he yearns to please.[52] Deprived in his dungeon of all but the most rudimentary sense-perceptions, he is almost infinitely open to the powers of suggestion. Given the conditions under which the second group of confessions were obtained, it seems not unlikely that the victims, acting perhaps on a hint from their examiners, revealed elaborate fantasies from within the resources of their own imaginations. And what more natural than that some of them should have elaborated on the stories they had heard, like everyone else at the time, about the abominable practices of the heretics who worshipped the devil in the shape of a cat, and made sacrifices to him from the bodies of murdered children?

We need not assume that in recording and crediting these confessions, the inquisitors were necessarily acting in the spirit of bad faith. The degree of correspondence between the first group of confessions we have already explained by referring to the proclamation. No further collusion on the part of the examiners is necessary. The fact that the second group of confessions strays further from the outline of the proclamation suggests the opposite case from a deliberate conspiracy on the part of those in authority. If they had merely been concerned cynically with carrying out the king's wishes, by 'framing' the order, we would have expected the second group of confessions to follow closely on the first, in the spirit of the king's instructions. In fact, the opposite is true: the number and variety of admitted contradictions in the evidence suggests the absence of any collusion between the episcopal inquisitors.

The rest of the story is briefly told. The four leaders of the order – Jacques de Molay, Hugues de Pairaud, Geoffroy de Gonneville and Geoffroy de Charnay – declined to defend themselves before the papal commission and insisted on being heard personally by the pope. This was to prove a serious error since it deprived the remainder of the defenders of leadership, and correspondingly strengthened the hand of Philip, who proceeded to destroy the order piecemeal, using the episcopal inquisition. In April 1310, he persuaded the pope to appoint Philippe de Marigny, the twenty-two-year-old brother of one of his ministers, to the archbishopric of Sens, which included Paris. Acting on the king's orders, the new archbishop at once summoned his council to deliver judgement on the Templars who had been examined in their jurisdiction. Those who stuck to their original confessions were offered reconciliation and liberty; but those who had revoked their confessions (there were fifty-four of them) were to be relaxed to the secular arm for burning as 'relapsed' heretics. All of these bravely chose martyrdom in defence of the order, and were burnt without delay. According to one chronicler, the courage they displayed at the stake placed their souls in great peril, for it led the common people into the error of believing them innocent.[53]

It is doubtful whether the archbishop was acting within his rights in treating those who refused to withdraw their revocations as relapsed heretics. The original rules of the inquisition required proofs for relapse into heresy as for any other offence. Proof should therefore have been given that the brothers had returned to their abominable practices subsequent to their original confessions and abjurations – i.e. during the period of their confinement. Those who merely revoked their confessions were not normally treated as lapsed heretics, but as 'obdurates' who rendered themselves liable to further torture in order to 'purge' their retractions. The faculty of theology at Paris voted 19–3 *against* the opinion of the council of Sens. When it came to the point, Philip and his stooges were strong enough to ignore the customary restraints of the law.[54]

A number of burnings followed in other dioceses. The message was now abundantly clear: those who elected to defend the order before the papal commission could expect no protection from the bishops or the king. This was enough to break the nerve of most of the defenders. The papal proceedings dragged on, but few came forward to defend the order. A last show of resistance was made by the rest of the Church against the French king and his bishops. At the council of Vienne, convened during the winter of 1310–11, the assembled cardinals and bishops refused overwhelmingly to condemn the Templars without a full hearing of all the evidence – which would have meant, of course, new commissions, new inquiries and more tortures. But by now the pope had become a puppet in the hands of the French king. At Philip's bidding, he overruled the verdict of his council and disbanded the order. Those who stuck to their confessions were distributed to various monasteries throughout Europe; those who stubbornly maintained their innocence were condemned to perpetual imprisonment. The order's goods and properties were given to the Hospitallers (but only theoretically in France, where the government had already grabbed the best part of them).

There was a final, heroic, scene in this dismal story of royal ambition and papal pusillanimity. The four leaders of the order were brought to the public scaffold in Paris to receive formally their sentences of life imprisonment. Hugues de Pairaud and Geoffroy de Gonville remained silent as the catalogue of abominations was read to them. But Jacques de Molay suddenly and unexpectedly spoke out, and made before the assembled crowds a last, ringing proclamation of innocence.[55] He was supported by the preceptor of Normandy, Geoffroy de Charnay. Both were sent to the stake without more ado, before the pope or even the bishops had been consulted. But this final act of defiance by the Grand Master did something to vindicate his memory and that of the order his own feeble leadership had played so notable a part in ruining.

SIX

The great witch-hunts

... It has indeed lately come to our ears, not without afflicting us with bitter sorrow, that in some parts of northern Germany, as well as in the provinces, townships, territories, districts and dioceses of Mainz, Cologne, Trier, Salzburg and Bremen, many persons of both sexes, unmindful of their own salvation and straying from the Catholic faith, have abandoned themselves to devils, incubi and succubi, and by their incantations, spells, conjurations and other accursed charms and crafts, enormities and horrid offences, have slain infants yet in the mother's womb, as also the offspring of cattle, have blasted the produce of the earth, the grapes of the vine, the fruit of trees, nay, men and women, beasts of burthen, herd beasts as well as animals of other kinds, with terrible and piteous pains and sore diseases, both internal and external; they hinder men from performing the sexual act and women from conceiving, whence husbands cannot know their wives nor wives receive their husbands; over and above this, they blasphemously renounce the Faith which is theirs by the Sacrament of Baptism, and at the instigation of the enemy of mankind they do not shrink from committing and perpetrating the foulest abominations and filthiest excesses to the deadly peril of their own souls, whereby they outrage the Divine Majesty and are a cause of scandal and danger to very many. ... Wherefore We, as is Our duty, being wholly desirous of removing all hindrances and obstacles by which the good work of the Inquisitors may be let and tarded, and also applying potent remedies to prevent the disease of heresy and other turpitudes from diffusing their poisons to the destruction of many innocent souls, since Our zeal for the Faith especially incites us, lest that the provinces, townships, dioceses, districts and territories of Germany, which we have specified, be deprived of the benefits of the Holy Office thereto assigned, by the tenor of these presents in virtue of Our Apostolic authority We decree and enjoin that the aforesaid Inquisitors be empowered to proceed to the just correction, imprisonment and punishment of any persons, without let or hindrance, in every way as if the townships, dioceses, districts, territories, yea, even the persons and their crimes in this kind were named and particularly designated in Our letters...[1]

The bull *Summis desiderantes affectibus*, issued by Pope Innocent VIII on 5 December 1484 is one of the most terrible documents in European history. Though many people had been burned as sorcerers, magicians or witches previously, the bull's appearance marked the beginning of a new era of intensity in the persecution which was to reach its climax in the century between 1560 and 1660. It had been drafted by two German Dominicans, Heinrich Kramer (Institoris) and Jacob Sprenger, who are best known as co-authors of the most notorious of all the manuals on medieval witchcraft, the *Malleus Maleficarum* or 'Hammer of Witches'. Pope Innocent's bull made an admirable preface to the work and unlike previous papal instructions to the ecclesiastical authorities it received the maximum publicity because of this. The *Malleus* was a beneficiary of the new invention of printing and, reflecting as it did the growing fears throughout society in western Europe about the activities of witches, it ran to a great many editions during its first forty years. From the time of its publication in about 1486, none of the authorities, either lay or ecclesiastical, could be in any doubt about the Church's attitude. Witch-hunting, with all its attendant horrors of torture and burning, was now official policy.

It would be impossible to estimate with any degree of accuracy the number of people, most but by no means all of them women, who were arrested, tortured and dragged to the stake in the two centuries following the publication of Pope Innocent's bull. A recent study, covering southwest Germany, gives a figure of 3,229 executions in a little over a century.[2] But it would be necessary for the court records for the whole of Europe to be analysed before it could be judged whether or not such a figure might be representative. Scholars have produced estimates varying from 200,000 to one million over two centuries.[3] In the absence of more information, we must be content with assuming that the figure lies somewhere within these very broad margins. Whatever the true figures, however, they only become meaningful when it is realized that they were not evenly distributed over time or territory, that country districts were often severely affected, and that the population of Europe was much lower than it is today. At Quedlinburg in Saxony, 133 witches were burned on one day in 1589.[4] Four years before, in the territory of Trier, the populations of two entire villages were executed, barring two persons.[5] The diocese of Como saw a thousand witches burned in a single year, while the prince bishop of Wurzburg is said to have sent 900 to the stake in eight years, including his own nephew.[6]

These peaks of intensity, often in sparsely populated districts, suggest a level of social destruction comparable to the totalitarian onslaughts of our own era.

Like the *Malleus* itself, Pope Innocent's bull was directed at the lay as well as the ecclesiastical authorities in Germany. Witchcraft and sorcery had been civil crimes before they acquired their increasingly heretical significance in the eyes of the Church. The two inquisitors were empowered to seek out and prosecute witches; but unlike their counterparts in the Languedoc they were not acting as members of a more or less autonomous institution. The developments of the previous centuries had made the inquisition virtually redundant. The inquisitorial process, so useful for the discovery of the secret and impalpable crime of heresy, had thoroughly permeated both ecclesiastical and secular law. The aim of the *Malleus* was to give the benefit of its authors' unrivalled knowledge of witchcraft and allied practices to the civil authorities as well as the bishops; in this they were entirely successful. From about 1500 all the prosecutions in France and most of those in Germany were carried out by the civil authorities. Neither the reformation nor the wars of religion which followed diminished the zeal of the witch-hunters. Indeed, the split in the Church seemed to intensify the persecution, as Protestants competed with Catholics in hunting down the enemies of Christianity. Lutheran magistrates adopted and improved on the methods of detection devised by Dominican friars: the famous judge and jurisconsult, Benedict Carpzov, is reputed to have personally signed 20,000 death sentences in the course of his career.[7] The lawyers and churchmen of the time found themselves engaged in a three-sided war for the soul of mankind. Protestant fought Catholic over questions of doctrine and church allegiance. But they joined forces in facing the common greater Enemy who, they believed, was working ceaselessly to subvert and destroy the human race through his agents, the witches.

In the *Malleus*, the means by which Satan and the witches conspire to ruin mankind are revealed in hideous detail. Care is taken to stress that everything the devil does has God's permission, for to assert the contrary would amount to heretical dualism.[8] But, granted the divine permission, the devil and the witches who adore him as their deity are endowed with formidable powers. Once they have made the 'pact' renouncing God, Christ and the Virgin (whom they call 'the anomalous woman')[9] – and this renunciation, of course, is an act of free will, for to assert the contrary would also be heretical – the witches belong body and soul to the devil, and their powers over nature derive entirely from him. To one unversed in the skills of dialectical scholasticism, these powers can hardly have seemed less potent than those of the Creator himself:

> ... they raise hailstorms and hurtful tempests and lightenings; cause sterility in men and animals; offer to devils, or otherwise kill, those children whom they do not devour ... They can also, before the eyes of their parents, and when no one is in sight, throw into the water children walking by the waterside; they make horses go mad under their riders; they can transport themselves from place to place through the air, either in body or in imagination; they can affect Judges and Magistrates so that they cannot hurt them; they can cause themselves and others to keep silent under torture; they can bring about a great trembling in the hands and horror in the minds of those who would arrest them; they can show to others occult things and certain future events, by the information of devils ... they can see absent things as if they were present; they can turn the minds of men to inordinate hatred; they can at times strike whom they will with lightening, even kill some men and animals; they can make of no effect the generative desires and even the power of copulation, cause abortion, kill infants in the mother's womb by a mere touch; they can at times bewitch men and animals with a look, without touching them, and cause them to die; they dedicate their own children to devils; and in short ... they can cause all the plagues ... this is, when the justice of God permits such things to be.[10]

Most of these acts are inspired by pure malice, the evil which the devil seeks to spread among humankind for its own sake. But there is also an ulterior purpose: the failure of crops, or animals and their products, or the ailments and incapacities of humans may be the result of spells the witches have made, and which they themselves alone know how to undo. Thus they drive many good Christians in despair to seek their help: and for such assistance Satan, of course, exacts his price. The witches who perform 'good' magic are really his recruiting officers, and those who seek their help usually end by making the 'pact'.[11] This was especially true in cases of impotence where only witches could undo 'the knot'.

The devil has other ways of proselytizing – the most effective being the arousal of sexual passion, 'for', say the authors, 'the Devil's power lies through the privy parts of men';[12] God has allowed him more power in this act than any others, by virtue of its 'natural nastiness' and because 'the first corruption of sin by which man became the slave of the devil came to us through the act of generation'. According to these authors, it was Adam's susceptibility to the wiles of Eve, not his pride or disobedience, that caused the Fall.[13]

Sex, it hardly needs saying, was at the heart of the witch cult and the worship of Satan, according to these celibate Dominicans: 'All witchcraft comes through carnal lust which is in women insatiable; wherefore for the sake of fulfilling their lusts they consort even with devils.'[14] The devils appeared in many forms, since they had the power to transform themselves into men or beasts. In their sexual personae they were called succubi and incubi, respectively female and male demons who copulated with mortal men and women, sometimes visibly in the shape of humans and sometimes, apparently, not.[15]

Among other writers, there was some scholarly disputation about the offspring of such unions. Some believed that the devil sired the infants himself and that the women gave birth to toads or monstrosities. The Dominicans, however, were too orthodox in their theology to allow such notions. The devil was a spirit: he could not therefore take on mortal flesh – that prerogative had been God's, in Christ, alone. The devil and his demons used borrowed matter: a woman received from an incubus the semen obtained in its previous role as a succubus.[16] In that way the child was mortal – though its mother, if already a witch, would almost certainly consecrate it to Satan as soon as it was born.[17] The inquisitors assumed that witchcraft ran in families, and a strong *indicium* against anyone, especially a girl or woman, was to have had a mother who had been burned as a witch.

The devil also lured the poor and ignorant with lavish promises of money; but, as with sex, the Dominicans were careful to dampen any enthusiasm the foolish might secretly entertain for his favours. Either he never paid his debts, or the coin in which he paid soon turned to clay.[18] A similar disappointment lay in store for those whose incontinence might tempt them to lust with demons. The picture is usually of joyless, even painful, orgiastic frenzy. The authors describe these manifestations with the same morbid relish with which public schoolmasters used to warn their pupils of the perils of self-abuse. Little in all this was new or original. Its unprecedented influence derived from the support it received from the pope, and the energy of its authors who were active inquisitors.

In 1475 there had appeared the first printed edition of a treatise by another German Dominican, the *Formicarius* or 'Ant Hill' of Johann Nider, written originally in about 1435. Nider claimed to have acquired most of his information about witches from a judge, Peter of Berne, who had been actively involved in persecuting them in Switzerland. From him he learned of a grand wizard in Lausanne called Städlin, who was able to appropriate magically a third of the manure, hay or grain from the fields of his neighbours; to cause hail and lightning, or destructive winds, and sterility in men and beasts; drown children in the sight of their parents, make mounted horses mad – indeed, he was able to perform most of the magical feats mentioned in the *Malleus*. When Städlin was finally arrested, he confessed under torture to having caused the deaths by miscarriage of seven unborn babies, sterility in cattle and the raising of tempests. Other witches in the Lausanne area and in Berne had confessed to eating their own children and those of other people, whom they had caused to die whilst sleeping peacefully in their cradles, minded by their parents. After the funeral, the witches would dig them up and cook them. The soup thus made was drunk at nocturnal assemblies presided over by the devil – in diabolical parody of the Eucharist. The solid residue was made into an ointment which, when rubbed into the body, enabled the witches to turn themselves into animals.[19] Similar legends of cannibalism and nocturnal orgies were told, as we have seen, about the Cathars and other heretical groups, as well as the early Christians, and appeared in some of the confessions of the Templars.

The belief in incubi and succubi was also of ancient origin. According to a Talmudic legend, Adam had been separated from Eve for some time, during which he had had intercourse with female spirits.[20] The notion of union between mortals and immortals was, of course, familiar from the writings of the ancients. In the thirteenth century Caesar of Heisterbach related several stories about demon lovers, including one about a priest who kept his beautiful daughter locked in the attic to safeguard her chastity, only to discover that she had been seduced by a demon in the shape of a man. Eventually the girl repented and confessed, and the priest sent her off to a convent – but the demon suddenly appeared and struck him so hard in the chest that he vomited blood and died within three days.[21] The scholastic view that demons inseminated vicariously bore the seal of St Thomas Aquinas himself – which at that time was rather better than Holy Writ. It was repeated in several demonological tracts, including one by Alphonso de Spina, a Franciscan, in about 1460. He described how nuns at their prayers were softly lulled to sleep by demons, to find to their horror upon waking that they 'had been polluted as if they had mixed themselves with men'. But the same author denies as the fantasies of ignorant simpletons the popular theory that it is demons which cause men to dream of women during the night, in order to extract their semen.[22]

Many of the details in the *Malleus*, therefore, were derived from literary sources, although the authors supplemented this knowledge from their own experience. There was, however, one striking omission. Several previous writers on witchcraft, including Nider, had mentioned the nocturnal assembly (variously called the *barilotto*, the sabbat or the synagogue) where the witches adored their master, the devil.[23] Thus an anonymous tract, dating from about 1450 and probably written in the French part of Savoy, gives a detailed account of the meeting where the novice witch, after swearing to kill as many children under three as she can get hold of, kisses the devil (who appears in the form of an animal, usually a black cat) under the tail, before settling down to a feast of roasted infant.[24] Other accounts of nocturnal assemblies appeared in tracts by Nicholas Jaquier, an inquisitor in France and Bohemia, written in 1458, and Girolamo Visconti, a Milanese Dominican, about 1460. Jaquier's witches, who evidently came from the affluent classes, indulged in extravagant but pleasurable orgies on Thursday nights – a fact confirmed by their servants, who testified that they sometimes kept to their beds all day on Fridays.[25] Visconti's tract, like most of the others we have mentioned, was written with the express purpose of confounding the sceptics, especially those who dared deny the truth about the nocturnal assemblies or who asserted that the witches' confessions were valueless because extracted under torture.

The authors of the *Malleus* cannot have been unaware of the stories about the sabbat; nor can they have been deterred by scepticism in this matter when they accepted so many other equally fantastic tales without demur. The reasons they ignored the sabbat were theological – or rather, political: unlike the other attributes of the witches, which were widely accepted, the sabbat was a highly controversial question which they found it wiser to leave alone. It involved the thorny problem of dogma raised by the *Canon Episcopi*, a text dating from the ninth century which became firmly embodied in the canon law. The relevant part of the text reads:

... there are wicked women who, turning back to Satan and seduced by the illusions and phantoms of the demons, believe and openly avow that in the hours of the night they ride on certain animals, together with Diana, the goddess of the pagans, with a numberless multitude of women; and in the silence of the dead of night cross many great lands; and obey her orders as though she were their mistress, and on particular nights are summoned to her service. Would that they alone perished in their perfidy, without dragging so many others with them into the ruin of infidelity! For a numberless multitude of people, deceived by this false view, believe these things to be true and, turning away from the true faith and returning to the errors of the pagans, think that there exists some divine power other than the one God.[26]

The Canon was an important obstacle to the development of the witch persecution because it implied quite clearly that those who believed themselves to have been transported magically to nocturnal assemblies were the victims of illusions caused by the devil. This did not necessarily mean that those entertaining such illusions were not guilty of heresy if they were practising witches: throughout the period of persecution, up until the eighteenth century, theologians who stood by the Canon would nevertheless argue that the witches were guilty on account of the 'pact' with Satan by which they obtained their magical powers.[27] They had renounced God, and therefore deserved to die. However, if this had remained the attitude of the Church and of the secular authorities who were under its influence, large-scale persecutions of the kind that developed during the late sixteenth and seventeenth centuries would have been impossible. For the means by which sporadic and isolated witch-hunts developed into epidemics was through the denunciation by one person, usually under torture, of several others whom he claimed to have seen at the sabbat. Implicit in this idea was that the witches were not simply isolated sorcerers, practising heretical magic, but members of an organized sect similar to the Cathars and Waldensians. So long as the sabbat continued to be officially designated as an illusion, it would have been illogical for the inquisitors – and most of them were men with trained and logical minds – to have accepted a denunciation as evidence.

When the *Malleus* was published, the subject was still highly controversial. The authors, who had encountered some resistance in their activities as inquisitors from secular and ecclesiastical authorities were anxious not to create further difficulties for themselves. They took an equivocal position which, they hoped, would satisfy both parties.[28] The witches, they said, 'can transport themselves from place to place through the air, either in body or imagination'.[29] Beyond that, they carefully avoid the vexed topic by making no references to illusory or actual assemblies. On the question of denunciations they make no allusion to torture, merely recommending that senior witches should be offered their lives in return for information leading to the conviction of others.[30] The promise may be honoured by sentencing the witch to perpetual prison on bread and water (though nothing, of course, is to be said of this at the time) or, less scrupulously, by passing her over to a different judge for sentencing to death.

Other writers were less cautious. Jaquier (1458) had tried to avoid the difficulty by stating that the 'sect' of witches he had been involved in prosecuting was not the same as the followers of Diana mentioned in the *Canon Episcopi*.[31] He argued that since God's counsels were inscrutable to men, it would in any case be presumptuous to set a precise limit to the degree of power he allowed the devils. Therefore when someone accused by accomplices of having been seen in the sabbat defended himself with the argument that the demon must have produced a false image of him, this was not to be accepted unless he could actually prove that the demon could produce this image. Otherwise, the sect would be encouraged to proliferate.[32] The debate continued for a century or more, with the believers in the reality of the sabbat gradually gaining ground. In the early years, the strongest resistance came from the civil lawyers. Thus Ambrogio de Vignati (1468), a well-known jurist who taught at Padua, Bologna and Turin and whose influence lasted throughout the sixteenth century, reaffirmed the thesis of the *Canon Episcopi*: if the devil caused a man to hallucinate, it did not necessarily mean that he was a heretic; while, if accomplices confessed to impossibilities, this was not an *indicium* even against one who otherwise confessed. Similar views were held by Ulrich Molitus (1489), Gianfrancisco Ponzibio (*c.* 1520) and Andreas Alciatus (1558).[33]

A change in the legal point of view appears in a tract of Paulus Grillandus, already familiar as author of an important essay on torture. Grillandus' account is interesting because he claimed to have changed his mind as a result of personal experience. Moreover he was a highly influential writer whose authority was constantly referred to in subsequent works. Writing in the 1520s, at a time when the civil law was of growing importance in witch prosecutions, his book, according to H.C. Lea, 'unquestionably did its share in establishing the belief in witchcraft',[34] especially among secular jurists. Grillandus started, according to his own account, by holding the traditional view of the

Canon Episcopi that the sabbat was illusory, until a personal experience convinced him that it was real.

In September 1524 [he wrote] while at a certain *castrum* of the monastery of S. Paolo de Urbe, I was asked by the abbot to go to Castro Nazareno ... to examine three women held in prison there and advise him what to do. I did so and commenced with one who seemed the easiest and finally persuaded her to confess everything. She had been fourteen years an Expresse Professa and named another woman as her Magistra who had inducted her. In that time they had performed many *maleficia* in which three men died and four cattle, and had devastated many harvests with hail and tempests, and also numerous other evil works, in revenge for injuries. I led her to tell me all the details of the Profession and adoration and Sabbats ... Among other details of the Sabbat is that all the reverences paid to Satan and all the dances are done backwards; also that after the feast the lamps are extinguished and the demons, as incubi and succubi, serve all the women and men present. [Unlike what we hear in more northern regions – comments Lea – this is *maxima cum voluptate*'.] ... The demons must carry their mates back before the church bells sound the Ave Maria; if they hear it on the way they drop their burdens at the instant, no matter where they be. But this very rarely happens, on account of the speed of the transit. She stated that after being at a Sabbat she was so exhausted that she suffered for three or four days.[35]

This and other similar statements were evidently obtained without torture, and Grillandus was satisfied that they proved that the sabbats really happened. While he did not state outright the conclusion that the denunciations of accomplices at the sabbat should be accepted, the implication would have been clear to anyone familiar with the legal arguments; in any case, he recorded with evident acquiescence a similar case in which attendance at the sabbat had produced denunciations and subsequent burnings.

A similar experience, of hearing at first hand the confession without torture of a witch, convinced the great French jurist and writer on demonology, Jean Bodin, of the reality of witchcraft. After Grillandus Bodin was, perhaps, the most formidable of the secular believers who accepted without question the whole body of witchlore which had developed by the middle of the sixteenth century. His views are more extreme than those of Grillandus – but that need not surprise us, for the debate between the two schools of demonology had intensified over the years. This was not, as will be shown in due course, a division between sceptics and believers, as used to be suggested; but rather a continuation of the previous century's argument around the *Canon Episcopi* – as to whether the witches were merely individual sorcerers who had made the pact with the devil or whether they formed, in addition to this, an organized heretical sect.[36]

The case that converted Bodin was that of one Jeanne Harvilliers who was arrested for witchcraft in April 1578. At first she denied the charge but eventually confessed without torture that when she was twelve her mother – who had subsequently been burned – had consecrated her to the devil, who appeared as a tall dark man, booted and spurred and wearing a sword. He had intercourse with her there and then and continued to visit her after her marriage while her husband was lying asleep at her side. She was arrested following the death of a man soon after she had sprinkled a certain powder across his path. She confessed to having attended the sabbat, to worshipping Beelzebub, engaging in promiscuous intercourse, flying through the air and so forth, and denounced a tyler of Genlis. She was unanimously condemned to death and sentenced to burning. After this Bodin insisted that anyone who disbelieved in witchcraft must himself be a witch (a charge he directed at the celebrated cabbalist and astrologer, Cornelius Agrippa, whose famous black dog 'Monsieur' Bodin considered a demon).[37]

Like other works of demonology, Bodin's *De Magorum Daemonomania* is both a polemical tract and a scientific manual. It explains the origins and describes the aetiology of witchcraft, drawing on the usual classical sources and citing Sprenger (author of the *Malleus*), Grillandus, and, significantly, the experiences of the Italian inquisitors in the Alpine district. But Bodin was also a judge of the *parlement* of Paris, and it was his technical advice that had such disastrous consequences: for his reputation as a jurist was second to none. He argued forcefully in favour of special procedures against witches: if normal legal procedures were followed, not one in a hundred thousand would be punished. The evidence of accomplices at the sabbat must be accepted; for how else could their attendance be proved? There was still continued reluctance in France and elsewhere in Europe to accept such evidence. It was inspired partly by the attitude of the papal and Spanish inquisitions, which continued to adhere to the tradition of the *Canon Episcopi*. This infuriated Bodin, who saw it as allowing those involved in the execrable crime of witchcraft to conceal their infamy. He urged caution in the use of torture – but only because of the *maleficium taciturnitatis*, the power of witches to render themselves immune from pain. His own practice, which he urged other judges to adopt, was to use torture mainly on children and delicate persons rather than the old or hardened. No punishment was cruel enough for the wickedness of witchcraft – and on no account should children be spared the stake – though, in consideration of their tender years, they might be strangled before being burned. (This was hardly a concession, since most executioners mercifully strangled their victims anyway.)[38]

By the end of the sixteenth century the sabbat had become the dominating theme of the active witch-hunters. The *Daemonolatreia* of Nicholas Rémy, witch-hunter of Lorraine and privy councillor to the duke, contained the most detailed and graphic accounts yet published on the subject. Drawn mainly from his experience of fifteen years as a judge in the area, it replaced the *Malleus* as the principle source of intelligence on Satan and his agents, until it was itself replaced a few years afterwards by the definitive compilation of Martin Delrio. As its title implies, the *Daemonolatreia* is more concerned with the activities of Satan and his demons than with the witches themselves, who by now have been reduced to a condition of abject and tortured slavery. At the sabbats, which invariably take place on Wednesday or Saturday nights, they are beaten almost to death for unpunctuality. The food is disgusting, satisfying neither hunger nor thirst, consisting of such things as rotting meat and garbage as well as, occasionally, human flesh. After the meal the witches are forced to dance exhaustingly to the accompaniment of hideous music played on such weird and horrible instruments as horses' skulls. The copulation is painful and unsatisfying, and afterwards the reluctant revellers are forced to kiss the devil, who takes on the hideous form of a stinking goat, on the anus. The witches are continuously tortured. Anyone who refuses to join in the dance, however old or sick, is savagely beaten. The devil rules by terror – every witch who fails to report an impressive list of storm-raisings, poisonings, child-murders and the like is cruelly punished. All admit that the burden is intolerable, and eagerly seek to throw it off – which suits his purpose exactly, since they are often driven to suicide, enabling him to reap their souls for eternal damnation. They are bound by fearful oaths never to confess, and believe that if they break under torture they will be condemned to eternal torture after death. Yet many so hate the devil that they confess spontaneously, and welcome death so they may be reconciled with God.[39]

Although the tradition of the sabbat was by now firmly established,

Catholic demonologists still had to wrestle with the *Canon Episcopi*, for at no time, as we shall see, was the persecution without vociferous critics. The last great Catholic compilation was that of a Jesuit, Martin Delrio, printed in about 1600. It was written, like all the other similar works, to confound the critics – those secret allies of the witches:

> We see the witches growing more audacious through impunity and untiringly adding to their numbers, for there is nothing more ardently desired by the devil than that this cancer should infect all who as yet are clean. This has always provoked the wrath of God, but now much more since he has given his Son for our redemption. What hope remains for us now, when every day there multiply defenders of these maleficient sorcerers in the councils of judges, consuls, fiscals, parliaments and even of princes themselves.[40]

Delrio then proceeds to go further than any of his Catholic predecessors by actually challenging the authenticity of the *Canon Episcopi*. He states, unconvincingly, that this is not through necessity, but because of the obstinacy of the other side. However, the intensity of his argument betrays his motives – as does the rather lame conclusion that the matter is of no account anyway, since the women described in the *Canon* are not the same as modern witches.

Protestant witch-hunters were less likely to find the *Canon Episcopi* a formal obstruction, though at its best, the spirit of the reformation acted as a moderating influence. Martin Luther in his later years became obsessed with the power of the devil; in consequence, his pronouncements on the possibilities of physical transportation are contradictory. Thus, in a public sermon in Wittenberg in 1518, he cited the *Canon Episcopi* to prove that the sabbat was an illusion – and narrated the case of a woman who tried to 'prove' its reality to a sceptical Dominican preacher: she anointed herself with magic ointment, went into a trance – and fell off the bench on which she had been sitting, hurting her head. Later, however, Luther seems to have changed his mind, and admitted that Satan could physically transport those who had already made the pact.[41] Protestant thinkers, departing from the tramlines of scholasticism, appeared to have lost sight of the fundamental distinction between the actual bodily presence of the witches at the sabbat and the mere illusions caused by the devil – despite their preoccupations with the similar dilemma of transubstantiation. Thus Thomas Erastus, the great Swiss theologian, could argue simultaneously that the devil made his physical mark on the witches, that they were justly executed not for what they had done but for what they wanted to do, and that torture was essential because without it no thieves or ordinary criminals would ever be punished.[42]

The confused attitudes of the seventeenth century, a period of legal and theological as well as civil chaos in most of Europe, are exemplified by one Johann Jacob Faber, Lutheran minister of the city of Esslingen during one of the worst witch-panics there. While asserting that witches actually did harm the cattle, he also maintained – in the *Episcopi* tradition – that much of their work, including the raising of storms, was illusory; and that, while the 'almost inhuman' practice of torture might force even the innocent to confess, it was nonetheless necessary in order to ferret out the witches' associates. The belief that the witches formed an organized conspiracy had become so ingrained that there no longer appeared a contradiction between questioning the efficacy of their powers and accepting the legal validity of denunciation.[43]

An example of the dynamics of one such epidemic, in which a single accusation led to others and, by a geometrical progression, to the creation of a nexus of terror involving a whole community, has been described from the records of Ellwangen in Germany by Erik Midelfort. On 7 April 1611 one Barbara Rufin, a housewife of seventy from a village in the district, was brought into Ellwangen on suspicion of desecrating the Eucharist. She evidently already enjoyed some notoriety, for even her husband thought her a witch, and during the next few days, in response to appeals by the authorities, denunciations from various neighbours and relatives began to pour in. By 12 April she was suspected of killing livestock by witchcraft and of trying to poison her own son, who publicly accused her of being a witch. One man described how after many horses and cows had died in his district, he had consulted a known witch, one Biren Ketterin, who undertook to reveal the culprit. The latter told him that as soon as she left his house, a person would come and ask for three things: if he gave them, his livestock would deteriorate further. Hardly had the witch left when Barbara Rufin appeared and asked for a shawl, a butterbox and a candle. The deponent and his father sent her away empty-handed, and after this the livestock began to recover. This testimony affords an interesting example of witchcraft accusations beginning with counter-witchcraft – a tendency confirmed by modern anthropology. After this, Barbara Rufin's legal situation deteriorated badly. Her daughter-in-law, with whom she had quarrelled, denounced her. Under questioning, she swore she knew nothing of witchcraft and that she herself had eaten of the allegedly poisonous soup without ill effects. On 20 April, after assembling a mass of testimony, the investigators decided on torture. The old woman was stretched twice, for fifteen minutes each time, but would not give anything away. But two days later, after she had been tortured seven separate times, she finally made a confession, only to make a complete revocation when required to confirm it three days later. On 6 May she was examined on eighteen articles drawn from her previous statements. Worn down by the relentless questioning, backed no doubt by the threat of further tortures, she was finally brought to ratify her confession. On 16 May she was executed with the sword (an act of mercy usually carried out in Ellwangen) and her body was burned at the stake.

Further denunciations followed with increasing rapidity as the authorities, under the pressure of events and convinced of the emergency, hastened the procedures and lowered the criteria for torture. Gone were the days when Barbara Rufin's torture had to be preceded by a voluminous and painstaking collection of evidence. Three denunciations, plus the devil's mark, sufficed for torture – in most cases, the witch-hunters had little difficulty in finding the latter by 'pricking' for the insensitive spot. By the end of the year, more than a hundred people had died in seventeen executions; the following year, a hundred and fifty or more. In 1615, three priests were executed for, among other things, secretly baptizing infants in the devil's name – a fact which lent added weight to the previous executions, since it explained the presence of so many witches in the area. Meanwhile, the interrogatories accompanying torture were standardized; a questionnaire was drawn up full of leading questions such as 'who seduced you into witchcraft?' The resulting confessions were predictably standardized. Most of the Ellwangen witches confessed first to some form of sexual seduction, often at the instigation of another witch. Only later did it transpire that the seducer was the devil. The discovery, however, never stopped the witches from renouncing God and His saints, and their own Christian baptisms. Then they usually confessed to desecrating the sacrament – by stamping on the host, mixing it with dung or employing it in magical potions, and to digging up the bodies of dead babies for the same purpose. The next section of the typical confession concerned the actual harm done – the *maleficia*: first the storms, then the sickness and death of livestock and people. Finally, in a third section, the witches described the sabbaths they attended and were obviously under great pressure to name as many other witches they had seen (there) as possible . . . These sabbaths were often the only time or place that one witch was thought to have contact with others, and they therefore provided the crucial link from one accusation to the next.[44]

These denunciations maintained the persecution in the Ellwangen district and ensured its spread to other regions. One woman denounced twenty-nine persons, another twenty-four, a third seventeen; in some cases the names thus obtained by the authorities were used in proceedings twenty years afterwards. In addition, witches often denounced people from other towns and other jurisdictions. To help the neighbouring officials the authorities at Ellwangen kept a book of those denounced from other regions, listed alphabetically by towns. Guilt was assumed before confessions were obtained: this was not only implicit from the inquisitorial proceedings, but it is evident from the fact that inventories of a suspect's belongings were started beforehand. The degree of correspondence in the confessions, already helped by the standardized interrogatories, were further helped by leaks from two of the guards, who publicly revealed some details of the confessions, including the names of some of those denounced. There is also evidence of blackmail and sexual extortion by the guards, one of whom was eventually executed for 'selling' the name of one suspect to another, as well as extorting valuables and sexual favours from a woman in exchange for letting her off the torture.[45] The abuses inherent in the system were evidently recognized. An instruction by the ruling *Fürstprobst* of Ellwangen written between 1605 and 1613 stated that confessions, with or without torture, had to be made in the presence of senior officials including the city bailiff, the supervisor, two or three members of the court and the town clerk. The confessions also had to be ratified afterwards before seven men, to prove that the culprit was now telling the truth. But there is evidence that these procedures were not in fact followed.[46]

Such is the anatomy of a fairly typical seventeenth-century German witch-hunt. The dynamic processes are similar to those we shall encounter in the Soviet Union when we come to consider the great purges of the Communist party during the 1930s. There is, however, an essential difference. Throughout the period of the great witch-hunts in Europe, persecution remained sporadic and localized. Sooner or later there appears to have come a point in every witch epidemic when the local authorities recognized that continued persecution threatened to destroy the whole community, and that a decisive show of solidarity would halt the inexorable process. Midelfort describes this 'crisis of confidence' as it arose in the free city of Offenburg in about 1630. Not surprisingly, the point was reached as the accusations gradually spread to the wives of the city's councillors. In order to avoid forcing individual councillors from ruling in matters affecting them so closely, the council agreed that members whose wives were under accusation should not attend the proceedings. Suspicions soon began to arise that the exclusion was being used as a way of eliminating political opponents. Councillors whose relatives were executed publicly accused the judges of being animated by personal spite. Eventually, the trials claimed a member of the council itself. As Midelfort comments,

One does not need an especially vivid imagination to visualize the frantic situation in Offenburg as councillors, who normally got along well enough, turned into bitter enemies. Accusation and insinuation must have hung like a cloud over the town. The cold language of the reports from the Council masks the most vicious of factional battles.[47]

Significantly, a heroic resistance to torture may have been the turning-point. In December 1629, two weeks after the execution of the councillor, a woman, one Gotter Ness, who refused to confess was put in the 'witches' chair' (This was a metal stool under which a fire was lit – a torture widely used in Germany.) Still she refused to confess – the first person to withstand this grade of torture. The council sent her home, and declared a 'truce' till after Christmas. When the holidays were over, they set the judicial machinery in motion again. Three women were arrested, including the daughter of Gotter Ness. Confronted with the chair, all three confessed and were condemned to be executed on Friday, 25 January. On the Thursday, however, all three of them protested their innocence. The priest (who had previously shown no compunction in breaking the secrecy of the confessional where witchcraft was concerned) was asked if he had absolved them of anything, and reported that all three had 'revoked their confessions and insist on the peril of damnation that they are not witches, and would answer in the presence of God for their statements'.[48] After further consultations, the council decided to let the women go – despite the fact that one of them, the daughter of Gotter Ness, had been denounced on five separate occasions. After that, there were no more bloody trials in the city of Offenburg.[49]

Such local crises of confidence were not the only moderating forces. The influence of the *Canon Episcopi* continued to make itself felt among Protestants and Catholics during the last hundred years or so of the witch-hunting era. The best-known Protestant opponent of the witch-hunts was Johann Weyer, physician to the duke of Cleves who, like many of the scientifically-minded men of his time, was fascinated by magic and demonology. He opposed the witch-hunts on the grounds that the power of the devil and his demons was such that he needed no intermediaries. In the tradition of the *Episcopi*, he maintained that the witches merely deluded themselves into thinking they had powers over nature. The witches could not really raise storms, but the devil sometimes told them when one was coming, and the witches then went through the ritual of throwing stones behind them, and consequently convinced themselves of their powers. As an expert on ritual magic, Weyer considered the witches far too ignorant to be able to master the black arts; and as a professional physician he was especially scornful of the 'uninformed and unskilled physicians (who) relegate all the incurable diseases to witchcraft'. He also roundly condemned the torture of witches:

> ... these wretched women, whose minds have already been disturbed by the delusions and arts of the devil and are now upset by frequent torture, are kept in prolonged solitude in the squalor and darkness of their dungeons, exposed to the hideous spectres of the devil, and constantly dragged out to undergo atrocious torment until they would gladly exchange at any moment this most bitter existence for death, are willing to confess whatever crimes are suggested to them rather than be thrust back into their hideous dungeon amid ever-recurring torture.[50]

Though Weyer did not disbelieve in the sabbat, he urged caution in the acceptance of confessions which, he said, ought not to be enough for condemnation. The testimony of different witnesses as to dates and other details should be carefully compared for corroboration. Weyer's views eventually became more radical, and it is not surprising to find him attacked for having 'consecrated himself to the witches' and for being himself 'a wizard and a mixer of poisons who has taken on himself the defence of other wizards and poison mixers'.[51] Nevertheless, his views strongly influenced the rationalist outlook of Reginald Scot, the

Elizabethan opponent of witch persecution, who went even further than Weyer in virtually denying the powers of the devil altogether.[52] The moderating views of the Lutheran reformers appeared to have had some effect. They were well represented in the theological faculty at the university of Tübingen, and their denial of the reality of the sabbat had legal consequences, as is shown by a ruling of the same university's legal faculty in 1598, that denunciations were insufficient to justify torture.[53]

Among the leading Catholic upholders of the *Episcopi* tradition were three Jesuit fathers, Adam Tanner, Paul Laymann and Friedrich von Spee. None of them went so far as the earlier writers who were prepared to state categorically that the sabbat was an illusion. By the seventeenth century, practically no one on the Catholic side dared go beyond the median position of the *Malleus* that the sabbat could be both a reality and an illusion – though Father Tanner ventured to suggest that God would permit the illusion more often than the reality. The position of the Jesuits was basically a pragmatic one: all three had, during their careers as confessors, reached the conclusion that witches sometimes put their souls in mortal jeopardy by making false denunciations. Tanner merely suggested a mild procedural remedy: the judges should bring witches to make their denunciations after condemnation, when they had nothing to gain by inculpating the innocent. He strongly condemned the use of torture by German judges who, he claimed, were usually applying it illegally.[54]

The dilemma of the father confessors was poignantly explained by Father Laymann, whose prime concern, as he made clear, was for the witch's immortal soul, rather than human justice:

> If ... after confessing judicially, she asserts her innocence and says it was extorted by torture, and on consideration he believes her ... he should console her with the example of the martyrs and [tell her] that God will know the truth ... If she persistently asserts that she has, through fear of torture or enmity, denounced the innocent, he should urge the obligation to retract even though she exposes herself to fresh torture – if there is any hope that the judge will listen to the revocation.[55]

This last matter was acutely embarrassing to confessors who believed the final confession of those condemned to die: for bearing false witness, even under torture, was a mortal sin that could only be pardoned if the falsehood were revoked. As a rule the judges refused to accept revocations made after the final condemnation, which meant in effect that the witch who was sentenced without revoking a false denunciation was doomed to suffer eternal misery in the next world as well as an excruciating death in this. Revocations made before sentence had to be purged by renewed torture – and this, of course, was a powerful disincentive against making them. The confessor himself could not intervene without breaking the seal of the confessional. If it became known that he did intervene, said Laymann, it would encourage the guilty to make false sacramental confessions 'with great sacrilege and damage to their souls'.[56]

The most strident and influential Catholic attack on witch-hunting was Friedrich von Spee's *Cautio Criminalis*, published in 1631. Running into sixteen editions, including translations, in a hundred years, it had a decidedly moderating effect. Queen Christina was impressed by it, which may account for the fact that Swedish troops put an end to many witch-trials in Germany during the Thirty Years' War.[57] Leibniz, who knew Spee through their common patron the archbishop-elector of Mainz, gave his book the credit for eventually persuading most of the princes of Germany to abandon witch persecutions in their territories. He recalled how Spee had once explained, in reply to the archbishop's question, that his hair had gone prematurely white through the nerve-shattering experience of accompanying witches to the stake, every one of whom he knew to be innocent. Although he published his book anonymously, Spee's views were known to the authorities whom he irritated considerably by sometimes giving advice to those under suspicion. The protection of his patrons probably saved him, though he may have spent a period in prison.

The *Cautio Criminalis* is a searing attack on the whole witch-hunting institution in Germany, beginning with those 'theologians and prelates who quietly enjoy their speculations and know nothing of the squalor of prisons, the weight of chains, the implements of torture, the lamentations of the poor, all of which are beneath their dignity'.[58] His concern is the result of his conviction, based on practical experience, that the great majority of those actually condemned to burn are innocent – not five, or even two in fifty are guilty, he estimates. The whole of the judicial process, he argues, makes it virtually impossible for an innocent person, once arrested, to escape the death penalty. With political acumen he blames the scandal of such innocence suffering on the *real* witches – who deliberately help accusations fall on the innocent in order to divert attention from themselves.

Having carefully established his orthodoxy, however, Spee goes on to demolish the case of the inquisitors with such thoroughness that very little room is left for the activities of the devil and his minions. For the whole of their case is constructed from evidence obtained under torture:

> What is to be thought of torture? Does it bring frequent moral peril to the innocent? In revolving what I have seen, read and heard I can only conclude that it fills our Germany with witches and unheard-of wickedness, and not only Germany but any nation that tries it. The agony is so intense that to escape it we do not fear to incur death. The danger therefore is that many to avoid it will falsely confess whatever the examiner suggests or what they have excogitated in advance. The most robust who have thus suffered have affirmed to me that no crime can be imagined which they would not at once confess to if it would bring ever so little relief, and that they would welcome ten deaths to escape a repetition. If there are some who will submit in silence to be torn in pieces, they are rare nowadays and are fortified by evil arts against pain. Experienced confessors know that there are those who have made false denunciations under torture and, when told that they must withdraw the accusations of the innocent, will say that they would willingly do so, if there were any way without incurring a second torture, but they cannot risk it even to avoid damnation.[59]

Even when the judges claim that a witch has confessed without torture, says Spee, and that therefore the confession must be true, this is in fact no more than a legal fiction. When he inquired the precise meaning of the phrase, he discovered 'that in reality they were tortured, but only in an iron press with sharp-edged channels over the shins, in which they are pressed like a cake, bringing blood and causing intolerable pain, and this is technically called without torture, deceiving those who do not understand the phrases of the inquisitors'.[60]

One of the gravest abuses exposed by Spee was the way in which leading questions were employed to achieve the desired confession from the witches, and especially the denunciation of accomplices – a practice expressly forbidden by Roman and German law. This was 'not only customary in many places, but special crimes, places and times for the Sabbat, and other details (were) suggested in the questions'.[61] Some inquisitors would even tell their victims the names of those they wished them to denounce; they would also inform them of what others had said about them, so they would know exactly what details to confess. Once arrested, there was no hope for the accused witch, even if she survived the torture.

I have never seen, though I could have seen it in many places, a woman discharged who had purged herself in the first torture [though this should have happened according to law]. It is with the utmost difficulty and scarcely ever, that one is acquitted who has been thrown in prison. They [the judges] want to burn *per fas et nefas*. They think it a disgrace if they acquit, as though they had been too hasty in arresting and torturing the innocent.[62]

Finally, Spee made this devastating comment on the *maleficium taciturnitatis* and other supposed characteristics of the behaviour of witches under torture:

It is assumed that a woman cannot endure two or three tortures unless she is a witch; it requires the aid either of the devil or of God . . . But this is to admit that the torture, as beyond human endurance, was excessive – and therefore illegal, and the accused [should] neither be tortured again nor condemned.[63]

Why is it always assumed, he asks, that it is the devil who supports the guilty in this way, not God who supports the innocent?

What are the signs ascribed to the *maleficium taciturnitatis*? They say that some do not feel [pain] but laugh. This is a lie, and I speak knowingly. If to endure great torment, one grinds her teeth, compresses her lips and holds her breath, they say she laughs. They say that some are silent and sleep. This is also a lie; some faint under torture and they call it sleep; some shut their eyes and, exhausted with pain, bow their heads and remain quiet, and this they call sleep . . .

How then can the innocent escape? Then why not at first confess? Foolish and crazy woman, why do you wish to die so often, when you can die once? Take my advice, and before these pains, call yourself guilty and die. You cannot escape, for this is the final result of German zeal . . . [64]

*   *   *

What, then, was the reality behind the witch persecutions? As has been suggested, the essential problem around which controversy raged for more than two centuries was that posed by the *Canon Episcopi*, concerning the reality of the night flight and the sabbat. Those who upheld the tradition of the *Episcopi* that at least *some* of the orgies described by the witches under torture were illusions caused by the devil felt very uneasy about the denunciations, yet the weight of judicial opinion, as revealed by the actual conduct of the trials, accepted these denunciations as primary evidence. It was the denunciations, more often than not under torture, that introduced the dynamic element into the witch persecutions. It is therefore not surprising to find, as we have demonstrated, that those who argued most forcefully in favour of torture believed in the reality of the sabbat; while those like Spee and the other Jesuit confessors who held that the sabbat might be illusory, were convinced that torture was abused and forced people into false confessions. At the same time, no one, if one excepts Weyer and Scot, argued that all witches were innocent, and that the whole persecution was a vast delusion. It was accepted, almost without question, that there were real witches, and that they were wicked and deserved to be punished, because they had made a pact with the devil and indulged in harmful magic. Even those who denied that the witches had any powers over nature would argue that they were evil because their will was corrupt.

Despite this evident paradox, the historical controversy about witchcraft centred for many years on an essentially false definition of the problem. Historians argued about whether or not the witch-hunters were victims of a *delusion*. To sum up a complex debate in the crudest possible terms, there were two schools of thought – the sceptics, who believed in the 'delusionary' thesis, and those who believed that there really were such people as witches. In the English language, the former school was represented mainly by Americans, H.C. Lea and his disciple, George Lincoln Burr.[65] In England they had a solitary representative in C. L'Estrange Ewen.[66] The other side, those who believed in a literal reality behind the witch persecutions, found their most famous exponents in Margaret Murray[67] and Montagu Summers.[68]

Murray is now something of a *cause célèbre*: having built up a reputation in egyptology, she turned to anthropology and for many years occupied the chair at London University. She dedicated herself, in two famous books, to proving that there really had been a 'witch cult' in western Europe, the relic of an ancient fertility cult based on the 'horned god' of ancient Egypt. Murray's theories, subjected to critical examination by historians and anthropologists, turned out to be almost wholly imaginary. She used her evidence in a highly selective manner, excluding from consideration almost anything that did not suit her thesis. Yet her theories not only became popular, but were supported by scholars of proven reputation.[69] Summers was an Anglo-Catholic antiquarian who lifted much of his material, without acknowledgment, from German scholars, while ignoring the results of their later researches. In contrast to Murray, he believed without question in the reality of witchcraft, as perceived by Sprenger and Kramer, Bodin, Rémy and Delrio. A sample of his writing is instructive:

> At the end of the sixteenth century, France was literally honeycombed by the vast secret society of witches, whose members, ever-busy at their evil work, might be found everywhere, in crowded capital and remote hamlet, in palace and cottage, of both sexes and of all ages, even the very youngest for . . . the older adepts trained up their children almost from the cradle in their diabolic craft.[70]

Summers and Murray, while violently disagreeing with each other, had common ground in supposing there really was an organized cult behind the persecution. For Murray, it was the worshippers of the horned god, with their sabbats, esbats and covens. For Summers it was the conspiracy of Satanists, black magicians and devil-worshippers, in the best tradition of the witch-hunters. Not surprisingly, Summers also believed the Abbé Barruel's reactionary fantasies about freemasons (see Chapter 7). Both believed, however, that the struggle was real and, in a sense, inevitable. Even though her sympathies lay with the 'pagans', Murray, like Summers, accepted that a real battle had taken place in which Christianity emerged victorious.

The sceptics gradually gained ground, once it became apparent that the weight of evidence was behind them. Lea, and Burr following him, built up the attractive hypothesis that the whole witch conspiracy was really an invention of the inquisitors – first the Dominicans, and after that the secular witch-burning judges. Naturally, they placed much greater stress on torture than their opponents – a point emphasized by Burr in attacking Margaret Murray who, he points out, makes barely a single reference to torture in all her work.[71]* Thus the debate over the great witch persecution depended, to a certain extent, on the emphasis the protagonists placed on the value of testimony extracted by torture. Those who believed in the conspiracy theory had a con-stitutional tendency to minimize the distorting effects of torture. Those who believed the whole witch craze to have been a delusion naturally placed the greatest emphasis upon it. But while the 'delusionist' case accorded in general with historically ascertainable facts such as court records, it had one very fundamental disadvantage. While accounting

---

* It is worth noting here that Lea's study of torture (in *Superstition and Force*, first published in 1878) was for nearly a century the only monograph in English. I exclude G.R.Scott's *History of Torture* (London 1940) and similar works as being devoid of any legal or historical value.

for the delusions of the inquisitors, it did little to explain the delusions of their victims. Consequently, though torture was used in a general way to discredit the veracity of confessions, its function as a mechanism of distortion was never made clear.

Recent historical and anthropological research have made the task of disentanglement easier. The essential problem is to define firstly what the witches themselves might be expected to have believed; and secondly what their inquisitors and judges believed about them. The gap, if there is one, will surely be bridged by torture. A comparatively reliable source of evidence about popular witch beliefs comes from England, where witchcraft as a common law felony was normally subject to jury trial. Torture was rarely if ever employed. With the notable exception of the Essex trials of 1645, there is very little to suggest that English witches were ever regarded as members of a sect or were believed to indulge in devil-worship. Even the pact with Satan, lynch-pin of the Continental doctrine joining heresy and witchcraft, is usually absent from the trial records. Of three acts of Parliament against witchcraft passed in 1542, 1563 and 1604, only the last refers to the 'compact' with the devil, in terms much too guarded to have satisfied a continental inquisitor. Moreover, the 1604 act was also unusual in that it was passed by James I, author of a notorious treatise on witchcraft, who accepted most of the Continental doctrines.[72]

In essence, English beliefs were limited to the view that witches practised maleficent sorcery by such means as 'fascination' of the eyes, or homeopathic magic. They might solicit the aid of demons or familiars, which could be detected by a number of means, including searching or 'pricking' for the 'devil's mark' or insensitive spot upon their bodies. In his *Handbook for Magistrates*, first printed in 1618, the Master of Chancery, Michael Dalton, warned his readers that against witches they must 'not always expect direct evidence, seeing all their works are the works of darkness, and no witnesses present with them to accuse them . . .' and he then went on to list the kind of evidence upon which a number of witches were convicted in Lancashire in 1612:

1. They have ordinarily a familiar or spirit which appeareth to them.
2. Their said familiar hath some bigg or place upon their body where he sucketh them.
3. They have often pictures of clay or wax (like a man) found in their house.
4. If the dead body bleed upon the witches touching it.
5. The testimony of the person hurt upon his death.

6. The examination and confession of the children, or the servants of the witch.
7. Their own voluntary confession, which exceeds all other evidence.[73]

Undoubtedly coercion was sometimes used to obtain these confessions. In the famous Essex persecution of 1645, Matthew Hopkins, the 'Witchfinder Generall', and his colleague John Stearne, used methods of divination which sometimes amounted to torture. They included continuous immersion in cold water – evidently an adaptation of the swimming ordeal – and prolonged interrogation involving deprivation of sleep. Nevertheless, Hopkins himself 'utterly denies that confession of a witch to be of any validity when it is drawn from her by any torture or violence whatsoever ... '[74] Hopkins was well versed in the Continental doctrines, and it is not surprising to find that the Essex trials, together with trials in Suffolk and Cambridge where Hopkins and Stearne were also active during the same period, are almost the only ones in the English records in which there are allusions to the sabbat and intercourse with the devil.

As professional prosecutors of witches, Hopkins and Stearne were the nearest England ever produced to Continental inquisitors of either the ecclesiastical or lay variety. Moreover, they were operating in the exceptional circumstances of political and judicial disruption caused by civil war.[75] The great majority of witch prosecutions resulted from actions by people who claimed to have suffered loss or damage through witchcraft. There are also a number of cases of counter-proceedings, in which people accused of witchcraft brought actions for defamation against their accusers. To judge by the number of cases in which the accusers were penalized, the possibility of oneself ending in court must have been a deterrent to many a would-be accuser.[76] Under common law witchcraft was thus a difficult though not impossible crime to prove. Ewen's study of the court records of the home circuit from 1558 to 1736 reveals that eighty-one per cent of those arraigned avoided the death penalty (which for a felony was hanging, not burning).[77] Projecting these figures on the national scale, he estimated the number of executions for the whole period at less than one thousand – a record of considerable moderation when compared to the minimal Continental figure of 200,000 from the fourteenth to seventeenth centuries, or of 4,400 in Scotland, where torture was used, between 1590 and 1680.[78]

That popular beliefs in witchcraft were largely confined to maleficent sorcery is also clear from those Continental sources least contaminated by judicial coercion. The records of most Continental trials consist of summaries drawn up after interrogation detailing the charges 'proven' against the accused. However, in a small number of cases dating from the fourteenth and fifteenth centuries, most of them from Switzerland, the original depositions of accusers or witnesses have survived. As in England, most of them are complaints by the suspected witch's neighbours, seeking her conviction. There are also, as in England, a number of cases of defamation containing the gist of the original accusations. None of these cases, according to the historian who has recently examined them, features the complex of charges associated with diabolism – adoration of the devil, the pact, the night flight, the sabbat or intercourse with incubi and succubi. Similar conclusions about the absence of diabolism from popular belief are stated to emerge from a recent, as yet unpublished, study of witchcraft in northern France during the sixteenth and seventeenth centuries. As in England, the great majority of court cases arose in the first instance from malicious damage.[79]

Thus at the popular or local level where witchcraft accusations originated there appears to have been no essential difference between English and Continental views of witchcraft. The disparities in the scale of persecution between England and the Continent are the result of the grafting of learned or intellectual ideas of witchcraft on the substratum of popular superstition by means of the inquisitorial process, and in particular through the application of torture, the threat of torture or allied forms of judicial coercion. In a number of cases, historians have actually been able to pinpoint the 'surgery' by which the learned ideas were interpolated. Thus in the trial of a woman from Lausanne in 1464 the original depositions of witnesses survive, indicating that the worst of which she was accused was poisoning and attempted kidnapping through sorcery. Within two days of the intervention of an inquisitor, she confessed to attendance at diabolic assemblies, having intercourse with the devil, raising storms and murdering children.[80] In another, similar case, a woman of Savoy evidently admitted some form of magic, but only confessed after two days of torture to taking part in diabolic assemblies.[81]

How did the more complex and terrible notions of witchcraft – or, more properly, diabolism – come to be confused with the older popular notions of sorcery? Various answers have been offered to this question. One reason may have been the result of the same tendency towards intellectual rationalization which led to the replacement of the ordeals by the inquisitorial process. The Aristotelian cosmology which steadily gained ground in the schools during the thirteenth century relied on the notion that natural forces were propelled, in the first instance, by spiritual beings whose source was God, the Prime Mover. If God delegated his natural work to angels, it followed that evil works such as maleficent sorcery must be performed by demons in the service of Satan. It became a theological impossibility for acts of *maleficia* to be performed without a pact, implicit or explicit, with the devil. The gap between making the pact and actual devil-worship was bridged in 1298 by a ruling of the theological faculty of Paris University that *maleficium* was tantamount to heresy.[82]

However, the scale reached by the witch persecutions from the fifteenth century cannot be explained by purely theological developments. The old orthodoxy of the *Canon Episcopi* gave ground to the belief that witches were members of a heretical *sect* because the inquisitorial machinery had originally been set up to combat heresy. From the thirteenth century when torture was introduced it had been assumed, *a priori*, that certain heretics such as the Cathars and Waldensians were not merely guilty of spiritual crimes or wrong thinking. They were believed to constitute an underground *sect* which, because of its errors, posed a threat not only to the Catholic Church, but to Christianity itself. As has already been suggested, the key role of torture after its introduction in 1252 was to procure denunciations. The strict inquisitorial rules, based on Roman law, rationalized the employment of torture largely in terms of the degrees of proof against the person under investigation; and these rules continued to function with more or less latitude against 'ordinary' criminals until the eighteenth century. Yet the volume of writing and commentary that developed around these rules should not mislead us into supposing that the only, or even the principal purpose of torture was to supplement the difficult requirements of legal proof. The whole edifice of the inquisitorial process had been built on the foundations of the fight against heresy in the thirteenth century. It was as a consequence of torture that nonsectarian heretics, such as people practising maleficent sorcery, were assumed to be members of a sect.

Whether or not this consequence was unavoidable, given the nature of the inquisitorial process, is another question. The inquisition of Spain took a notably lenient view of witchcraft, weighing accusations of *male-*

ficium with a caution worthy of the most enlightened English judge.[83] Having been set up to combat the 'judaizing' tendencies among the recently converted Marrano Christians, its view of heresy was conditioned by a very different environment from that of its medieval predecessor. It adhered more strictly to the original inquisitorial rules, with their safeguards against the conviction of innocence, as did the papal inquisition in the latter period, which also refused to accept the denunciations of accomplices without other forms of proof.[84] The great witch-hunts of France, Switzerland, northern Italy and Germany were thus not only the result of the inquisitorial machinery, but the consequences of what one might call the systematic maladministration of that machinery. It is probably true that every case of a classic witch-panic involving a dynamic spiral of denunciations entailed serious violations of the original inquisitorial rules. In many cases this could be put down to the ignorance or inexperience of judges or inquisitors; but not always. It is chastening, and tragic, to see Jean Bodin, one of the great seminal minds of his day and its leading jurist, inventing rationalizations to justify the systematic violation of the rules in cases of witchcraft.

In part, at least, this malfunctioning of the system was the result of genuine confusion. Although two historians have recently cast doubt on the authenticity of the sources linking the first appearance of the sabbats with the Albigensian persecution in France, a similar confusion between witches and sectarians appears to have occurred in northern Italy and the southern Alps. Late in the fourteenth century Waldensians in the Turin area were indicted for witchcraft in addition to the standard doctrinal charges; while in about 1450 a number of suspected witches in Savoy were accused of simulating orthodoxy to avoid detection – a standard charge against Waldensians.[85] There is also evidence to suggest that innocent country rituals, relics of a forgotten paganism, were believed by over-zealous inquisitors to be diabolic assemblies.[86] By the mid-fifteenth century, the confusion between heresy and witchcraft was general – as is shown by the attachment of the word *Vauderie* (from Vaudois or Waldensians) to the great witch-hunt at Arras around 1460. The confusion was made permanent by the dissemination of 'learned' ideas through demonological tracts, and through the administration – or maladministration – of the inquisitorial procedure which, as we have seen, relied heavily on standardized interrogatories containing 'leading' questions.

Behind this confusion between popular and learned ideas lies a deeper and more complex confusion of two distinctive, but closely related, traditions of witch beliefs which appear to be common to many pre-literate societies. Anthropologists who have studied modern witch beliefs among primitive communities in Africa and elsewhere make a distinction between witch accusations as a social function, where the witch may be almost any member of the community, and 'witchcraft' may even be committed involuntarily; and the 'night witch' of fantasy or nightmare, an archetype of deviant behaviour whose mythical activities dramatize negative social values.[87] These two notions of witchcraft correspond in many ways to the popular and learned traditions in Europe. In his seminal work *Witchcraft, Oracles and Magic among the Azande*, E. E. Evans-Pritchard described an episode from his experience:

Shortly after my arrival in Zandeland we were passing through a government settlement and noticed that a hut had been burned to the ground the previous night. Its owner was overcome with grief as it had contained the beer he was preparing for a mortuary feast. He told us that he had gone the previous night to examine his beer. He had lit a handful of straw and raised it above his head so that the light would be cast on the pots and in so doing he had ignited the thatch. He and my (Zande) companions also were convinced that the disaster was caused by witchcraft.[88]

On another occasion, Evans-Pritchard met a boy whose toe had gone septic after he had knocked it against a tree-stump. The boy insisted that witchcraft was responsible. The anthropologist

told the boy that he had knocked his foot against the stump of wood because he had been careless, and that witchcraft had not placed it in the path, for it had grown there naturally. He agreed that witchcraft had nothing to do with the stump of wood being in his path, but added that he had kept his eyes open for stumps, as indeed every Zande does most carefully, and that if he had not been bewitched, he would have seen the stump.[89]

The argument was really about primary causality. The Englishman and the Africans were basically agreed about the immediate cause of the burning and the sore toe. Their disagreement was about the underlying metaphysics. The average Westerner would see the primary cause either in moral terms, as 'carelessness'; or as an 'accident' or 'bad luck'. The latter are really residual categories which defy logic or analysis. As many writers on Africa have pointed out, Western theories do not explain accidents or account for the selective incidence of disease.[90]

Like many people regarded by most Westerners as 'unsophisticated', the African who believes in witchcraft is really demanding greater intellectual rigour than is implied in most Western notions of causality. In incidents such as these, 'carelessness' or 'accident' will not do. When a man who has performed the same task hundreds of times with repeated success suddenly fails, an explanation is needed. The same applies to a normally healthy man who unexpectedly falls sick. In both cases witchcraft supplies the necessary explanation, because it relates to something specific and identifiable.

Among the Azande, one who believes his kinsman to have been bewitched first consults an oracle, usually supplying the names of those he suspects. Then if the oracle so advises he makes a public declaration calling on the witch, who is not named, to remove his magic. If the sickness continues, a poison oracle is administered to a chicken. If the chicken dies, its wing is cut off and sent to the prince or his deputy, who may then select a messenger to deliver it to the suspected witch. On receiving it the latter almost invariably says he had no idea that his witchcraft had caused injury to the sick man; and as evidence of goodwill he blows a spray of water over the chicken wing (a common gesture of conciliation in Africa) and beseeches the witchcraft in his belly to become cool. If the sickness continues, there are further oracular consultations. If the sick man dies his kin may take steps to execute vengeance but only after it has been established by oracles that the sickness was due to witchcraft.[91]

Since anyone may be accused of witchcraft, it is not normal for people to regard themselves as witches. How, then, does the man who receives the chicken's wing feel about the accusation? Some African peoples, according to Evans-Pritchard, bridge the contradiction between the proven act of witchcraft and the witch's sense of personal innocence by claiming that witchcraft may be involuntary. Not so the Azande, who maintain that it is impossible for a witch to be 'ignorant of his condition and of his assaults on others'.[92] The problem is avoided by shirking the conceptual jump between the particular and the universal. Since these questions are never discussed between Azande, one who has faced the accusation of being a witch may believe in his own innocence while still admitting in principle that others are responsible for their own actions.

So far as he knows he has never visited the home of the sick man whom he is said to have injured, and he is forced to conclude that either there must have been an error or that he has acted unconsciously. *But he believes his own case to be exceptional and that others are responsible for their actions.* People have always been of the opinion that witches plan their assaults, and the fact that he himself has not acted with intent is no reason to suppose that others do not act consciously. Indeed, a man in these circumstances must feel that if it is true that he is a witch he is certainly not an ordinary witch, *for witches recognize each other and cooperate in their undertakings, whereas no one has a secret understanding with him nor seeks his aid.* (emphasis added)[93]

Other anthropologists have noted consistent patterns in witchcraft accusations. General calamities involving the whole community do not usually result in witch accusations, though sometimes unknown witches will be blamed.[94] Accusations are made most often against people well known to the accuser, usually within the same village. Functional interpretations of witch accusation therefore stress its role as a means of creating divisions within a community or lineage when it becomes necessary for these to split.[95] They may also provide an outlet for tensions between people whose moral order prevents them from quarrelling publicly. Such tensions are of various kinds, between young and old, or between members of the same kinship group. They may involve the struggle for political power at village level with rival factions bandying witchcraft allegations against each other;[96] they may involve a challenge to the authority of older leaders by the young who accuse them of holding on to power by means of witchcraft; or they may, on the contrary, be directed to reinforcing existing hierarchies, in which case accusations are made against those who might challenge existing social or political arrangements.[97]

Many anthropologists have noted complaints that witches are everywhere on the increase in Africa as a result of colonial rule and Christian missionary activity.[98] An important reason for this is the banning of ordeals, especially the poison ordeal.[99] Unilateral ordeals, such as those employed in early medieval Europe, were in general use in pre-colonial Africa, including the hot iron and hot water ordeals as well as a version of the latter using hot sheep fat. The ordeal most widely used in connection with witchcraft, however, appears to have been the poison ordeal. Any suspected witches – or sometimes, indeed, the whole community, if the people wished to clear themselves of suspicion – were assembled together and given a poisonous drink. The innocent vomited up the poison. Those who failed to do so and became sick or died from the ill-effects, were guilty. Obviously many Africans regarded the permitted forms of divination, such as the use of oracles or professional diviners, as considerably less efficacious than the poison ordeals. During the breakdown of authority in Congo in 1959, poison ordeals were revived, and hundreds are said to have died as a consequence.[100]

Other reasons put forward to account for the supposed increase in the number of witches include the general rise in social stress and tension resulting from the breakdown of traditional economic arrangements and the introduction of a cash economy. People who might suddenly acquire wealth outside the traditional social context were, not surprisingly, believed to have made it through witchcraft.[101] An example of the way in which new technologies may be assimilated to old beliefs is the case of the garage-owner thought to have made money by bewitching lorries to break down on the stretch of highway near his premises. Some anthropologists have noted a rise in witch accusations among people recently moved to urban areas.[102] Christian conversions, it has also been suggested, may have contributed towards an increase in fears of witchcraft by removing alternative explanations for calamity, such as the vengeance of ancestors or local deities;[103] while the first effects of a Christian attack on magic would most likely be felt in the erosion of counter-witchcraft. Keith Thomas has noted a similar tendency during the Reformation period in England. He suggests that the Protestant attack on the magical aspects of Catholic doctrine and practice may have led to a rise in witch accusations, since people now felt deprived of the magical protection afforded them by certain Catholic rituals against maleficent sorcery.[104]

Other parallels between the role of witch beliefs in late medieval and early modern Europe and those still to be found in African societies are even more compelling. Alan Macfarlane found that in nearly ninety per cent of the witch accusations he examined in Essex the witch and her victim came from the same village – a fact which is fully in line with the observations of most African anthropologists.[105] As in Africa, many accusations arose out of bad relations between neighbours, particularly when the victims of witchcraft felt themselves to have been guilty of lack of charity or some other moral failing. The most common circumstance in England, according to Keith Thomas, was when the victim (or if a child, its parents) had been unneighbourly towards some old woman who had come to the door to beg or borrow food or the loan of some household utensil. The old woman might be sent away empty-handed, mumbling a curse or malediction. In due course, when something went wrong in the family

– a cow fell sick, or a baby died – she was immediately held responsible. In psychological terms the witch accusation represents a projection or inversion of the guilt the accuser feels towards the supposed witch. By blaming her for the subsequent misfortune, he relieves himself of the guilt he might have felt on account of his original lack of charity.[106] Similarly among the Cewa in Zambia, Max Marwick found that in some sixty per cent of his cases, the *victim* of witchcraft was guilty of some moral fault.[107]

Further similarities emerge when the social implications of witch accusations are considered. In Africa, it is more usual for social inferiors to make witchcraft accusations against their superiors, or juniors against their elders, since the latter usually have alternative methods of retaliation at their disposal. Similarly, in England 'before a witchcraft accusation could be plausibly made, the suspect had to be in a socially or economically inferior position to her supposed victim'.[108] In both cases, witch beliefs are double-edged in their social implications. On the one hand, by affirming traditional communal values and providing an outlet for suppressed resentments, they act as 'conservative social forces'.[109] On the other, they may have the more radical social function of articulating deeper divisions within the community, or helping to dissolve 'relations which have become redundant'.[110] A rise in the number of witchcraft accusations may thus reflect a general increase in social or economic tensions at community level. In Africa, as has already been suggested, such tensions may be brought about by colonial rule, urbanization and economic changes.[111] Similar findings have been made in Latin America, where witch accusations have been found to be most common in urban areas.[112] In Europe, during the early modern period, witch accusations may have been connected with the breakdown of traditional family structures in the towns.[113] In England especially, Keith Thomas has argued that witch accusations resulted from the 'conflict between the neighbourly conduct required by the ethical code of the old village community, and the increasingly individualistic forms of behaviour which accompanied the economic changes of the sixteenth and seventeenth centuries'.[114] Finally, another common point of comparison between the popular witch beliefs in Europe and those still to be found in Africa and elsewhere, is that witchcraft can reside in ordinary people and almost anyone can be accused of being a witch. At the level of witch *accusations*, neither in Africa nor in Europe do witches appear to have been conceived of as necessarily acting as members of a group. The activities giving rise to witch accusations are essentially disparate and uncoordinated.

Nevertheless in Africa, as in Europe, there has existed a stereotype of the witch district from the idea of witchcraft as popularly conceived, yet closely related to it. In Europe it has been shown that this stereotype, belonging to the heretic as well as the witch, was grafted on to the traditional witch accusation by means of the inquisitorial process, particularly by the application of torture. This has rarely occurred in Africa, with a few significant exceptions. There the 'night witch' or fantasy witch of popular nightmare, while associated in people's minds with ordinary witchcraft, has 'a quite different significance from that of the unneighbourly person who may one day be accused of witchcraft. It has the effect of asserting cultural values rather than specific social obligations. The real witch behaves badly in the accepted cultural context; the night witch rejects culture altogether'.[115]

Some African ideas about night witches are strikingly similar to those of the European witch manuals and demonological tracts. Thus some Azande women, not all of them witches, are believed to have sexual relations with cats, or to give birth to kittens which they suckle like human infants.[116] The Kaguru believe in witches who meet at night on mountain tops for orgies where they eat dead bodies and practise incest. They travel naked, walking upside-down on their hands, their bodies smeared white with ashes. Though they travel corporeally, they can elude capture in daylight by making themselves invisible. Sometimes they employ hyenas to dig up bodies for them. Their children are also witches and are initiated into the cult by being made to have sexual intercourse with members of their families. For the Kaguru, the witches' incest is a form of pact: 'Since these persons enjoy each other', they say, 'they will never betray each other to others'.[117]

The Mandari witches make a speciality of homosexual acts, bestiality with cows and goats and sex with immature girls; their favourite witch-salve is made from human excrement, which they drop on their victims' animal traps or rub on their belongings. They are born deceivers, often appearing as vigorous and good-looking young people – their children are especially charming.[118] The Wambugwe build their cult almost entirely around the hyena. Every witch owns at least one hyena, branded with an invisible mark which only he can recognize. He calls them his 'night cattle', milking them every night and occasionally they are ridden like horses to a saturnalian orgy where all the witches gather to boast their evil deeds and practise obscene rites. A visiting anthropologist received 'eye witness' evidence from his Wambugwe hosts:

> They had often seen the eerie light of a witch's torch as it flickered in the distance; one reported that he had been almost knocked over as a mounted hyena rushed past him in the dark; and it was a common experience to have smelled the acrid odour of burning hyena butter where a witch had recently passed. When these fragmentary experiences are put together, the evidence of the senses seems to reveal an authentic picture of a witch riding naked at full gallop through the night, mounted on a hyena and carrying a flaming torch which he refuels from time to time from a gourd of hyena butter slung over his shoulder.[119]

The night-witches of fantasy in fact embody everything that is considered horrible and detestable in the societies that believe in them. They practice incest and necrophagy, homosexuality, bestiality and the violation of young children. They are foul in their habits and ride dangerous or despicable animals. They are the personification of everything that is evil and anti-social. And the worst and most sinister of their characteristics is their secrecy and elusiveness, making it impossible to detect them. Among the Amba, for example, they are in constant league with each other, forming a secret association in each village. They do not attack people from other villages, but only members of their own communities:

> Not only have the witches killed and eaten their fellows in the past, it is certain that they will kill again. At any time a man himself, or a member of his household, may be chosen as one of their victims. The anxiety created by this belief is heightened by the uncertainty which surrounds the identity of the witches...[120]

In certain instances people have confessed to the horrible activities, some of them patently impossible, of the night witches. The colonial police in Rhodesia, who investigated witchcraft accusations in order to prove them false, found that many women confessed to acts of cannibalism and to impossible acts such as riding hyenas and pouring poison down the throats of sleeping men. In most cases, the women appear to have deluded themselves into witch fantasies: in a typical case of self-confessed cannibalism police dug up the corpse and found no traces of mutilation. But in one curious, and apparently unique instance, when the subjects admitted to having killed a child and cut its body in half, police only found half the corpse.[121] In this case the women may have actually acted out one of the witch fantasies suggested to them by society.* Generally speaking, however, there appears to have been a conceptual gap between the night witch of popular fantasy and the act of witchcraft which might be committed by one's neighbour. As Lucy Mair remarks, '... one cannot usually find a close connection between general ideas about witches and the direction of suspicion in individual cases ... '[123] The most probable reason for this is that, while large-scale witch hunts do occasionally occur, the procedures for dealing with witch accusations work primarily on an individual basis. Just as in England, the common-law procedure was primarily concerned with the *damage* done by witchcraft rather than the witch's diabolical activities, so in Africa most of the procedures for dealing with witches are of a practical nature, designed to persuade them to desist from their activities. In Zandeland, for example, a man has to be the object of repeated accusations before he can be executed as a witch.[124]

With a few exceptions, African methods of dealing with witchcraft are not designed to make the witches reveal themselves and confess their activities. On the contrary, witchcraft is so much taken for granted as part of everyday life that the purpose of the anti-witchcraft machinery is not to abolish witchcraft and exterminate all witches, an objective which would seem hopelessly utopian, but to appease the witches and to shame them into calling off their magic. The employment of witch doctors, diviners, oracles and elaborate forms of detection are primarily directed towards satisfying and appeasing the accuser, thereby making it unnecessary for him to engage in open conflict or vengeance. The night witch of fantasy belongs to a different conceptual framework: it is part of the propaganda necessary to maintain communal standards of behaviour and to define communal virtues in terms of their opposite. All the night witch's characteristics, such as walking upside-down, committing bestial acts, incest and so forth, are inversions of the standards society sets up for the individual. By the same token, the secret

---

* A similar conclusion might be drawn from the Affair of the Poisons, the scandal involving Mme de Montespan, mistress of Louis xiv, in 1680, in which a 'Black Mass' is said to have taken place involving the sacrifice of a new-born infant. This incident, taken by some as evidence of the sabbat, took place after three centuries of propaganda by those who believed in the reality of the sabbat. It would hardly be surprising if some unscrupulous individuals found it easy to persuade the rich and gullible to part with their money in exchange for gaining access to diabolical agencies.[122]

society of witches dramatizes the negation of the values of society as a whole. They are of course *internal* enemies, since aggression is usually legitimized when turned away from the community. Their nocturnal orgies are the counterpart of daily celebrations, necrophagy of proper burial and healthy food, incest of the principles of exogamy. In general the fantasy witch articulates good in terms of its opposite, and dramatizes evil by inverting the good.

However, as the Rhodesian cases suggest, the gap between the neighbourhood witch and the night witch of fantasy is not unbridgeable if means are available to discover the 'truth' about witches. It is ironic that the Rhodesian Witchcraft Suppression Act, set up to discourage witchcraft accusations, appears to have had the opposite effect. The machinery of normal police interrogation which, in this context, evidently contained the minimum of pressure, was nevertheless geared towards obtaining the witches' *confessions* – something which, in most cases, the native machinery seems to go to some lengths to avoid.[125] The novelty of a purely investigative procedure may have encouraged the Rhodesian witches to confess – or rather, to articulate their confessions in terms of the night witch stereotype. Under traditional African circumstances this would not normally have been required of them. It was, no doubt, for similar reasons that witches are frequently recorded as having made spontaneous confessions in Europe.

PART 3

Torture in modern history

SEVEN

Neapolitan dungeons and revolutionary brotherhoods

In 1851, Mr Gladstone, on a private visit to Naples, discovered that something was rotten in the Kingdom of the Two Sicilies. The problem that stirred this devout and brilliant Tory minister was the imprisonment under shocking conditions of forty of the kingdom's leading liberals, including a former prime minister, after a trial that bore only the faintest resemblance to a civilized judicial process. Mr Gladstone was not the man to let things rest once the volcanic resources of his moral indignation had been roused. The fate of the Neapolitan prisoners became within weeks a question of international importance, and probably enough a turning-point in the fortunes of the Tory party, whose lukewarm response to Gladstone's campaign led to his eventual apostasy. His revelations, published initially as open letters to his leader, Lord Aberdeen, after private remonstrance had failed, were further elaborated in refutations of the Neapolitan government's reply.[1] Their impact on public opinion was comparable to the publication of Burke's *Reflections on the Revolution in France* half a century earlier.[2] Appealing powerfully to the Englishman's native aversion to tyranny and violence, they permanently moulded British opinion against the Neapolitan government – a factor that significantly furthered the cause of Italian unity ten years later.

Torture was only one instance of this monumental system of misrule which Gladstone, borrowing a local phrase, denounced as 'the negation of God erected into a system of government'.[3] His primary concern was the way in which political prisoners were condemned to long terms of imprisonment under appalling conditions, after conviction on charges supported by the evidence of notorious police informers who had been bribed, blackmailed or otherwise intimidated. Men like Carlo Poerio, prime minister during the brief false dawn of liberalism that followed the revolution of 1848 when the king had been forced to grant a constitution (which he subsequently revoked); or the saintly and scholarly Luigi Settembrini, condemned to a Promethean punishment of 'double irons for life upon a remote and sea-grit rock'.[4] (The fate of Settembrini so affected Gladstone that he later joined in a conspiracy with Lord and Lady Holland, Anthony Pannizzi of the British Museum and others to rescue him with the help of some northern patriots.)[5] It was the fact that such men as these were chained to common criminals, forced 'to wear thick heavy dress of coarse woollen and leather' in the height of midsummer, and 'compelled to attend [but not, it seems, to suffer] the floggings of the vilest common criminals'[6] that aroused his fury and that of a large section of the educated British public against a system of government which he regarded as a standing invitation to republicanism.

Though Gladstone justified his attitude towards Neapolitan misgovernment on Conservative grounds, his attack marked the beginning of the turn to liberalism which culminated in his joining the Liberals. As an upholder of the twin principles of 'conservatism' and 'conservation' (or legitimacy), he argued

> ...for each of these principles it is a matter of deep and essential concern that iniquities committed under the shelter of its name should be stripped of that shelter... Nor has it ever fallen to my lot to perform an office so truly conservative, as in the endeavour I have made to shut and mark off from the sacred cause of government in general a system which I believed was bringing the name and idea of government into shame and hatred, and converting the thing from a necessity and a blessing into a sheer curse to human kind.[7]

In the event he found, as others in similar situations have found, that in politics party interests usually predominate over questions of principle, however immaculately stated. The Conservatives were less interested in the substance of the allegations than in the fact that they lent moral authority to the current Liberal government's anti-Bourbon policies.[8] Gladstone felt dutifully bound to apologize to Palmerston, which hardly endeared him to his colleagues. In the end, it was Gladstone, not his party, who changed. For in his concern with upholding the legitimacy of governments, he failed at first to draw the inevitable conclusion from what he saw. Illegality, he stated, had been the

> foundation of the Neapolitan system... illegality the fountainhead of cruelty and baseness and every other vice; illegality which gives a bad conscience, that

bad conscience creates fears, those fears lead to tyranny, that tyranny begets resentment, that resentment creates true causes of fear where they were not before; and thus fear is quickened and enhanced and the original vice multiplies itself with fearful speed, and old crime engenders the necessity for new.[9]

It only gradually dawned on him that there was no reformist escape from such a closed system of vice. By 1876, after the failure of his first administration, he had finally 'outgrown the view that governments in general, whether absolute or not, must be supported, and appealed to the conscience of British democracy to vindicate the right of people to revolt against oppression'.[10]

Whatever the effects of Mr Gladstone's exposures on British – and international – public opinion, there seems to have been no permanent improvement in the condition of King Bomba's prisoners. Committed supporters of Italian unification continued to make hideous revelations. In 1856, the *Morning Post* published a series of harrowing accounts of the tortures to which Sicilian patriots had been subjected in Cefalu in the repression after 1848.[11] Friends and relatives of patriots who had gone underground were tortured to reveal their hiding places. According to the principal source of the reports, most of these efforts were unsuccessful. One man was left naked in iron fetters for several days in a small damp cell with his two small sons (who had no one else to look after them) simply for failing to reveal the whereabouts of one of his relatives. A doctor found him unconscious after having suffered several epileptic fits, covered in bruises, while the two sons were almost dead from starvation. The standard method of torture seems to have been a type of thumbscrew nicknamed the *strumento angelico*; the victims were not apparently even permitted to scream; their mouths were clamped shut in a leather muzzle known as the *cuffia del silenzio*.

The tortures appear to have been conducted on the initiative of the local police, without the explicit sanction of higher authority, and some prisoners were released through the intervention of local doctors or priests. The Neapolitan government vociferously denied the allegations, claiming that the *Morning Post* had merely reproduced scandalmongering articles from the Piedmontese press. But from the chronology it seems clear that the plagiarism was the other way round: the *Morning Post's* were the first reports to be published, the accounts having been smuggled out through the good offices of the British consul. The governor also invited three foreigners to inspect the Cefalu prison: a Polish doctor, a Polish count, and a German officer who acted as the

Turkish sultan's agent in Sicily. Naturally, they found nothing to complain of.[12]

Naples was not the only part of Italy where torture appears to have been revived in the reaction after the fall of Napoleon. The restoration of papal rule in the central states produced an oppressive clerical autocracy, the French, with their enthusiasm for centralization, having destroyed the last vestiges of local and municipal independence. Clerical rule 'the clutch of dead men's fingers in live flesh'[13] blurred all distinction between religion and politics. The secrets of the confessional were passed to the restored inquisition, which passed them on to the police, and the bureaucracy which was dominated by priests. In the wave of repression after the collapse of the Roman republic in 1848, the Italian patriot Orsini's allegation that the *bastinado* was applied literally under the eyes of the pope, though possibly exaggerated, is not entirely surprising. The inquisition's famous tribunals were also revived under their traditional judges, the Dominican friars who, he says, subjected people to tortures of every description.[14]

Neither the efforts of the pope nor of King Bomba to contain the rising tide of Italian nationalism could have succeeded without the principal prop for the status quo in Italy, the Austrian army, whose grip on Lombardy and the Veneto was supported by military tribunals, special courts and a host of other sanctions. There is a special irony in the fact that the Austrians, who under the enlightened despotism of Joseph II had abolished torture, were the first people north of the Alps legally to permit its reintroduction, albeit under emergency provisions. Orsini (whose career ended on the scaffold after his attempt to assassinate Napoleon III by throwing a bomb at his carriage in 1858) describes the *bastinado* as administered in a Viennese prison in 1854:

Passing from my cell to the Examination Hall, I often saw a poor victim stretched on the *cavaletto*, a bench about eight feet in length, with his face downwards. By means of a movable vice in the centre, the body is screwed down, so that the patient cannot stir, the arms are stretched above the head, and the wrists are fastened to irons at the ankle, so that the foot remains beyond the bench. A corporal chosen for strength and brutality stands to the left of the victim, and commences administering the torture thus: holding a switch aloft in his right hand he swings it across his victim and up to the left with as much force as he can muster, saying EIN; returning to the right, he says ZWEI, and again to the left, DREI... If the victim speaks, the flogging is suspended to note down his depositions. At the conclusion of the operation the surgeon examines him, and he is borne back to his sack of straw. If he has remained firm in his refusal to confess, the punishment [sic] is renewed on the following day.[15]

According to Orsini, who as a professional 'revolutionist' was involved in most of the activities of the carbonari and their successors in 'Young Italy', the *bastinado* yielded considerable results for the Austrians in their struggle against Italian and Hungarian patriots. It was usually employed only as a last resort, after a prisoner had been thoroughly debilitated by prolonged imprisonment and near starvation. He recalls a Hungarian who held out for a year before admitting he was an army deserter. Promptly taken to the *bastinado*, he revealed everything about his friends.[16] A Milanese patriot, Giovanni Cervieri, was given twenty blows on eight successive days, on orders of the military governor, finally forcing him at death's door to reveal the whereabouts of a 'movable barricade' he had invented.[17] Orsini also credits the *bastinado* for revealing much of the information that led to the executions of nine patriots in 1852. But the outcry this caused in the rest of Europe, coming so soon after Gladstone's Neapolitan revelations, persuaded the Austrians to modify their methods. The most notorious of the torturers in Italy – a converted Jew from Prague who was believed to have become a Catholic to improve his chances of promotion – was dismissed and the military tribunal replaced by a civilian court containing two Italian assessors. The latter were supposed to make sure that prisoners were not *bastinadoed* or asked leading questions. Orsini dismisses these improvements as a 'farce' intended only to save appearances.[18] The assessors – he says – were themselves intimidated, and though the *bastinado* was discontinued 'other methods, less brutal in appearance, but more effective in reality' were resorted to. Prisoners refusing to answer questions were put in solitary confinement; they were then examined and subjected to leading questions, their statements were garbled and altered.

> When solitary confinement, unwholesome and insufficient food, combined with malaria have reduced the prisoner to a state of physical and often mental weakness, he is again, after a lapse of a year or more, brought into the court for examination. If he still failed to give information, he was liable to a further five years of *carcere duro* or hard labour with chains.[19]

Executions continued, though with less publicity than before Mr Gladstone's revelations.

Such were the expedients available to the Austrian authorities that it is hard to see how any patriot could have failed to succumb, if not to the *bastinado*, then to death by slow degrees as a result of the appalling prison conditions. Undoubtedly a large number of them did. Orsini, by remarkable courage and tenacity as well as good luck, managed to escape from his death cell in the castle of Mantua and succeeded in making his way to London where his account of his sufferings published in English sold 35,000 copies in one year (1856–7).[20] British public opinion, helped by Gladstone's own apostasy, was swinging firmly in favour of Palmerston and Italian unity, and was not to be deflected by Orsini's amateurish and bungling attempt on the French emperor the following year with a number of custom-made bombs purchased openly from a Birmingham iron-master.[21]

Nor did the facts of torture themselves, as distinct from the public indignation they aroused, prompt any useful reflections about its utility – whether in Naples, the papal states, or the Austrian north. Those who sided with the politics of the victims were merely confirmed in their views on the medieval barbarity of most of the peninsula's governments. Those, like the editor of the ultra-Catholic *Universe* who believed in upholding the status quo, challenged the facts as well as the motives of the exposeurs.[22] The editor was able to point to an apparently hypocritical contradiction between the humanitarian concern shown by Mr Gladstone and his friends for the fate of the Neapolitan prisoners, and the systematic torture to which a large number of Her Britannic Majesty's subjects were being subjected in India.[23] Even Gladstone himself paid scant attention to the function of torture in the Neapolitan case, as distinct from the grosser indignities to which the patriots had been subjected. It was left to one of his anonymous partisans in the polemics that developed after the publication of the famous letters to the Earl of Aberdeen to detail its uses in the Naples trial.[24] While the more prominent victims like Poerio and Settembrini evidently escaped torture or the threat of it, the court proceedings were rank with it, as was the evidence of two of the chief prosecution witnesses who were also among the co-accused.

One of Poerio's co-accused, Margharita, a Sicilian brought from Syracuse for the trial, retracted in court a statement implicating Poerio as having attended a meeting of the 'Great Council' of an alleged sect, the 'Unità Italiana'. Not only did he allege that the statement had been forced from him by keeping him without food for three days, as well as by constant threats of flogging, but he also claimed to be ignorant of the persons whom he had finally named – the names having been suggested to him by the examining magistrate. Another witness claimed that similar methods had been used, including threats to the life of his ailing mother, to elicit an incriminating letter from him – by 'il inquisitore'. In the latter case the court, far from challenging the statement or even commenting on it, appeared to accept it, for the witness, also one of the accused, got off with a light sentence.[25]

More ominous than these methods of intimidation, however, was the gist of the charges – that Poerio, Settembrini and their co-accused were members of a conspiratorial sect, the Unità Italiana, with the treasonable aim of overthrowing the monarchy in favour of Italian unity. Settembrini had previously served a term as a member of Mazzini's 'Young Italy', the revolutionary brotherhood of 1848. This, together with Poerio's admitted interest in the union (i.e. alliance) of Italian states, lent a semblance of plausibility to the charges, sufficient at least to impress foreign reporters. The equation of liberalism with subversion – subversion cunningly organized for devilish aims by secret revolutionary brotherhoods like the carbonarists – had long been part of the currency of reactionary politicians.

Ever since the French revolution had begun to tear Europe's social fabric apart, conservative princes and politicians had sought, in the secret revolutionary brotherhoods and in their predecessors the freemasons, the key to the cataclysmic events of their time. People for whom change was an affront, and quite unnecessary, clearly needed an exceptional explanation for exceptional events. Since all had been for the best in the best of possible worlds represented by the *ancien régime*, the disruption that engulfed Europe at the end of the eighteenth century must be the work of a malignant agency.[26] There was plenty of material to hand with which to construct a conspiracy theory of the French revolution based on the role of the freemasons. During the latter part of the eighteenth century, the masonic lodges had undoubtedly played a subversive role – though not necessarily intentionally. In a hierarchical order based on obedience and rigid feudal categories, the lodges provided a forum in which landowners and tradesmen, members of the aristocracy and the upper bourgeoisie, had been able to meet for a few hours at least on terms of relative equality. This together with their Anglo-Saxon origins made them a natural vehicle for the dissemination of the enlightened egalitarian ideas of the *philosophes* and the disciples of classical economy. * History does not record how many of the nobles

* One of these progressive ideas, as we have seen, was the abolition of torture.

who sided with the third estate in 1789 were masons. But their numbers must have been considerable, for in the year the revolution broke out there may have been as many as a hundred thousand masons in France alone, while the movement had spread rapidly throughout the rest of Europe.[27]

Not all the lodges were egalitarian and progressive – or, as believed by their enemies, atheist and anti-clerical. Many had remained loyal to the Scottish–Jacobite tradition introduced into France by the Old Pretender. But it was inevitable that a hysterical Catholicism, sensing itself under attack, should begin to persecute the order. The inquisition in Spain and Portugal began to harass freemasons spasmodically around the middle of the eighteenth century. In the 1740s the arrest and torture of an English mason, John Coustas, by the Portuguese, on grounds of suspected heresy, raised an outcry in England and prompted diplomatic intervention. In his indictment the inquisition stigmatized the 'sect' as 'a horrid compound of sacrilege, sodomy and many other abominable crimes'.[28] As with the Templars, the Cathars and numerous other persecuted groups, the charge of sodomy became the stock-in-trade of the enemies of masonry.* Masons themselves were to some extent to blame for what eventually became their predicament. The arcane mysteries, the theatrical emphasis on secrecy which had grown up in response to rationalist tendencies during the Enlightenment, naturally fuelled the superstitions of the now terrified Right. More disastrous, perhaps, was the masons' mythical foundation legend associating them with the Templars. Finally, there was an element of truth, which became the core of a widespread belief, that the masons contained a conspiracy aimed at overthrowing the social order.

In the late 1770s, a secret society with the 'genuinely' – that is to say, self-consciously – subversive aim of spreading egalitarian and anti-clerical ideas acquired ascendancy in a number of German and Austrian lodges. Known as the Illuminati, it was founded by a Jesuit trained scholar and to some extent imitated the methods of the Society – though its aims were diametrically opposed. It is believed to have numbered Goethe, Mozart and Schiller among its adherents. The exposure of the society's aims after the defection of some of its members added to the fears of conservatives about masons in general, seeing that these were now proven to contain a measure of truth. After the revolu-

---

* The association of freemasonry with homosexuality survived in France well into the 1950s. See Nancy Mitford, *The Blessing* (London 1951).

tion broke out, the darkest fears about the movement seemed to be confirmed. Marie Antoinette, at one time a supporter of masonry, warned her brother the Austrian emperor: 'Take great care over any associations of freemasons . . . It is by means of masonry that the monsters of this country count on succeeding elsewhere . . .'[29]

The coming war between France and Austria created the need to close ranks. All masonic lodges in Austria were forbidden to meet. The following year the authorities uncovered a 'plot' involving the establishment of a secret society similar to the Illuminati. It was led by discontented liberals and Hungarians, one of whom turned out to be a police informer. Agents provocateurs provided the evidence needed for the arrests. In the trials that followed, most of the accused were found guilty and hanged. From then onwards conservatives in Germany, Austria and Italy became increasingly alarmed, if not obsessed, by the dangers of secret societies.[30]

The most celebrated version of the conspiracy theory of revolution was that of Augustin de Barruel, a Jesuit-trained priest who left France shortly after the September massacres. His five-volume *Mémoires pour servir à l'histoire du Jacobinisme*, published from 1797 on, achieved immense popularity and was acclaimed by, among others, Edmund Burke. According to Barruel, the Jacobins had planned the events which brought them to power and destroyed so many lives and so much property at least two years before the revolution of 1789.

> . . . all was foreseen, premeditated, plotted, resolved, planned: everything that happened was the result of the deepest wickedness, because everything was prepared and managed by men who alone held the threads of long-settled conspiracies and who knew how to choose the right moment for their designs.[31]

Behind the Jacobin plot lay the converging threads of ancient conspiracies going back to the Templars and the Manicheans. The anti-monarchist conspiracy worked through the masonic network, disseminating republican ideas. Some individual masons, Barruel conceded, were innocent dupes of masters higher up in the hierarchy, while some apparently innocent lodges posed as 'front' organizations, the better to conceal the aims of the true conspirators. In 1789 this great underground machine was composed of at least 600,000 masons under the command of Lafayette and the Duc d'Orléans. Jacobin power was eventually achieved as a result of a take-over of the freemasons by the German Illuminati, a fundamentally anti-Christian sect dedicated to atheism, universal anarchy and the destruction of property. The tentacles of this vast conspiracy extended far beyond France. Peasant risings in Bohemia and Transylvania were attributed to its evil influence; while the success of General Bonaparte's campaign in Italy was the result of advance planning by the Illuminati. Inside France, even the guillotine was shaped in the form of a masonic triangle.[32]

A more respectable version of the conspiracy theory appeared in the writings of Joseph de Maistre, a man of immense learning and culture who was for some years ambassador of Savoy at the court of St Petersburg. De Maistre, who had himself been a mason, rejected most of Barruel's wilder claims – indeed he left among his unpublished papers a detailed refutation of them. Nevertheless, he endorsed some of Barruel's arguments about the malignant aims of the Illuminati whom he saw as Protestant-influenced enemies of the papacy and the house of Bourbon working through the agency of the secret societies. That such an enlightened man could hold these views is indicative of the general strength of the belief in the manipulative power of the secret societies in Catholic and conservative circles.[33]

The belief would never have become so firmly grafted into the minds of the restoration governments and their police forces had it not been shared, in a parallel sense, on the other side. The father of all left-wing revolutionary conspirators was, of course, the famous Gracchus Babeuf, who still occupies a high position in the Marxist pantheon. His ideas were disseminated by his friend and disciple, Felice Buonarotti, who shared a prison cell with him for a few months after the fall of Robespierre. Both were released after Bonaparte's 'whiff of grapeshot' at Vendémière, which staved off an attempted royalist coup. The shift to the left after Vendémière was not to last, and Babeuf's newspaper – the *Tribun du Peuple* – was closed down by police within a few months. Babeuf and his closest supporters, including Buonarotti, formed an 'insurrectionary committee' with the aim of overthrowing the Directory and driving the revolution back on its egalitarian course by seizing power and implementing the radical constitution of 1793. The method of the 'Conspiracy of Equals' was to infiltrate the army, the police and other branches of government with an organization built around twelve 'revolutionary agents'. The model evidently owed something to the masonic structure. Buonarotti, who had been born in Italy before joining the revolution in Corsica, may at one time have belonged to the Illuminati. Apart from the fact that the police appear to have known about the scheme from the start, the conspiracy met with little response. Hatred of Robespierre and Jacobin terror was still fresh in the public mind. In the summer of 1796, two hundred conspirators were arrested, and the trials took place at Vendôme the following year. The charge of conspiracy was not proved, and most of the defendants were acquitted. Several of the leaders were convicted for advocating and seeking to implement the Jacobin constitution; but only Babeuf was executed. Buonarotti was imprisoned, but released after only three years by Napoleon, who could afford to be reasonably indulgent towards political opposition on the republican side. Buonarotti may also have been helped by ex-Jacobins such as Fouché and Réal, who held prominent positions in Napoleon's police. In 1806, he settled in Geneva where he earned his keep by giving music lessons, and founded an international secret society, the Sublîmes Maîtres Parfaits, which caused the local prefect to send alarmist reports to Paris. Since freemasonry was generally popular under the empire, the Paris authorities paid little attention to Buonarotti's activities, though he was eventually ordered to move to Grenoble.[34]

With the defeat of Napoleon and the Bourbon restoration, supporters of the revolution precluded from legitimate political activity followed Buonarotti's example and organized themselves into secret societies. Inevitably, the authorities were inclined to attribute all subsequent disturbances to their influence. The troubles in Italy and Spain in 1820–1, for example, were seen as resulting from their machinations. The secret societies themselves were hardly likely to decline the credit. Thus during one popular demonstration in Naples, the carbonari displayed their banners, giving the impression that their organization was behind the agitation.[35] Similarly, when the Austrian police, through information obtained from two of Buonarotti's closest associates, succeeded in exposing his contacts with a number of different secret societies, Buonarotti, unabashed, was able to enjoy to the full his reputation as the grand maestro of his revolutionary orchestra.[36] It is hardly surprising to find Metternich urging the Tsar Alexander to suppress the secret societies as 'a real power, all the more dangerous as it works in the dark, undermining all parts of the social body, and depositing everywhere the seeds of a moral gangrene'.[37]

The finishing touch to the picture was placed by Buonarotti himself, with the publication in 1828 of his account of the Babeuf insurrection, *Conspiracy of Equals*, which firmly established the principle of insurrection by a small revolutionary élite as the dominant warcry of the left until the ascendancy of proletarian socialism and the emergence of Marxism a generation later. The masonic pattern of the secret society, with its elaborate rites and its principle of gradual initiation into the 'inner secrets' of the movements, came to be adopted both by the infant socialist movements in France and Germany, and by the liberal–nationalist movements in Italy, Hungary, Poland and Ireland.[38] Repression, of course, was inevitable; Austria introduced the death penalty for membership of secret societies in its Italian dominions. The pope banned the carbonari and excommunicated them. Freemasons were harried once again.[39]

What, then, was the reality behind this spectre that haunted the kings and policemen of Europe during the restoration period? What, if any, was the actual threat they posed to the social order? As with the masons during the eighteenth century, the answer lies less in what they did, or claimed to do, than in what they *were*. In a purely objective sense, the secret revolutionary brotherhoods commanded loyalties from their followers that were incompatible with the duties of good subjects. The elaborate rituals and initiation oaths, which created an aura of theatrical mystery around the societies, had originally been copied from those of the craftsmen or journeymen's fraternities going back to the Middle Ages. The original aim of such ceremonies was to provide illiterate or semi-literate workmen with a measure of trade solidarity and a way of protecting their chief economic asset – the 'secret' of the craft.[40] Once republican, or any other form of revolutionary (or counter-revolutionary) activity had been suppressed, such clandestine organizations provided a useful way for opposition groups to keep in touch with one another. In the field of action, however, it is doubtful whether they achieved anything significant. The carbonarist movement in southern Italy, though widely blamed for the Neapolitan revolution of 1820, was far too large and divided to hold on to any of its gains. The revolution was in any case largely spontaneous, born of peasant frustration with the failure of promised land reform and the disenchantment of upper-class constitutionalists hankering after the 'enlightened' days of Joachim Murat.[41] The very failure of the revolution indicated the absence of centralized control, either by the carbonarists, who had members in all ranks and stations, or any other sect. As for the manifold activities of the arch-fiend Buonarotti, no one has yet shown, according to a recent authority on the secret societies, that his Sublimes Maîtres Prafaits did anything positive of significance except strengthen Metter-nich's hand by being discovered.[42]

As the nineteenth century progressed, the appeal of the myth that events were being secretly controlled by international secret societies gradually declined. With constitutions in France and Piedmont Euro-pean politics began to take on a less monolithic appearance. The revo-lutionary movement divided into two main streams. One, accompany-ing the growing industrialization in France and Germany, abandoned the ritualistic brotherhood of the secret society in favour of the mass working-class organization favoured by Marx and Engels, who strongly condemned anything savouring of the 'superstitious worship of authority'.[43] The other stream irrigated the growing nationalism of the 'young' movements – Mazzini's Young Italy, with its imitators in Hungary, Poland, Ireland and among other subject peoples in Europe and Asia. Here, in a more authoritarian climate, the conspiratorial tradition survived. Mazzinians like Orsini were masters of intrigue and the use of invisible ink. Occasionally their expertise yielded practical results as, for example, when Orsini contrived his fabulous escape from the fortress of Mantua. But in terms of revolutionary effectiveness, their operatic methods were no more efficacious than those of Buonarotti. It was the conventional diplomacy of Cavour, the armies of Napoleon III and Victor Emmanuel, and above all, the military genius of Garibaldi – rather than the conspiratorial intrigues of Mazzini and Orsini – which brought about the birth of Italy.

Nevertheless the spectre of the secret societies, though no longer the prime concern of politicians, continued to haunt the minds and dossiers of Europe's policemen, even in France. A few days after the *coup d'état* which brought Louis Napoleon absolute power in 1852, the Minister of the Interior, M. Morny, wrote to the prefect of the Paris police, M. de Maupas, urging him to act against all members of the secret societies.

It is essential that the capital be freed from all impure and dangerous ele-ments . . . Paris must cease to be a refuge for bandits from all countries who meet there in order to put society in peril. Knowing well your zeal, I am sure that you believe as firmly as I do that the time has come to impress these men who have been troubling the country for the past thirty years, with a salutary terror . . .[44]

The search for conspirators extended to the provinces. According to a

republican deputy exiled to London, people were arrested and interrogated by examining magistrates to reveal the names of the heads of
secret societies. In more than one instance, pressure appears to have
been put on them by throwing them into freezing cells, though there
is no evidence that physical torture was used.

It seems fair to conclude, therefore, that regardless of the objective
or historical reasons for the great revolutionary upheavals between
1789 and 1848, the political police in most of the European countries
had an exaggerated view of the power, actual or potential, of the revolutionary conspirators. (England, of course, is always exceptional,
because the police lacked a central organization.) The delusion was
helped by the conspirators themselves, or more especially, those revolu-
tionaries-turned-police-informers who provided them and posterity
with most of their information about the secret brotherhoods. Yet there
is here a curious paradox: the frequency with which devotees of the
brotherhoods defected to the police, and the ease with which the organizations could be infiltrated and kept under police surveillance must
have limited their effectiveness in police eyes.[45] The myth, which made
such a notable contribution to the rise of the police states of the following
century, could hardly survive the wholesale penetration of the organizations by the police without being exploded.

There is no single explanation for this paradox, though a number of
reasons may be suggested. Among the reactionary régimes – in Austria,
Naples and tsarist Russia – the police were less slaves to the myth than
servants of political masters for whom the myth was a necessity. For at
a time when there were political alternatives to absolutism, the auto-
cratic rulers needed every ideological weapon they could lay their
hands on in order to justify the withholding of constitutions. Political
police were therefore under pressure to provide evidence in support
of the view that every kind of oppositionist activity was subversive,
and treasonable. The most convincing way of doing this, given the
climate of the restoration years and the susceptibilities of conservative politicians, was to fit oppositionists of any category into the
network of the old secret societies, or their revamped versions. This
at any rate, seems a reasonable inference from the rigging of evidence
in the Poerio trial.*

* See W. E. Gladstone, *Examination of the Official Reply of the Neapolitan Government* (London 1852), p. 42: 'It is a certain proposition that when a government treats enmity to
abuse as identical to the purposes of subversion it, according to the laws of our mixed

In less conservative societies, another factor may have been at work, what might be called the 'detective psychology' of the police – a legacy from the criminal to the political branch. Such a psychology will equate 'political' events with crimes of the conventional variety, with the result that when rioting or street fighting takes place, there will be a search for the 'criminals' or 'agitators' at the expense of wider explanations. Such presumption is rarely confined to the police, but is usually held by those politicians who stand to lose by these events. Obviously, there is a role for mob orators and others gifted with the power to influence their fellow men in every revolutionary situation. However, this is only compatible with a presumption of conspiracy if such leaders are credited with more or less supernatural powers. An alternative presumption is the venality of the mob which, incapable of strong feelings of its own, will riot or demonstrate on behalf of anyone who will pay for it. Paris police agents embellished their reports on the rioting in 1793 and 1794 (mainly caused by high food prices) with accounts of men and women 'carrying bundles of assignats or distributing handfuls of gold and silver' although not one of the witnesses interviewed about these events admitted seeing such bribery. The result of searches were invariably negative, although those arrested were often found to be carrying arms.[46]

However, the innate tendency of policemen to see conspiracies where none exist will remain in bounds provided torture is not used to obtain or manufacture (consciously or otherwise) the evidence. During the nineteenth century, police in France, Germany and Russia barely if ever resorted to torture, although they were just as predisposed to the conspiracy mythology as their Austrian and Sicilian colleagues. Whatever their revolutionary potential, the ritual brotherhoods were notoriously vulnerable to police infiltration. Where conditions for this were not forthcoming, other chicaneries were always available – the bribery of witnesses, forgeries, perjury, pressure on juries and so forth.* A willingness to believe, or to pretend to believe, in conspiracy theories is

---

nature, partially amalgamates the two, and fulfils at length its own miserable predictions in its own more miserable ruin.'

* A letter by Jenny Marx provides an example of German police harassment of her husband during preparations for the trial of the Cologne communists in 1852. Since police agents among the socialists were unanimous in reporting Marx's repudiation of armed risings and plots, they resorted to underhand methods. Homes were illegally broken into, files stolen and letters forged, including the minute book of a non-existent

therefore not a prerequisite for torture, although at times of great persecution torture and conspiracy have usually been associated.

The most striking example of this is the complete absence of torture in France during the nineteenth century, when, as the political laboratory of Europe, it went through every vicissitude of revolution, from a 'feudal' restoration to the world's first experiment with communism. The period was marked by increasing waves of revolutionary and reactionary terrorism, beginning with the September Massacres of 1793 and reaching its climax with Marshal MacMahon's wholesale slaughter after the collapse of the Paris commune, a massacre unprecedented in Europe for several centuries. The period also saw, in England as in France, a marked deterioration both in the status and treatment of political offenders as the power of the state bit deeper into society. Most of the instruments of modern totalitarianism – the political police, the politicization of the army, the use of terror by the state, the prison camps, the suspension of laws guaranteeing human rights, the plebiscitary dictatorship – were created in France during the nineteenth century. Yet for all that, torture, perhaps the most characteristically totalitarian practice of all, appears to have been entirely absent. The evidence on this seems conclusive.

*   *   *

'Humanity has suffered more degradation in France in a single year than in Turkey in a hundred years ... '[47] writes a Girondin during the height of the Terror in 1794, in a book which describes the roads crowded with prisoners, men and women chained together, or tied ignominiously to the tails of horses. Certainly, Europe had witnessed nothing like this since the religious wars of the seventeenth century. The prisons, built for a more leisurely age, were chronically overcrowded. Those who had the doubtful fortune of surviving more than a few weeks in Robespierre's festering jails were almost certain to die

---

meeting. 'The whole police case is lies' Jenny wrote. 'They steal, they forge letters, they break open desks, they commit perjury and give false evidence and consider they have a perfect right to do so in the case of the communists, who are beyond the pale. . . Marx has to work all day and half the night copying out proofs of the forgery to send via different routes to Germany.' Marx' diligence was partly rewarded. Some forgeries were unmasked and four of the eleven accused acquitted. See Nicolaievsky and Maenchen-Helfen, *Karl Marx: Man and Fighter* (London 1973), pp. 236–8.

on the scaffold – that is, if they were not first murdered by the enraged populace while being transferred from one prison to another, as happened in September 1792. Prisoners, especially those of gentle birth, were insulted by the warders, had their belongings stolen or were subjected to various forms of blackmail. Physical assault, however, seems to have been very rare indeed. The worst that could befall a woman was being made to strip, or if she were a member of the aristocracy, being subjected to a body search by a member of the lower orders, or being thrown into a common jail with prostitutes. And, to judge by the heartfelt cries of horror and outrage that still shriek from contemporary accounts, for an eighteenth-century aristocrat, this was defilement enough.[48]

The manner in which the judges of the popular tribunals interrogated their victims, causing them to trap themselves into admissions of guilt, was bitterly resented. Often, apart from cross-examination, they were not permitted to speak in their defence. 'Tu n'as pas parole' Fouquier-Tinville, the state prosecutor in Paris, would shout if one dared to utter in his own defence.[49] The judges were in league with the prosecutors: 'Ses réponses et ses moyens de défense sont sublimes', the prosecutor was overheard whispering to the judge during an interrogation at Arras, 'le jury mollit; prends y garde'.[50] But the fact that examinations were held in public courts or before groups of publicly appointed commissioners prevented the possibilities of torture. There was no political police, as yet, entrusted with the task of squeezing out counter-revolutionary secrets from reluctant victims. Judging by the victims' accounts, the cruellest thing the plebeian judges on the tribunals were capable of doing was to make damaging insinuations about a respectable woman's honour. A fellow-prisoner of Mme Roland, the Girondin leader, recalls the indignation of her jail-mates when she returned from one such interrogation: 'Quand elle revint ses yeux étaient humides; on l'avait traitée avec une telle dureté, jusqu'à lui faire des questions outrageantes pour son honneur, qu'elle n'avait pu retenir ses larmes tout en exprimant son indignation.'[51] Such fine sensibilities would not long survive a modern interrogation. But it was not just a matter of refraining from physical brutalities. The public interrogations were only one aspect of a whole system based on public vengeance and revolutionary justice. This is not to say that the victims were never innocent, or executed on the slenderest charges. But if they were murdered it was nevertheless an expression of 'general will', in effect of revolutionary violence, not at the hand of a special military or police caste that had separated itself entirely from the rest of society. Once the vengeance of the people had abated and the fear of foreign invasion had been averted, the Terror gradually subsided, and those who had been closely identified with it were first isolated and then destroyed.

What distinguishes torture from other forms of terrorism of either the revolutionary or counter-revolutionary variety is not its cruelty, or its illegality, but rather the purpose to which it is put – the desire to elicit the 'truth' from the condemned in order to give moral validity to his execution or punishment, or to obtain the names of 'accomplices'. The revolutionary tribunals in France did not need a public confession of guilt on the part of the accused to justify their sentences.

Expressions of support for the *ancien régime* were punished as severely as infringements of the law.[52] Up till June 1794, when the counter-revolution of the Vendée had been finally crushed and the battle of Fleurus made France the first military power in Europe, the vast majority of the victims of the terror appear to have been guilty of the charges brought against them.[53] Many of them admitted their guilt, arms were found on them, or correspondence with the enemy was produced in evidence.[54] Admittedly, many thousands were shot without trial, or drowned in the Loire, because neither tribunals nor prisons could be found to cope with them. But these illegal executions were in areas where an active civil war was in progress, where facilities for disarming and interning prisoners who would have had every intention of continuing the struggle did not exist.[55]

Only in the final months of Jacobin rule can the Terror be said to have evolved, under its own dynamic laws, into a system of government as such. The victory of the revolution, achieved at such a terrible cost in blood, produced a revulsion which cost the Robespierrists their popularity, while their threats to redistribute suspects' property, and their failure to carry these threats out, alienated both property-owners in the Convention and the intended beneficiaries.[56] The dictatorship could no longer rely on the support of any class, and terrorism became its sole means of existence. From that point onwards, until the fall of Robespierre, there is far more doubt about the guilt of the victims.[57] Those tried under the law of 22 Prairial were condemned without fore-knowledge of the charges against them, or even a hearing.[58] 'Conspiracies' were manufactured in the prisons, with the help of agents provocateurs, or, according to one source, by deliberately making the prisoners eat foul food.[59] Under these conditions, torture would clearly have been a useful additional weapon in the régime's struggle for survival, but it could not be used because there was no permanent, semi-secret élite force to administer it.

Napoleon's police minister, Fouché, is perhaps the first of the modern police chiefs to grasp that power counts for more than personal loyalty or ideological commitment, and that power in a modern state goes to him who controls not just its external trappings – the police, the army and their weapons – but the life-force on which these institutions depend for their existence – namely, information. A centralized police-system directly answerable to the king with spies in every nobleman's household had been a feature of the *ancien régime*. What distinguished Fouché from his royalist predecessors – La Reynie, d'Argenson, Lenoir – was his understanding that this gave him a personal power that could be used, if necessary, independently of his master. After his quarrel with the emperor in 1810, Fouché destroyed his files and fled to Italy – which made it necessary for Napoleon to restore him. He put his enormous power at the disposal of the monarchy in 1814, gave it back to Napoleon during the hundred days, and there betrayed his leader a second time after the final defeat at Waterloo.[60]

For Fouché, since accuracy of intelligence was the key to power, precise interrogations of suspects and agents were crucial. He had a network of agents and informers throughout France and among foreign émigrés.[61] In 1795, during his Jacobin days, he had joined Babeuf's conspiracy only to denounce it.[62] Infiltration and provocation were his favourite methods of operation. In his war against the Chouans (the royalist movement in Normandy and Brittany) he had frequent recourse to various terroristic methods, including threats to families or friends of suspects, or even their landlords.[63] There is no evidence however that he employed torture, although there is nothing in his character to suggest that he was prevented by any scruples other than the belief, a relic perhaps of his 'enlightened' background, that more effective results could be achieved by other means. However, two of his subordinates, Réal and Bertrand, are said to have used thumbscrew techniques in the campaign against the Chouans; and, in a single documented instance, Napoleon himself is recorded as authorizing one of his marshals to employ the breech-loader of a rifle as a thumbscrew to obtain information from a fisherman suspected of dealings with the

English.[64] But these are very few instances in a record that is remarkable for the absence of torture. The new state was threatened from both royalist and republican quarters, and the drastic step had already been taken whereby political opponents of the régime had become identified as enemies of the state and consequently outlaws. In the modern world, such conditions invariably lead to torture, even by those régimes which maintain a formal democratic structure.

If the first empire proved that a military dictatorship could be run perfectly efficiently without the use of torture, the experience of the second suggests that the same applies to a police state. Bonapartist sentiment retained its appeal in the police as well as the army during the Bourbon restoration and the July monarchy, and the intervention of de Maupas, the Paris police prefect, was decisive in achieving the success of Louis Napoleon's coup d'état.[65] Fouché's techniques of provocation and infiltration came into their heyday. It was the high summer of the agent provocateur, when the police themselves provoked riots against the government in order to gain the credit for having suppressed them.[66] Yet even now, although the treatment of political prisoners had deteriorated considerably since the revolution, cases of deliberate torture appear to have been very exceptional.

In the polemical literature of any era, the word 'torture' itself is often a useful guide to what might be called the 'threshold of outrage'. For what is torture for one generation may very well be a minor inconvenience for another. This usually provides a useful clue as to whether real torture of the kind already defined actually exists. No writer, however hysterical or prejudiced, is going to waste invective on a minor abuse or inconvenience when there are greater cruelties to expose. An example may be found in the attacks on the dictatorship of Louis Napoleon by one of the ousted republican deputies, Victor Schloecher. For men of education and culture, to be detained for several days in an overcrowded prefecture without a change of linen was, he said, 'an excess of pain approaching torture'.[67] Those unfortunate enough to be deported were marched, in awkward wooden shoes, to Le Havre.[68] Once on board they were shut in fetid holds below the deck, and given nothing to eat beyond some watery soup, to be shared among ten or more prisoners using a single spoon. The latter indignity outraged the writer: 'Who were those to whom, by a refinement of implacable hatred, the torturers gave a single spoon for ten, a single cup for twenty? ... They were men of business and property, lawyers, doctors, officers, journalists, politicians, poets, scientists and so forth ....'[69] Nevertheless, there is no mention of physical violence.

The second half of the nineteenth century saw a progressive deterioration in the treatment of political prisoners, not only in France but in Britain as well. The suppression of the Paris commune in 1871, in which 20,000 people were massacred by the soldiers of Marshal Mac-Mahon, foreshadowed in its details many of the horrors of the twentieth century. Some 40,000 people were arrested, 7,500 of whom were sentenced to transportation to New Caledonia.[70] In one makeshift prison, aptly named the 'Grenier d'Abondance' the guards are said to have quelled any trouble among the eight hundred women prisoners by beating them on the breasts.[71] Though in one case a twelve-year-old boy is said to have been beaten to force him to reveal the whereabouts of his father,[72] there is little evidence that interrogative torture was practised systematically.

Generally speaking the same applies to Britain, though flogging was liberally applied in the armed forces and as a punishment for convicted prisoners. Irish prisoners who were treated comfortably in the 1850s,[73] were reduced to the status of common criminals in the 1860s, and suffered forced labour and solitary confinement.[74] The latter was recognized at the time as inhuman and worse than physical assault. Charles Dickens encountered it in America during the sixties:

> I believe that very few men are capable of estimating the immense amount of torture and agony which this dreadful punishment, prolonged for years, inflicts upon the sufferers ... I hold this slow and daily tampering with the mysteries of the brain to be immeasurably worse than any torture of the body; and because its ghastly sights and tokens are not so palpable to the eye and sense of touch as scars upon the flesh, because its wounds are not upon the surface, and it extorts few cries that human ears can hear, therefore I denounce it as a secret punishment which slumbering humanity is not roused up to stay.[75]

Solitary confinement was part of the American 'Philadelphia' system, which aimed at reformation rather than punishment. It was discontinued in the United States after protests about its cruelty.[76] It had an affinity with torture in more than one sense: not only was it designed to coerce conformity upon the prisoner, by effecting a total change of personality, but it employed techniques of sensory deprivation similar to those recently in use in modern police and army units.[77] At Mountjoy prison in Dublin, where solitary confinement was practised long after it had been stopped in the United States, several prisoners were certified insane.[78] The instance of insanity among prisoners in Ireland was more than ten times that of England, a fact which one medical observer attributed to poor diet and the systematic use of solitary confinement.[79] This too foreshadowed developments that were to occur in the course of the same political struggle in the following century.

This brief and inadequate survey of prison literature in Europe during the nineteenth century yields two conclusions. Firstly, torture was applied under reactionary régimes in Italy and Austria after the collapse of the revolutions of 1848. Secondly, the absence of torture in France proved to be a permanent gain for the revolution, despite the fact that some French policemen were as obsessed with the machinations of the secret societies as their colleagues in Austria or Italy. How can this contrast be accounted for? Can it have been that a small kernel of liberty survived the tornadoes of destruction unleashed by the French revolutions? After the suppression of the commune, the socialist writer, P. Lissagaray, described the executions of some of these first martyrs of the proletarian revolution. They died, he wrote, 'like the Arabs after battle, with indifference, with contempt, without hatred, without anger, and without insult to their executioners'.[80] Despite the arrogance and brutality of the Versailles troops, this dignity was to some extent reciprocated. The socialist martyrs were accorded the last sovereign right of a human being, the right to die for one's beliefs. Two or more generations were to elapse before Stalin's torturers, trained in the habits of Asiatic despotism, and mindful of the martyr's time-bomb, would force their victims to denounce themselves before being shot or herded into labour camps.

The liberty which Marx and his followers were to denounce as no more than the hypocritical cant of a section of the bourgeoisie, licensing the strong to despoil the weak, contained something more than this: the idea of freedom of conscience, as it arose from the religious conflicts in England and Germany. This notion, which went to the very core of the doctrine of the rights of man, implied a division of sovereignty between God and the king in accordance with the Christian maxim 'render unto Caesar ... ' Before the revolution, the king's sovereignty had derived from God, and depended upon his role as defender of the Christian faith. The ultimate sovereignty therefore belonged to God alone who ruled the temporal world through his anointed kings and the spiritual world of the human 'soul' through the Church. Both Church and state were headed by God's representatives on earth who had an absolute duty to defend them against temporal and spiritual attacks. In practice, the two kinds of attack were identified as one. Heresy was 'treason against God's Majesty'. Treason was heresy against the king. Both were sins as well as crimes, whose inception lay in the innermost chambers of the human mind, recesses which could be uncovered, so it was believed, by the use of torture.

The French revolution destroyed the temporal power of the king, and substituted for it the sovereignty of the people. In practice, the people came to be identified with the nation – a development which was to have disastrous consequences, as those who lay beyond the boundaries of the nation-state were made into outlaws and slaves.[81] But God's sovereignty over the spiritual world was left untouched. The 'bourgeois' revolutionaries were not doctrinaire atheists: they simply believed that human affairs, that is to say the political realm, should be the concern of men, not of God or of men claiming to be his earthly appointees. Their Terror, compounded of 'virtue' and 'justice', embraced rituals that had to be performed in public, in accordance with the doctrine of popular sovereignty and the 'general will'.*

The Austrian, papal and Bourbon régimes in Italy which resorted to the old methods of the inquisition were the last outposts of the *ancien régime* at a time when the anti-clericalism unleashed by the French revolution created a closer identification between Church and state than at any time since the Reformation. The attitude of these régimes was set out in a *Catechismo Filosofico* devised by the Church for use in Neapolitan schools to counteract the 'false' philosophy of the liberals and to justify King Ferdinand's suspension of the 1848 constitution. The only true sovereignty, says the *Catechismo*, is the Divine Right. Since constitutions represent an attempt to put limitations on this sovereignty, they cannot have any validity. The sovereign's oath to the constitution is therefore binding only insofar as 'it is not opposed to the general interests of the state' – a matter upon which the sovereign alone is qualified to judge. The catechism outraged Mr Gladstone, who called it 'a complete systematized philosophy of perjury for monarchs . . .'[82] It also implied the ancient prerogative of the theocratic monarch to probe the inner mysteries of the human brain, if necessary by torture. In theocratic monarchies, the state, as embodied in the sovereign, is

* For further remarks on revolutionary terror see Chapter 9, p. 257 ff.

above all merely human law, and there can be no limitation on the means by which it chooses to protect its interests. In the civilized world as represented by France during the nineteenth century, the division of Church and state into separate areas of sovereignty under God and the people was a guarantee which placed torture, for a period at least, *hors de combat.*

Two developments, however, would erode this distinction during the following century. One was the coming to power of secular ideologies in Russia and Germany which effected a new synthesis between religion and politics. The other was a progressive erosion of European political values by the imperial bureaucracies with their police and military forces. In India and the Far East, especially, torture was endemic in the systems of government taken over by the colonial régimes. The case of India will be described in some detail in the next chapter.

EIGHT

The Madras revelations

In 1846, a Mr Theobald, an 'English gentleman of high standing at the Calcutta bar' was travelling to Barrackpore with three companions in a *palkee gharrie** when a thief stole a bag containing four hundred rupees. He informed the local *darogah* and within the hour a native had been arrested, but without the money. The *darogah* obligingly offered to torture the wretch, in accordance with local custom, to make him reveal his hiding-place. Mr Theobald was either genuinely or affectedly unfamiliar with local custom. He made inquiries, and came to the conclusion that torture was a more or less standard practice not only in Bengal, but throughout the rest of India. Even more scandalous was the discovery that its use was not confined to obtaining confessions about criminal acts. It was applied throughout the East India Company's dominions in collecting land revenues and other taxes from the peasants. This was not entirely surprising, since in most country districts the *darogahs* combined the duties of police chief and revenue officer.[1]

Mr Theobald had influential friends in London. Questions were asked in the House of Commons. In 1854 Mr Danby Seymore, MP, a leading member of the India Reform Society, accused the Honourable East India Company of using torture and coercion 'to get ten shillings from a man when he only had eight'.[2] The Bengal government indignantly denied the accusations, supported by *The Times*, which pronounced that 'there is no reason to believe that torture is employed in India under any circumstances'.[3] But the reformers enjoyed the support of a powerful lobby which had been strongly opposed to the Company's hegemony in Indian affairs ever since

---

* A wheeled carriage drawn by two ponies; see E. Braddon, *Life in India* (London 1872), where it is described as a 'weak-springed, dirty, insect-haunted box upon wheels'.

Warren Hastings had been dragged to the pillory before parliament. It was inspired by resentment at the enormous power wielded by its officers, mixed with Edmund Burke's fear that 'the breakers of the law in India' would end by becoming the 'makers of the law' in England.[4]

The governor of Bengal adamantly refused an inquiry.[5] But in the Madras presidency where a new governor had recently been appointed the reformers were more successful. In 1854 a commission was set up to inquire into the allegations. Its chairman was a prominent Liberal barrister, a member of the India Reform Society and the editor of a local newspaper distinguished, according to those who disagreed with it, 'by its hostility to the civil service and the present system of administration.'[6] At first, the commission's brief was confined to investigating the use of torture for revenue purposes. But it received such a torrent of complaints against the *darogahs* in their police capacity that the mandate was extended to include police torture as well.[7]

The commission sat for seven months, and heard several hundred allegations from people who travelled from every part of the presidency. One witness actually *walked* a thousand miles to appear before it.[8] It avoided dealing with allegations against individual officers, which, it believed, should be handled according to existing court procedures. Prisoners could always retract their statements in open court, though there was rarely any substantive evidence of torture, since the police could hold people long enough for the marks to wear off, or could have used methods that left no marks at all. In practice, everything depended 'upon the opinion which the particular Judge entertains of the purity of the police'.[9]

The problem was therefore to establish the general extent to which judicial confidence in the police was justified. In any case, there were comparatively few allegations from the victims themselves – most of whom were already 'on the roads' – i.e. serving sentences of hard labour. Most of the complaints came from friends or relatives.[10] The commission's conclusions were forthright and unequivocal. Having invited complaints by advertizing its existence in every village and district in Madras, and offering to pay the travelling expenses of those willing to appear, it received a mass of spontaneous complaints from individuals 'the great majority of whom could have had no means of acting in concert, dwelling at great distances and totally unknown to each other, using even various languages'. Yet 'one and all speak of similar facts, detail similar practices and ascribe similar causes for their treatment. If this be a concerted plan ... it is the most singular conspiracy in the world's history.'[11]

Torture was used throughout the presidency for obtaining both revenue and confessions from criminals. It was also employed as often as not for wholly illegitimate aims – the personal enrichment of the *darogahs* and their friends. The commonest fiscal torture was, aptly enough, the *kittee* – 'a very simple machine, consisting merely of two sticks tied together at one end, between which the fingers are placed...'[12] Many other forms of duress were used in the collection of revenue. They included:

... keeping a man in the sun, preventing his going to meals and other calls of nature; confinement, preventing [his] cattle from going to pasture by shutting them in the house ... pinches on the thighs, slaps, blows with the fist or whips; running up and down, twisting the ears, making a man sit on the soles of his feet with brickbats behind his heels, putting a low-caste man on his back, striking two defaulters' heads together, or tying them by the back of their hair; tying them by their hair to a donkey or buffalo's tail, placing a necklace of bones, or other degrading or disgusting materials round the neck....[13]

The standing torture was described to the commission by an English merchant who saw it in the Cuddapah district:

[I saw] at least a dozen *ryots* [peasants] in arrears of *kist* undergoing the ordeal. They were all ranged in the courtyard under a meridian sun in the hottest period of the year [May]. They all had heavy stones placed either on their heads or on their backs between the shoulders. Their bodies were bent double and several were kept in that position standing on one leg, the other being raised from the ground by means of a string going round the neck and round the big toe too.[14]

The police tortures were even more severe. They included:

Twisting rope round the arm to impede circulation; lifting up by the moustache; suspending by the arms tied behind the back; searing with hot irons; placing scratching insects, such as the carpenter beetle, in the navel, scrotum and other sensitive parts; dipping in wells and rivers till the party is half suffocated; beating with sticks; prevention of sleep; nipping the flesh with pincers; putting peppers and red chillies in the eyes, or introducing them into the private parts of men and women; these cruelties occasionally persevered in until death sooner or later ensues.[15]

Far from being dismayed at the revelation of these atrocities, the Madras government welcomed them, and agreed to act immediately on the committee's recommendations. The president, Lord Harris, expressed his 'unqualified satisfaction' at the way the report had been drawn up which, in his opinion, left 'no manner of doubt of the existence of those practices which have been properly designated as "torture"'.[16]

The police and judicial functions would be separated. Later the Indian Evidence Act was introduced, rendering confessions to the police inadmissible as evidence in court, unless subsequently ratified before a magistrate. The report was much less popular with the old East India Company hands, who not unreasonably suspected it would be used to discredit their administration. The reformers would undoubtedly have made more use of the commission's findings in that way, had not the question of torture become submerged in the much wider changes that followed the outbreak of the Mutiny in 1857, which brought to an end three centuries of Company rule.

The Mutiny, according to an unsigned article in the *Calcutta Review* which clearly reflected the local opposition to the report, had provided the strongest proof that the report had exaggerated the oppressive rule of the *darogahs* for partisan ends. For of all the regions in India, Madras was the only one that had remained almost wholly loyal. Surely, if all the stories of torture and extortion had been true, the population would have risen as one to destroy their oppressors.[17] This argument was of course unconvincing, for oppression and rebelliousness do not necessarily function in precise correlation. Moreover, as the Madras report had shown, the *darogahs* were not generally associated in the popular mind with their British overlords. The committee's opponents further weakened their case by changing their ground in the course of the revelations, from categorically denying that torture had ever polluted any part of Her Majesty's dominions to conceding that it had of course been one of the evils of the old Moghul system which would naturally disappear with the course of progress and civilization. 'The practice' said the *Calcutta Review*'s anonymous writer 'has greatly diminished through the exertions of the European officers' though he dared not yet hope 'that it is altogether eradicated, either in Madras or in the other presidencies'.[18]

In fact, torture had been endemic in India long before the British extended their power beyond a few trading posts, and even possibly before the Moghul conquest, though neither Hindu nor Muslim codes had any provision for it.[19] A military surgeon who spent most of his career with the Bengal army recorded that the ordeal by tears (prescribed in the *Malleus Malificarum*), was used in Bihar in cases of suspected witchcraft. The accused witch had powdered chilli rubbed into her eyes to see if she would cry. If the smarting failed to draw tears, she was tied to the branch of a tree and left to swing there for four or five days, until she confessed. An Indian orderly writing in the 1850s described how he had helped place a woman in a sack filled with dried chillies to make her confess to poisoning – an apparently normal procedure.[20]

The proverbial cruelty of some of the Moghul rulers exercised a powerful hold on the European imagination. Seventeenth- and eighteenth-century travellers' tales abounded with accounts of nawabs who made their subjects wear leather trousers filled with live cats or 'drink buffalo's milk mixed with salt till they were brought to death's door by diarrhoea'[21] and nizams who had their Hindu subjects tied to palm trees and smeared with honey to attract the red ants. *Zemindars* and *chowkidars* were tortured into paying their feudal dues, and in turn tortured the *ryots* beneath them. The irregular system of taxation – the result of a climate where superabundance often alternated with famine – encouraged farmers to hoard; and this was probably the root of the system. Panchkouree Khan, the Indian orderly, explained to his English readers: 'It is well known that no native, how rich soever, will pay money the moment it falls due, unless he has the dread of punishment or disgrace before him.'[22] As the old feudal order disintegrated in the eighteenth century, the violence that underwrote the Moghul power became dissipated throughout society. Organized crime and gang-robberies or *dacoities* increased markedly as whole tribes turned to robbery, some of it with the active protection of the old *zemindars* and the police. Cruelties that had once been 'official', in that they related to the exaction of legal dues, became part of the normal currency of social relations. In the 1940s Dr Chevers, the Bengal military surgeon, found that: '... the poor practise torture on each other, robbers on their victims and vice versa; masters upon their servants; *zemindars* upon their *ryots*; schoolmasters upon their pupils; husbands upon their wives; and even parents upon their children'.[23] Even the priests consecrated instruments of torture before their idols.[24]

Nor were these cruelties restricted to the hierarchical relationships between superiors and inferiors. The double habit of hoarding and torture also ruled in the political realm. Hoarded wealth in a pre-capitalist economy took the tangible form of precious metals, coins and jewels. The fabulous riches which dominated the imagination and excited the greed of European adventurers were really the distilled toil of an impoverished peasantry. Members of ruling families tortured each other to reveal the whereabouts of hidden treasure. Warren Hastings was acting according to the traditions of the Indian nobility when he starved one hundred and twenty thousand pounds out of the begums of Oudh and almost tortured their eunuchs to death. This and the other excesses that led to his impeachment may have horrified Burke and his fellow traditionalists in England, and ruined any ambitions Hastings may have had in politics at home; but they did not injure his standing or reputation in India, where he was perhaps the most popular governor-general England produced.[25]

Indeed, the greatest obstacle to the abolition of torture and the kindred vices of extortion, servility and petty tyranny was that they were so deeply ingrained in the habits of the population. As one witness put it to the Madras commission, it was utterly absurd to expect English standards of justice

from a people who are utter strangers to a sense of honour, faith or honesty and among whom lying and duplicity are inherent and predominant vices. They themselves declare that no man is silly enough voluntarily to confess the crime of robbery or murder till he be subjected to torture. The whole body of *ryots* believe in the existence of the system, and are practically acquainted with its effects and consequences, but not a single individual can be found bold or resentful enough to make it a matter of public complaint, simply because the idea is prevalent among the people that such acts are tacitly tolerated by the government ... The police establishment ... has become the bane and pest of society, the terror of the community and the origin of half the misery and discontent that exists among the subjects of the government ... corruption and bribery reign paramount among the whole establishment; violent torture and cruelty are the chief instruments for detecting crime, implicating innocence or extorting money ... While the people entertain such a lively horror of the police, it is not possible to expect a single victim to come forward and arraign his tormentors or to bring the charge home to any of them after the deed has been perpetrated in some ruined fort or deep ravine situated miles away from the town or village ... The public are too apt to charge all the misery of the country to the neglect of the collectors and other European officers, whereas the crying evil is bred and fostered by the people and no system of government can eradicate it. They are thoroughly corrupt, immersed in gross ignorance and superstition and will never be able to shake off the incubus of oppression till a radical change takes place in their moral and social condition; or till they display a becoming pride, independence of spirit and manly decision of character.[26]

Another witness pointed out, perhaps with stricter accuracy, that the natives were in fact prepared to complain of abuses, but only when they suspected the native officers of acting in their private interests. The officers of course could always conceal their private motives behind their public duties, which prevented more than a few complaints from ever reaching European ears.[27]

During the period between the suppression of the Mutiny and the rise of the nationalist movement at the turn of the century, relatively few accounts of torture were printed in English. However, the absence of documentary evidence does not necessarily mean that the practice itself had been abolished. The Madras commission obtained most of its evidence from country districts, where a large proportion of the population was illiterate. Its method of operation, actually inviting complaints and according complainants the full protection of the law, was based on the assumption that existing procedures were wholly inadequate, and that the absence of complaints in no sense indicated the absence of torture. None of the subsequent investigations into police abuses spread such a wide net or approached the question so openly. Allegations continued to be occasionally made public, suggesting that the administrative changes urged by the Madras commission had been inadequate to deal with the problem. With few Europeans available to supervise activities of the police, only a tiny proportion of cases can have been documented. But the frequency with which torture allegations came to be repeated after the emergence of a vigorous nationalist press and legal profession suggests that the barbarity of the police only diminished marginally, if at all.

Moreover, during the intervening years, there are a number of hints and clues that support this view. For example, a pamphlet in 1860 summarized the proceedings of two trials in which the district police had been found guilty of torture and in one case, of murder. It warned that 'cases of torture are notoriously of frequent occurrence in

Bengal; but as no police objective can be served by taking notice of them they are looked upon with perfect placidity by the government.'[28] The accusation does not appear surprising, in view of the previous governor's attitude during the controversy of 1854. Both of these cases only came to the attention of a higher court because of exceptional factors. In one of them the victim had evidently been accidentally asphyxiated while undergoing the water torture, and the police bungled their efforts to conceal the murder. The other case concerned an elderly woman whose shoulder was permanently dislocated by the *strappado*, so that three weeks after her interrogation she still carried the marks of her injuries. The local magistrate's report, however, indicated that no permanent injuries need result from torture if the police learned to concentrate on techniques that left no physical marks. In commenting on the evidence in one of these cases, the local European magistrate's report had stated that it was impossible to form any view of the allegation that the victim had also been beaten with the *hatha*, a leathern instrument said to leave no marks.[29]

In the meantime few British writers, official or otherwise, had much good to say for the district police. Thus a writer of the eighties described the police of the Panjab area in Bengal as stupid, corrupt and brutal, fully deserving Lord Napier's aphorism that they were 'useless in time of peace and dangerous in time of war'.[30] Lack of intellect though did not prevent them from operating what appears to have been a lucrative prostitution racket.[31] According to the same writer, the police felt no compunction even if innocent men were hanged, so long as they received 'favourable reports in their service books and the good opinion of their superior officers'.[32] In a similar vein, a former English superintendent argued that the inadequacies of the police could no longer be excused by reference to the 'primitive and semi-barbarous condition of Indian society', in view of the 'steady march of progress of the past twenty years'.[33]

In a country where few ordinary people were disposed to cooperate with the police, forced confessions made up for slack detective work. That much was widely admitted in official circles. Some observers went a good deal further, claiming that the police actively connived at organized crime. A Bengal detective came to the conclusion that the local police were involved in most of the gang-robberies in his district. The police split the booty with the robbers, and then forced innocent people to confess to the crimes in order to prove their efficiency to their English masters.[34] Similar charges were made by Panchkouree Khan in the fifties.[35] Other sources suggest that the police actually committed the robberies themselves, and then 'framed' innocent people previously arrested on trumped-up charges.[36] They were not above 'planting' incriminating evidence on innocent people either so that even when uncorroborated confessions to the police were ruled inadmissible in court, the police were not necessarily prevented from winning their cases.[37]

Dacoity, or gang-robbery, was one of the evils in India the British had less success in suppressing than such organized ritual crimes as thuggee and suttee. These had increased dramatically with the decline of the old Moghul order when the *zemindars* had been obliged to compensate the peasants for their losses, and they continued to plague society throughout the nineteenth century. Some officials believed the *zemindars* actively encouraged the dacoits. Often they included complete families, sometimes whole tribes, and until the end of the century the district police was the only weapon available to the authorities. Like the 'thugs' some of the dacoits were inspired by religion. In some respects they approximated to the secret brotherhoods of bandits that flourished in parts of southern Europe during the same period. In the first decade of the twentieth century dacoity appears to have merged with political terrorism in Bengal and the Punjab.[38]

The close association in crime between the dacoits and the police resulted partly, no doubt, from their similar social backgrounds. If the increase in gang-robbery was a symptom of the breakdown of the old protective feudal relationships, the robbers were victims as well as criminals. They were misfits in the new social landscape emerging under British rule. The police were recruited from a similar social layer, the lowest in India's ancient human pyramid, individuals who, deprived of other means of support, would otherwise have been drawn to crime. Indeed, in 1855 a Cawnpore magistrate, Mr Spankie, argued quite seriously that the only way to deal with disbanded dacoits was to recruit them into the police.[39] Police malpractices, then, were generally admitted. The difficulty remained over what to do about them. In 1871 the government introduced the Indian Evidence Act, the first systematic codification of the laws of evidence in line with the best traditions of the English courts. The aim was partly to give guidance to officials charged with the administration of justice, many of whom were civil servants without legal training. But the act was also specifically designed to prevent the recurrence of torture by laying down precise rules against coerced confessions. Confessions caused by an 'inducement, threat or promise' were declared irrelevant (section 24); those made to a police officer inadmissible (section 25); those made by anyone in police custody inadmissible unless made in the presence of a magistrate (section 26).[40]

Though a model of its kind, and a milestone in the law of evidence, the act proved a less than complete remedy against torture. Policemen, if sufficiently unscrupulous, could still force confessions from innocent people and plant incriminating evidence on them, since the act did not disallow evidence 'discovered' by means of improperly induced confessions. Moreover an improper confession could still get through the courts if the junior magistrates were in league with the police – an allegation that was to be made in due course.

The effect of the act in suppressing torture would be difficult to establish. If allegations are any guide to actual instances, its effect was the opposite of what was intended – for as the nineteenth century drew to its end allegations of torture appeared with increasing frequency in the nationalist press. The truth, however, may have been that while actual instances of torture remained at the same level, or even declined, the act supplied defence lawyers with a very effective weapon, while in no way leading to an improvement in actual police practice. Nationalist lawyers made Indian prisoners conscious of their rights; and the latter tended increasingly to withdraw in court all statements previously made to the police in accordance with the provisions of the act. The government became alarmed, as notorious criminals were seen to escape the course of justice with as much ease as those who had really been forced to make false confessions.

By the turn of the century the government had been forced into action. In 1901, the governor of Bengal demanded in public that police reform must take precedence over every other project. The investigating staff in his own province were 'dishonest and tyrannical'.[41] This view was upheld by the Curzon commission set up the following year to investigate police oppression. Its report, published in 1905, stated that there was no province in India to which the governor's remarks might not be applied. It condemned the 'unnecessary severity' and 'unnecessary annoyance' with which the police discharged their duties, but exonerated them of 'actual physical torture' which, it stated, was 'now rarely resorted to'.[42] The comment would have carried more conviction if the commission had not also quoted a similar remark made by Mountstuart Elphinstone a century before (and therefore half a century before the Madras revelations).[43] It was the habit of British officials (including several witnesses to the Madras commission) to refer to torture as a 'thing of the past'.

Nevertheless, while shrinking from the word 'torture', which (in contrast to the Madras commission) it explicitly restricted to meaning 'such physical violence as leaves its traces on the victim', the Curzon commission roundly condemned the 'improper inducements', 'threats' and 'moral pressure' used by the police to get confessions from suspects and sometimes innocent persons as a result of their 'want of detective ability' and 'indolence'. It also admitted that 'deliberate association with criminals in their gains, deliberately false charges against innocent persons on the ground of party spite or village faction, deliberate torture of suspected persons and other most flagrant abuses occur occasionally'.[44]

The language of the Curzon commission's report was a good deal more restrained than that of the Madras report, but it would be simplistic to infer that the practice of torture had diminished proportionately. The commission's method of operation and the political context in which it was set up suggested that in reality conditions may have changed but little. The Curzon report is much shorter than its predecessor, and its brief was formulated in much vaguer terms. It operated less publicly and it resorted to bland generalizations where the Madras report was precise and specific. Whereas the annexes to the Madras report, running to several hundred pages, are full of specific allegations, the Curzon commission's testimony and verbal proceedings were never made public. It is an altogether less satisfactory document from the historical point of view. Its aura, if not exactly whitewash, has the flavour of bureaucratic obfuscation.

The reality was that little could be done to improve things short of abolishing the police and rendering the courts unworkable. The commission was hard put to make any recommendations at all, except the negative one of insisting that there should be no relaxation in the restrictions governing the admissibility of confessions made to the police. The prevalence of extorting confession 'by all possible means' had led to the enactment of provisions in the Code of Criminal Procedure and the Indian Evidence Act which imposed stringent limitations on the admissibility of confessions made to the police. Many witnesses to the commission had demanded relaxation of these provisions which, they argued, placed obstacles in the way of investigation. Yet many third-class magistrates had shown themselves 'unfit to judge the circumstances of confession'. The commission concluded by recommending that only those magistrates having jurisdiction in the case should ratify confessions. Above all, there should be no weakening of the safeguards in the Indian Evidence Act: 'The Commission are wholly opposed to any relaxation of the law in this matter. The evidence before them shows that the practice of working for confessions is still exceedingly common.'[45]

The Indian government was not happy with the commission's report. It had appointed the commission 'in the belief that the increase in serious crime resulted from administrative defects'. The commission had made it clear that the defects had much deeper causes; the unfortunate fact that 'the people of India are not generally actively on the side of law and order . . . [and] are not inclined actively to assist the officers of the law',[46] it suggested was partly because the police were brutal, tyrannical and corrupt. The government found these conclusions unacceptable. The commission had been influenced by the innate tendency of Indian witnesses to hyperbole. It had 'painted an exaggerated picture in vivid colours'.[47]

Despite the commission's professed belief in their 'comparative rarity', disturbing allegations of 'actual physical torture' continued to appear in the nationalist and in some cases the English press. One notorious case occurred in the Punjab in 1908 where a local court had sentenced a woman, Gulab Bano, to death after she had confessed to having poisoned her husband. The high court at Lahore upheld her appeal, after a civil surgeon supplied medical evidence confirming her story that she had been hung upside down from the roof of the village police station and a baton smeared with green chillies had been thrust up her anus. The most alarming feature of the case had been the attitude of the local sessions judge, Mr Kennedy, and the governor of the Punjab. Kennedy, whose conduct was criticized by the appeal judges, had frequently referred in his conduct of the trial to another case which should have been inadmissible. The chief court ordered the governor to 'institute a most searching inquiry'. After nine months, the governor issued a resolution based on a 'confidential' police inquiry which, despite the woman's acquittal, completely exonerated the police and attempted to discredit the opinions of the two British high court judges and the civil surgeon.[48] The following year, at the same chief court in Lahore, a murder case had to be dropped after the alleged victim, rather embarrassingly, turned up. Again, the governor refused to criticize the conduct of the police, merely pointing out that they had been right to drop the charges![49]

Far more alarming, however, were the implications of one of the famous conspiracy trials in Calcutta, in 1909. The decade before the first world war saw the development of a terrorist movement based originally in Bengal. A bomb factory had been discovered in Calcutta in 1907.[50] In April 1908, two Englishwomen, Mrs Kennedy and her daughter, were killed by a bomb thrown at their carriage as they were passing the house of the chief magistrate of Calcutta, Mr Kingsford. It was not the first outrage of its kind – the previous year a sanitary engineer had been murdered in similar circumstances – but, the victims being a mother and her daughter, it sent a ripple of alarm throughout the British community, for whom the terrors of the Mutiny were never far below the surface. The following May, the police arrested a number of youths in possession of arms, explosives and ammunition. Their trial, subsequently known as the Alipore conspiracy case, revealed a link between the murder of the Kennedy ladies and the arms find. According to the prosecution, the conspirators had employed one of the youths accused of the Kennedy murder to kill Mr Kingsford. The youth had mistaken the ladies' carriage for that of the magistrate. He had had a personal grudge against Mr Kingsford, who had recently sentenced him to fifteen strokes of the lash in connection with the prosecution of a local nationalist newspaper. Before the trial was over the alleged accomplice of the accused assassin who had turned king's evidence had been murdered in pre-trial custody. The authorities feared they had a full-blown terrorist organization on their hands.[51]

Events appeared dramatically to confirm this view. Police raided houses in several Bengal towns. Arms, ammunition and explosives were found. Over the next five years, several hundred young men were rounded up. All of them were charged with 'Conspiracy to wage war against the king-emperor' (contrary to section 121A of the Penal Code), in a dozen or so 'conspiracy trials'. Most of them were acquitted for lack of evidence. In one of the trials held in Calcutta in 1909 three had been convicted out of a total of 154 defendants. Their appeals against conviction were upheld on the grounds that their confessions had been extorted illegally by the police and (in the words of an English judge who did not take part in this case) 'that the theory of the defence that the police themselves had planted the bombs on the accused was not one to be wholly rejected'. The court found that the pressure on the prisoners had included beating and stoning, solitary confinement, sleep deprivation and threats to one of their parents. The magistrate had accepted their confessions and according to the high court ignored the all-important fact that the prisoners had been held for seven days in police custody. An inquiry into police conduct was ordered but the results were never published, though a number of officers were given leave of absence.[52]

The conspiracy trials continued, bombs were produced by the police (they rarely seem to have exploded) and more young men were arrested. Torture allegations abated somewhat, with the suppression of the more vociferous nationalist organs under the Newspapers (Incitement of Offences) Act, 1908. However, a number of English judges continued to draw attention to the scandal of police confessions by writing letters to English as well as Indian newspapers. Though their campaign was ignored by most of the judges and officials in India, they met with a more ready response in England, where there was a Liberal majority in the House of Commons. There were demands in the House and the Imperial Legislative Council that all pre-trial records of confession should be prohibited, or at least that 'no conviction could be based on a confession once made but subsequently retracted unless commission of the offence was materially corroborated by direct evidence'.[53]

The Indian government, supported by a majority of the senior judges whom it consulted, resisted the proposals with a variety of arguments, including the circular one,

That high judicial officers are unwilling to approve of any such prohibition is a valuable indication of the fact that these confessions are not regarded in the majority of cases as false or tainted; in fact, the instances in which the courts express a positive opinion that a bogus confession has been obtained by reason of the tutoring or ill-treatment of the prisoner by the police are, we believe, few.[54]

In the Indian government's view, not only did the absence of complaints indicate the absence of torture (an inference specifically rejected by the Madras commission), but the fact that the courts only rarely upheld such complaints as were made must mean that there was nothing much to complain about. The underlying assumption, of course, was that British courts and British judges were beyond suspicion. In fact, British judges in India, unlike their colleagues in England, were really tools of the administration who could be transferred or dismissed on the viceroy's orders. Their condition was illustrated by the fate of a Bihar sessions judge, Mr Justice Pennel, who had the temerity to allow an appeal against imprisonment by an Indian who had suffered a serious assault at the hand of a European district engineer. Lord Curzon had the judge transferred, and the judge was publicly criticized by the governor of Bengal for the 'vindictive rancour' with which he attempted to bring a policeman involved in the case to justice.[55]

Equally disingenuous was the government's assertion that 'experience shows that confessions are frequently willingly made in circumstances that afford no ground for doubting their truth'[56] – an opinion which flatly contradicted the Curzon commission's conclusions.

The evidence adduced to support this argument was that confessions were frequently corroborated by material evidence in the form of stolen goods, etc. It virtually implied a concession to the utilitarian case for torture:

> ... the obtaining of the confession is not the sole, or even the principal, motive which induces incompetent or dishonest police officers to resort to a mixture of threatening, coaxing, worry or ill-usage; their object is rather to induce the accused to give up the stolen property or to indicate where some clue may be found ...[57]

Understandably, the government forbore to suggest that the 'dishonest and incompetent police officers' who did not scruple to resort to 'threatening, coaxing, worry and ill-usage' might not scruple to plant the evidence, as was suggested in the Calcutta conspiracy case.

Similarly, the notion of 'spontaneous' confession, dismissed as inherently improbable by the Madras commission, now received the full weight of official and judicial approval, backed by sixty years' experience of native 'psychology':

> It seems to us unwise to ignore the *proved fact* that the novice in crime in this country is frequently unable to keep his guilty knowledge to himself, while even the more hardened criminal not infrequently insists on unburdening his mind,

and the prohibition of confession would only deprive the courts of evidence which in many cases may be quite reliable and of value . . .[58]

The lieutenant-governor of Bengal added a short essay on the peculiarities of the native temperament:

. . . the influence of public opinion in an Indian village has more effect on an Indian villager than any public opinion in England on an Englishman. [Therefore] it cannot be regarded as surprising that confessions are volunteered in this country to an extent that would seem hardly credible in England . . . . Some of the reasons which make for the large number of confessions in India also make for their subsequent retraction. The mental condition that drives a criminal to unburden himself is naturally more intense among the unbalanced peasants who for the most part commit crimes of passion in this province. But the frenzy that induces such a criminal to exalt his crime, or the impulse that impels declaration to obtain a momentary respite is succeeded frequently in such an organization by a reaction under the influence of which the instinct of self-preservation reasserts itself. Under the second influence, retraction follows.[59]

An Indian judge expressed similar views in rather less abstruse terminology:

. . . one fact, which is patent to anyone who knows the character of our people, especially the illiterate and ignorant portion of them . . . is [that] our people cannot successfully conceal their acts or motives. Hence it is that, when a man who has committed a crime is arrested, he will, after a little questioning, make a clean breast of it. The unsophisticated man in this country may be given to lying, but he does not know, because he has not learnt, the art of persisting in his lie, and keeping his own counsel so as to mislead others for any length of time . . .[60]

The genuineness of the confessions then depended on the assumption that the native suspect was basically honest. The almost universal tendency to retract in the course of trial was simply a judicial ploy by clever Indian defence lawyers, bent on exploiting a legal loophole in order to secure acquittals. As one English judge saw it, the criminal law was for historical reasons quite apart from India, 'extraordinarily tender to the accused', because in England it had been reasonable to assume that the individual citizen was 'willing to help the state, willing to give information of crime brought to his knowledge, willing to give evidence in court against the accused'. This assumption was 'grotesquely untrue' in India, where the only willing witness was the false witness or the personally interested one. For those conducting the campaign against the police, it was evidently a matter of 'serene indifference' whether or not offenders were punished.[61]

It remained for one of the few dissenting voices, Mr Justice Beaman, to point to the obvious contradiction in this position. For the assumption of a childlike incapacity for sustained falsehood necessary to support the thesis that most of the retracted confessions had been genuine could hardly be made to square with the opinion that 'the only willing witness was the false witness or the personally interested' one. As Judge Beaman succinctly put it:

The average low-caste native of this country is not, by common consent, addicted to the truth. Why is it that the average criminal who is drawn from this class should suddenly show himself a marked exception and volunteer the truth? . . . Why should the most untruthful people in the world become in one set of conditions and one only the most confessing set of people in the world? And why, again, should this phase coincide precisely with the period during which they are helplessly at the mercy of the mofussil [rural district] police?[62]

Not content with commenting on the various ways the 'native character' was interpreted to suit the arguments of those who wished to retain the existing system of confessions, Judge Beaman went so far as to accuse most of his colleagues on the bench of deliberately avoiding the facts. The current practice required sessions judges

to do violence to their conscience or intellect every time they admit a retracted confession. Every sessions Judge of any experience, who knows the native, would, upon rigorous self-examination, admit that the average mofussil criminal would never confess if left entirely to himself. In fact, he confesses, literally in shoals. The sessions Judge of experience who knows the mofussil police as well as he knows the native, in his heart knows very well WHY. It is in my opinion safe to say that, excepting violent crimes . . . all other retracted confessions have been directly or indirectly induced by improper means . . . Where actual torture is not used . . . the knowledge that it will be used may induce a number of criminals who would not otherwise confess to do so in anticipation of the methods they dread being employed on them . . . The opinions of judges whose experience has been restricted to the criminals and police of the Presidency towns is relatively valueless on this point. They do not know and cannot know what goes on in the mofussil. I feel that I must enter this protest, because judged by numbers only, I shall be in a minority . . .[63]

Although the most outspoken of the dissenters, Judge Beaman was not entirely alone in his view. A colleague from the Madras presidency, while avoiding the direct accusation of torture, pointed out the futility of relying on procedural changes to improve police practices.

> I am no believer in the efficacy of any of the [proposed] measures designed to protect accused persons from police influence. It would be most unsafe to send prisoners charged with grave crimes to a first-class magistrate with only peons for escort and such a measure would not prevent the police having as much opportunity as they like while on the journey to influence the prisoners . . . No doubt a first-class magistrate can be better trusted to put his foot down if he sees reason to suspect improper influences. But it all depends on the prisoner himself complaining and throwing himself on the magistrate's protection. I do not remember ever hearing a case where this was done. The fact is the police do not put up a man whom they have induced to confess, unless they are pretty sure he will not give them away: and the preliminary questioning etc., by a busy magistrate with plenty of other work to do is apt to be of a somewhat perfunctory character.[64]

There were plenty of means at the disposal of the police to prevent anyone giving them away. As Judge Pennel, the Bihar sessions judge victimized for his attempt to uphold the rights of an Indian attacked by a white official as well as the police, had stated in one of his judgements: 'In this country the only people who will come forward to give evidence against (police) officers . . . are those who do not mind their houses being burnt, their shops looted, their relations turned out of government employment and members of their families dragged up on false charges and sent to jail.'[65]

But such protests, as Judge Beaman had intimated, were doomed to futility. The attitude of the majority of the judges, accepted with evident relief by the Indian government, was that most of the complaints against the police had been motivated by malice or a desire to escape the consequence of crime, and that nothing beyond a few minor procedural changes should be allowed to interfere with the existing system. To have acted otherwise and countenanced the abolition of confessions would have threatened the whole rickety structure of Anglo-Indian justice at its foundations. As it was, attempts must be made to preserve appearances. The sum of official thinking was best expressed in a letter from the chief secretary of the Bengal government:

> The Governor in Council does not deny that abuses exist and that from time to time cases occur in which confessions are alleged or prove to have been obtained by means of violence or threats of violence and which magistrates who have recorded confessions have, by neglect of the rules of the subject and by

want of the exercise of proper care and intelligence failed to detect that the confessions were not made voluntarily... It is important, however, not to lose sight of the first principle involved. The object of criminal proceedings is to find out whether persons accused of offences have in fact committed them or not, and this result can best be aimed at by examining all the evidence obtainable on the subject. *No one is able to give more conclusive evidence as to what was done than the person who did it and any general rule to exclude that person from giving the assistance which he is so obviously in a position to give amounts to an artificial obstruction of the attainment of the object for which the whole judicial system has been created.* (emphasis added)[66]

A contradiction of the principle that men be judged innocent until proved guilty.

*   *   *

A striking omission in the 1913 correspondence was any reference to terrorism, despite the background of politically inspired violence against which the discussion was conducted. A scant reference was made to the value of the confessions in the Alipore bombing case,[67] but it was not suggested that this might be important to the discussion.

Despite some forty prosecutions for 'conspiracy' in which more than a thousand people were arrested and charged, the violence in Bengal continued unabated until the outbreak of the first world war. In the ten conspiracy trials, nearly two hundred individuals were accused by the police of 'waging war against the king-emperor'. But for lack of evidence, only sixty-three of the police prosecutions were successful. Even the number of attempted prosecutions was considerably smaller than the number of 'outrages' committed by the terrorists. According to the authorities, there were 210 outrages between 1906 and 1918, plus some hundred or so attempts.[68]

In 1912, an attempt was made in Delhi to assassinate the viceroy, Lord Hardinge. He escaped unhurt, but one of his attendants was killed. With the approach of war, the government became increasingly alarmed, especially over the Punjab which was the principal recruiting ground for the empire's Indian armies. Just after the outbreak of war a group of militant Sikh emigrants, returning to India after being refused admission to Canada, staged a riot near Calcutta in which a number of people, including police, were killed. They appeared to have been strongly influenced by a militant emigrant organization based in San Francisco, whose newspaper, *Ghadr* (revolt), was urging the people of Punjab to terrorism and mutiny.[69]

In 1915, the government was able to introduce emergency provisions including the right of indefinite administrative detention under normal wartime measures (the provisions were similar to those in force in Britain itself). The threat of rebellion in the Punjab proved exaggerated; in Bengal several hundred terrorist suspects were interned, and the wave of violence appeared to subside. But the end of the war brought a new and uncertain political climate. The nationalist movement's support for the empire had been conditional on some tangible reward for Indian loyalty. In 1919, the principle of self-government was formally conceded; but this was only the beginning of the political difficulties that lay ahead. The problem of a timetable was critical, as nationalist ambitions were fed by the explosive example of the Versailles settlement, which conceded the principle of national self-determination to the former subjects of Austria and Turkey.[70] Finally, the Russian revolution, with its ominous example of the supposed possibilities of revolutionary conspiracy, struck fear in the hearts of India's rulers. They believed that the pre-war revolutionary conspiracies had only been checked by the exceptional measures of the Defence of India Act. In the new and more uncertain post-war climate, they were in no mood to relax any of its provisions. In 1918 the imperial government appointed a committee to assess the dangers of these conspiracies, with a brief to recommend the legislation that should follow the demise of the Defence of India Act.

The Rowlatt committee – named after its chairman, Mr Justice Rowlatt – made a detailed review of all the evidence in the pre-war conspiracy trials, together with a study of the revolutionary literature of the various nationalist movements and a quantity of police evidence – the alleged confessions of some two hundred and fifty detainees – that would have been inadmissible under normal court proceedings. It concluded that a revolutionary conspiracy or conspiracies existed to destroy British power in India, and recommended legislation to counter the threat. The legislation – which was duly incorporated in a series of bills generally known as the Rowlatt acts – provided for a progressive series of measures to be taken in the event of public order being threatened by 'revolutionary or anarchical crime'. They included the suspension of normal legal processes, including preliminary hearings before magistrates, the presence of Indian 'assessors' (which usually replaced the jury system of lower courts in India) and, where the gravity was regarded as exceptional, administrative detention.

So, despite the concern of pre-war British governments and the Curzon commission about the tyrannical and arbitrary methods of the police, legislation had been introduced which incomparably strengthened their powers. The step had been taken in spite of liberal opposition in London and in the teeth of nationalist hostility in India. It was achieved by arbitrarily dissociating the 'political' from the 'procedural' aspects of police power. Despite the background of political violence against which the question of police confessions had been discussed, no reference had been made in the Curzon commission's report to the political arguments in favour of retaining existing procedures, or to the fact that retractions were forcing the courts into acquittals at a time when the authorities were growing increasingly alarmed about the state of public order. In the Rowlatt report, on the other hand, only scant reference was made to the fact that most of its evidence came from 'confessions' that would have been wholly inadmissible under normal procedures, and none at all to the fact that such confessions had within recent memory been the subject of serious concern in London and had given rise to torture allegations by some of India's senior judicial officers. The policy of 'divide and rule' is the hallmark of tyranny in the bureaucratic as in the territorial realm.

The Rowlatt committee's conclusion that a conspiracy or conspiracies existed to destroy British power was based on three principal categories of evidence, all of which are suspect. Into the first category came the material evidence – the arms, ammunition and explosives collected by the police in various raids in Bengal, usually after tip-offs from informers. This evidence itself was dubious because, as the Calcutta conspiracy case showed, the police were not above planting the evidence when it suited them. Some of the evidence, such as the revolutionary tracts alleged to have been found in the raids, may have been genuine: it was the inferences drawn from them in the wider political context that were questionable. For example, anti-British manifestos were discovered in shops where burglaries had been committed, and in one case the victim of 'expropriation' was left a promissory note undertaking to repay the missing sum, with interest, on the achievement of 'liberty'. However, no attempt was made to compare the politically motivated raids with the traditional or 'non-political' dacoities troubling the continent at that time; and no arguments were advanced to explain why special measures were needed in the former case which did not apply to the latter.

The British claimed to have had considerable success in dealing with ordinary dacoities in the areas under their administration. This, however, did little to solve the general problem of organized crime, since the dacoits could always take refuge in the 'badly governed' native states.[71] According to the Curzon commission, the suppression of dacoity, as well as thuggee, had been achieved through the extensive use of informers and by enlisting the services of ex-convicts in exchange for a free pardon.[72] The case for emergency legislation, however, would have been weakened if due consideration had been given to the long history of dacoity in the Rowlatt report. It had never been suggested that emergency legislation was needed to deal with 'normal' dacoities. By failing to mention these, the Rowlatt committee avoided having to explain why 'traditional' methods, which had evidently been adequate in suppressing 'normal' dacoities, were insufficient to deal with the political ones.

Indeed, in the climate of uncertainty, following the first world war, the committee exaggerated the threat posed by 'political' dacoities. The distinction between political and non-political dacoities was not a clear one, given that many of the earlier robber gangs, like the nationalists, had drawn their inspiration from religion. For example, the committee cited documents of the Bhawani Mandir, a sect it believed to have been inspired by a combination of Japanese militarism, Russian anarchist terrorism and the desire to found a new order of political devotees who would worship Bhawani in a spot 'far from the contamination of modern cities and as yet little trodden by man, in a high and pure air steeped in calm and energy' – a curiously unworldly ambition for a revolutionary movement.[73] It failed to mention, however, that the Bhawani group of dacoits had been well known during the nineteenth century. They were organized into sworn bands at an oathing ceremony during which a fowl or a goat would be sacrificed. Their season closed with the monsoon each year, when the spoils would be divided and members would repair to their winter quarters.[74] Even if the aims of the group had become more overtly political (which is not unlikely, given the widespread dissemination of nationalist propaganda) there was no reason why methods successfully used against the Bhawani Mandir in the nineteenth century should suddenly have become inefficacious in the twentieth.

Even more doubtful was the second category of evidence, the two hundred and fifty or so confessions alleged to have been made by the terrorist suspects to the police. The committee stated unblushingly that the fact that such statements were inadmissible under the India Evidence Act actually added to their veracity.[75] At the same time, it used the restrictions of the act as an excuse for treating the statements as confidential, and admitted that there were very few other statements 'and those only as to particular incidents, made by police agents and members of the public'.[76] The implication is clear that whereas evidence of individual incidents or crimes might be corroborated by a variety of independent witnesses, including police informers, the critical information that fitted such incidents into the wider framework of the 'revolutionary conspiracies' came only from the mouths of the detainees themselves.

For those familiar with the 'spontaneous confession' thesis advanced by several magistrates, judges and provincial governors in 1913, the Rowlatt committee's account of how the police managed to come by the confessions of the terrorist suspects must have had a familiar ring. The Defence of India Act introduced in 1915 allegedly 'broke the morale' of the conspirators, in consequence of which they appeared to have inundated the police with unsolicited statements:

At this time, the leaders, when arrested, sometimes after a long period of hiding, have in many, though not all, cases been ready to tell the whole story freely. Some speak under the impulse of a feeling of disgust for an effort which has failed. Some, of a different temperament, are conscience-stricken. Others speak to relieve their feelings, glad that the life of a hunted criminal is over. Not a few speak only after a period of consideration during which they argue with themselves the morality of disclosure.

Although the committee added that information of this kind could not always be relied upon, 'least of all in India', it claimed to have had 're-markable facilities' for testing the statements. In fact, the corroborative value of these 'facilities' depended utterly on never calling police integrity into question.[77]

The third category of evidence upon which the committee based its conclusions was the records of the pre-war conspiracy trials, before the Defence of India Act rendered criminal proceedings unnecessary. These were subjected to a highly selective interpretation: the absence of a jury system placed a great deal of discretion in the hands of the judges, and the attitude of the judges varied considerably. Some of them were inclined to see in every manifestation of nationalist activity, regardless of its legality, part of a hidden design to overthrow British power. Their views were thoroughly endorsed by the committee. Others, of a more liberal and rational disposition, pointed out contradictions in the prosecution case. Here the committee cited their opinions to support its conclusion that normal judicial processes were inadequate to deal with the terrorist threat.

For example, the committee developed an elaborate thesis that the *samitis*, or young men's clubs for physical culture and education, were really fronts for secret revolutionary groups dedicated to overthrowing British rule, despite a contradictory suggestion that some of the militants who tried to turn the clubs to revolutionary objectives had been obliged to resign for lack of support.[78] One of the judgements cited with approval stated that the accused had, among other things, been members of a *samiti*, 'one of the ostensible objects of which was the improvement of physical culture by exercises in *lathi*-play, but the real object of which was to bring about a revolution'.[79] The notion that a revolution could be 'caused' in this manner is reminiscent of the attacks on the freemasons and the Illuminati in the years that followed the French revolution. The same hysterical tone echoed from some of the judgements concerning the nationalist press and the activities of a number of teachers. In the Alipore conspiracy trial the accused were stated to have 'employed newspapers in the furtherance of this criminal conspiracy', of which one paper in particular, the *Jugantar*, was described as a 'limb' by the judge. Two of the Dacca conspirators were described by their judge as having acquired degrees and taken to teaching with the sole object of 'poisoning the minds of the students'.[80]

On the other hand, the judgement in the Howrah conspiracy case, where the prosecution case was thrown out by the judge, was invoked to justify the retention of emergency measures. Not only did the court find the testimony of two police informers unreliable, but the charge of conspiracy itself internally inconsistent. The accused had been described both as being members of a variety of organizations, and with entering into a conspiracy to wage war against the king-emperor. The judge declared that it was a 'legal impossibility' when several persons were charged with the same conspiracy that some should be found guilty of one conspiracy and some of another.[81]

This judgement, in fact, tended to undermine the whole premise on which the report was based. For the charge of 'Conspiracy to wage war against the king-emperor' obviously belonged to a very different order of possibilities from the pedestrian and workaday conspiracies to cause explosions, rob shops or banks or even assassinate European officials, including the viceroy himself. Whatever the long-term aims of the revolutionaries or the fantastic hopes they might have entertained, it was grotesque to endow them with the dignity of war, unless one granted them a preternatural efficacy far beyond the range of normal human capacities. A hundred, even a thousand, armed men organized in disparate groups with a handful of home-made bombs and Mauser pistols did not, in themselves postulate a military threat to a large and powerful army fresh from defeating its strongest rival. They could only hope to achieve their ambition in the context of a much broader-based political movement embracing a majority of the politically active part of the population. Under no common sense definition of the word does such a movement which in the nature of things must be public and largely open to scrutiny constitute a 'conspiracy'.

Actually, the Rowlatt report hesitated to take the final step of linking all the disparate signs of rebelliousness and unrest into a single Grand Conspiracy in the manner of Barruel or the *Protocols of the Elders of Zion*. It relied on insinuation and innuendo rather than explicit analysis. It conceded that there might not have been 'one conspiracy, in the sense that the individuals of one group or party could not be held legally responsible for the acts of another group' and that 'particular outrages were not always approved as a matter of policy by groups other than that which committed them'. But it insisted vehemently that 'there was one movement, promoting one general policy of outrage', whose connections lay in the similarity of their tactics, similarity of bomb-types, overlapping membership and above all 'the statements made by the persons arrested' which were 'too closely interwoven to be invented, anticipating their own corroboration by way of subsequent discoveries and strikingly connected in important matters by documents'.[82]

There was no end to the mischief caused by the Rowlatt report and the ensuing acts. Mahatma Gandhi denounced them as 'unjust, subversive to the principles of liberty and justice and destructive of the elementary rights of individuals on which the safety of the community as a whole and of the state itself is based . . .'[83] The passing of the acts produced a wave of disturbances the continent had not seen since the year of the Mutiny. Gandhi may be said to have built his career on the agitation. Despite his commitment to non-violent opposition to the bills, there were a number of incidents in which angry crowds attacked and burned government buildings, assaulted Europeans and in one case brutally murdered them. Most of India's larger cities were affected, but the greatest disturbances were in the Punjab, where feelings had been brought to fever-pitch by five years of martial law and the strains of bearing by far the heaviest burden of the war effort.

The worst of the riots was at Amritsar, a traditional stronghold of nationalist feeling. The story of the massacre of nearly four hundred unarmed demonstrators by Brigadier-General Dyer is well known. The local riots had been precipitated by the arrest of two nationalist leaders, both of them supporters of Gandhi. A bank was set on fire in which three European clerks were burnt to death. Miss Sherwood, an English schoolteacher, was brutally assaulted by the mob and left for dead. The local police and army units being unable to control the situation, the deputy commissioner called for reinforcements. Dyer arrived to take command of some nine hundred British, Indian and Gurkha soldiers. He issued a number of proclamations at the beat of the drum, ordering a dusk-to-dawn curfew and prohibiting gatherings of more than three persons. Partly in defiance of, partly in ignorance of these prohibitions, a crowd of some twenty thousand assembled in the Jallianwalla Bagh, a large open space surrounded by houses. The general marched there with some ninety native troops and without further warning opened fire on the crowd from a vantage point at the only entrance to the square, so the people were unable to escape. He continued firing until 1,650 rounds had been spent, and then withdrew his force without making any provision for the care of the injured and dying. Later, he established a whipping post at the point of Miss Sherwood's assault, where the three alleged culprits were publicly flogged. He also issued the notorious 'crawling order'. Everyone who passed the spot was obliged to crawl on hands and knees, including local residents who had no other means of access to their homes.[84]

The massacre was the worst in Anglo-Indian history, and proved a decisive turning point in the relations between the government and the nationalist movement. It killed the chance of a peaceful evolution towards independence as envisaged in the Montagu–Chelmsford proposals of 1919 and the Government of India Act of the same year. It decisively polarized native and Anglo-Indian opinion. Even the commission of inquiry divided along racial lines, the Indian members, though unquestioning loyalists, insisting on a much stronger condemnation of the General's conduct and that of the military as a whole than the British were prepared to entertain. Dyer's dismissal, on the other hand (he was relieved of his command but not cashiered) consolidated a substantial section of Anglo-Indian and British opinion behind him. For them he became first a hero – the saviour of 'India' from another Mutiny – and then, after his dismissal, a martyr for the upright military virtues in the face of time-serving political duplicity. In Britain itself, the controversy put strains on the Liberal-Conservative coalition government and may have helped bring about its demise.[85]

There is a twofold connection between the Amritsar massacre and the Rowlatt acts. In the first place, as the Hunter committee found, the main cause of the riots throughout the Punjab and elsewhere was a spontaneous demonstration against the passing of the act and the arrest of Gandhi who symbolically disobeyed one of its provisions. This, of course, undermined one of the main assumptions upon which the act was built: that because the 'revolutionary conspiracies' were the work of a malignant minority, ill-disposed towards the 'true' interests of the population (as represented by British rule), the 'temporary' restrictions on individual liberty embodied in the act would meet with the approval or even indifference of the majority.[86] The spontaneity of the demonstrations that greeted the passing of the act proved the opposite. Whereas the majority of the population might not necessarily agree with the aims or methods of the terrorists, they were not so far out of sympathy with them as to be prepared to sacrifice their own liberties (which in India were few enough anyway) to help the authorities fight them. The myth of the secret 'organization' standing between local crimes and incidents and the wider social and political forces was exploded.

Secondly, there is the decisive connection between the belief that events were being controlled by a secret revolutionary organization and the conduct of General Dyer and his military and civilian colleagues. When he arrived at Amritsar, local railway stations had been sacked and telegraphic communications cut, and Dyer found

... a clear conviction on the part of local officials that a determined and organized movement was in progress to submerge and destroy all the Europeans on the spot and in the district and to carry the movement throughout the Punjab and that the mob in the city and the excitable population of the villages were being organized for the purpose ... When, contrary to previous expectation, violence broke out, such organization quickly showed itself and ... we found by experience there was sufficient organization down in the lowest stratum to go and spread with wonderful rapidity to do acts of violence.[87]

Thus, as he explained to the Hunter committee: 'It was no longer a question of merely dispersing the crowd but one of producing sufficient moral effect from the military point of view, not only on those who were present, but more especially throughout the Punjab. There could be no question of undue severity.'[88] The fact that the people had assembled in the Jallianwalla Bagh in defiance of his orders was to Dyer, proof that there was something 'much more serious' behind the disturbances than he had imagined, that the people were therefore rebels who should not be treated 'with gloves on'. 'They had come to fight if they defied me, and I was going to give them a lesson.'[89] He admitted that his action had been designed to 'strike terror throughout the Punjab'[90] but he sought to obtain sympathy for the unpleasant duty he had been obliged to discharge. Asked if it had occurred to him that his action might be a *disservice* to the British government, he replied:

> No, it only struck me at the time it was my duty to do this and it was a horrible duty. I did not like the idea of doing it, but I also realized that it was the only means of saving life and that any reasonable man with justice in his mind would realize that I had done the right thing; and it was a merciful act, and they ought to be thankful to me for doing it.[91]

Dyer was not alone in supposing there was something 'much more serious' behind the disturbances. The lieutenant-governor of the Punjab, Sir Michael O'Dwyer, supported Dyer's action on the same grounds. However, when asked by the Hunter committee if there was a central organization behind the disturbances, he replied:

> 'I have no proofs of it. But I am strongly inclined to believe that it did exist. There was some organization.'
> 'There was some central organization directing them?'
> 'Certain phases of them.'
> 'There was some common agency which worked out certain phases of the occurrence that took place?'
> 'Yes, that is what I believe.'
> 'You have no evidence in support of this?'
> 'I cannot give it. As I say, I left the province directly after these disorders were put down and did not have the opportunity of investigating the matter further.'[92]

Even more revealing was the cross-examination of Colonel O'Brien, deputy commissioner of the Gujranwala district, who had claimed in his written submission that the unrest had been 'organized' from outside his province:

'So . . . the organization that you refer to was in the Punjab, outside Gujran-wala?'

'I don't say that. I say it was certainly outside Gujranwala.'

'Was it outside the Punjab or inside?'

'That I cannot tell you.'

'You cannot say where the organization was?'

'No, I have no information.'

'You do not know whether there was any organization at all?'

'No.'

'Then why do you say here [i.e. in the statement] "it was organized . . ." when you never knew whether there was an organization at all or not?'

'As I said, it was only my assumption. I don't think that the Gujranwala people would have started it off of their own accord, therefore I assumed that it must have come from outside.'

'You assumed the existence of an organization without any evidence at all? You never made any inquiries?'

'It is not for me to take into consideration every individual thing outside my own district.'

'Colonel, you have made a statement, and surely you must base that statement on some material?'

'I did not expect to be cross-examined.'

'Therefore you thought that it did not matter if you made that statement, and it would not be challenged?'

'I was asked to give my opinion by the Punjab government, and I gave it.'[93]

All the conspiracy theories, in fact, tended to evaporate in the unexpected heat of cross-examination, including some far more outlandish than the mysterious 'organization' of Dyer, O'Dwyer and O'Brien. One witness linked the disturbances with similar outbreaks in Egypt and Afghanistan, suggesting they were connected with, if not financed by, the 'Russian–German–Bolshevik organization'.[94]

Both the majority and the minority of the Hunter committee rejected the idea of a pre-arranged conspiracy to overthrow the British government.[95]* The occasion of the disturbances, they agreed, had been the passing of the Rowlatt acts and the arrest of Gandhi whose campaign of civil disobedience had inevitably led to disorders and breaches of the peace. The underlying causes were both more 'legitimate and

*The action taken by General Dyer has . . . been described . . . as having saved the situation in the Punjab and having averted a rebellion on a scale similar to the Mutiny. It does not, however, appear to us possible to draw this conclusion, particularly in view of the fact that it is not proved that a conspiracy to overthrow British power had been formed prior to the outbreaks (Hunter majority report, para. 43)

potent' than a conspiracy – the result of an implicit contradiction between the promise of self-government contained in the Montagu–Chelmsford proposals and the 1919 Government of India Act on the one hand, and the wartime emergency provisions and the threat of their continuation under the Rowlatt acts on the other.[96] The main point of divergence between the two sections of the committee was whether the disturbances amounted to a 'rebellion' justifying the continuation of martial law. The majority faction argued that it was possible to have a rebellion without an antecedent conspiracy, the minority countering that the absence of any attempts to steal arms ruled out rebellion in any meaningful sense of the word.

The contrast between the Hunter committee's report and that of Mr Justice Rowlatt could not have been more striking. The latter articulated the deepest fears of India's white community, was the work of a reactionary Anglo-Indian judge and relied decisively on police 'confessions' which it refused to make public. The Hunter committee, in contrast, was chaired by a senior Scottish judge, uncontaminated by years of obsequious deference on the part of native subordinates. It dared to subject a governor, a general, several senior officers and civilian officials to rigorous cross-examination of a kind that they had clearly never experienced before, and never expected. The minority dared to express its reservations about the character of a senior native police officer whom it interviewed.[97] It exploded the fantasy world into which all but the very top levels of the British administration had retreated. But though it added a tiny push to the fall of Lloyd George in England, India was no climate for cold Scottish common-sense. The report was ignored, and with the accession of an all Conservative administration in England, Hunter's voice of moderation was drowned in the strident tones of Rowlatt. An act indemnified the conduct of the officers criticized by the commission,[98] giving, in effect, the military and police the go-ahead to pursue a policy of terror.

The first phase was the repression in the Punjab where according to Nehru 30,000 persons were given prison sentences during December 1921 and January 1922.[99] The brutality of the police in rounding up terrorist suspects had already been condemned in the Hunter report, and was the subject of a continuous stream of complaints from Gandhi, who claimed that ninety per cent of those convicted were wholly innocent of the charges against them.[100] The result was a revival of terrorism and in particular, the assassination of policemen. The most spectacular incident occurred at Chauri Chaura in the United Provinces in 1922, when complaints of police brutality led to a demonstration in which police opened fire. The crowd retaliated by setting fire to the police station, and hacked to pieces those policemen who tried to escape. The remainder were burned alive.[101]

In 1928, a nationalist leader died after being assaulted by the police during a demonstration against the Simon commission.[102] The British officer who led the assault was subsequently murdered; and in what almost seems a repetition of the Alipore conspiracy trial of 1910, a number of suspects were arrested on conspiracy charges linking the murder of the policeman with the discovery of a bomb factory in Lahore.[103] Allegations of torture became increasingly frequent. The authorities' search for conspiracies began to acquire a left-wing twist, as they began to suspect the ubiquitous finger of the Comintern behind local disturbances and labour troubles. The British government took the threat seriously enough to conduct a search for proof in a raid on Soviet offices in London. The results were predictably barren, and the government attempted to conceal its blunder by breaking diplomatic relations with the Soviet Union.[104] Undeterred by this set-back, the authorities in India proceeded to conduct two communist show-trials, known as the Cawnpore and Meerut conspiracy trials.[105]

As police brutality increased and the treatment of political prisoners progressively deteriorated, the line between interrogative torture and punishment became indistinct. Once the government had armed itself with arbitrary powers of arrest and detention, confessions were no longer needed for juridical reasons. Even the communist conspiracy trials themselves suggest a reflex action more than a serious search for conspirators. A government publication admitted that the communist leader M. N. Roy had disowned all belief in bombs, secret societies and individual outrages, relying only on the organized mass of industrial workers.[106] The violence reached its height during the civil disobedience campaign of the thirties. Apart from a revival of political dacoity in Bengal for which some 2,700 suspects were detained administratively,[107] it was largely the work of the military and the police. Though the *satyagrahis* confined themselves mainly to symbolic infringements of the laws, the authorities reacted with uncompromising severity. Gandhi complained, in a letter to the viceroy, that

whilst known leaders have been dealt with more or less according to legal formality, the rank and file have been often savagely, and in some cases, even indecently assaulted ... Accounts have come to me from Bengal, Bihar, Uthal, United Provinces, Delhi and Bombay confirming the experiences of Gujerat of which I have ample evidence ... Bones have been broken, private parts have been squeezed for the purpose of making volunteers give up, to the government valueless, to the volunteers precious, salt.[108]

Similar brutalities are alleged to have been applied, often on direct orders from European officers, during subsequent civil disobedience campaigns. In 1942, for example, demonstrators were said to have been beaten and 'forced to lick spittle from the ground' for deliberately breaking the forest laws. At some police stations, victims were reported to have been forced to drink urine. Hundreds of homes were burned or demolished. Nationalist pamphlets also accused the police of more traditional tortures, including the *strappado*, the application of chilli-powder to the genitals of men and women and anal pentration with a variety of instruments.[109] Methods associated with Stalin's GPU, although not yet widely known in the West, began to be employed. And, as in Russia, prominent political figures were no longer exempted from the treatment meted out to the rank and file. Ram Lohia, the socialist leader, told Harold Laski that he had been subjected to sleep deprivation for ten days continuously. Another socialist, Jayaprakash Narain, complained of 'continuous' interrogation sessions in the manner of the Soviet 'conveyer'. A nephew of the nationalist leader, Subhas Chandra Bose, alleged that he had been beaten, kept continuously awake and personally threatened with having a bamboo cane pushed up his anus by a European deputy inspector general of the Punjab CID.[110]

As Gandhi's complaint to the viceroy indicated, violence was both retributive and coercive, designed to punish nationalist supporters and to force them to abandon their campaign. The need for 'information' at such a stage in the struggle was nugatory. Revolutionary violence belonged to the fringes of the movement, and had been consistently denounced by nationalist as well as communist leaders. The penal service became an instrument of political coercion, blurring the distinction between interrogation and punishment. Lester Hutchinson, one of three Englishmen accused of complicity in the communist Meerut conspiracy trial, described how political prisoners sentenced to hard labour were often beaten by convict-overseers who qualified for their privileges by acting as stool-pigeons. The 'punishments' auth-

orized for alleged infringements of prison discipline included the standing torture (the prisoner was usually handcuffed to a tree in a manner
forcing him to stand on his toes), bar fetters designed to cause maximum
discomfort, solitary confinement and flogging. Officially, beatings
were prohibited except when ordered by a superintendent, but this rule
was observed only in the breach:

> The warders and even the convict-overseers entertain themselves through
> the long hours by striking and torturing prisoners, and the jailer often holds
> what is known . . . as a 'blanket parade'. The prisoner against whom the jailer
> has a grievance is placed flat on the ground and covered with blankets; he is
> then beaten through the blankets with bamboo rods wielded by the jailers'
> trustworthy minions, so that although he receives all the pain of the beating,
> he has no wounds to show the superintendent to justify his complaint, and in-
> deed, it is not wise to complain; for complaints do not lead to rectification of
> evils, but to further punishment and torture.

These brutalities were far from being arbitrarily sadistic. That they
were part of a wider system of coercion is indicated by the fact that convicted prisoners could have their sentences reduced or even abolished
in exchange for 'an apology for past conduct'. The torments described
by Hutchinson were 'tortures' in the strict Benthamite sense.[111]

*   *   *

On 26 June 1975 Mrs Indira Gandhi, daughter of Nehru and heir to
the viceregal legacy, locked up a thousand or more of her political
opponents and declared a state of emergency – thus becoming in effect
the world's first female dictator. The powers she gathered to herself
were already on the statute book, having lain there, in abeyance, since
the war with Pakistan. Using the same tactics as her colonial predecessors, she sought to adapt the war-time measures designed to meet an
external threat to the task of bolstering a political position that had
become untenable at home. It is probably too fanciful to suppose that
she consciously imitated the colonial administration of more than half
a century back, or that some bright civil servant succeeded in unearth-
ing the Rowlatt report from somewhere in the state archives and placed
it on her desk. Political cultures are inclined to endure in a manner
scarcely flattering to the self-esteem of politicians – especially those
claiming legitimacy from a revolutionary break with the past. But

whether consciously or not, in announcing her measures Mrs Gandhi lapsed comfortably into the language of Mr Justice Rowlatt and General Dyer. In her message to the Indian people explaining the declaration of the emergency she said:

> I am sure you are all conscious of the deep and widespread conspiracy which has been brewing ever since I began introducing certain progressive measures of benefit to the common man and woman of India. In the name of democracy it has sought to negate the very functioning of democracy.[112]

As with similar pronouncements by other leaders tired of constitutional inconveniences, Mrs Gandhi's claim that her opponents were conspiring to destroy democracy in the name of saving it supplied a succinct and accurate description of her own actions.

Mrs Gandhi's dictatorship was incomplete and short-lived – factors which may one day help to vindicate her reputation. Her government may have been too corrupt and incompetent to function according to the constitutional rules; but it was insufficiently ruthless when it came to dispensing with them altogether. Lacking the dogmatic assurance of a marxist ideologue, she sought to legitimate her rule at the polls once more, and lost catastrophically. Yet in the aftermath of her defeat in 1977 a number of facts came to light which proved that state terrorism was far from being an exclusive characteristic of the colonial government. Indeed, how could it have been when the colonial rulers had themselves acquired the habit of torturing their opponents from their native subjects?

Opposition leaders sought to make capital out of the ugly revelations of police methods under the emergency. Dr Subramanyam Swamy, Janata Party leader, claimed that police in Kerala had acquired their ideas of torture from Mrs Gandhi's ally, the Soviet Union. It was only there, he claimed, 'that the police made people drink their own urine, ducked them in ice-cold water, administered electric shocks, denied water and food continuously for days together' and indulged in various other methods of torture attributed to the Kerala police.[113] Politicians are inclined to have short memories, and only look into history when it suits them.

Colonialism then may already be ceasing to be the universal scapegoat, as memories of western domination recede in former colonial territories to be replaced by less evident, but many more insidious forms of suzerainty. But whether it is seen as a legacy of foreign rule – as it must seem to be in those parts of Africa such as Uganda currently governed by former colonial lackeys; or, as Edmund Burke might see it, as a result of the contamination of the westerner's free institutions by Asiatic despotisms, torture is part of the common inheritance of the post-colonial world. Kenya, Aden, Cyprus; Indo-china, Algeria – and recently a part of the so-called 'United Kingdom'. All these countries have, in recent memory, provided confirmation of Burke's grim warning that the arbitrary nature of colonial rule, however well-intentioned, would prove subversive to those hard-won rights that add up to the abstract noun 'freedom'.

NINE

Stalin and the Russian devils

On 1 December 1934, a shot rang out in the corridors of the head-quarters of the Leningrad Communist Party whose velocity by a strange inversion of the laws of ballistics increased with every ricochet to the point where the life of approximately half the Soviet Union's 170,000,000 citizens was put at risk. The assassin was a comparatively unknown young man – a disillusioned communist called Leonid Niko-layev; the victim, the rising star in the soviet hierarchy, whose popu-larity in the party was second only to Stalin's: Sergei Kirov. Judged by its consequences, the pistol shot has every right to be compared with that other crime of the century, the shot that killed the Archduke Franz-Ferdinand at Sarajevo.[1]

The facts of the Kirov murder are still open to dispute, but only in a vestigial sense. It has not yet been formally admitted that Stalin was primarily responsible.[2] The truth appears to lie in a singular combina-tion of circumstances: a lone assassin with a personal grudge whose in-tentions were known in advance, and whose access to the closely guarded party secretary was facilitated by deliberate negligence ordered from on high. A veteran of the civil war, Nikolayev belonged to the youngest generation of revolutionaries who were most likely to feel resentful at the drift of events. The old revolutionary leaders still occupied the commanding heights of the party; the younger generation – the first fruits of an all-communist education system – were already beginning to emerge beneath them; the party was becoming increas-ingly 'bureaucratized'. Although he does not appear to have suffered personally in the clean-up of the Leningrad party that followed the defeat of the left opposition and Zinoviev's first fall from grace in the late twenties, Nikolayev appears to have shared some of their feelings. Frustrated in his emotional need for heroics and desperate to recall the now-forgotten days of revolutionary brotherhood, his thoughts had turned increasingly to the dramatic deeds of Russia's revolutionary past. His diary showed that he had read widely into the history of the Russian terrorists, the Narodniks and Social Revolutionaries who had successfully plotted the assassinations of tsars and their ministers.

The story has Dostoyevskian proportions. Nikolayev was doubtless not alone in his views, and moved in circles where subjects like terrorism were guardedly – but daringly – discussed. It may even be true that he confided in a friend that he intended to assassinate some major party figure as a protest. The friend was a police informer; but instead of arresting Nikolayev, the NKVD ordered him to smooth the assassin's path by providing him with a gun and turning his thoughts in the direction of Kirov. Things did not go smoothly at first. Nikolayev was twice arrested with his revolver near the Smolny before his third, successful attempt. It is difficult to believe that his unaccountable releases (on the first occasion he was not even searched) did not lead him to suspect he was playing the dupe.[3]

Obviously, only a section of the Leningrad NKVD was involved in the plot. The key man was Zaporozhets, who had the tricky job of securing Nikolayev's access to Kirov without arousing too much suspicion. The most difficult part was detaining the personal bodyguard, a man called Borisov, well known for his devotion to Kirov. The day after the murder, Borisov became suspicious and had to be killed in a faked (and partly bungled) motor accident.[4] Zaporozhets, his superior, and several other members of the Leningrad NKVD were given astonishingly light sentences for their failure to protect a senior member of the politburo; and rumours began to circulate in senior NKVD circles, though the affair was considered to be far too dangerous to know much about.[5] Four years later, when thousands had already died for alleged terrorist plots that included a solitary instance where violence had actually happened – the murder of Kirov – one of the true culprits confessed to the crime. That was Yagoda, former head of the NKVD, who claimed he had been acting under orders from Yenukidze, a Georgian, formerly close to Stalin. Conveniently, Yenukidze was already dead, shot after one of those secret trials held for defendants who failed to confess.[6] With the benefit of hindsight, it hardly seems necessary to look beyond the obvious facts of political rivalry for an adequate motive for Stalin's complicity in the murder. The man who in the course of half a dozen years procured the deaths of every one of his revolutionary peers by judicial and para-judicial means, or plain assassination, long after any of them had ceased to enjoy any vestige of his previous reputation in the party, did not require a special provocation to allow the elimination of the one man in all Russia who at that time could be accounted a potential rival.

Kirov's advance had been rapid since being picked by Stalin to take charge of the Leningrad party organization after Zinoviev's fall in 1925. At first he appears to have encountered considerable opposition from the right-wing elements in the city who had hoped to benefit from Zinoviev's disgrace. But in recent years his local popularity had grown. His régime was a comparatively liberal one and former oppositionists were invited to return from exile and work as advisers – much to Stalin's annoyance. He did much to restore the tradition of intellectual and scientific independence that Russia's 'window on Europe' had enjoyed in Zinoviev's heyday.[7] Though unquestioningly loyal to Stalin, Kirov carried his conciliatory style into national politics. True, he never hesitated to endorse the wholesale terrorism employed against the kulaks at the beginning of the first five-year plan, when Stalin made his sudden bid for rapid industrialization; he never protested – as the 'rightist' leaders did – at the more or less infinite extension of the category of 'kulak' to include the vast majority of middle and poor peasants – the muzhiks – who objected, often violently, to being coerced into collective farms. Moreover, the notorious prison camps of the Kem and Murmansk coasts fell within his jurisdiction and he was in charge of the construction of the Baltic–White Sea canal which cost many thousands of convict lives, most of them political prisoners. As one of his contemporaries put it, Kirov was hardly a man to be reproached 'with any undue tenderness in the manner in which he disposed of human lives'.[8] Yet, for all his toughness – and largely, in fact, because of it – he became the chief candidate of moderation and conciliation in the party and as such by 1934 constituted Stalin's most formidable rival.

The reasons are well known. The party was sickened by the bloodshed and terror – worse than anything since the civil war – that inevitably accompanied Stalin's war on the kulaks. Millions of families had been deported from the land, according to arbitrarily reached decisions of local soviets or Bolshevik action squads specially drafted from the cities. Often the poor and middle peasants, far from turning on the 'exploiting' kulaks whom they were supposed to hate, sided with them against the expropriators. The struggle became a war between the city and the countryside; and when the superior arms of the city carried the day, the peasants who remained on the land to be forced into collectives retaliated by the wholesale slaughter of livestock and the destruction of farm machinery. The result was a famine infinitely worse than the shortfall of grain (two million tons) that had precipitated the crisis. The disasters of the peasantry therefore in no way assisted the condition of the workers, who were doubly worse off: in the short term, the accumulation needed to finance Stalin's ambitious industrialization plans had to come from their mouths as well as from those of the peasants. The whole of Russia starved (excepting, of course, the party elites) while precious food was sold abroad to earn the foreign currency necessary to purchase industrial machinery. Meanwhile, the party's standing in the country reached its nadir and terrorism erupted in the villages, with communist party workers and offices the primary objects of attack.[9]

Naturally, since Stalin bore the entire responsibility for this policy, there were rumblings about his leadership. They came from the former left opposition, whose policy he had suddenly adopted and taken to lengths that none had dared contemplate, as well as from the 'rightists', who could claim greater consistency. At bottom, there was the justified fear that Stalin had, by his impetuousness, rocked the soviet revolution at its very foundations – the alliance between workers and peasants that had made possible the Bolshevik victory in the revolution and civil war. Moreover, another spectre was looming on the horizon: the rise of Hitler in Germany. Not everyone was yet able to take the full measure of this danger. But for those who could sense it, another aggressive Germany was there – and for that, too, the general secretary bore a major responsibility. Wasn't it Stalin, after all, who paved the way to Nazi victory by turning the German communists against the social democrats in 1928, instead of closing the socialist ranks in face of the fascist danger? By 1932 the grumblings in the party had already reached a serious level, as various documents opposing Stalin's policy began to circulate. The most outspoken – and possibly influential – was the so-called Riutin Platform, a massive indictment of his leadership which went so far as to demand the removal of the general secretary as the 'great agent provocateur, destroyer of the party' and the 'grave-digger of the revolution, and of Russia'.[10] Heeding the warning-lights, Stalin had already reduced the tempo of his programme. But he was always intolerant of opposition, especially of a personal variety. When the OGPU demanded that Riutin be shot Stalin concurred but found himself blocked in the politburo – and by Kirov of all people, his favourite protégé. Stalin was forced to give way, and Riutin was simply sent to exile.[11]

Meanwhile, the members of the former opposition, frightened by their recent brushes with Stalin, continued to grumble, and rather ineffectually to join hands tentatively behind his back. But both factions, the left and right, had been damaged by public renunciations of their views. Trotsky was in exile abroad, maintaining increasingly remote contact with his supporters. His former left-wing rivals Zinoviev and Kamenev had joined him much too late to be of any use and, after Trotsky's central Asian exile, had further lost face in the eyes of their followers by returning to make grovelling renunciations at the feet of Stalin and the party. The leaders of the right opposition had put up even less of a fight against Stalin when he abandoned their policy and turned against them than had the livelier personalities of the left. They had allowed themselves to be outmanoeuvred behind the closed doors of the politburo without making any appeal to their supporters outside – all to maintain the appearance of party unity. By the time Stalin's new policy was fully launched and into the hurricane, Bukharin, Rykov, and Tomsky had already made their renunciations, and were in no mood to rock the boat. And so those in the party who were thinking of an alternative leader – and there were many – inevitably looked in the direction of Kirov. Vigorous, energetic, good-looking – and a Great Russian to boot, there was no taint of heresy about him, nor had he ever compromised himself by denouncing his past errors. Now that the fateful decision to collectivize had been taken, the question of policy was secondary to personality: it was Stalin's style, his immoderation, boorishness and cruelty that aroused the deepest apprehensions of those around him.

The mood of the party found its fullest expression at the seventeenth party congress – dubbed prematurely the Congress of Victors – in July 1934. Stalin received the usual ovations, the immoderate and obsequious adulation that had now come to grip the party like a deathly virus escaped from the grave of the old régime. But Kirov, by all accounts, received an equal amount of applause – a matter which caused a burble of interested speculation during the recesses. According to some accounts, an attempt by Stalin's fellow Georgian, Sergo Ordjonikidze, to replace him as general secretary by Kirov was only checked by Kirov's own refusal to countenance such a move. In elections for the central committee Stalin received fewer votes than any other candidate; 270 votes were cast against him to three against Kirov. At the end of the congress his official title was changed from general secretary to secretary, an indisputable downgrading in a party that had come to set the greatest store by the minutiae of hierarchical nomenclature. There could be no doubt about it: Kirov's star was in the ascendant, Stalin's was on the wane. Yet in less than a year Kirov was dead.

As soon as he heard of the murder, Stalin travelled to Leningrad to take personal charge of the 'investigation', but not before issuing a decree (which must have been previously drafted) speeding up the investigations in cases of terrorism, abolishing the right of appeal for those sentenced to death and making provision for immediate execution following sentence. It is an indication of the enormous power he had already concentrated in his hands that he did this without consulting the politburo, who merely approved the emergency measures the following day. As Khruschev – one of Stalin's own henchmen – put it in his famous 'secret' speech to the twentieth party congress in 1956, Stalin's directive

> became the basis for mass acts of abuse against socialist legality. During many of the fabricated cases the accused were charged with the 'preparation' of terrorist acts; this deprived them of any possibility that their cases might be re-examined, even when they stated before the court that their 'confessions' were secured by force, and when, in a convincing manner, they disproved the accusations against them.[12]

Following the tradition of Nicholas 1 and the Decembrists, Stalin personally interrogated the first batch of suspects. According to some accounts, Nikolayev was severely beaten in Stalin's presence after he claimed he had been forced to commit the murder by members of the NKVD.[13] Yet he stalwartly refused to implicate the other young communists, his former associates, who had been arrested with him. His diary, portions of which were shown to politburo members, contained no references to any organization, an awkward fact which the NKVD later attempted to explain away by claiming it had been a forgery.[14] The first victims of the new decree – other than Nikolayev and his 'associates' – were groups of so-called White Guards, in Leningrad, Moscow and various other cities, who were shot for preparing various 'terrorist acts' none of which included specifically the Kirov murder. They may have been genuine counter-revolutionaries, arrested before the crime, whose cases were in various stages of completion. After Stalin's return to Moscow the deputy chief of the NKVD, Agranov, was put in charge of the investigation.[15] Taking his cue from Stalin, Agranov remorselessly pursued the connections between Nikolayev and the young communists, and the former opposition circles in Leningrad associated with Zinoviev. He was only partially successful: the links were insufficient for public exhibition.

Nikolayev himself may have been tortured into confessing to having committed the murder on orders from a secret 'Leningrad' centre; but it seems that none of his supposed accomplices would admit to any crime beyond membership of an illegal 'Zinovievite' group. Such a group of young intellectuals no doubt existed; it had been known to the NKVD for months before the murder. Kirov had been informed but, preferring persuasion to force, he had refused to allow police measures against them. Thus only the indictment was ever made public; and after a secret trial Nikolayev and thirteen of his alleged 'Zinovievite' accomplices were shot.[16] Despite what must have been, from Stalin's point of view, an unsatisfactory conclusion, a great taboo had been broken: Bolsheviks could be executed at last, and Stalin was free to destroy his old political enemies, as well as the larger and better part of the old communist party. A wave of arrests hit the party like the plague. Secret directives were sent all over the Union calling on party committees to hunt down and expel all former oppositionists. Nests of 'Trotskyites' were uncovered throughout the country. There were mass deportations to Siberia and the Arctic. Zinoviev and Kamenev were tried in secret, and imprisoned for 'influencing' the terrorists: they were not yet accused of direct involvement. But the trial marked a new and ominous departure, as the first occasion on which political opposition from within the communist party had been made the subject of an open criminal charge.

It took several more months to forge the direct connecting links between the Komsomol terrorists and the disgraced opposition leaders and, more importantly, with the arch-fiend in exile, Trotsky. This crucial link was provided by a NKVD agent obliged to confess – in the line of duty – to having been the contact man between the Berlin Trotskyites and a terrorist group in Gorki. Some fifteen further confessions were required to provide the supporting evidence for the 'Trotskyite–Zinovievite–Terrorist Centre' publicly unveiled at the first great show-trial – the Trial of the Sixteen in August 1936.[17] These confessions were employed indirectly, to bring added pressure on the accused. It speaks much of the difficulties facing the NKVD interrogators at this early period that at least three hundred people had been interrogated to produce the required confessions, a failure rate of approximately 95·5 per cent.[18] But eventually all was ready. The principals in the trial – Zinoviev and Kamenev, and the 'Trotskyites' Smirnov and Mrachkovsky (among others) eventually capitulated in the face of a multitude of pressures, including threats to their families and followers, and agreed to confess in open court to charges which included forming the terrorist 'group' responsible for killing Kirov and for plotting the assassination of Stalin and of the other politburo leaders. During the trials, ominous hints were dropped in the cross-examinations. One of the accused spoke of 'negotiations' with the three principal rightist leaders – Bukharin, Rykov and Tomsky; and a 'Red army assassination squad' was also mentioned.[19] Further trials were evidently being contemplated.

Twenty-four hours after being sentenced to death, Zinoviev and Kamenev were shot in the cellars of the NKVD, in violation of Stalin's promise to spare their lives in return for a full confession.[20] Kamenev reportedly died with stunned indignation; Zinoviev may or may not have finally broken down weeping and calling on the God of his forefathers.[21] They were the first of the leaders of the revolution, Lenin's close comrades-in-arms, to be killed in this ignominious fashion, illegally deprived of their right to appeal to the central committee. The general secretary was on holiday.

Not a single communist party in any part of the world protested or put in a word to save the former president of the Communist International. A good many of the foreigners who attended the trial found nothing objectionable, despite the obvious flaws: the almost complete lack of documentary evidence for the alleged 'plot'; the failure of certain prominent witnesses to appear in court; the absence of any reference to some of the previous trials held in connection with the Kirov murder (for example, the trial of the Leningrad NKVD).[22] Neither were European communists or fellow-travellers shaken when facts were advanced to refute specific evidence given in the trial – the fact, for example, that the hotel in Copenhagen where one of the defendants allegedly met Trotsky had been demolished in 1917. It was this reaction which, no doubt, emboldened Stalin to proceed with the second public trial already being prepared by the NKVD. From the hints dropped during the Trial of the Sixteen, it is clear that he intended to move against the leaders of the right opposition immediately. Tomsky pre-empted his fate by committing suicide; but the standing of Bukharin and Rykov in the party was still too high, and Stalin apparently met strong opposition in the central committee of which both were candidate members.

Nevertheless, Stalin continued to press ahead with the purges. The rightist leaders were spared – for the time being. But Yagoda was sacked as head of the NKVD for being too backward in the hunt for enemies. His place was taken by Yezhov, whose name will forever be identified with the darkest of all periods in Russian history – the Yezhovschina. Meanwhile, a new show-trial was in preparation. The second group of victims consisted of Piatakov, Radek, and a number of 'Trotskyite saboteurs' accused of trying to wreck the soviet economy with the ultimate aim of overthrowing the government in conjunction with the Nazis and the Japanese.[23] Clearly, these charges against men who had devoted the whole of their lives to the revolution and the Communist party, were far more fantastic, and less credible, than those levelled against Zinoviev, Kamenev and company. The leaders of the former left opposition had, at least, (together with Trotsky) been Stalin's most prominent political rivals. They shared power with him during the period of the 'Troika' after Lenin's death, until he had succeeded in outmanoeuvring them, and it was not wholly inconceivable that they might have plotted his and Kirov's assassination, seeing no other way of returning to power, even though individual terrorism ran strongly counter to their Bolshevik principles. The new charges, on the other hand, belonged to an entirely different order of probability. Politically, they had the function of further blacking the arch-fiend Trotsky. In the first trial, the Zinovievites had been much more prominently displayed than the supporters of Trotsky – the principal one of whom, I. N. Smirnov, had cast some doubts upon the proceedings by refusing to admit to all the charges.[24] While prominent Trotskyites were still not available for the second trial – having mostly been destroyed or made too many previous recantations – the new defendants could at least be represented as his agents and creatures of his true masters, the Nazis. The second improved version of the 'Great Trotskyite Conspiracy' had two somewhat contradictory aims: the assassination of Stalin and his colleagues (it became the mark of the highest political favour to be included on the list of intended 'victims'), and the spreading of sabotage throughout the soviet economy. It had been hatched, predictably enough, during another famous hotel meeting – this time between Trotsky himself and Rudolf Hess, Hitler's deputy.[25]

The most interesting feature of the trial were the allegations of sabotage: though these were far from being a novel feature of soviet judicial life, this was the first time detailed accusations of 'wrecking' had been levelled against leaders of the communist party. The first sabotage trial occurred in 1928, when fifty-three engineers and technicians – three of them Germans – were charged with creating an espionage and sabotage network in the coal industry in the Shakhty area (southern Ukraine). Ten of the accused made full confessions, six made partial ones. Eleven were sentenced to death, five of whom were shot. Most of the remainder received terms ranging from three to ten years. During the trial, one of the accused attempted to withdraw his confession in the Moscow court, stating he had only signed it after being driven to distraction by threats; but then after pressure from the prosecution he withdrew the allegation. Another retracted, then confirmed his confession; then withdrew it again when his wife cried from the public gallery: 'Kolya, darling, don't lie. You know you are innocent!' – which caused him to break down and tearfully admit he had not been permitted to sleep for eight nights. (The following morning, though, he affirmed his confession once more.)[26]

As with the subsequent trial of the opposition leaders, it seems to have been intended that admissions made during the Shakhty trial should form the basis for further charges of wrecking and sabotage against non-party technicians, this time on a nationwide scale. Alexander Solzhenitsyn believes that the star of the second trial was to have been P. A. Palchinsky, a distinguished industrialist during the first world war who became a consultant to the state planning commission (Gosplan) after the revolution. However, Palchinsky and the two colleagues arrested with him refused to confess; and they were either shot (with or without a secret trial) or died 'during interrogation'.[27] It was not until December 1930 that the OGPU managed to obtain a suitable 'lead' for the second great wrecking trial, the case of the so-called 'Industrial party', headed by Professor Ramzin.

This alleged organization also consisted mainly of former engineers and non-party technicians, but its so-called plans were much more ambitious and far-reaching than those of the leaders accused in the Shakhty trial. Palchinsky was posthumously accorded the honour of leading this group, whose activities were no longer confined to simple counter-revolutionary wrecking and sabotage. The conspirators now included such internationally known foreigners as President Poincaré,* Lawrence of Arabia, and Sir Henry Deterding (an oil magnate), and the plan involved the overthrow of the soviet government and the awarding of handsome concessions to capitalist powers. The leader of the alleged plot, Professor Ramzin, director of the Institute of Heat Engineering, indignantly denied foreign allegations that he and his co-defendants had had their confessions wrested from them by torture: 'Our presence here is sufficient proof that we were not subjected to tortures or torments!'[28] It seems probable that Ramzin actually rehearsed his part, in the manner of the post-war trial in Prague. Within two years of his sentence he had been released from prison; within five he had been fully rehabilitated and restored to office, and awarded the Order of Lenin.[29]

The Industrial party allegedly had a membership of two thousand, though only eight of the 'leaders' appeared at the trial. It was not just a 'centre' of political opposition, but a fully-fledged political party, complete with a central committee (to which five of the defendants were supposed to belong). Not content with infiltrating its saboteurs into practically every industrial plant in the Union, it had also formed links with other arch-enemies of the communists – the so-called 'Working Peasants party' led by the kulaks, with a membership of 200,000, and underground groups in the large cities and agricultural cooperatives. It also had links with the co-called Bureau of Mensheviks, whose 'leaders' were brought to public trial the following year (1931) after two of them had been so badly tortured that they tried to commit suicide.[30] The trial turned out to be one of the GPU's less successful performances as the crucial evidence – the secret visit to Russia by the Menshevik leader Abramovitch – was immediately refuted by news photographs of his appearance at a conference of the Socialist International in Amsterdam.[31]

But the most sensational of the earlier non-communist show-trials was that of a number of British and Russian technicians employed by the Metropolitan-Vickers Company (Metrovick). On 11 March 1933 a number of Metrovick works were raided and six British engineers – Monkhouse, Thornton, Cushny, Macdonald, Nordwall and Gregory – were arrested, together with eleven Russian employees of the firm.

---

*Poincaré's official statement of denial was published in *Pravda*, 3 December 1930, and entered into the official court record.

All were subjected to prolonged interrogation by the GPU, at the end of which two of the Britons – Thornton and Macdonald – and the Russians signed confessions. Under cross-examination during the trial, Thornton repeatedly denied that torture or 'third-degree' methods had been used against him, though like some of the others, he had been subjected to the stress of sleeplessness and prolonged interrogation. Macdonald likewise denied that 'special methods' had been used, or that he had been 'forced' to write his deposition – though when pressed to say why he had signed it, he remained silent.[32]

According to the indictment read at the trial, the accused Russian and British technicians had all been members of a counter-revolutionary group discovered after a number of repeated and sudden breakdowns at power stations in Moscow, Chelyabinsk, Zuevka and Zlatoust. Not only did the group engage in deliberate sabotage with the object of undermining soviet industry and thereby weakening the state; they had also engaged in industrial and military espionage and had bribed soviet state employees to carry out further 'wrecking' activities on their behalf. The charge was supported by the findings of a technical commission of experts which concluded that in all the cases investigated there had either been criminal negligence or deliberate sabotage.*

Following the report of the commission, the Russian chief of the Zlatoust station, V. A. Gussev, was arrested, and after interrogation revealed that he had organized a group of wreckers at the station after receiving money from Macdonald. Under interrogation, Macdonald substantially confirmed Gussev's statements in a signed deposition, in which he revealed that he had been acting on a 'veiled' suggestion of Thornton's made in the summer of 1929 that he should collect information about the production of military supplies, the power situation and

---

*Typical of the commission's findings was its account of sabotage in the Zlatoust electrical power station and metallurgical works in April 1932:

1. The displacement of the stator iron laminations and the subsequent damage to the rotor could take place as a consequence of the presence of an extraneous metallic body in the air gap of the motor. The displacement could take place particularly easily due to the absence of control of the tightening of the bolts which fastened the iron core.

2. The presence of an extraneous piece of iron in the air gap of the motor must lead to the breakdown of the motor, to the deformation of the iron laminations, the perforation of the insulation of the motor, i.e. in the last resort to putting the motor out of action.

3. Under normal working conditions, extraneous pieces of iron cannot work their way into the motor, but can only be introduced into it deliberately.

G. W. Keeton, *The Problem of the Moscow Trial* (London 1933) p. 4.

so forth at the Zlatoust works, and that he should endeavour to inter-
rupt the work at the plant by organizing breakdowns. These activities,
according to the indictment, were linked with a wider system of
espionage organized by British intelligence through the director in
charge of Metrovick operations in Russia, Richards and his chief
engineer, Monkhouse. The fact that both Richards and Monkhouse
had served with the British Expeditionary Forces in Archangel during
the intervention against the Bolsheviks in 1919 gave more than a touch
of plausibility to the charges especially, for the Russian public since it
was never disputed that Richards had been a captain in military intelligence. The chief prosecution witness, Gussev, had also fought on the
White side during the civil war.[33]

Both Thornton and Macdonald repudiated their statements in
court. Of the Englishmen, only Macdonald pleaded guilty. Thornton's
plea of not guilty indicated that he considered the acts admitted in his
confession, almost exclusively the collection of information, to be non-
criminal. Macdonald, who had admitted to wrecking charges in his
deposition, went back on them, and here at least prosecutor Vyshinsky
made no serious attempt to dislodge him. The nearest admission to
wrecking by any of the British defendants was that of Monkhouse, who
did not attempt to deny in court his earlier admission to the OGPU that
there had been defects in some of the equipment supplied by his company. He had even gone so far as to state that if he had been in the Russian service he would not have bought some of the machines supplied
by his firm. But these admissions, which could have been inflated into
charges of sabotage, were not pursued by the prosecutor.[34]

The charges of spying, however, were a different matter. Thornton's
repudiation of his confession, part of which was read out in court, was
unconvincing even to independent observers of the trial. In his signed
deposition Thornton had named twenty-seven members of the company's British staff, including those under arrest, who he claimed had
been engaged in political or economic spying. Some had been engaged
in military espionage as well. Despite his subsequent repudiation of this
document which he claimed he had written 'under great pressure',
Thornton continued to admit during the trial that he had gathered information of a political and economic nature on behalf of the firm.[35]
As an English lawyer who studied the trial records observed:

... Thornton's whole evidence in Court labours under the disability that
these damning admissions had been made before the OGPU, and there was no

way of escape except by repudiating them entirely; but if a complete repudiation was made, he was immediately involved in a network of queries concerning his conduct which automatically brought fresh admissions relating to the collection of information which he could only protest was innocent. Even judged by his evidence in court alone, apart from his confession before the OGPU, Thornton must be regarded as having shown an interest in Soviet power stations which surely transcends that of the normal engineer in Russia.[36]

The problem of espionage, then, was as much one of interpretation as of fact. What Thornton and his fellow engineers might have regarded as a perfectly legitimate activity – the collection of information about general social and political conditions, about other industrial projects and the work of rival firms, all in the interests of the company – could be construed in the minds of the ever-suspicious OGPU men as 'political and economic spying', while the passing on of general gossip about military affairs could be easily inflated into military espionage. Inevitably, ideological questions entered into the choice of definition. Thornton's defence lawyer, Braude, who was far from being the obsequious toady depicted in accounts of the later show-trials, skilfully drew out this aspect in his final plea on Thornton's behalf:

What we in our country, in the land of planned economy, in the country of State trade, call economic espionage is, in the capitalist world, with its anarchy of production, its dominating private trade and dominating private property, the ordinary, everyday, perfectly usual phenomenon of the competitive struggle within capitalist economy. There, every firm, every commercial enterprise tries to discover the secrets of the other firm, of its customers, of its partners, of its competitors, and of its rivals, and it is a great pity that the accused brought into our land of planned economy the methods of the capitalist world and without the slightest doubt studied our industry not only as its customer, but also as its indisputable rival on the world market in the near future.[37]

All the accused, except Gregory, were found guilty. The Britons received relatively light sentences: Thornton three years imprisonment, Macdonald, two; Monkhouse, Nordwall and Cushny were expelled from the Soviet Union for five years. With the lifting of the trade embargo in July 1933, Thornton and Macdonald were deported, having served only a few weeks of their sentences.[38]

Thus by the time Piatakov and his associates appeared in court in 1937, the soviet public must already have become accustomed to the idea that 'saboteurs' and 'foreign agents' were at work in mines and factories and farms, right up to the highest level. As will be suggested in due course, this idea did not arise out of the blue; nor was it simply the invention of cynical toughs in the GPU. There are enough ambiguities in the Metrovick case to suggest that the gist of the charges was believed in by those who made them, at least in the initial stages. What was astonishing was the name of the principal accused: Yuri Piatakov. For more than any other individual (excepting, of course, Stalin), he was credited with the miracle of the first five year plan. Although theoretically subordinate to Stalin's Georgian comrade, Sergo Ordjonikidze – commissar for heavy industry – he was in fact the brains of the department as well as the driving force. A lean, austere man, he was a fanatically hard worker whose dedication and ability had been fully recognized by Lenin, who singled him out for commendation in the famous suppressed 'Testament'. Ordjonikidze did his best to defend his subordinate, but committed suicide when it was clear that his protests were useless.[39]

Piatakov confessed to most – though not all – of the charges, including the particularly outlandish one that he had secretly flown to Norway during one of his visits to Berlin for a meeting with Trotsky. The evidence was soon refuted by the Norwegian authorities (who pointed out that no aircraft had landed during the month of the alleged rendezvous); the German firms who had had dealings with Piatakov deliberately confirmed these obvious errors in his confession to embarrass his accusers.[40] However, during cross-examination, Piatakov explicitly denied that torture or any other pressure had been used against him.[41]

His fellow-accused, Radek, went a good deal further in his self-denunciations, and outstripped the prosecution in the vindictiveness with which he attacked himself and his colleagues for their vile and reptilian treachery; in so doing he subtly undermined the whole of the prosecution's case, by emphasizing how all the evidence against his co-defendants depended, initially, on his own confession – a point on which he was not contradicted. He is even said to have written the record of his own interrogation himself– having rejected the version presented by his interrogator as amateurish and ham-fisted. By all accounts, the finished version was a masterpiece: plausible in its tone of abject surrender for the party faithful, with the hint of irony needed to alert subtler and more sceptical minds. Radek, like Ramzin, was rewarded for his collaboration: whereas all the others were sentenced to death and immediately shot, he received the comparatively light sentence of ten years.

As in the first of the major show-trials, there were plenty of hints in the proceedings to point to the next batch of prominent victims. The 'Red army' group mentioned in the first trial achieved a more concrete form and the famous name of Tukachevsky, the most prestigious of the civil war generals, was dropped (though in an innocent context), as well as the less unexpected names of Bukharin and Rykov – by now fallen in and out of grace a number of times. The Red army generals, however, were never tried in public, a fact which led some NKVD men to suspect that there really had been a plot to get rid of Stalin, who was forced to strike swiftly to pre-empt a military coup. The most likely explanation, however, emerged after the second world war, when it transpired that the Nazis had planted the evidence of Red army treason on the Russians, with results that must have exceeded their wildest dreams – Russia's leading and most experienced generals were shot, and the officer corps of the armed services was decimated.[42]

The last of the great set-pieces was the trial in Moscow of Bukharin, Rykov and nineteen other defendants. They included the third surviving member of Lenin's politburo, Krestinsky; the Ukrainian leader Rakovsky, and Yagoda – former head of the NKVD who now had to pay for his part in the Kirov killing. Chernov, a former commissar for agriculture was also in the dock, as were three eminent doctors charged (in addition to the other plots) with 'medical murders' Maxim Gorky and others.

The third and final great show-trial was by far the most spectacular with so many illustrious leaders in the dock charged with a conspiracy whose ramifications extended into every root, branch and twig of soviet society, not to mention the chancelleries of Britain, Germany, Poland and Japan. To the now familiar accusations of wrecking and sabotage in industry and agriculture, trade and finance were added espionage (in conjunction with the military plotters and foreign intelligence services) as well as complicity in the plan to 'restore capitalism' in conjunction with the Trotskyites, Zinovievites, Rightists, Mensheviks, Social Revolutionaries, and Bourgeois Nationalists. Bukharin, the chief and most illustrious of the accused, was also charged with having planned the murder of Lenin – way back in 1918. The three doctors, who had been thrown into this seething cauldron of iniquity, were charged with the medical murders of the few soviet celebrities who had actually died natural deaths during the past few years – Maxim Gorky; the Old Bolshevik, Kuibyshev; Menzhinsky, the former head of OGPU

– and Gorky's son, Peshkov. The vastness and complexity of the conspiracy could only be appreciated from the huge multicoloured diagram that covered the whole of one wall of the NKVD campaign headquarters:[43] for the indictments against the twenty-one men in the dock were only, of course, the tiny visible tip of the submerged iceberg composed of hundreds of thousands of individuals – party members, intellectuals, workers and peasants, most of whom were never destined to appear in a public court.

Thus one of the defendants at the Bukharin trial, Zelensky, confessed that some fifteen percent of the staff at the central cooperative union 'consisted of former Mensheviks, Socialist Revolutionaries, anarchists, Trotskyites, etc. In certain regions the number of alien elements, former members of other parties, Kolchak officers and so on . . . was considerably higher'. These elements, he said, were assembled to 'act as a centre of attraction for all kinds of anti-Soviet elements'. As Robert Conquest points out, the way in which Zelensky's denunciation would snowball automatically is obvious.[44] Denunciations by 'professional' informers, or forced from people by threats, pressure of interrogation or physical violence, were the means by which the purges extended themselves into every area of soviet society. For every party member, Conquest estimates, eight to ten ordinary citizens were arrested.[45] By mid-1937 practically the entire urban population had become 'purge fodder'. Physical violence had to be introduced in order to process the growing number of prisoners. Prisons were chronically overcrowded, as cells designed for ten to fifteen people were filled with a hundred or more. Prisoners were packed in their cells like sardines, so that when one person moved, everyone had to move with him.[46]

The denunciations were fantastic. 'In one district sixty-nine persons were denounced by one man, in another over a hundred. In Odessa a single communist denounced 230 people. In Poltava a party member denounced his entire organization.'[47] In Kharkov, a secretary of the local medical council denounced all the doctors in the city.[48] A foreign journalist living in a block of about 160 apartments in Moscow noted that arrests had been made in more than half of them. In the office of the newspaper *Izvestia*, as Ilya Ehrenburg noted, they had given up putting nameplates on the doors of the department heads: 'Here today and gone tomorrow,' as the messenger girl explained.[49]

Sometimes prisoners managed to devise ingenious ways of avoiding denouncing the innocent. An Armenian priest named as members of his 'counter-revolutionary organization' all the parishioners he had buried during the past three years.[50] Prisoners sometimes presented each other with lists of 'unused' dead men.[51] A group of Ukrainians played 'hunt the slipper' with a fictitious arms hoard to which one of them had confessed under torture. Each admitted to having passed on the arms to another member of the group, until the last in the line had the inspiration of naming his dead geography teacher. He was rewarded by his interrogator with a good meal and some tobacco.[52] Those already sentenced could be denounced without guilt.[53]

The charges themselves usually belonged to the same world of fantasy. Most of those who came before a court – and there were hundreds of trials, most of them held in camera, all over the Union – were charged under Article 58 of the Criminal Code which designated as counter-revolutionary crimes 'Any act designed to overthrow, undermine or weaken the authority of the workers' and peasants' soviets and the workers' and peasants' government of the [USSR, etc.] . . . and of the basic economic, political and national achievements of the proletarian revolution. . .[54]

The article had long been given the broadest interpretation: a Supreme Court ruling of 1928 had laid down that counter-revolutionary offences were committed 'when the person who committed them, although not directly pursuing a counter-revolutionary aim, wittingly entertained the possibility of this arising or should have forseen the socially dangerous character of his actions'.[55] People were sentenced to three or more years under this article for such charges as smiling in sympathy with anti-soviet anecdotes;[56] for saying, after his arrest, that Marshal Tukachevsky was a handsome man;[57] for failure to inform on others – or for simply being born to a mother of the wrong political party.[58] The wife of an Austrian Jewish physicist, Mrs Weissberg, was charged with secretly inserting swastikas in the pattern of some tea-cups she designed.[59] A Jewish architect faced a similar charge in the shape of a building he designed.[60] A potter designed an ash-tray resembling the zionist star of David.[61] A German communist doctor was charged with injecting patients with VD. A working man was charged with attempting to blow up a bridge across the Dnieper with – of all things – a lump of arsenic.[62] Most of the offenders, of course, were directly involved in the various interlocking conspiracies to destroy communism and restore 'Trotskyite' capitalism; and a great many people were obliged to include in their confessions plans to assassinate

Stalin. Mrs Weissberg, for example, was charged with keeping two pistols under her bed for this purpose.[63]

The numbers of those who perished in the great purges of the 1930s will probably never be known. An informed consensus, including moderate soviet dissidents as well as foreign scholars, accepts a figure of around eight million: and sources in the Italian communist party indicate that this was the figure suggested by the soviet leadership during the period of 'de-Stalinization'. It breaks down, roughly, into four categories: firstly, the 600,000 to 1,000,000, most of them party members, condemned to death and immediately executed, some 40,000 of them on warrants personally signed by Stalin; secondly, an indeterminate number of illegal executions of those sentenced to forced labour 'without right of correspondence', (which appears to have been a ruse, comparable to the Nazi 'deportation' orders, concealing the true rate of execution). The third category comprises an unknown number of prisoners subsequently massacred in the labour camps, as, for example, in the Baikal-Amur area, where some 50,000 prisoners were executed, more or less secretly, during 1937 and 1938.[64] The final group, by far the majority, were those who died of sickness, starvation, exhaustion and exposure under appalling conditions in the labour camps themselves where even the healthiest and most robust could not expect to survive more than ten years. (The most pernicious aspect of the labour camp system was the policy of linking a prisoner's food to the amount of work he did, according to norms apparently established for horses rather than humans.)[65] The cost in human suffering of the Yezhovschina and the surrounding years was in no sense less than that inflicted on humanity by the leaders of the third Reich; in one respect, the cost has been higher, since the régime of terror lasted nearly twice as long as the twelve-year Reich, it has yet to be completely abolished, and its beneficiaries comprise the present leadership of the Soviet Union.

Since the effect of the purge was the destruction of every kind of social solidarity beyond the tightly-knit group of Stalin and his supporters, historians have assumed, *a priori*, that its purpose was intentional. Thus Robert Conquest argues

Right through the purge Stalin's blows were struck at every form of solidarity and comradeship outside that provided by personal allegiance to himself. In general the Terror destroyed personal confidence between private citizens everywhere. The heaviest impact of all was, of course, on the organizational and communal loyalties which still existed in the country after eighteen years of communist rule.[66]

Similarly, it has generally been assumed, excepting of course by latter-day Stalinists who minimize their effects or seek to justify them, that the great show-trials were part of a deliberate 'frame-up' aimed at the destruction of Stalin's former rivals and their followers. Such was the conclusion of the Dewey commission set up in 1938 to investigate the charges against Trotsky, and the only body of a judicial type to have examined them in detail;[67] and a similar assumption runs through most of the more recent accounts of the purges.

On the face of it, the machiavellian version of Stalin's purges obviously fits the facts – so much so, that it is generally accepted without question. Granted that Stalin was, with Yagoda, privy to the Kirov murder, there can be no doubt about his moral responsibility. In the years prior to the murder, Stalin had acquired complete mastery of the party apparatus, including the GPU–NKVD machine. By dominating the central committee and filling it with his own stooges, he undoubtedly used the security apparatus for purely political ends; in Kirov's case, for a criminal purpose as well. Proceeding from these facts, many writers assume that everything that happened was a direct consequence of Stalin's will. The power which sustained the purges originated with the dictator and was forced down into society by means of the 'transmission belts' of the party and security apparatus. Even such politically distinct writers as Robert Conquest, an anti-marxist, and Roy Medvedev, the soviet marxist dissident, share this assumption of Stalin's total responsibility. As Conquest argues, 'The nature of the whole purge depends in the last analysis on the personal and political drives of Stalin.' While, for Medvedev, Stalin's responsibility for perverting the basically sound institutions bequeathed by Lenin and the revolution is the principal theme of his book *Let History Judge*.

The shortcoming of the machiavellian thesis is its failure to explain why the destructive forces unleashed by Stalin encountered so little resistance. It also takes insufficient account of the evidence, which is well documented, that the accusations and denunciations necessary to sustain the purges often originated at local level. Moreover, by stressing the role of judicial malpractices such as torture and forced confessions, it leads to the conclusion that the whole of the security and judicial apparatus was involved in creating a conscious and deliberate 'frame-up' at the behest of one man. While there are elements of truth in this view, (which, admittedly, has been summarized here much more crudely than its authors would like) it is much too simplistic to account for what was at all times a very complex process involving a mixture of credulity and cynicism, faith and fabrication, and above all, the mixing of communist ideas and peasant beliefs. If in the course of this holocaust, probably the greatest in human history, Stalin was to emerge triumphant, it was not because he was its 'architect', but because he understood how to manipulate it. Similarly, the 'totalitarian' system of government in the Soviet Union was less the principle behind the terror than its consequence.

At the trial of Bukharin and others in 1938, all the accused admitted their guilt except Krestinsky, who unexpectedly told the judge: 'I do not admit my guilt. I am not a Trotskyite. I never took part in the "Right-Trotskyite Bloc" and was not aware of its existence. I never committed a single one of the crimes imputed to me, and in particular I do not confess myself guilty of contacts with German intelligence'.[68] The judge adjourned the proceedings for twenty minutes, and after the recess the order of questioning was changed. Instead of continuing with Krestinsky, Vyshinsky, the prosecutor, examined Bessonov, a former diplomat in Germany alleged to have been the link between Krestinsky and Trotsky. Bessonov admitted the charge and when the prosecutor mentioned Krestinsky's denial, Bessonov smiled.

'Why are you smiling?' asked Vyshinksy.

'The reason I am standing here,' Bessonov replied, 'is that Nikolay Nikolayevitch Krestinsky named me as the liaison man with Trotsky. Besides him and Piatakov, nobody knew about this.'[69]

Krestinsky continued to maintain his innocence under strong pressure from Vyshinsky. Finally, Vyshinsky asked Krestinsky why he had gone back on the testimony he had given during his preliminary investigation. Krestinsky's reply produced a 'shocked hush' from the audience: 'I simply considered that if I were to say what I am saying today – that it was not in accordance with the facts – my declaration would not reach the ears of the party and the government'.[70] At the afternoon session of the same day, Krestinsky stood by his retraction. But the following afternoon, when further evidence was given against him, Krestinsky gave in and affirmed the original deposition he had made at the preliminary investigation, admitting his guilt. Asked why he had engaged in 'Trotskyite provocation' by denying his guilt, he replied that he had affirmed his innocence 'mechanically':

> I didn't have the strength to tell world public opinion the truth, that I have all this time been carrying out Trotskyite work against the Soviet regime. I ask the court to record my declaration that I wholly and completely confess myself guilty of all the serious accusations made against me, and I confess myself completely responsible for the betrayal and treason done by me.[71]

There are various accounts of the pressures which made Krestinsky withdraw his retractions and return to his original confession. According to one version, he was tortured so badly that his left shoulder was dislocated – an injury that would not have been noticed while he was sitting in the dock.[72] Other versions say he was faced with very bright lights that damaged his already injured eyes. Bessonov, the principal witness against him, was also, it seems, tortured during the preliminary investigation. Roy Medvedev, the historian, records that Bessonov told a man with whom he shared a cell in 1938 that he had been subjected to seventeen days continuous interrogation by relays of examiners, without food or sleep. Whenever he fell down, he would be forced to stand up again. This system, known as the 'conveyer' was the most widely used form of pressure; Bessonov was also seriously beaten on the kidneys.[73]

Yet despite these allegations, which seem plausible enough in the light of other evidence, it is clear that none of the principals in the show-trials capitulated solely or even primarily as a result of torture or physical pressures amounting to torture. Moral and psychological factors predominated. From Bessonov's own testimony in the trial, it would seem that his breaking point arrived when Krestinsky denounced him during the preliminary investigation. The resentments resulting from these betrayals, regardless of the pressures that induced them, were the source of bitterness inspiring further accusations and of a sense of guilt that undermined the capacity of many individuals to resist. In general, the reasons for the capitulation of the old Bolsheviks are complex, and cannot be attributed to any single cause, least of all to purely mechanical methods of torture or 'brainwashing'. Physical pressures were employed very widely in Russia during the thirties, especially after they were formally authorized by Stalin after 1937. But they cannot be treated in isolation, as something separate and distinct from the general psychosis that gripped soviet society during this period.

Blackmail and extortion were widely used. Zinoviev and Kamenev had given in on the understanding that Stalin would spare their lives if they cooperated at the trial. In any case, Zinoviev was already a sick man, and his health was not improved by the rigours of prison, especially when the NKVD turned on the heating in his cell, though it was mid-July.[74] Moreover he was promised that his former supporters, who numbered thousands, would be spared. Wives and relatives were used as hostages. At one point during the preliminary investigation Kamenev's interrogator ostentatiously picked up the telephone and ordered his son's arrest.[75] Smirnov was persuaded to capitulate by his former wife, on the understanding that she would be spared.[76] Rykov was a heavy drinker, an easy subject for manipulation.[77] Before the first trial, Stalin had subtly raised the expectations of the accused that their death sentences would, after all, be commuted, by restoring right of appeal which had been suspended under the anti-terrorist decrees.[78] In the event, all the accused were shot. But this did not prevent the defendants at the second (Piatakov) trial from lying to save their families. Radek's virtuoso performance saved him (though he was destined to perish under a later wave of shootings); Piatakov died, but his wife and child were spared, and the same went for Bukharin, who had married late in life and had a young family.[79] Krestinsky had a fifteen-year-old daughter.[80] It should not be forgotten, of course, that several other leaders refused to capitulate, and died in dignified silence. They included Bela Kun, leader of the Hungarian communist rising of 1919 and Budu Mdivani, the Georgian leader.[81]

It would be wrong to conclude that physical pressures were the main reasons for the capitulation of the old Bolshevik leaders between 1936 and 1938. In most cases, it was the *moral* pressure that was decisive – the belief that by confessing their 'crimes' the accused were performing a necessary service to the party and the soviet state. Many years after Bukharin's death his widow, Larina, gave an account of his final interview with Stalin shortly before his arrest. Bukharin had been on hunger strike in protest against the accusations that were being made against him in the party and in the press. When he appeared before the central committee, it was Molotov who took the lead in denouncing him. According to his widow, Bukharin said:

'I am not Zinoviev or Kamenev, and I will not tell lies against myself!'
'If you don't confess,' replied Molotov, 'that will prove you're a fascist hire-

ling. Their press is saying that our trials are provocations. We'll arrest you and you'll confess!'

'What a trap!' Bukharin exclaimed, before returning home.[82]

Blackmail was moral as well as physical. In the last resort the old party leaders believed they had to cooperate because not to do so would have confirmed the accusations of the enemies of the soviet state. With the growing danger of war with Germany, an attack on Stalin would amount to collaboration with the enemy. In Bukharin's case, especially, this attitude may have some historical justification. As it was, General Vlasov, who went over to the Nazis, was able to raise an army from among disgruntled soviet prisoners, while nationalists in the Ukraine collaborated wholeheartedly with the Nazis. Bukharin's endorsement of the Stalin line, his repeated insistence that opposition to the régime led 'objectively' to counter-revolution and collaboration with fascist and foreign intelligence services, exemplified by his own conduct, was the last gesture of a man who remained a devout patriot as well as revolutionary.

The view that in confessing the accused leaders were performing a 'last service to the party' – essentially the thesis developed in Koestler's masterly novel *Darkness at Noon* – is much nearer the truth than the lurid accounts of torture and 'brainwashing'. Some of the smaller fry, such as Bessonov, may have been physically tortured. But suggestions of drugs and hypnosis – which Medvedev thinks worth consideration – sound very far-fetched. Similar tales were circulated at the time of the Metrovick trial to account for the behaviour of Thornton and Macdonald. They proved to have been without foundation. The 'general inertia and sluggishness' of the prisoners at the Bukharin trial, noted by Ilya Ehrenburg, are sufficiently explained by sleeplessness and general stress. Citing Ehrenburg, Medvedev states that the prisoners '. . . gave their testimony in a kind of mechanical language, without the intonation and temperament peculiar to each of them. Although each one used some of his stylistic peculiarities, for the most part they used the language of an average office clerk, with turns of speech that they had never employed previously'.[83]

In the case of some of the defendants this may have been so; but most certainly not in the case of Bukharin whose strategy, to which he held with absolute consistency throughout the trial, was to acknowledge his overall responsibility for the actions of the 'bloc' while refuting most of the specific charges of sabotage and terrorism which the prosecution tried to pin on him. In this, according to one of the most perceptive of the foreign observers of the trial, he 'displayed all his old dialectical skill' despite a twenty-four hour recess evidently called to 'induce in him a more amenable frame of mind'.[84] The official record substantiates this view: not only does Bukharin sometimes embarrass the president, Ulrich, by giving an all too candid and plausible account of his past 'errors' – to the point where they might be construed as an apologia for the opposition's views and by implication an indictment of Stalin's policies; he even succeeds, on one occasion at least, in muddling the usually clear-headed and quick-thinking Vyshinsky.

Bukharin's attitude displays a princely arrogance more reminiscent of Milton's Lucifer than the brainwashed zombies of Orwellian nightmare.

> ... I want to say that I was not one of the cogs of the counter-revolution, but one of the leaders of the counter-revolution; and as one of the leaders I play and answer in a far greater degree, bear far greater responsibility than any of the cogs. And so I cannot be suspected of wanting to wriggle out of or repudiate responsibility, even if I were not a member of the Right and Trotskyite organization. The court and the public opinion of our country, like the public opinion of other countries, as far as progressive mankind is concerned, can judge how people sank to such depths, how we all became rabid counter-revolutionaries, traitors to the Socialist fatherland, and how we turned into spies, terrorists and restorers of capitalism, and what, in the end, were the ideas and political standpoint of the 'bloc of Rights and Trotskyites'.[85]

So far, for the prosecution, so good. But when it came to specific charges of terrorism and sabotage, Bukharin was harder to pin down. One of the accusations, for example, concerned an alleged attempt at a coup d'état with the help of Abel Yenukidze, Stalin's fellow-Georgian and one-time commander of the Kremlin guard. Tomsky, the head of the trades unions and Rykov, prime minister, were supposed to have been involved. Bukharin admitted the general intention, but since the coup had never occurred, attempted to explain why:

BUKHARIN: The inception of the idea of a coup d'état among us Right conspirators relates approximately to the years 1929–30 and at that time this coup d'état in its embryo form was conceived, or rather was spoken of as a coup d'état on a relatively narrow basis. I would say that it was an idea of a circumscribed coup d'état, or rather, of a 'palace coup'.

VYSHINSKY: What is the meaning of the expression 'palace coup'? Am I to understand that this means the direct seizure of power by the forces of your bloc?

BUKHARIN: Absolutely correct: politically – by the forces of the bloc. But why do I say 'palace coup'? This means by forces organizationally concentrated in the Kremlin.

VYSHINSKY: By such forces as would prove to be at your disposal, but not necessarily by forces that were in the Kremlin?

BUKHARIN: Absolutely correct.

VYSHINSKY: Then would it not be better to speak not of a 'palace coup', but of an attempt to seize power by means of an armed uprising?

BUKHARIN: No, it is not quite correct to speak of an armed uprising.

VYSHINSKY: Why not? You wished to seize power with arms in hand?

BUKHARIN: An armed uprising is a mass affair, while here it was a matter of a narrower . . .

VYSHINSKY: What masses? you had no masses with you.

BUKHARIN: Consequently it is not an uprising.[86]

Vyshinsky, no doubt, objects to the term 'palace coup,' for its obvious tsarist overtones. By doing so, he exposes a crucial weakness in the prosecution case. 'Armed uprising', according to Marxist theory, demands mass support. Such a situation must imply mass discontent with Stalin's rule.

The whole passage in fact illuminates one of the contradictions that runs like a fissure through the mountains of evidence. How was it that, with the tentacles of the grand Trotskyite–Bukharinite conspiracy reaching into the innermost circles of power, the party and its leader, Stalin, managed to survive? The vigilance of the security organs in uncovering the threads of conspiracy does not provide an answer; for is not Yagoda, former chief of the OGPU, the self-confessed murderer of Kirov, of Gorky and Mendzhinsky, now facing the People's Judges in the dock? Yagoda's confession is part of the crucial evidence of the prosecutor. Both Bukharin and Rykov denied knowing anything about the plans for assassinating Kirov. Yet here was Yagoda, who we now know was certainly one of the real participants in the Kirov murder-conspiracy, directly accusing them:

YAGODA: Both Bukharin and Rykov are telling lies. Rykov and Yenukidze were present at the meeting of the centre where the question of assassinating S. M. Kirov was discussed.[87]

The Kirov murder worked through Yagoda and Yenukidze's complicity. Why not the 'palace coup', which would have also have been carried out on Yenukidze's instructions? Despite denying direct involvement in the former case, one can see why Bukharin, anxious to preserve theoretical and logical consistency, felt it necessary to explain why the 'palace coup' was never carried out.

A similar contradiction occurs in the area of sabotage. The presence of nests of saboteurs in every industrial and agricultural organization was clearly upsetting to the image of Stalinist Russia as a proletarian paradise where, free at last from exploitation, the happy workers and peasants were hard at work breaking every norm of production. Indeed, with so many men in key posts secretly pledged to the enemy, it was difficult to see how anything can have functioned properly. This problem was especially evident in the second (Piatakov) show-trial in 1937, in which sabotage allegations were prominent. One of the accused at this trial was Livshitz, assistant commissar for railways who, despite his secret Trotskyite activities in engineering train-wrecks, also had to carry out his official duties with apparent efficiency. This resulted in a curious exchange:

LIVSHITZ: ... It must not be thought that as assistant People's Commissar I was engaged only in wrecking work, in that only.

VYSHINSKY: No, of course, not in that only.

LIVSHITZ: I also performed useful work. I do not want to talk about that now, because that is not the question ...

VYSHINSKY: I put that question, I said that in relation to Order no. 183 of the People's Commissar, you should have, as I understand it ...

LIVSHITZ: Yes, and not everything I did in connection with Order no. 183 was to disrupt it.

VYSHINSKY: And why did you not do everything to disrupt it when that was your aim, when you organized people to disrupt it, when you gave these people instructions to disrupt it? Why did you not do everything to disrupt it, but did some things not to disrupt it? Why?

LIVSHITZ: If I did all that alone, I might be in a position to decide to disrupt everything. But millions, thousands of people are working on the railways.

VYSHINSKY: That is, it did not depend upon you?

LIVSHITZ: And not only because it did not depend upon me. I repeat, not everything I did was bad.

VYSHINSKY: What induced you to do something good? After all, you were a member of the Trotskyite organization and did that organization set itself the aim of doing good work on the railways, or disruptive work?

LIVSHITZ: Disruptive work.

VYSHINSKY: That was your aim? Naturally, you could not do everything in pursuit of this aim; you could not destroy everything. Why?

LIVSHITZ: The aim was not to destroy the railway system to such an extent as to bring it to a standstill.

VYSHINSKY: What aim did you set yourselves?
LIVSHITZ: To complicate and hamper the work of the railways.[88]

Here, as in the Bukharin trial, it is the accused, rather than the prosecutor, who tries to bridge over the ludicrous disparity between the aims of the conspirators and their negligible results.

Such discrepancies and contradictions in the evidence raise the following question: if the show-trials are really to be understood in terms of a judicial frame-up, why are there so many contradictions in the evidence? In the post-war show-trial of Löbl and Slansky in Czechoslovakia, for instance, all those who appeared in the dock had learned their parts by heart like actors after repeated rehearsals.[89] But, as we have seen, deliberate and conscious fabrication, with physical and moral blackmail, do not adequately explain either the confessions or the charges themselves in Russia. An element of conscious guilt, of voluntary submission, was there in the case of Bukharin and it was his determination to prove to the court that it was his heresy according to the judgement of history, not any squalid involvement in minor criminal conspiracies, that had brought him into the dock. The other charges – murder, terrorism and wrecking – he either forcefully denied (as in the plots to murder Lenin and Kirov) or dismissed with the telling phrase that he had not been concerned with 'dotting the i's'.[90] The prosecution went to great lengths to dot the i's by pinning specific charges on him, but one cannot conclude from a reading of the transcripts that they were successful. Bukharin, subtly triumphing over Vyshinsky, emerges as his own best prosecutor.

Bukharin, of course, was exceptionally tough-minded: we do not find the same arrogance in Rykov or in Chernov, the former commissar for agriculture. In his case, the i's are diligently dotted:

The chief task assigned to me by the German intelligence service at that time was to arrange to spoil grain within the country. This involved delaying the construction of storehouses and elevators, so as to create a discrepancy between the growing size of the grain collections and the available storage space. In this way, Scheffer [the German agent] said, two things would be achieved: firstly, the grain itself would be spoilt; and secondly, the indignation of the peasants would be aroused, which was inevitable when they saw that grain was perishing. I was also asked to arrange for the wholesale contamination of storehouses by pests, especially by corn-beetle ... The German intelligence service made a special point of the organization of wrecking activities in the sphere of horse-breeding in order ... not to provide horses for the Red Army. As regards seed, we included in our programme muddling up seed affairs, mixing up sorted seed and thus lowering the harvest yield in the country. As regards crop rotation, the idea was to plan the crop area incorrectly and thus place the collective farm peasants in such a position that they would be virtually unable to practise proper crop rotation and would be obliged to plough up meadows and pastures for crop growing. This would reduce the size of harvests in the country and at the same time rouse the indignation of the peasants, who would be unable to understand why they were being forced to plough up meadows and pastures when the collective farms wanted to develop stock-breeding and required fodder for the purpose.

As regards the machine tractor stations, the aim was to put tractors, harvester combines and agricultural machines out of commission, to muddle the financial affairs of the machine and tractor stations, and for this purpose to place at the machine and tractor stations useless people, people with bad records, and above all members of our Right organization.

As regards stock-breeding, the aim was to kill off pedigree breed stock and to strive for a high cattle mortality ... to prevent the development of fodder resources and especially to infect cattle artificially with various kinds of bacteria in order to increase their mortality .... I instructed Ginsburg [chief of the veterinary department] and Boyarshinov, Chief of the Bacteriological Department, to artificially infect pigs with erysipelas in the Leningrad region and with plague in the Voronezh region and the Azov–Black Sea Territory. I chose these two bacteria because the pigs are inoculated not with dead microbes, but with live ones, only of a reduced virulence. It was therefore quite simple from the technical standpoint to organize artificial infection ...

For this purpose, three factories were selected at my suggestion ... In these factories serums were made with virulent bacteria and given special serial numbers. Boyarshinov was informed of these serial numbers and he transmitted them to the chiefs of veterinary departments in the localities who could be relied on in this matter, and they in turn transmitted them to veterinary surgeons who had anti-Soviet feelings and who in case of a heavy cattle mortality would not raise a big fuss.[91]

What is particularly striking about Chernov's statement is its lunatic coherence. In stark contrast to Bukharin, Chernov not only sings in harmony with Vyshinsky, he invests his statement with plausible details drawn from his experience as commissar for agriculture. It is through his own bureaucracy that he transmits the secret instructions of German intelligence. All that is necessary is to know where other members of the right organization stand in the departmental network, that they may change the serial numbers on the appropriate batches of serum, initiate the appropriate acts of maladministration and so forth. The disasters themselves – the destruction of seed grain, the livestock epidemics, the failure of agricultural machinery – were not inventions, they actually occurred, as a consequence of maladministration, incompetence, or plain ignorance among the peasants. Such things were the consequence, possibly unavoidable, of a sudden agrarian revolution in a backward country. As many commentators have pointed out, men like Piatakov and Chernov who were in charge of industry and agriculture during the first five-year plan, when so many such disasters must have occurred, were put in the role of scapegoats. The rational aim of the show-trials, so it would seem, was to load on their shoulders all the failures of the five-year plan, while Stalin and his friends could reserve for themselves all the credit.

Such no doubt was Stalin's intention. However, there was more to these charges than a deliberate and cynical motivated conspiracy by Stalin and his henchmen to frame certain high officials into becoming scapegoats for the inevitable failures in his policies. The public trials were not confined to Moscow. As Medvedev points out, 'Almost every republic, *oblast* (region) and even *raion* (district) had its own "open" trial'. He argues that since it was usually the same officials – the local party secretaries, directors of machine tractor stations, collective farm chairmen, senior agronomists, and so forth – who were put on trial, a uniform scheme must have been worked out at the centre, implying, it would seem, that the local judicial bodies were acting under direct orders from Stalin.[92] While this may be true of the actual legal processes, it does not account for the nature of the 'wrecking' charges, or explain why they were so readily accepted at local level. If it is assumed *a priori* that the régime of terror was already total, the fact that the officials were acting under orders on pain of themselves being executed would provide an adequate explanation. But there is evidence to suggest that this was not the case. On the contrary, the charges do not necessarily seem to have originated in Moscow – which merely issued from time to time general directives to seek out 'enemies of the people'.[93] What they really seem to have represented was the struggle for power at local level. This in itself is enough to account for the fact that it was usually the same officials who found themselves put on trial.

The trials of local officials were usually preceded by expulsion from the party at local open purging sessions. Purges had been conducted fairly regularly since 1921, after it became apparent that the Bolsheviks as the ruling party in a one-party state were attracting careerist and self-seeking elements. After Trotsky's defeat in 1924, the party was purged of his supporters, while in 1928 the first purge of rightists occurred after Stalin's *volte face* in favour of collectivization and industrialization. From 1933 onwards, after the disastrous effects of collectivization became apparent, the party was in an almost continuous state of purgation prompted by a commission headed by Yezhov.[94] In theory it was the purge rather than the NKVD apparatus that constituted the main instrument of Stalin's dictatorship over the party. In practice the situation was rather more confused, since the complexity of relations between the party and the internal security apparatus both at national and local level was considerable.[95] Until the mid-thirties party members were immune from arrest until expulsion; and even afterwards they continued to enjoy, theoretically at least, the right to appeal to higher party organs in cases of wrongful arrest. The theoretical limitations on the NKVD have an important bearing on the conduct of interrogation, indicating a voluntary element behind the investigation of party members who had not yet been expelled. The party purge was an important line of defence for party members faced with expulsion and subsequent arrest.

Although the purging commissions nominated by Stalin exercised a considerable influence on the proceedings, the evidence available does not suggest that their control was absolute. In certain cases they might decide in advance that a particular individual should be expelled, and here they would have no difficulty in dominating the decisions of the 'open' session – by producing, for example, incriminating evidence unknown to rank and file colleagues, or compromising documents. But this treatment certainly did not apply to every case, indeed probably only a minority were singled out for purging in advance. The whole purpose of the open session from a Stalinist point of view was to manipulate existing animosities in the villages, the factories, the scientific and educational institutions, with the object of flushing out deviations or potential deviations from within the party rank and file. Far from depending on an 'omniscient', 'omnipotent' police state apparatus for its efficacy, the party purges testify to the absence of both. The totalitarian state was the ultimate consequence of a system which originated not in the fear inspired in ordinary citizens by men in uniform but in the unrestricted scope given to the petty vindictiveness of ordinary men and women under conditions of social stress.

A sufficient number of accounts of the party purges have become available to indicate that the system had its positive side. In the absence of a functioning electoral system the purges provided the means by which the party rank and file were able to air their grievances against the local leaders and their coteries or 'family circles'. The central control commission which organized the purges at the all-Union level had been created to counter 'bureaucratizing' tendencies within the party apparatus, and although Stalin appears to have succeeded into converting it into a weapon of autocracy by using it to enforce the party line at regional and district level, it never ceased to maintain its original purpose. Like the OGPU–NKVD itself – the 'eyes and ears' of the party – it had the positive function of exposing corruption and inadequacies within the system in addition to the negative one of rooting out dissent.

A valuable source of information about party purges is the Smolensk archive, captured by the Germans during the second world war and later taken to the United States. These documents, which have been summarized by Professor Merle Fainsod of Harvard University, provide a candid and, so far as one can judge, unbiased account of the life and work of the party in this part of the Soviet Union during the period between the revolution and the second world war. They are the only records not intended for publication which have become available in the West. The picture of the purging process they present leaves a distinctively different impression from the accounts of events as viewed from the centre in Moscow.

They abound with reports of local party leaders abusing their position of trust, feathering their nests at state expense and sharing the spoils with friends and relatives or 'family circles' as they were known. This evil was particularly prevalent in rural districts, where communist power was traditionally weak and where, like it or not, the authorities had been bound to collaborate with the wealthier and more influential peasants or kulaks until they were destroyed in the upheaval of collectivization.[96] The purge in fact was a necessary accompaniment to the 'de-kulakization'. For it is obvious that the party's radical change of tack on the agrarian question involved the wholescale uprooting of the network of vested interests that had developed throughout the soviet state in nearly twenty years of communist rule. The upheaval within the party was by no means restricted to the villages, where local party cells could be expected to sympathize with those peasants – often influential rather than wealthy – who were designated as 'kulaks'. But outside the capital cities, the ties between the towns and countryside were still very strong. Indeed, Marxist distinctions between 'workers' and 'peasants' had little psychological significance where the overwhelming majority of factory workers were emigrants from the countryside, or the children of emigrants. The change of tack necessitated the purging of any elements who might be disloyal to the new policy and, given the social realities, that meant practically everybody. So, in effect, the party purges became a free-for-all in which anyone could be expelled provided a sufficient number of his fellow members harboured a grudge against him.

An illustration of this process is provided by a case history dating from 1937 in the Smolensk archive. It concerns the decline and fall of the party secretary in the Belyi district (in the Smolensk region), a man by the name of Kovalev who up to then enjoyed much power in his district. The first signs of trouble came when he had to face considerable but indirect criticism at a meeting of his local executive called to discuss a resolution of the central committee urging a revival of intra-party democracy and strict observance of the rules governing party elections. Shortly afterwards, at a general meeting of the district party organization, chaired by Golovashenko, a member of the regional committee, the whole question of Kovalev's tenure of office was raised. The session, which went on for four days, was attended by some two hundred and twenty members and candidate members.

The meeting was opened by Kovalev with a report on the February plenum. Immediately afterwards his former colleagues and subordinates moved in to the attack. The first speaker, the director of accounting courses, condemned the report as contrary to the Party line. He denounced Kovalev as a dictator who constantly abused his subordinates and accused him of holding Trotskyite views. Others joined in the attack, most of them men who had been closest to the party secretary. One of them charged him with having deserted the Red Army during the civil war. Many others piled up evidence of his abusive and dictatorial conduct. The only reservations came from the rank and file. As the chairman of one of the village soviets put it: 'Everyone now blames Kovalev – but why, if it's all true, didn't they do something about it?'

In contrast to these attacks, the speech of the regional representative, Golovashenko, was relatively moderate and responsible in tone. He criticized Kovalev for his poor leadership, his bad attendance record at district and town party meetings and for co-opting too many members of his district committee. But he refused to associate himself with the charge of Trotskyism. 'Personally,' he said, 'I do not have sufficient basis to call Kovalev a Trotskyite. We need to understand what a Trotskyite is – an agent of fascism, a restorer of capitalism, who must be destroyed as an enemy of the working class.' The evidence must be investigated and, in the meantime, a new party secretary appointed. In his final speech, Kovalev admitted his shortcomings, which, he said, had been made clear to him by Rumyantsev, the Smolensk party leader. The onslaught he had just suffered had been a sad experience to live through. But, apart from his admitted shortcomings, his record was clear. He had fought in the Red Army as a volunteer in the civil war. He had never been a Trotskyite, nor had he ever had any connection with such groups. He promised to remedy his deficiences. The meeting concluded with a resolution listing his shortcomings and removing him from his post. His duties were temporarily assigned to Karpovsky, the second secretary.

Karpovsky, however, was not destined to hold on to his job for long. At first, the district committee requested that an outsider be appointed by the Obkom (regional party) leadership, there being an understandable reluctance among the local party leaders to take on such a hazardous responsibility; but the man appointed was rejected, despite Karpovsky's own recommendation, and Karpovsky was eventually appointed instead. Meanwhile, the regional party boss, Rumyantsev, had fallen in a storm of sabotage and wrecking allegations at the Smolensk headquarters, where a special resolution of the plenum made it clear that the 'unmasking' of the top men was only beginning, and that agents and wreckers in the district would also be rooted out. The hysteria soon spread to Belyi, where Kovalev's former colleagues began to denounce each other in an endeavour to dissociate themselves from him.

'One by one [writes Merle Fainsod] those who had held high office ... under Kovalev found themselves compromised and victimised by the association.' Karpovsky's turn came at a meeting of the raikom in September 1937. It was chaired by Frolov, editor of the local party newspaper, with Shirozyan, the regional representative, in attendance:

The material on Karpovsky was read. He was accused of having been an agent in the raion of the former Oblast leadership, of having once been a participant in a bandit gang, of having relatives abroad, of maintaining connections with a sister who had married a former merchant, and of continuing his contacts to the last with 'enemies of the people'.... Karpovsky tried in vain to counter the accusations. He denied any relationship with enemies of the people. He claimed instead to have been a member of a band, he had participated in the extermination of one and had himself killed two bandits. He admitted receiving a letter from an aunt in Rumania, but insisted that he had never met her since she had left Russia in 1908, when she married a Rumanian. He acknowledged that his sister had married a former merchant, but pointed out that they were both now employed in useful work. One brave friend, a Comrade Moskalev, even rose to Karpovsky's defence and testified that they had participated together in the liquidation of 'bands', but all the explanations and denials proved wasted breath. Karpovsky was unanimously excluded from the party, and Frolov was temporarily charged with performing the duties of first secretary.

The wave of denunciations and recriminations gathered momentum. At a general meeting of the raion party organization the following day,

> speaker after speaker denounced Karpovsky as a bandit, and even the loyal friend who had testified that they fought together against bandits, and who now found himself attacked on all sides, said weakly that he had not known that Karpovsky belonged to a band. Shirozyan, the Obkom representative, charged that Karpovsky had been sent into the raion by the old leadership to protect Kovalev's cadres, that there were still many enemies in the raion, and that it was necessary to eliminate them. The meeting obliged with a new hail of denunciations and expulsions. Now the heat turned on Frolov, who was accused of displaying 'liberalism' and of having been closely associated with Karpovsky ... [Later] Frolov was removed as second secretary, but was left temporarily to serve as editor of the raion newspaper while a commission investigated his past. A new second and a new third secretary were chosen ... By the end of the year 1937, a completely new team had taken over in Belyi, and they were all strangers to the raion.[97]

Two points emerge from this account of obscure party meetings in an obscure district of the Union. The first is that the denunciatory pressures came mainly from below; the second, that the Obkom representative, the most senior party member present, played a relatively passive role in the proceedings, and on the first occasion especially, the removal of Kovalev, exercised a moderating influence. In the second instance, the removal and expulsion of Karpovsky, one senses that the Obkom representative, Shirozyan himself, joins in the denunciations because he cannot any longer exercise restraint, afraid as he is of his own position in the Obkom (where, no doubt, he is subject to the same kind of pressure Karpovsky is facing at this meeting).

One explanation for the hysterical vindictiveness of the denunciations that cannot be sustained is that the raikom men are simply afraid of their superiors in the Obkom, that their actions are dictated by blind obedience to party orders. After the removal of Kovalev, the district executive requests the Obkom to send 'an experienced worker who will work better than Kovalev' as the new first secretary, but the Obkom candidate makes a 'bad impression' in the district party, and they turn him down. Regional headquarters is obliged to accept this rebuff without demur.[98] This episode as well as the torrent of denunciations directed against each of the local party leaders in turn suggest something different from the idea of a totalitarian police state where every move is under the eye of the secret police. On the contrary, the terror at this level is primarily a revolutionary process, in which the older generation of leaders is being continually denounced by former colleagues and rank and file members determined to remove and possibly replace them. From this point of view, the purge is the logical outcome of a revolution with a *self-styled* revolutionary party, where the rising social forces cannot form themselves under an independent revolutionary label for the obvious reason that to do so would expose them to the charge of being 'counter-revolutionary'. Nor, for the same reason, can the whole of the old hierarchy be attacked *en bloc*. The result is a local guerrilla campaign against individuals within the apparatus, using the weapon of denunciation and the classic tactics of Bolshevism – the merciless dictatorship of the majority at party meetings, where the losers are given no quarter and are cast into outer darkness.

So much for the denunciations. But what of the actual charges, the allegations of 'terrorism' and 'sabotage'? It is customary to assume that these and similar charges which were admitted by defendants in the show-trials were part of a deliberate attempt by Stalin to 'frame' certain high officials into becoming scapegoats for his disastrous policies. This, though partly true, is a superficial view. Stalin was certainly instrumental in having such charges heard in a public court, and there is no doubt that he took advantage of them to divert the blame from himself. But the propaganda campaign that made 'sabotage' and 'wrecking' accusations part of the normal currency of social relations in the farm and on the shop floor was not something that he conjured out of the fiendish resources of his imagination. There is evidence that those who made the accusations believed in them. The assumption that anyone even suspected of opposing official decisions, for whatever reasons, was guilty of 'sabotage' had been deeply ingrained in post-revolutionary society. And just as the bitter polemics of the leaders had resulted in mass arrests of oppositionists, so the sabotage and wrecking allegations had developed out of the combat rhetoric of the civil war years, when acts of sabotage had really happened.* The assumption was embodied in the legal code, as well as in official documents.[99] The idea of sabotage was certainly very far from being the invention of a few senior NKVD officers, who then transmitted it down the totalitarian telephone wires. One such allegation was made at the height of the 1937 purge against Victor Kravchenko, a rising young soviet industrialist, whose defection to the West in 1944 and publication of memoirs caused a major political storm in France in the 1950s. It illustrates among other things a fact that is almost invariably overlooked: that it was possible for an individual falsely accused to vindicate himself by providing documentary evidence in refutation of the charges – something which would have been impossible if the NKVD had been as unconcerned with the veracity of the charges as is usually made out.

Kravchenko's ordeal began in November 1936, at a meeting in the industrial complex at Nikopol, where he was the head of the pipe-rolling sub-plant. His first denunciation came from a colleague, and concerned his father's Menshevik background.[100] A second denunciation was clearly activated by social resentment and jealousy (Kravchenko had achieved a high position in the plant at an early age): 'Kravchenko is a doubter!... At the Institute, he criticized collectivization. Everyone knows that much. And the same at the factory, always a long face, nothing to his grand taste!... Why has he such a high position at all? Because he has his friends in Moscow and in Kharkov! Not ability but connections!'[101]

Finally Yudavin, an NKVD agent (according to Kravchenko), makes his sabotage accusation from the floor – but not before he has established that there is a strong current of opinion hostile to Kravchenko at the meeting:

Yes, a saboteur! This Kravchenko has deliberately frozen a million roubles worth of Soviet currency and any amount of foreign *valuta*. How did he do it? A simple device, much too simple! He has ordered all sorts of expensive instruments and piled them up at his sub-plant. His department is jammed up with

---

*The most celebrated instance of sabotage during the civil war was the flooding of the Donetz coal mines by the White armies of General Denikin.

costly machine-parts, none of which are ever used. Some of it has never been unpacked! I charge that this is all deliberate and calculated to do harm to the government and the country![102]

Kravchenko fights off this accusation, giving plausible reasons why there is expensive and unused machinery at his sub-plant, and the meeting accepts a compromise proposal: Kravchenko retains his job and party membership while a commission investigates his case. Next day he finds himself pilloried in the local newspapers – another indication that the purges still retained a 'democratic' or populist character, at least at this level – for the newspaper editor, usually an important party official, evidently awaits the outcome of the party meeting before giving his approval to the attacks. There are further meetings, in which the campaign against Kravchenko gathers momentum; at the same time, a reaction develops in his favour. Most of the 'establishment' at the Nikopol plant – representing the soviet technocracy of senior engineers and managers – are on his side. They commit themselves to his cause, and know they themselves will fall if he does. The issue turns on whether Kravchenko can produce copies of documents proving that the orders for his equipment were a legitimate consequence of higher planning decisions. After weeks of anxious searching, he finds the documents, and for the present at least the case against him is dropped.[103]

Kravchenko's book was denounced by western communists as a blatant fabrication (a charge they failed to substantiate in a Paris court) and has been widely considered primarily as a work of propaganda. In fact, though the tone is often smug and self-congratulatory (one finds it sometimes hard to believe the author's continual claims that he somehow managed to survive those years without denouncing anyone while at the same time keeping out of prison), the facts correspond with what is known from more reliable sources, such as the Smolensk archive. The essential point that both sources reveal is that the denunciations that look so outrageous in the context of the show-trials were standard terms of abuse in the struggle in the villages and the factories. There is no reason to believe that those who made them at this level necessarily made them in bad faith.

Part of the invective behind the charges of course can be put down to the rhetoric with which a rising layer of the bureaucracy hoped to challenge the entrenched position of its superiors. But the underlying malice does not account for their fantastic nature. The allegations could only be politically effective if they were regarded by the majority as plausible; and, as Kravchenko and the official documents from the Smolensk archive suggest, the more outrageous the charges, the greater their demagogic appeal. The explanation for this lies in the first instance in the low educational level of the party during the thirties and its predominantly peasant background.

It is usually forgotten that the history of Russia until the first third of the twentieth century is the history of rather less than a quarter of its population. Illiterates leave no documents: a fact that is too often overlooked by historians.[104] Yet illiteracy and peasant backwardness are probably the single most important factor in accounting for the scale of the purges. As late as 1927, only one percent of party members had completed higher education, less than eight percent had even received secondary education. About a quarter were officially classified as 'self-taught'; while only two percent were officially classified as 'illiterate', the real figure was probably a good deal higher, since even in advanced societies illiterates are notoriously adept in concealing the fact.[105] Added to the general lack of education was the specific absence of trained communists to direct state enterprises. An analysis of 1928 disclosed that although the great majority – about ninety percent – of directors were party members, less than three percent had received higher education (compared to fifty-eight percent of the non-Party directors).[106] Finally, another factor already mentioned should be stressed: the predominantly peasant background of the great majority of industrial workers. Country habits die hard: yet in less than a century Russia had undergone an agrarian and industrial transformation equivalent to more than five centuries of change in western Europe. People who had tilled with the wooden plough in their youth suddenly found themselves in charge of sophisticated machinery. The time-honoured fluctuations of peasant existence were replaced suddenly and without any provision for mental adjustment by the accelerating rhythms of modern industry. The Church, the tsar, and the shackles imposed by the world's harshest climate, where the ground was frozen half the year so that the whole cycle of food-production had to be completed in a few summer months, had been shattered to be replaced by the arbitrary, uncertain and bewildering discipline of the shop floor. In a few decades, the muzhik had been deprived of nearly all the familiar props of his daily life. His predicament, therefore, was not far different from that confronting people in other pre-literate societies, faced with sudden social and ideological change. Deprived of the psychological support of the church and the autocracy, it is not surprising that he should have fallen back on atavistic beliefs in supernatural forces – in particular, the age-old universal belief in witchcraft or *maleficium*, the supernatural manipulation of the physical order by those of evil intent. Only, since the muzhik was now supposed to be part of a socialist, industrializing society, based on rational principles and using modern machinery, the forms which the malevolent supernatural forces took had to be supplied with contemporary labels.

*   *   *

It is generally understood amongst the Russian peasantry that swarms of spirits – good, bad and indifferent – wander at will through the universe, and nothing will shake from him this belief which again, let me add, is sedulously fostered in his all too credulous brain by the ubiquitous representatives of the Church. Every spot on the world's surface harbours these spirits: not even the sanctity of the Orthodox Churches is respected. These immaterial beings are, as a rule, the personification of evil, and the bitter and unrelenting foes of mankind. They penetrate into private houses, into human bodies, into holy edifices; they swarm in river, lake, pond and swamp. They wander at will through forest and valley, and across the boundless plains, bringing disease, temptation and every conceivable form of misfortune in their train. Their number is legion, and they are blessed by the peasantry with all kinds of names – *Tchort*, *Diavol*, and others – all of which can be translated by the one word 'devil'.[107]

Once again we are in the familiar, numinous world of a pre-literate society where those misfortunes that contravene the predictability of a timeless universe of custom and repetition, and which do not fit the categories of ordinary human malevolence, are relegated to the realm of evil spirits or demons. But this is not medieval Europe or darkest Africa: it is Russia in 1907, a mere decade before the revolution. The writer is an English physician, Dr Kennard, who travelled and lived among the peasants in 'all parts of European Russia'.[108] Although he is an amateur his testimony is confirmed by anthropological evidence.

Like his European counterparts in the Middle Ages, the Russian peasant is not entirely at the mercy of these malignant deities. Beliefs in the demons are to be inferred mainly from the practice of counter-magic and the way in which he tries to divert the spirit from its evil course by bribery. The women propitiate the *domovoi* or household demons by leaving provisions, such as bread and a bottle of *kvas*, for them outside the door; the farmyard demon, the *domovoi dvoroff*, she cheats by leaving the head of a fowl she has taken hanging in the poultry shed. Peasants avoid visiting the communal bath-house at times when the *bannik*, the demon of the bath, is believed to be present. In winter a bonfire is lit outside the village barn so that the *ovennik*, or barn demon, will resist the temptation to warm himself by setting fire to it. For, says Dr Kennard, 'Village barns are ill-built wooden constructions, and owing to the peasants' carelessness are frequently burned down; but simple and natural reasons are not admitted for these catastrophes. All evils of this nature are placed to the credit of the barn spirit'.[109]

The *leshi*, or wood spirit, like the satyr of antiquity or the medieval incubus, has a reputation for lechery, seducing women and girls unwise enough to get lost in the forest. But he is sometimes the hunter's friend, and will lead him to his prey if propitiated with a dead rabbit or hare.[110] In the *polevoi* or field-spirit we encounter the phenomenon of 'wrecking'.

> If agricultural tools will not work, or some part of the mechanism breaks, or if the soil is too hard to allow of sufficient working, all these difficulties are put down to the account of the evil *Polevoi*; he again is bribed by the peasantry. I have seen an intoxicated *muzhik*, before lying down to sleep in the field, place another *vodka* bottle full of the stuff by his side, and with the words '*Vot deliar tebye Polevoi!*' ('There! that's for you, Polevoi!'), sink to slumber.[111]

The most dangerous of all the spirits is the *keekeemona*, which lies in holes in the ground and is the cause of famines and epidemics. During the great famine of 1891, the peasants of Kharkov addressed a petition to the tsar through the governor: '. . . seeing that that child of the Devil, the *Keekeemona*, was absolutely and solely to blame for the terrible want of provisions, would His Majesty take the necessary steps towards the extermination of that spirit'.[112]

Among the Russian peasants *maleficium* is not confined to supernatural beings. Demons sometimes work through human – or apparently human – agents, such as changeling babies planted on careless mothers. Kennard records the case of one such suspected changeling, a young woman who had been kept chained to the wall of a peasant *izba* (hovel) for thirteen years.

> The facts are as follows: At the age of nine she developed a coarse, guttural cough and a peculiar, rather vacant expression . . . At the same time . . . it was

noticed that into whatever house she entered there was sure to be illness. A consultation of the elders of the village was held, and it was decided ... that this unfortunate girl was no human child, but the child of one of the numerous devils, which had been placed as a substitute in the cradle during the period of suckling. A wise *babooshka*, or old woman, was called in to give her opinion, and without any hesitation gave it on the side of the majority. The mother was informed of the terrible decision, and such is the faith of the peasant in devils, and all things appertaining to them, she acceded to their inhuman request, which was that the wretched girl, in order to stop her wandering in the village and doing harm, should be chained to the wall of the *izba*. This was done, and after a more or less lengthy period the child became mad, but was kept chained for thirteen years, until she died only a few months back. Other similar cases have been brought to my notice, and I have no doubt that, if the truth were known, such instances of credulity and cruelty are very numerous.[113]

Although there is a general paucity of anthropological evidence – neither the tsarist nor the Stalinist bureaucracy were in favour of studies which might draw attention to peasant 'backwardness' – there is no reason to suppose that the changes in Russian society immediately after the revolution saw a sudden and dramatic decline in these beliefs. It seems more probable that economic and social changes, plus the decline of the Church, produced an upsurge of superstition. Despite Kennard's manifest anti-clericalism, the evidence from other countries in a similar stage of development, for example, England during the high Middle Ages, suggests that the Church helped to stabilize, if not discourage, belief in *maleficium* by sanctioning magical antidotes and remedies. Kennard himself suggests an example, in the priest's ritual spitting at the departing devil during the orthodox ceremony of baptism.[114] In England, as Keith Thomas suggests, the reformers' assault on 'works' and the superstitious or magical elements in Catholic belief may have led to the increase in witchcraft accusations during the sixteenth and seventeenth centuries. Deprived of the magical protection of the Church, people in general felt more exposed to the dangers of maleficent powers. As we have seen, a similar tendency has been observed with the coming of missionaries in several parts of Africa.

Anthropological evidence confirms the vitality of similar beliefs during the twenties. In a survey carried out in Subcarpathian Russia (then under Czech rule) from Prague University in 1923–6, P. Bogatuirev dismissed the idea that popular beliefs were merely 'survivals' of old traditions.

Not only are we in the presence of traditions; but we are seeing the creation of new rites and magical operations ... in reality there are no survivals, because each corresponds to one of life's needs, to some passing nuance of thought ... Contemporary superstitions are in the same relations with pagan myths and rites as modern poetic formulae are with those of the past: they provide the framework in which thought is conditioned and without which it could not exist.[115]

In some districts Bogatuirev found a resurgence of paganism following the ending of tsarist rule. Sorcery, formerly forbidden, was now openly practised. In all the villages studied, the sorcerer received up to twice as many visits per year as the local health officer. The sorcerers practised conjuration, divination and the invocation of all kinds of spirits. Homeopathic and contagious magic, as well as sympathetic love-magic, were widely used. Modern adaptations consisted in the use of photographs as magical objects.[116] *Maleficium* or harmful magic was also practised: a man's shirt might be burned by his enemy to make him suffer the same fate. Though such cases rarely came before the courts, Bogatuirev cited one instance, dating from 1908. An unknown malefactor destroyed a farmer's fruit trees. The owner practised sorcery in his orchard and announced that whoever entered without permission would break his leg. A neighbour, returning home after a long absence and unaware of the spell, entered the orchard where she slipped and broke her leg. Immediately, the local inhabitants took her for a dangerous witch and ostracized her. The case came up in court when she brought a charge of defamation.[117]

Clearly, then, it is more than probable that the essential elements of popular belief in *maleficium* or harmful magic conducted through the agency of evil spirits or demons were present in early twentieth-century Russia, just as they were in medieval Europe. At the lowest level the accusations of 'sabotage' and 'wrecking' made by peasants or the children of peasants at party meetings were essentially the same concepts translated into the vocabulary popularized by Stalinist propaganda. Just as the 'cult' of Lenin, with its ikons and hagiology was substituted by Stalin, the ex-seminarist, for the old state religion of the Orthodox Church, so the notion that 'Trotskyite' agents and saboteurs were secretly at work, preventing the good muzhik from fulfilling his norms, interfering with agricultural and industrial machinery and 'causing' disease among animals and crop failure neatly replaced the demonology of the peasants under the old régime. The essential belief, at popular level, was that no untoward incident can be attributed to accident or incompetence. The idea was assiduously fostered by party propaganda, covered by a thin veneer of Marxist verbiage. In this we find a conjunction of ideas similar to the 'popular' and 'learned' notions of witchcraft in Europe. The popular beliefs are given coherence by a superstructure derived from current metaphysical doctrines. In the late Middle Ages the superstructure was created from the scholastic philosophy of the neo-Aristotelians. In communist Russia, of course, it borrowed the vocabulary of Marxism. Thus, according to an educational publication of 1932:

> One of the inescapable conclusions to be drawn from the Marxist-Leninist doctrine of the unity of theory and practice and of Party vigilance in science is that every theoretical mistake, every error in the field of methodology is inescapably transferred into a political error. Similarly, in the present state of things, every such error not only weakens the front of socialist construction, but it arms our enemies.[118]

Theoretical errors, of course, lead to practical mistakes; and they are in any case the consequence of political errors. The conclusion of this syllogistic style of reasoning is that a mistake, or act of inefficiency, is a political crime. There is no distinction therefore between incompetence and sabotage. Both are 'objectively' counter-revolutionary and must be punished accordingly.

Similarly, the coherence of the superstructure forbids the possibility that the act of *maleficium* or sabotage can be committed in isolation. Witchcraft postulated devil-worship which in turn demanded attendance at the sabbat. In Russia the counter-revolutionary act of sabotage postulated membership of a counter-revolutionary organization. In tsarist times, revolutionaries had belonged to underground organizations. It was inconceivable that a counter-revolutionary could be acting in isolation. And just as all European witches were ultimately tools of the devil, so in every case of counter-revolutionary sabotage, the hidden connections had to be traced linking its perpetrator to the archfiend Trotsky.

While Stalin did everything to encourage these assumptions, not least because he shared most of them himself, perhaps on a semi-conscious rather than an intellectual level, it is simplistic to suppose that he deliberately invented them, or consciously manufactured falsehood. The charge of sabotage was made at the Metrovick trial in a context that was to prove highly embarrassing to the soviet government. The probability that they were made in good faith is increased by the fact that they were rejected by the court. If this trial had been ordered from on high for political reasons, the charges would most probably have been made to stick. Several British observers of this trial including a senior barrister were of the opinion that the authorities genuinely believed in the 'wrecking' charges. In view of the international storm raised by the case, the soviet authorities went to great lengths to ensure that proper procedural rules were observed. In the opinion of several foreign observers, the defendants had the fairest possible trial in the circumstances.[119]

If in the face of peasant superstition and the revolutionary dynamic of the party purges we are forced to modify the machiavellian thesis that all the charges, from the highest levels down to the humblest party functionaries, were deliberate, cynically motivated 'frame-ups' ordered by Stalin and dutifully carried out by his minions in the NKVD, a similar revision must be made *a fortiori* in evaluating the techniques of interrogation and torture used to elicit confessions. The purpose of confession and the means used to extract it seems to have been misunderstood by several writers. Thus Robert Conquest, pursuing the machiavellian thesis, finds it odd that confession was insisted upon in cases that were never intended to come up in a public court – and that, of course, applied to the overwhelming majority:

In fact, confession is the logical thing to go for when the accused are not guilty and there is no genuine evidence ... In general, moreover, in the public trials of Zinoviev and the others, the confession method can be easily accounted for. Stalin wanted not merely to kill his old opponents, but to destroy them morally and politically ... Even if confessions seem highly implausible, they may have some effect, even on sceptics, on the principle that there is no smoke without fire and that mud sticks ...

These are rational considerations. But it is also clear that the principle of confession in all cases, even from ordinary victims tried in secret, was insisted on. In fact, the major effort of the whole police organization throughout the country went into obtaining such confessions. When we read, in cases of no particular importance, and ones never to be made public, of the use of the 'conveyer' system tying down team after team of police investigators for days on end, the impression one gets is not simply of vicious cruelty, *but of insane preoccupation with a pointless formality. The accused could perfectly well, it seems, have been shot or sentenced without this frightful rigmarole.* (emphasis added)[120]

Indeed, granted Conquest's premise that all the confessions were consciously fabricated for a political purpose regardless of whether or not the victims were destined to appear at a public trial the whole operation appears highly irrational. But this, as has been suggested, was far from being the case. The confessions were necessary because a very substantial proportion of those making denunciations, as well as the NKVD men entrusted with investigating the charges, believed in them. Even in criminal investigation as practised in western countries, confessions provide by far the greatest source of evidence. Where the investigators believe themselves to be confronted with a criminal conspiracy, only the suspect can reveal the names of his accomplices. Since there was no real conspiracy, we may surmise that most of the suspects considered themselves innocent, although this must be qualified in the light of the assumptions by the leaders such as Bukharin that certain opposition tendencies led 'objectively' to counter-revolutionary activity. But the victims' sense of innocence need have no bearing on the operation of the system, particularly where torture and other forms of judicial coercion were used. Many loyal communists, though knowing themselves to be innocent, were prepared to accept their fate for the 'higher good' of the party;[121] while generally speaking, the same would apply to interrogators who had doubts about the truth of their investigations. Any private doubts they might have had about the guilt of individual subjects would not necessarily call into question their general belief in the reality of the various conspiracies. In any case, though there were some who in private expressed scepticism or were prepared to 'call a spade a spade', they were always in a minority, and risked denunciation by their subordinates or colleagues if they ever revealed 'cynical doubts'.[122]

True, the confessions were hardly ever backed up by corroborative or factual evidence. Cases of house searches in which the NKVD men overlooked genuinely 'counter-revolutionary' or illegal documents are sometimes mentioned, as are cases of real spies escaping detection.[123] This, however, merely testifies to the rudimentary police training and low educational level of the average NKVD man, who was usually of peasant stock. Moreover judicial confession, though by no means a necessity under the soviet criminal process, was to some extent encouraged by it. As with Continental procedures in general, more emphasis is placed on discovering the 'truth' than on safeguarding the rights of defendants. With the law defined as an instrument of social policy, the emphasis is placed on the educational role of the courts in sentencing 'anti-social' criminals for their own good and for the good of society.[124] The confession thus acquires an exemplary function as well as a procedural one. Moreover, among the peasantry, it was rooted in the tradition, not just of the Orthodox Church, but of the old tsarist customary law enforced by village communities, which regarded it as 'the most satisfactory proof of guilt'.[125]

People whose mental conditioning equipped them to register most accidents as acts of sabotage were hardly likely to exhibit a constitutional scepticism about the value of confessions extracted under torture, especially when confession itself enjoyed a high position in the hierarchy of proofs. The habit of regarding confessions as deliberate fabrication reflects the outlook of 'Westernized' Russian writers, and leads them to some very naive conclusions. Thus several writers, noting the similarity between the methods of the NKVD and those of the inquisition, drew what was to them the obvious conclusion that coerced confessions in the latter as in the former case must have been known to be fraudulent. For example, two writers who were imprisoned during the worst period of the Yezhovchina state that

> There are plenty of examples in history of confession having been required as the indispensable proof of guilt. One is reminded of the Inquisition and the witches' trials, with their tortures and improbable self-accusations. Precise instructions for the extortion of confessions and for the interrogation of witches have been handed down to us in the *Malleus Maleficarum*, which leaves it doubtful whether or not the interrogators themselves believed in the reality of the 'legends' they extorted.[126]

The dissident Marxist, Roy Medvedev, is even more categorical in assuming that torture must always have been consciously employed to manufacture falsehood:

> Torture not only conflicts with the principles of a proletarian state, it is the least effective method of investigation. In most cases torture yields not the truth but a distortion of the truth, since the accused will say anything to stop the unbearable torment. Thus torture is aimed not so much at finding the guilty person as at making the innocent one guilty, forcing him to calumniate himself or others. Medieval inquisitors were well aware of this when they forced their victims to testify about their contacts with the devil. The intelligence agencies of capitalist countries are also aware of it . . . Stalin and the NKVD officials understood this very well when they forced devoted Communists to testify about their connections with genuine enemies of our nation.[127]

The analogy with the inquisition is illuminating, since it exposes the essential flaw in the machiavellian thesis. In not one of the sources or histories we have studied for the earlier chapters of this book has it been suggested that the inquisitors were conscious of perpetrating a fraud.

Medvedev may be correct in arguing that despite his frequent attacks of 'morbid suspiciousness' Stalin basically knew what he was doing when he signed arrest warrants on the slenderest pretexts, without ever demanding confirmatory evidence. Even here, however, he probably underestimates the extent to which Stalin, in contrast to the more Westernized Bolshevik leaders, shared the credulity of the masses. In the first place, any dictator possessing enormous power is likely to fear assassination for perfectly sound reasons: a certain disposition towards paranoia is a 'rational' consequence of dictatorship. But beyond this Stalin seems to have had from an early period in his career the habit of seeing hidden designs at work in apparently unconnected circumstances. As Robert Conquest remarks,

> The Stalin method of argument, which is still prevalent in the Soviet Union, can be traced as early as his first articles in 1905. Its particular marks are expressions like 'as is well known' (*kak izvestno*), used in lieu of proof to give weight to some highly controversial assertion; and 'it is not accidental' (*ne sluchayno*), used to assert a connection between two events when no evidence, and no likelihood, of such a connection exists. Readers will find many examples of these and similar expressions in current Soviet speeches.[128]

Conquest calls the idea that nothing is accidental 'a strictly paranoid formulation',[129] and this is how most Westerners would conceive of it. However, it is simplistic to infer from this, as Conquest's argument suggests, that the terror originated from this flaw in the dictator's personality. The idea that 'nothing is accidental' is characteristic of pre-literate societies everywhere. It was this which set Stalin apart from his Westernized peers among the Bolshevik leaders and which paradoxically accounts for his extraordinary success in outmanoeuvring them politically. The man who formulates his own tactics on the premise that his rivals are conspiring against him will have an immediate advantage over those whose actions are dictated by the assumption that all men are motivated by broadly 'rational' assumptions. To this day the triumph of Stalinism in Russia represents the dominance of a peasant psychology, formulated and fossilized into institutions, over the rationalist tradition of the Enlightenment as transmitted to the Russian intelligentsia through Marxism–Leninism.

How did the institutionalization of terror come about? Although we have suggested that the Terror was driven by accusations very similar to those encountered in many pre-literate societies, this in itself is not sufficient to account for the particular forms it developed. The dynamic spiralling of witch accusations in continental Europe was conditional on an inquisitorial procedure which made torture a virtual juridical necessity. No such provision existed under the Soviet Code of Criminal Procedure. Article 136 categorically laid down: 'The interrogator does not have the right to extract testimony or confession from an accused by means of compulsion or threats'.[130] Nevertheless, torture, or other equally effective forms of judicial coercion, became institutional in Russia after the revolution, despite sporadic attempts by the Communist party to prevent malpractices. They resulted from circumstances created by the revolution and civil war. There is no evidence before 1937 that they were ever ordered or approved of by higher authority.

Torture had belonged to an undercurrent of violence in social relations in Russia which many have seen as the legacy of Tartar rule.[131] It was a distinctive aspect of the government of Peter the Great, whose special political police, the Preobrazhensky guard, were encouraged to torture those suspected of treasonable or disrespectful conduct towards the tsar. People were liable to arbitrary arrest under a formula known as 'the Tsar's Word and Deed', in which little, if any, distinction seems to have been made between treasonable thoughts and actions. Beating with the 'knout', a flail-like whip of Tartar origin, was the usual mode of application, and no one was sacred. The Tsarevitch Alexis was knouted to death by the Preobrazhensky after quarrelling with his father in 1716. The 'Word and Deed' remained in force until 1762. Torture continued to be used sporadically in the provinces, as is evidenced by a decree of Alexander I forbidding it in 1801, and a similar decree by his successor Nicholas I in 1827.[132] The Third Section, Nicholas I's political police, appears to have been correct in its treatment of suspects. Allegations of torture do not occur until the terrorist campaigns of the 1870s and 1880s, when they appear in Narodnik and other anarchist literature.[133] Karakazov, an ex-student who tried to assassinate Alexander II in 1866, is said to have been driven mad by his interrogation which combined deprivation of food and sleep and threats of torture.[134] Nicholas Rysakov, one of the five executed for the successful murder of Alexander in 1881, confessed everything to the police and was treated with contempt by his accomplices. When

brought to the public gallows he is said to have showed a pair of mutilated hands to the crowd, and was heard to shout, above the drum-rolls,
that he had been tortured.[135] Apart from this, however, there is little
evidence that the Third Section or its successor, the Okhrana, regularly
employed torture.

Nevertheless, the violence of social relations in Russia under the old
régime is evident from the harshness of the corporal punishments
employed in the prisons, and the occasional brutalities inflicted on
peasants.[136] For the most part they were accepted passively, which possibly accounts for the brutalities of the civil war, once the torpor of the
peasants had been roused by revolution. These atrocities exceeded anything in the experience of western Europe. Thousands of people on
either side were literally tortured to death: there is nothing comparable
even in the *jacqueries* of the French revolution. The mutilations and dis-
memberments discovered in the wake of both Red and White armies
bore all the marks of mental derangement. They received publicity
from both sides.[137]

It would be wrong to suggest that the Bolshevik leaders bore direct
responsibility for such atrocities. On the other hand they were responsible for ordering shootings on a considerable scale. Thus after the
murder of Commissar Uritsky in 1918, five hundred 'counter-revolutionary' hostages were shot in Petrograd; in Moscow three hundred
more were shot after the attempt on Lenin's life.[138] Trotsky, in his
polemical *Defence of Terrorism* against Karl Kautsky, justified the shooting of suspected counter-revolutionaries by arguing that prison would
be no deterrent to them, since they did not expect the revolution to
endure.[139] More generally, Bolshevik leaders attempted to justify a
policy of terrorism by reference to previous revolutions. Thus Lenin
exclaimed:

The English bourgeois have forgotten their 1649, the French their 1793. The
terror was just and legitimate when it was applied by the bourgeoisie for its own
advantage against the feudal lords. The terror became monstrous and criminal
when the workers and poor peasants dared to apply it against the bourgeoisie.[140]

The weakness of this analogy was that the Bolsheviks made no distinction between the aims of terror and its means. The French revolutionary terror had for the most part been conducted publicly. Its public
nature was essential to its function. Robespierre had been quite explicit
about this:

If the attribute of popular government in peace is virtue, the attribute of popular government in revolution is at one and the same time *virtue* and *terror*, virtue without which terror is fatal, terror without which virtue is impotent. The terror is nothing but justice, prompt, severe, inflexible; it is thus an emanation of virtue.[141]

However far the terror in France departed in practice from Robespierre's maxim, the public forms of trial were in most cases observed, the executions took place in public. In the last resort, the forms of legality acted as a brake on the dynamics of terror. Popular government retreated from the acts of 'virtue' committed in its name, and the terrorists were removed from power. Once the crisis of the republic had passed, the accelerating tempo of the guillotine and the diminishing fears of the people became seriously out of phase.[142]

Justice, either popular or revolutionary, played no part in the Bolshevik conception of terror, at least not in the sense in which it had been understood in Robespierre's time. Here Russia's native tradition and the subversive doctrines of Marxism coincided to attack the abstract and formal idea of justice at its root. In a society conditioned by centuries of despotic government the very idea that terrorism must nevertheless acknowledge its own judicial principles was thoroughly alien. Power remained uncontaminated by notions of lawfulness or legitimacy; indeed, the triumph of the Bolshevik party over the state represented above all the triumph of a doctrine inspired by purely ethical over constitutional values. In this respect the Russian revolution differed fundamentally from the English and French revolutions, both of which, in different ways, began by asserting the traditional rights and freedoms embodied in ancient but eroded institutions against the radical threat of arbitrary power. Marxism completed the attack on justice by undermining its ethical basis. For Marxists, 'justice' was meaningless outside its concrete historical setting, 'justice for whom, and at whose expense?' Since justice, like every other social and political idea, changed according to the relations of productive forces, the law did not exist in the abstract but only as 'a set of concrete rules enacted by an economically dominant class for the maintenance of its privileges and authority'.[143]

Thus the only justice Bolsheviks could bring themselves to acknowledge was the justice handed out at the bar of history, that is to say, the justice enacted by one dominant class at the expense of another. In France, the revolutionary context had blurred the distinction between justice and terror – or the naked exercise of power. But in Russia, such a distinction barely existed. The dispensation of justice according to a received set of customary laws had never formed part of the Russian monarch's sovereignty, the 'supreme and unlimited power' of the tsar deriving only from God.[144] The inheritors of that sovereignty were not in consequence under any obligation to dispense their terror, as Robespierre had dispensed his, in accordance with judicial forms which in any case, they regarded as meaningless and hypocritical. History was their judge, not public opinion. If the party was the sword chosen by history to complete the revolution, terror was the sharp edge of its blade.

Dzerzhinsky, founder and first head of the Cheka which after 1922 became the OGPU and later the NKVD, was quite explicit in rejecting a judicial basis for the principal organ of terrorism:

> The Cheka is not a court. The Cheka is the defence of the revolution, as the Red Army is. And just as in the civil war the Red Army cannot stop to ask whether or not it may harm individuals but is obliged to act with the one thought of securing the victory of the revolution over the bourgeoisie, the Cheka is obliged to defend the revolution and conquer the enemy, if its sword does by chance sometimes fall on the head of the innocent.[145]

Since each new step in the direction of communism could be expected to produce new waves of counter-revolution, in accordance with the 'scientific' laws of Marxism, the sword could never be sheathed, nor the cutting-edge of social progress allowed to become blunt. Every advance must encounter new hordes of enemies. Thus it was with the rhetoric of combat, not of justice, that the organs of terror were unleashed on soviet society. The legal trappings were either discarded altogether, or treated as so much hypocritical bourgeois cant. So long as the crisis lasted, the terror was conducted administratively, and in a country whose whole tradition of administration tended towards an obsessive secretiveness, the foul business of revolution, which should have been open and public, was conducted in the secrecy of the Cheka's cellars. Of the Bolshevik leaders, only Radek seems to have been farsighted enough to have seen the dangers of permitting the Cheka always to act administratively.

> The public execution [he wrote] of five bourgeois in the presence of thousands of approving workmen on the strength of a verdict of the soviet would be a far more effective terrorist act than the secret shooting of five hundred per-

sons on the ground of a decision of the Cheka, without the cooperation of the working masses.[146]

It was in the secrecy of the Cheka cellars, away from public scrutiny, that torture evidently took root. It is therefore impossible to establish the extent to which it enjoyed official connivance or approval. The claim by two recent writers that the party leaders and the Cheka 'approved ... the use of torture for the extraction of information and confessions' is not provided with any documentary basis.[147] On the other hand, a commission of inquiry set up after the civil war to investigate allegations of brutality and torture by the CID of Stavropol was confronted with a secret circular allegedly emanating from the central Cheka in Moscow, laying down that '... if, during a process of investigation of prisoners, or a preliminary inquiry with regard to prisoners, the latter should resist circumstantial evidence, confrontation and threats, and refuse to confess to their imputed crimes, the "old and proven" remedy should be applied to them'.

The circular was reportedly issued in 1921, after complaints about the inquisitorial methods of one of the People's Prosecutors attached to the Moscow Cheka, a man named Voul. The latter had allegedly threatened to resign if he were prevented from using the 'old and proven remedy' in suppressing 'banditry' in the city – a prospect that frightened Menzhinsky, deputy head of the Cheka, into authorizing it.[148]

There was no theoretical reason to encourage the use of torture in obtaining confessions in justification of the acts of revolutionary violence authorized by the Bolshevik leaders. The Marxist doctrine of class conflict, as interpreted by them, assumed that certain social categories were class-enemies regardless of their political views or current loyalties. Thus M. Latzis, one of the senior officers of the Cheka, proclaimed in November 1919:

> We are out to destroy the bourgeoisie as a class. Hence, whenever a *bourgeois* is under examination the first steps should be, not to endeavour to discover material of proof that the accused has opposed the Soviet government whether verbally or actually, but to put to the witness three questions:
> 'To what class does the accused belong?'
> 'What is his (social) origin?'
> 'Describe his upbringing, education and profession.'[149]

This attitude was consistent with the first soviet constitution which disenfranchised and effectively outlawed members of the employing classes (or 'former people' as they came to be known) who in consequence were left to the mercies of the Cheka. It certainly helped create a 'torturable' category of people, even if it did not contribute to the practice of extracting confessions.

The use of torture probably had different though related origins. As in India, the spread of torture was helped primarily by the fact that it was first employed on a large scale under conditions where it was capable of yielding concrete results. For during the period of chronic food shortages during and after the civil war it was often the quickest and most successful means of forcing the peasants to reveal their hidden stocks of grain or pay their taxes. Most of the evidence of this comes from the Social Revolutionary party, including the left-wing faction that formed a coalition government with the Bolsheviks during the civil war. For example, Steinberg, the SR people's commissar for justice, in a pamphlet quoted *Pravda* and *Izvestia* reports which described how kulaks in the Bologda district were put in an ice-cold barn, stripped and beaten with ramrods to force them to reveal the whereabouts of their grain stocks. In Kostroma province, the peasants put on five shirts apiece in a vain endeavour to protect their backs against beatings with whips of twisted wire.[150] Another SR memorandum on the disorders in Tambour in March 1919 describes how some peasants were indiscriminately flogged in front of others.[151] Another writer described how levies of the 'extraordinary revolutionary tax' were made in a manner that recalls the standing tortures of India, except that cold rather than heat was applied; living persons were forced to stand out in the cold until literally transformed into statues of ice.[152] The practice of holding hostages against deliveries of grain, officially encouraged by Lenin,[153] inevitably led to the use of 'mock executions' for the same purpose. The victim was given to believe that he was being executed – and all the usual paraphernalia of the firing squad was applied except that the bullets were blank. The practice frequently yielded the desired results – indeed *Pravda* in February 1919 approvingly cited a case to illustrate the advantages of this method, in which

a well-to-do peasant who had refused to meet a requisitional order for 20 *poods* of grain by way of the 'extraordinary food tax', and had been imprisoned, and still refused to pay, and had then been stood up against the local churchyard wall, and again refused to pay, and lastly, had had a shot fired about his ears....

– which finally did the trick.[154]

What could be done so usefully against recalcitrant peasants might be applied – *a fortiori* – against members of the bourgeoisie. Since these people were not allowed to join trade unions, they were often condemned to unemployment and penury. Not surprisingly, many were forced to live on their few remaining possessions, including jewellery and precious metals, and a vigorous black market developed which the government was obliged to suppress. Here again the Cheka found that tortures and mock executions often yielded concrete results. One SR account described the 'revolutionary' rape of a Madame Dumbrovskaya who was repeatedly assaulted and had her fingers nipped with pliers until she revealed the whereabouts of a valuable hoard of jewellery. After that she was no longer fit to fulfil any function and was shot.[155]

For those accustomed to using torture for the obtaining of tangibles like grain or jewellery it was a short and barely perceptible step to using it for information. Many observers at the time of the civil war, among them General Knox, noted that Bolshevik prisoners were sometimes tortured into giving evidence before being shot. According to a contemporary account by the Russian-born correspondent of a German newspaper, in the early days the Chekists mainly contented themselves with obtaining confessions by threats, promises and chicanery.[156] With the development of the Terror after the attempt on Lenin, however, torture appears to have been employed on a widespread scale as part of the general system of repression. Ordinary citizens were arrested, according to the same source, not even upon suspicion, but merely in order to be tortured in the hope that 'something interesting could be learnt' from them.[157] The claim may have sounded far-fetched and propagandist at the time, but sounds less implausible with the hindsight of the Yezhovschina. The same may be said of a similar claim that as early as 1924 many, if not the majority, of prisoners in the Siberian and Solovetsk concentration camps had been sentenced on the basis of forced confessions.[158]

Thus the practice of extracting confessions as 'proof' of guilt when wide powers of administrative detention were available seems to have been a feature of soviet repressions from the earliest days of the régime, probably before the death of Lenin and certainly before the fall of Trotsky. It is difficult to believe that deliberate considerations of policy were involved. At the level of the politburo administrative powers were seen as a necessary corollary of the 'dictatorship of the proletariat' – the doctrine that a period of class rule was necessary before the revolutionary ambitions of communism could be achieved. While this created a category of detainee who could be maltreated with impunity, there remained the practical difficulty of precisely determining class boundaries. It was easy enough for the intellectuals at the head of the party to talk in grandiloquent terms of class warfare. But the revolutionary shock-troops charged with actually carrying out the official policy of terrorism needed more specific guidance as to which individuals constituted 'enemies' in the confusion of a no-man's-land in which it was not easy to tell friend from foe. 'Bourgeois' arrested by the Chekists were hardly likely to tell the truth about their social origins if they could possibly avoid doing so. Documents could be wilfully or accidentally destroyed; and, with the development of anti-Bolshevik terrorism, 'class-enemies' were in any case no longer limited to the 'former people'. The 'old and proven remedy' had been used successfully against recalcitrant peasants with implicit approval from the party leaders. In the circumstances, it must have seemed neither unjust nor unreasonable to the ordinary Chekist to use it to determine the 'guilt' of suspected counter-revolutionaries or class-enemies, even though the formalities did not require a signed confession.

There are plenty of indications that the leadership at times attempted to impose restraint. Dzerzhinsky, like many police chiefs since his time, had the double role of defending his organization against its critics and of weeding out the men who brought it into disrepute. Stung by criticisms from the party, he insisted that the Cheka never murdered people secretly and that every execution was the result of a unanimous decree by its council which represented both the party's central committee and its executive. After the council of people's Commissars called for 'compulsory publication both of the names of those shot and of the reasons for applying the supreme punitive measure' (the current Bolshevik jargon for the death penalty, the latter phrase having unacceptable pre-revolutionary overtones), the Cheka weekly journal published a list of ninety persons shot for complicity in the attempt on Lenin – though without mentioning the majority of their first names or patronymics.[159] Dzerzhinsky's insistence that his organization had sought 'to impart wise direction to the chastening hand of the proletariat' lest the 'centuries-old hatred for its oppressors might express itself in senseless, sanguinary episodes which arouse such elements of popular fury as would sweep away friends as well as foes'[160] may sound like the purest humbug, in view of what happened in places like Kharkov, where the advancing Whites found thousands of mutilated corpses at the Cheka headquarters. But it could equally well be seen as an expression of intentions which circumstances prevented him from carrying out. Once the civil war was won several officers were punished for excessive cruelty in addition to those already mentioned at Stavropol. They included the head of the Doubosarsky CID as well as a member of the Archangel revolutionary tribunal who specialized in torturing his victims before shooting them.[161]

On the whole, there is comparatively little evidence of physical torture in the period between the end of the civil war and 1937. What there is comes mainly from the provinces. Thus a construction engineer, arrested in the White Sea canal area in connection with the 'Industrial party' trial in 1930, claimed to have been repeatedly punched in the stomach and to have witnessed a fellow-prisoner die in hospital from this treatment.[162] According to Solzhenitsyn, lighted cigarettes were used to burn the hands of prisoners under interrogation in Georgia in 1926.[163] Torture first appears to have been used in a more formal judicial role in connection with the trial of the Shakhty engineers in 1928.[164] In 1931 two of the defendants in the Menshevik trial were, according to a recent soviet account, badly tortured.[165] Subsequently it was used in most of the political trials at national and regional level, though not as a rule against the principals. During the great purges, its application was virtually guaranteed by the interpenetration of the judicial and security apparatus; most of the interrogators were officially 'examining magistrates' such as are found on the Continent. This fusion of the functions of policeman and lawyer was the consequence of the application of Marxist doctrines concerning the subservience of legal institutions to class domination.

It cannot be established at what precise point physical violence became official policy. As heirs to the Cheka, the NKVD operated in secrecy and enjoyed for a period what amounted to complete extra-legal immunity. Nevertheless as it was subject to strict bureaucratic control, its operatives went by the book. This was probably the reason for what became known as the conveyer system, in which the perfectly legal interrogation by examining magistrates became in effect a form of torture. Alexander Weissberg, who was kept sitting on his stool for six continuous days and nights, regarded it as far worse than being beaten: 'With a flogging a man could grit his teeth and bear it, knowing that it must end, or lapse into unconsciousness if the pain got too bad. Sitting on the stool you did not lapse into unconsciousness and the torment never ceased'.[166] When at one point Weissberg fell off his stool, the examiner summoned his superior who delivered a formal reprimand.[167]

Actually, physical violence seems to have been the result of the pressures to which interrogators were subjected rather than a deliberate effort to induce false confessions. A former NKVD man who shared a cell with Weissberg in 1938 described the stages by which a 'request' from Stalin became, in effect, an unofficial order to employ physical methods of violence. In the first instance, Stalin might call Yezhov and 'suggest that inquiries should be instituted to discover whether any connections exist between the former followers of Bukharin and the German Gestapo'. Yezhov would then summon his district chiefs and say: 'We must uncover the connections between the Bukharinites and the German Gestapo' – a small, but significant step from Stalin's phraseology. In its next modulation the order, as delivered orally to individual interrogators, would take the form: 'We must take the most energetic measures to uncover the connection between the Bukharinites and the German Gestapo.' Since it would be highly unlikely that any communist would admit to connections with the Gestapo except by physical violence or the threat of it, the ordinary interrogator would know what was required of him, although he would also know that physical violence was illegal.[168] Pressure to provide 'evidence' of the 'connections' would in almost every case be greater than fear of breaking the law, since an interrogator who 'acquitted' more than one or two suspects would soon be denounced and arrested. The NKVD men were of course in an impossible trap, as it was for using illegal methods of interrogation that many of them were subsequently tried and sentenced to death.[169]

Like the bull of Pope Innocent IV authorizing the use of torture against heretics in 1252, Stalin's directive allowing physical violence was only the formal acknowledgement of something which, for practical reasons, had already become a necessity. The instructions were evidently issued secretly in late 1936 or 1937 and only confirmed retrospectively in 1939, in a coded telegram to the heads of party committees and NKVD organizations:

The Party Central Committee explains that application of methods of physical pressure in NKVD practice is permissible from 1937 on, in accordance with permission from the Party Central Committee . . . it is known that all bourgeois intelligence services use methods of physical influence against the representatives of the socialist proletariat and that they use them in their most scandalous forms. The question arises as to why the socialist intelligence service should be more humanitarian against the mad agents of the bourgeoisie, against the deadly enemies of the working class and of the collective farm workers. The Party Central Committee considers that physical pressure should still be used obligatorily, as an exception applicable to known and obstinate enemies of the people, as a method both justifiable and appropriate.[170]

The effect of physical methods, of course, was greatly to increase the speed with which prisoners could be processed, since the older methods of the conveyor and prolonged interrogation could endure for months before 'breaking' them, tying down teams of examining magistrates and interrogators. The authorities were evidently embarrassed by having recourse to illegal methods. According to some prisoners, one way to counter a beating was to 'shriek like a stuck pig' to make oneself heard in the cells.[171] The examining magistrates – never police or prison staff – were the only officials to use them, and their irregularity was apparent from the fact that improvised objects such as broken-off chair legs were used rather than regular instruments such as whips or rubber truncheons.[172]

*   *   *

The second world war saw the end of the great purge and a general stabilization of the machinery of terror. The shock of the German invasion broke into the Russian nightmare, facing the soviet people with a real crisis and a real enemy. The effects of the Terror on the conduct of the war cannot be discussed here: enough to say that the devastating losses of the first two years cannot but have resulted from the defloration of the army in the Tukachevsky purge; while Russia's remarkable recovery after Stalingrad may have owed much to the redirection of the prodigious aggressive forces unleashed in the thirties.

The purges were never revived in their wholesale form, though there are signs that Stalin may have been on the brink of unleashing a new wave of terror in conjunction with the Jewish doctors' plot shortly before his death.[173] In the nature of things, a large-scale purge cannot be sustained indefinitely, as some students of totalitarianism suggest. Sooner or later, as in the witch-hunts of the late Middle Ages and

Renaissance, there comes a 'crisis of confidence' in which the socially destructive effects of the terror are seen to exceed the positive need to exterminate the hidden enemy. To all intents and purposes, this crisis point coincided in the Soviet Union with the death of Stalin and the murder of Beria by his successors.[174] Kruschev's break with Stalin proved that in the last resort the Communist party could still triumph over its destroyer. Though the present soviet leadership is authoritarian and exhibits many traces of Stalinism in its thinking, there are no signs of a return to the terror of the thirties. If the distinguishing characteristic of a totalitarian régime is its inability to discriminate between guilt and innocence, or rather between genuine and phantom dissent, then the present Russian state falls short of the wholly totalitarian. The dissenters who are persecuted today are for the most part genuine oppositionists who have sought publicity for their causes. To those accustomed to Western political values, that such people should be persecuted at all is bad enough.

Nevertheless, though the purge itself ground to a halt, its characteristic institution, the show-trial with its tortured confessions, survived the second world war in a formalized, rationalized state as an instrument of soviet *realpolitik*. The trial of the leaders of the Polish underground in 1945 saw its use for the first time against foreign non-communist politicians. The methods by which they were brought to confess to collaboration with the Nazis during the occupation were the same as those used against the fallen communist leaders in the thirties. Here however the element of credulity and voluntary submission was wholly lacking. The accused were brought to confess by purely 'mechanical' means, including all the methods of continuous interrogation, accompanied by constant lack of food and sleeplessness.[175] The discrediting of national communist leaders in Hungary and Czechoslovakia was achieved in the same manner, through the ministration of soviet advisers in the local intelligence departments. In the latter case, all pretence to belief in the charges was abandoned. Examining magistrates were replaced by junior functionaries of a low educational level who were never informed of the general charges against the accused. Each interrogator was merely presented with a list of the answers he was required to obtain from his subject by almost any means he cared to use. Physical violence was frequent; and the accused, no longer subjects of interrogation, were required to rehearse in detail the 'lines' they were to speak at their trials.[176] After Stalin's death, similar methods were employed to discredit religious leaders in Hungary and Bulgaria,[177] and were imitated by the Chinese communists against British and American prisoners during the Korean war.[178]

The latterday use of the tortured confession in communist states has led many observers into the error of projecting their evidently cynical aims retrospectively on to the pre-war soviet trials. Yet beyond a few individual cases there is little evidence to suggest that the earlier showtrials were entirely the result of conscious fabrication. The soviet experience is darker and more tragic than befits the philosophy of the neomachiavellians. Perhaps if its atavistic and anthropological roots are taken into account, the next generation of soviet leaders will have less difficulty in coming to terms with it.

EPILOGUE

EPILOGUE

When in the eighteenth century Beccaria, Verri and Voltaire set in motion the reforms which were to culminate in the abolition of torture, it can hardly have occurred to them that in barely two centuries that relic of medieval barbarism and religious fanaticism would become entrenched once more, not only in Europe but throughout the civilized world. Yet it is a paradox of our time that though torture is against the law of every nation, physical violence and other forms of severe compulsion are, to a greater or lesser extent, regular features of police and military interrogation in very many, possibly a majority, of the world's states. According to Amnesty International, the independent human rights organization based in London, torture has been practised with official connivance in at least sixty states during the 1970s: this figure, however, can only apply to those states for which information is available, where there are various unofficial channels of communication between prisoners and the outside world. The practice, according to Amnesty, is far from being confined to the police or military:

> ... doctors, scientists, judges, civil servants, politicians are [also] involved in torture, whether in direct beating, examining victims, inventing new devices and techniques, sentencing prisoners on extorted false confessions, officially denying the existence of torture, or using torture as a means of maintaining their power. And torture is not simply an indigenous activity, it is international; foreign experts are sent from one country to another, schools of torture explain and demonstrate methods, and modern torture equipment ... is exported from one country to another.[1]

It would be beyond the scope of this book to try to explain this baffling recrudescence by investigating or describing the use of torture in modern states. Nevertheless, with some of the foregoing historical perceptions in mind it may be possible to suggest a general line of approach.

To begin with, it would be useful to make a distinction between the *purpose* of torture as perceived by its practitioners, and its *function* in the broader sociological sense, which may not necessarily be clear to them. Several purposes may be served by applying physical or mental pain to someone against his will. There is the penal or retributive purpose properly described as corporal punishment. Although some definitions, both traditional and modern, include the concept of punishment in the word 'torture', I have generally followed Bentham in drawing a distinction between compulsive violence (torture) and retributive violence (punishment). The essence of the distinction is that in the former case the victim may have it in his power to stop the pain by complying with the wishes of his torturers. At the same time, it is doubtful if this distinction has always been evident where torture has been employed. The original rules of the inquisition *sentenced* people to torture on the basis of the *proofs* (*indicia*) against them, and the severity of the torture was correlated to the degrees of proof. The same torture techniques, such as stretching, which were employed in the examination of suspects, were sometimes used as forms of corporal punishment – usually as aggravations of the death penalty in cases of treason. Moreover, some 'torture' instruments such as the hot iron were during the early Middle Ages employed as ordeals to determine the judgement of God. Hence the phenomenon of torture (or rather torment, to use the broader term) is antecedent to any of the purposes to which it may be put.

Granted, however, that the purpose of torture is coercive, two principal objectives may be served. Torture may either be used to compel someone's allegiance, by forcing him to renounce rival loyalties; or it may be applied to extort goods or information from him. As Tertullian point out in his *Apologetic*, these two objectives may be in conflict. Christians were forced under torture to renounce Christ, that is to say, to *deny* their faith. Ordinary criminals, on the other hand, were expected to confess – or *affirm* their guilt. In later persecutions Christians were apparently simultaneously expected to *deny* that they were Christians (which the braver ones of course refused to do), and to admit that as Christians they had eaten children and performed similar bestial acts.

Renunciations of loyalties or beliefs and confession as to acts are therefore different things. Both however are often present where torture is used. Albigensian heretics, coerced into abandoning their opposition to the Church, were also tortured into confessing their heretical beliefs. The dissident is not only forced to renounce his dissent: he is required in his confession to place a criminal construction on that dissent, in line with the prejudices of his tormentors.

Recent examples of this double purpose are furnished by the Greek island of Makronisos, where after the civil war communists were interned under conditions of considerable brutality until they publicly abandoned their beliefs.[2] In subsequent repressions, however, the Greek political police rounded up former communists and left-wing sympathizers, and tried to force them under torture to confess to participating in terrorist conspiracies with the aim of destroying the state.[3] Similarly in Kenya, during the campaign against the Mau Mau in the 1950s, the colonial authorities rounded up and tortured to death a number of guerrillas who refused to break their oath to the movement. At the same time, rumours based (according to nationalist sources) on tortured confessions were circulated by the government alleging that the Mau Mau oathing ceremony involved the performance of bestial acts.[4]

In all such instances, and they appear to be increasingly common in the modern world,* torture appears to have both a primary and a secondary function. In the first instance, which may be apparent to the torturer, the object is simply to compel the victim's allegiance: it has already been suggested that this practice originated in the enslavement of prisoners in war. This function was implicit in the tortures meted out to traitors and heretics both as punishments and as special methods of investigation. Its basis was the notion that torture purges contempt. This function was implied in the treatment, known as the *peine*

---

*It would, of course, be impossible to demonstrate with any precision the degree to which torture is increasing in the modern world. Reliable information is notoriously difficult to come by. No doubt such bodies as Amnesty International, by drawing attention to the problem, help to generate the evidence, giving the possibly false impression that torture is on the increase, whereas in fact it is the consciousness of the problem which is growing. Nevertheless, a quantitative increase in the use of torture as a system of government seems more than probable, if only because methods that were once sporadic and localized – as, for example, in early nineteenth-century India – have become standarized or bureaucratically administered in so many modern states. Within the context of institutions based on European models, the contemporary recrudescence of torture is undeniable. So even if the phenomenon itself cannot generally be proved to be increasing, institutions, such as the police, army and courts, which were relatively free from it a century or so ago, are being progressively corrupted. Such institutions, moreover, form the organizational superstructure of most of the states of the modern world.

forte et dure, meted out to those refusing to plead in English courts. The prisoner was bound and weights were placed on his body until he changed his mind and agreed to plead.[5]

The secondary function of torture is to provide the confession which validates the first. The confession of the accused, which became a legal necessity in Continental law during the Renaissance, affirmed the validity of the trial in effect by compelling the acquiescence of the criminal in his sentence. This was subsequently rationalized in the evidential requirements of 'legal proof'. However, in both France and Germany torture first appears to have been used on a large scale against members of alienated groups – respectively the heretics and the Jews. At this stage, the objective was not to fulfil evidential requirements – since these had not yet been formalized – but to procure the confessions which alone could validate the proceedings which had already been taken against them. Above all, it was essential that these confessions would confirm the prejudices of the persecutors. The Jews duly confessed to child-murder and poisoning, the heretics to Manichean beliefs and forbidden rituals.

The affinity between these medieval precedents and the pre-war soviet show-trials hardly needs stressing. The defeated Trotskyites and Bukharinites had been branded as counter-revolutionary conspirators, terrorists, wreckers and so forth. The confessions in open court provided a judicial validation of these claims. This may even have been Stalin's conscious purpose in holding the trials. However, as has been suggested, it is simplistic to see all the charges as conscious fabrications. The element of credulity, especially at popular level, has to be taken into account. When the system first developed, the average soviet investigator was as credulous as his medieval predecessor.

Left to itself, the tortured confession has a static function. It is the denunciation which introduces the dynamic element into the torture system. The dissident must betray his accomplices, in the first instance, because without this betrayal his submission would be less than complete. As Jean-Paul Sartre has observed:

The purpose of torture is not only to make a person talk, but to make him betray others. The victim must turn himself by his screams and by his submission into a lower animal, in the eyes of all and in his own eyes. His betrayal must destroy him and take away his human dignity. He who gives way under questioning is not only constrained from talking again, but is given a new status, that of a sub-man.[6]

The aim of dehumanizing the victim is not necessarily a conscious one. The denunciation has to be rationalized: the dissident 'sub-man' must give details about the 'secret organization' of which he is assumed to be a member. Confederates must be denounced, regardless of whether they are members of real or phantom organizations. Just as in his individual confession he is forced to accept his designation as 'heretic', 'counter-revolutionary' or 'terrorist', whose errors are permeated with 'anti-Christian', 'bourgeois' or 'Marxist' beliefs, so in his denunciation the dissident is forced to accept his role as a limb of a malignant conspiracy to destroy society. Only thus can the possibility that his dissent arose from legitimate grievances or justified causes be excluded from consideration.

Consciously or otherwise, torture thus becomes the pretext for dehumanizing a real or supposed enemy. Just as the confession will usually supply the 'proof' necessary to justify the application of torture in the first instance, so the victim's dehumanization contributes to the continuance of the system. The victim who talks becomes his torturer's accomplice – or, as Sartre expresses it, he 'becomes one with his executioner'.[7] Not only does he betray others, whether known to him or not, innocent or guilty, committed or indifferent. By his grovelling he accepts his role and that of his 'accomplices' as a creature who, being less than human, need no longer be treated as such. On the psychological as on the logical level the torture system is self-confirming.

In this respect torture serves, or reinforces the function of, racism, which is to provide the emotional and psychological basis for the process of dissimilation necessary for persecution. People will not willingly acquiesce in the destruction of those whom they regard as their own kind. The inquisition, aided by Catholic propaganda, dehumanized the heretic before destroying him by torturing him into betraying his fellows. The witches were placed beyond the pale of humanity by their association with the devil, obscenely confirmed by copulation. Stalin's victims were talked, tortured or blackmailed into denouncing each other as spies, counter-revolutionary agents and saboteurs.

In British India and other colonial, or post-colonial situations, on the other hand, the work of alienating the subject from the dominant group by dehumanizing the former had already been partly achieved by years of colonial government in which all the important posts were held by white men. The Europeans regarded themselves as inherently superior to the natives. They had brought peace and 'civilization' to a people whom they regarded as backward and uncultured. Only when their dominance came to be challenged by the rising nationalist movements did torture, previously seen as a manifestation of native barbarism, come into the white man's service. The European became the native torturer's apprentice, then his accomplice.

Torture and racism may mutually reinforce each other. But it would be wrong to see one as depending on the other. In some colonial situations the torture of the native by the settler may unconsciously serve to confirm the latter's sense of superiority, by providing direct and palpable evidence of the former's degradation. With the extreme forms of racism represented by the German Nazis, this function was virtually apparent from the start. However, since terror amounted to a whole culture under the Nazis, the characteristic rationalization of torture within an inquisitorial system never evolved. It is partly for this reason, and partly in order to limit the scope of this book, that it has not been possible to devote a full chapter to the Nazis.

Although the word 'Gestapo' has become almost synonymous with 'torture', it tends to be overlooked that both the Italian fascists and the Nazis consciously modelled their organs of repression on those of soviet Russia, just as they imitated many of the rhetorical devices of Bolshevism in their progaganda.[8] In other respects Nazi 'racism' was a revolutionary extension in a European context of the racism which was inherent in the expansion of European power overseas. The difference, however, was that racism overseas was taken for granted (as was that natural consequence of racism, genocide). Within Europe, it appeared outrageous, even insane.[9]

The Nazis were conspiracy theorists *par excellence*. Indeed, as an example of the literature of paranoia, Hitler's *Mein Kampf* is only excelled by that other classic of anti-semitic literature, *The Protocols of the Elders of Zion*. The latter, though a forgery, is in a similar vein to the anti-masonic fantasies of the Abbé Barruel. It consists of plans, allegedly by a secret Jewish organization, to create a totalitarian world government under a Jewish leader, by fomenting revolution and economic chaos through the agency of the freemasons and other societies which have been penetrated and taken over by the Jews. According to Hermann Rauschning, Hitler took the *Protocols* as his primer for politics,[10] while the Nazis, as Hannah Arendt has noted, more or less consciously modelled themselves on the secret society of the Elders of Zion.[11]

However, the Nazis never developed an inquisitorial style of machinery for uncovering this diabolical conspiracy, whose existence seems to have been taken for granted. There are historical reasons for this which have to do with the nature of anti-semitism.

The image of the Jew as child-murderer, cannibal, sorcerer and poisoner has the same affinity with the night witch of African fantasy as has the medieval image of the heretic-cum-witch. Whereas the faithful worship God, Christ and the saints, both the Jews and heretic-witches were accused at various times of worshipping Satan or Anti-Christ, and having recourse to the intercession of demons. There was, however, an essential difference. Whereas the heretic-witch was conceived of as the 'enemy within' who could not be discovered without an elaborate process of detection, the Jew was a member of an identifiable group whose social distinctiveness was upheld by discriminatory laws and by his own exclusive religious customs. Jewish persecution *per se* never required the establishment of an inquisitorial machinery. Only if one had been born into the Jewish faith, or was a descendant of a Jew and suspected of feigning Christianity while remaining secretly attached to the religion of his forefathers, was an inquisition necessary to discover him.[12]

Historically, anti-semitic persecution has functioned in two opposite directions: one towards forcible conversion and assimilation, the other towards isolation, expulsion and extermination. The Spanish inquisition had no competence over Jews who refused to convert to Christianity. (They were eventually expelled and settled for the most part in North Africa.) It was set up originally to combat 'judaizing' tendencies among the newly-converted Christians, thereby enforcing the conformity of the converts. Although in the course of time the persecution in Spain developed a 'racist' character in which mere possession of Jewish 'blood' came to be regarded as warranting investigation, the aim of the Spanish inquisition always remained basically the same: not the alienation of the Jews, but the elimination of Jewish cultural and religious traces. Only the impenitent, or those who persisted in maintaining their innocence despite the weight of *indicia* against them, were sent to the stake. Similarly in Portugal the Jewish 'problem' was solved by coerced assimilation through forced intermarriage.[13]

Modern anti-semitism has exhibited both these tendencies, often in contradictory association. Some nineteenth-century anti-semitic writings, of which traces survive in the pronouncements of Hitler and other Nazi leaders, convey the idea of Jewishness as a degenerate human characteristic or set of values, rather than the attribute of a specific group.[14] In this sense, Jewishness is associated in Nazi ideology with Bolshevism as representative of ideas and values which are quintessentially 'un-German'. Had Nazi conceptions remained confined to these essentially abstract definitions, it is likely that a machinery of ideological coercion comparable to the Spanish inquisition would have been established with the aim of 'Germanizing' Jews and Marxists. However, the racist elements in Nazi ideology dictated the opposite course. Racism, in the extreme intellectual form advocated by the Nazis, postulates a biological definition of nationality or confessional identity: 'race' is an unalterable fact of nature which cannot be changed. Nazi policies were aimed at creating a German Reich whose Jewish citizens had been removed through voluntary or forced emigration or extermination.[15]

Because racism assumed *a priori* that certain categories, including the Poles and gipsies as well as the Jews, were 'subhuman' and therefore unassimilable within German society, the Nazis never needed to develop an inquisitorial machinery for identifying the 'enemy within'. In the initial stages ordinary bureaucratic methods – the examination of birth-certificates and so forth – were sufficient to enforce the dissimilation of Jews from German society. This process was facilitated by the initial defiance of many of the Reich Jews, who 'wore their badges with pride' and swelled the ranks of Zionist organizations. Financial inducements, the pressure of concentration camps and Zionist influence completed the work of the Nuremberg laws. Once a decisive majority of the Jews had accepted their designation by the Nazis as an unassimilable group, the way to wholesale collaboration was opened. Little resistance was offered to the deportation and 'resettlement' programmes which were the necessary prelude to extermination.[16]

The racist character of Nazism permeated most of its institutions – so much so, indeed, that Marxists and other political dissidents were accorded the same treatment as 'biologically inferior' types. Both were seen *a priori* as threats to 'social hygiene' or 'racial purity' which needed to be isolated in 'protective custody' camps. Except in the case of the Reich Jews, some of whom were released from custody on agreeing to emigrate, the concentration camps had no coercive function. Rehabilitation and indoctrination ran counter to the racist idea that certain types were irredeemably beyond the pale of humanity. Terror reigned in the camps, which remained outside judicial control and were placed in the charge of sadistic individuals many of whom had personal grudges against 'respectable' society. Racism also underwrote the use of living human beings for scientific experiments. Once certain categories had been irreversibly designated as 'subhuman', it followed that they could be accorded the same treatment as animals.[17] In short, Nazi repression did not substantially differentiate between political opposition and racial or social undesirability. The category of the subhuman was assumed in advance. It did not need to be created in the course of an investigation. It is this, perhaps, which accounts for the evidently arbitrary and spasmodic use of torture by the Nazis.

Although torture appears to have been a standard weapon against resistance fighters, 'third-degree' interrogation procedures were also used against socially undesirable categories. An order signed by Heinrich Müller, head of the Gestapo, in June 1942, authorized the use of 'third-degree' methods 'where preliminary investigation had indicated that the person could give information on important matters, such as subversive activities'. The methods, according to the decree, could include bread and water, a hard bunk, a dark cell, deprivation of sleep, exhaustive drill and flogging. (For more than twenty strokes, a doctor had to be consulted.) The methods were restricted to certain categories, including 'Communists, Marxists, Jehovah's Witnesses, saboteurs, terrorists, members of resistance movements, Polish or soviet Russian loafers or slackers'. The decree, which was produced in evidence at the Nuremberg trial, states that these methods are to be used only for obtaining information and not confessions by the accused.[18]

According to the prosecution evidence at Nuremberg, actual methods of torture employed by the Gestapo went far beyond these restrictions. For example, in addition to the authorized methods the tortures applied in France were said to include 'whipping, chaining for several days without a moment of rest for nourishment or hygienic care, immersion in ice-cold water, drowning in a bathtub, charging the bathwater with electricity, electrification of the most sensitive parts of the body, and the pulling out of fingernails'. There is no documentary evidence, however, that these methods, though virtually standardized, were officially approved. Where torture was applied according to the rules, both outside and within the Reich, special printed forms were provided, some of which survived. Several witnesses denied that the 'unofficial' methods were ever authorized. The same applies to the ill-treatment of internees in the camps. Rudolf Höss, commandant of the Auschwitz camp, consistently denied that ill-treatment of the inmates in his charge had been ordered, although he readily admitted receiving and carrying out Hitler's order to exterminate the Jews. In the latter case, Höss sought to exonerate himself by blaming his superiors – Eichmann, Müller, Kaltenbrunner and Himmler. It seems likely that if tortures had really been ordered from above, Höss would have similarly blamed his superiors. In fact, he claimed that Himmler had given strict instructions that individual sadists among the SS should be punished.

Judging from the evidence at Nuremberg, it seems that the worst Gestapo tortures were only semi-official, the result initially of excesses condoned at the highest level and subsequently standardized. An American report after the liberation of Paris suggests that tortures were applied unsystematically and inefficiently. 'The tortures were all the more horrible because the Germans in many cases had no clear idea of what information they wanted and just tortured haphazard.' This impression is certainly at variance with the idea of a centralized process under bureaucratic control, on the lines of Hitler's 'Final Solution'. The French prosecution failed to substantiate its argument that the 'systematic repetition of the same methods of torture' proved 'that a common plan existed, conceived by the German government itself'. The final judgement of Nuremberg only included a single indictable reference to torture, in the case of Kaltenbrunner (Heydrich's successor as head of the RSHA, which included the Gestapo and the SD). The terms in which his offence were framed were relatively vague and unspecific: 'During the period in which Kaltenbrunner was head of RSHA, the Gestapo and SD in the occupied territories continued the murder and ill-treatment of the population using methods which included torture and confinement in concentration camps, usually under orders to which Kaltenbrunner's name was signed'.[19]

None of this proves of course that the Gestapo were necessarily less brutal than they are usually depicted in books about the second world war. There is abundant evidence of extreme and wanton cruelty of the most inhuman kind. But it does not seem to have been confined to interrogation, nor, with the exception of the third-degree order cited above, was the need for information invoked to justify it. Most of it seems to have been part of the wider policy of terrorism and intimidation authorized by the Nazi leaders. In this context it is worth quoting an order of General Keitel's on 'the combating of guerrillas' dating from December 1942:

The Führer has been informed that certain members of the Wehrmacht who took part in the struggle against the guerrilla bandits were later called to account for their behaviour while fighting. In this connection the Führer has ordered:

'The troops have the right and duty to use in this struggle any and unlimited means, even against women and children, if only conducive to success. Scruples of any sort whatsoever are a crime against the German people and against the front-line soldier who bears the consequences of attacks by guerrillas, and who has no comprehension for any regard shown to the guerrillas or their associates ... No German participating in combat action against the bands is to be held responsible for acts of violence either from a disciplinary or a judicial point of view.'[20]

Such an order obviously overrode the more specific and scrupulous instructions referring to 'third-degree' interrogation for certain categories. Nazi terror-tactics included the wholesale shooting of hostages and the elimination of political opponents by secret deportation and murder. With methods such as these, and above all with the systematic and officially authorized extermination of millions of gipsies, Jews, Poles and Russians, torture has a secondary place in the catalogue of Nazi crimes.

It would be wrong, therefore, to overestimate the contribution made by the Nazis to the spread of torture after the second world war. Racism, which provides a climate in which torture flourishes, was not their invention; nor was torture. The habit of treating certain categories as 'subhuman' was certainly fostered by Nazi ideology, but this was also inherent in the measures adopted by many of the colonial powers against their overseas subjects. King Leopold II of the Belgians was responsible for the massacre of at least as many unarmed civilians as Hitler.[21] Torture was used in Indo-China, India and Algeria long before the second world war. Certainly there is evidence that local collaborators who worked with the Nazis in the occupied territories subsequently used torture against their own compatriots. In France the Department of Internal Security is reported to have used electrical tortures as early as 1949; while many of the methods used in Algeria during the 1950s and early 1960s were similar if not identical to those alleged against the Gestapo. In Greece, where Allied governments were more concerned with communism than the relics of fascism, the security police, who had collaborated with the Germans against the partisans, remained in the service of post-war governments, and maintained a tradition of torturing 'subversives' which became an international scandal in the late 1960s. The Papadopoulos and Ioannides dictatorships merely extended and brought into prominence practices which had been endemic in the post-war monarchy.

But torture has also flourished since the war in countries which were never occupied by the Germans – in Spain and Portugal and most of Latin America. It survived the war in eastern Europe, to be employed with spectacular *éclat* in the preparations for the Slansky and Loebl trials. It survives to this day in fact, wherever governments believe themselves, or choose to believe themselves, to be beset by conspiracies and subversion. The institutionalized paranoia which we have seen as a common feature of the torture system, at least during its initial phase, was certainly a characteristic feature of Nazism. But it is also a feature of many other régimes of differing complexions and ideologies.

The conspiracy scenario to which this attitude gives rise is often the reaction of a régime with a weak moral or social base. In such cases the varied and disparate manifestations of dissent born of evolutionary changes or contradictions in the social structure are perceived as the result of machinations by a 'hidden' enemy. The inquisitorial machinery with torture at its centre is established to 'root' the enemy out. Denunciations are extracted under torture. Since most people faced with torture will confess to whatever is demanded of them (with the possible exception of the tested militants belonging to real underground organizations), the system becomes self-fulfilling and self-extending to the point where the initial aim of interrogation gives way to intimidation and ultimately to mass terror. Thus torture can become the means by which a relatively small and unrepresentative élite, such as a political party, a foreign-based régime, a local police or a military formation can obtain, monopolize or increase its political power. Unchecked, these tortured denunciations will attack every form of solidarity and group cohesion, resulting ultimately in a society of atomized individuals which has sometimes been defined as the end of totalitarian rule.

The conspiracy scenario is not necessarily adopted with conscious intent. Anthropological evidence suggests that the notion of a society under attack from 'hidden' forces may be rooted in the fantasy of the night witch, whose behaviour represents the opposite of what is socially acceptable. Among the Amba of western Uganda, for example, the witches, though in league with witches from other villages, only attack people from their own. If they were thought to be victimizing people from other villages, their actions would not be considered immoral, since the village is the largest 'moral universe' possessed by the Amba. '. . . If the Amba are to believe in the existence of witches, they must also believe that each village contains within it a group of people who are secret enemies of the social order, a fifth column which is constantly attempting to destroy the village from within.'[22] The same ideas are to be found in the much larger moral universe of the modern state, and its predecessor, the Catholic Church. The idea of Manicheans or magicians secretly working on behalf of Persia to destroy the peace-loving Romans by occult means is implied in the strictures on Manicheans in the Theodosian codes. The same tradition was taken over by the Church in the twelfth century, and helps to explain why the Manichean label was applied prematurely to various dissenters and heretics from the eleventh century. The fantasies surrounding the heretics were duly applied to the neighbourhood sorcerers or witches with devastating consequences. Similar fantasies, dressed in an increasingly secular garb, lay behind the attacks on the European freemasons and the secret societies in the eighteenth and nineteenth centuries; and they emerge once more in the related conspiracies of the Jews and the Trotskyites in Nazi Germany and soviet Russia.

Nor are these fantasies confined it would seem to any particular state or culture. A similar tradition, in which the activities of freemasons are equated with those of the devil, runs through a whole subculture of literature in the United States, dubbed by one scholar the 'paranoid style'. In the 1950s, at the height of the Cold War, it broke surface in the congressional hearings of Senator Joseph McCarthy, whose own words supply a telling description of this outlook:

How can we account for our present situation unless we believe that men high in this government are concerting to deliver us to disaster? This must be the product of a great conspiracy, a conspiracy on a scale so immense as to dwarf any previous such venture in the history of man. A conspiracy of infamy so black that, when it is finally exposed, its principals shall for ever be deserving of the maledictions of all honest men . . .[23]

In all societies, it would seem, the idea of conspiracy has a profound emotional appeal, particularly at periods of tension, or economic or social stress. Even in democratic states within the common-law tradition, such as Britain and the United States, the ordinary laws of conspiracy come perilously close to ideas of 'thought crime'. The notion that a *combination* to commit a crime is inherently more dangerous than the crime itself, is both illogical and unprovable. Since conspiracy laws tend to prescribe punishment for 'little more than a state of mind', proof is notoriously susceptible to coerced confessions in countries lacking the most stringent legal safeguards.[24]

What is the basis of this appeal? Psychologically, though conspiracies may be terrifying, they are also in a sense comforting. They explain and give coherence to events that would otherwise seem incomprehensible or unacceptable. They are rooted in feelings of insecurity and power-lessness. According to one Freudian writer, they have an essentially in-fantile character based, perhaps, on the child's unconscious fear of its parents' sexuality:

> ... attributing a conspiracy to an event amounts to an assertion that events do not occur without an act of conscious, more or less rational, human will. It may be that this suggests a regression to that developmental stage where child-ren tend to regard their parents as omnipotent with respect to the world. If something happens, the parents must have had a hand in it or at least be able to do something about it.[25]

This reaction is especially characteristic of groups whose standing in society is threatened by economic and social developments. In the up-heavals of revolution, we have suggested, the Russian muzhiks fell back into age-old witch-beliefs as an explanation for agricultural or mech-anical disasters. The German middle classes, whose livelihoods were almost destroyed in the successive crises of inflation and un-employment, were seduced into Nazism by a skilful blending of age-old conspiracy fantasies surrounding the Jews and the spectre of Bol-shevism. A similar reaction has been observed on the part of the British authorities in India after the first world war, where it found expression in the Rowlatt report.

The conspiracy scenario is especially attractive to the military or police in situations where they are confronted with hostile or potenti-ally hostile populations. The manifestations of political unrest, usually disparate and spontaneous, are at an early stage welded in the minds of the authorities into a single 'movement, promoting one general policy of outrage'. The 'organization' behind this movement becomes the basis for all subsequent military strategy. It is assumed from the start that this organization, structured on military lines, has an almost preternatural capacity to *manipulate* the population. It is isolated conceptually from its environment: for at no point can it be admitted that the success of rebels and dissidents is determined principally by the attitudes of the people to whom they belong and in whose name they are acting. The authorities regard it as axiomatic that they are defending high moral principles, which include the 'true' interests of the people. Riots and explosions cannot be accepted as the work of people who conceive themselves to be acting in the same interest: for once this were admitted, a political dimension would be introduced into what the military or police regard as a 'security' matter. The generals invariably win these wars: it is the politicians who lose them.

The riots and explosions therefore must be the work of malignant forces, usually working for a hostile 'foreign' power. The terrorists are organized in secret, hermetically sealed groups who rule the peace-loving majority by terror. They cannot be prosecuted in the courts, since no one will dare give evidence against them. It cannot be admitted that the reluctance of witnesses may be due to sympathy with the rebels; or that reprisals against collaborators could under different circumstances be translated as punishment for treason. Emergency measures suspending civil liberties are introduced. Members of the supposed organizations are rounded up and herded into internment camps. Torture is usually resorted to in order to discover information about their membership and composition, armaments and supply lines.

Of course, such organizations do exist in most colonial or quasi-colonial situations. They are implicit in the repressive measures adopted by the régime where all opposition activity is banned or driven underground, and where anyone intending to pursue political objectives is bound to resort to secrecy. Bombings, murders and other acts of violence are also of frequent occurrence: they are resorted to initially when the militants among the majority believe their aims cannot be achieved by other means. Violence is also endemic in certain political cultures, either for historical reasons prior to colonization, or by borrowing the methods of the occupying power. The manifest violence of the nationalists feeds on the latent violence of the military. Nevertheless, in its early stages it tends to be sporadic and unstructured, and relatively spontaneous. It is the military repression which creates the need for strategy, and the strategy which in turn creates the need for a secret, centrally controlled organization. The military, in effect, creates its own mirror-image in the rebel organization.

Military theorists, however, tend to postulate the rebel organization as antecedent to the activities they attribute to it. The notion that the initial violence may be relatively uncoordinated and spontaneous and symptomatic of a deep malaise within certain sections of the community would threaten their sense of moral superiority. Moreover, the complex behavioural patterns involved in localized and sporadic acts of violence do not fit the more rigid cast of mind of those charged with the control of conventional armies. In most countries hierarchical relationships in every branch of civil life have been under attack for a century or more. Because of the exigencies of war, where obedience must be unquestioning and unconditional, the army (or militarized police formation which closely resembles its structure) is almost the only remaining organization where decisions flow in a single direction from top to bottom. Soldiers carry out orders: they do not negotiate with their superiors or belong to trade unions. Inevitably, military theorists with little understanding of politics or civil life are content to see, in the civil opposition with which they find themselves confronted, the reflection of their own hierarchical formation. The 'communist' or other 'subversives' are assumed *a priori* to be organized into command structures. Local or sporadic events are assumed to have been determined by decisions taken away from the centre of events, possibly even in a foreign capital. Rebel leaders of course turn the military point of view to their advantage: it greatly improves their local standing and prestige to be credited with the manipulative capacity to mastermind every local incident or disturbance. Internment in special camps completes the process: with or without torture, these institutions became the training-grounds for rebels, for anyone subjected to a period of imprisonment without charge or trial is likely to emerge with a grievance, the more so if he has been subjected in camp to the influence of more militant fellows.

Once it is assumed that every disturbance or act of violence is the result of conscious planning, pressure for the unofficial introduction of torture becomes irresistible. It is impossible to rule out circumstances in which innocent lives might be saved by the application of torture to the right people at the right moment. Kidnappings, bombings, hijackings and assassinations, the standard tactics of the guerrilla in modern society, all require secrecy and careful planning – the essence of conspiracy. Theoretically, the bomber caught in the act of planting a murderous device in a crowded area could be compelled by torture to defuse it.[26] Torture might also lead the authorities to the supplier of arms or explosives, or to their hiding places. Such arguments are invariably used to justify the introduction of 'special interrogation techniques' under emergency conditions.

In practical terms, the circumstances under which torture can yield the information necessary to forestall an act of violence are extremely limited. How can the authorities know that the man in their custody has the information they want? If they do get the information, will they be able to act on it before it is out of date? In a well-organized guerrilla campaign, arms and explosives are constantly moved from one place to another. 'Bomb factories' can be rapidly disassembled and dispersed as soon as it is known that a member of the team has been arrested. Moreover, the hardened guerrilla or terrorist who continuously flirts with death and even welcomes it is perhaps the least likely of men to speak under torture. Like the Cappadocian bandits, members of underground organizations may learn the techniques of resistance. In practice, then, torture will be most efficacious against the 'softer' targets – the 'fellow-travellers' or sympathizers rather than the militant operators. It is these softer targets who provide the link between the small conspiracies of the militants and the Grand Conspiracy which is uppermost in the minds of the authorities.

The small conspiracies are implicit in the tactical operations of the guerrillas. The Grand Conspiracy is a fantasy in the minds of the authorities, born of a paranoid response to the dissidence around them. The small conspiracies are only one manifestation of a much more general malaise or unrest permeating society, whether this revolves round the struggle for political independence, civil rights, better living conditions or demands for a more even distribution of wealth or property. The Grand Conspiracy is the reaction of the élite groups, especially in militarized societies, who stand to lose by social change. Once torture is institutionalized on the basis of the need to deal with the small conspiracies, the Grand Conspiracy becomes a model of repression to be applied to every contingency. The softer targets embrace an ever-widening circle of people. The 'contacts' of the terrorists who must be arrested and tortured in order to control the security situation eventually include everyone who might possibly have had some remote dealings with them. Lawyers, doctors, poets, journalists, students and scientists are eventually dragged into the net. The Grand Conspiracy takes on an increasingly ideological tone, as a growing proportion of intellectuals are interrogated. 'Foreign' ideas are seen as the source of the poison that is corrupting youth and destroying society. Not only are political or social ideas (whether Marxist or 'bourgeois', depending on the context) attacked, but anything, including religion and psycho-analysis, that could lead an individual to question the prevailing military values. The infantile nature of military repression is sometimes revealed in attacks on young people exhibiting a desire for sexual equality or freedom. The child's primeval fear of its own parents' sexual power is, it has been suggested, the psychic root of all fears of conspiracy.[27] Certainly, the unconscious identification of sexual with political potency would explain the tendency of police and military torturers in many countries to focus on the genital organs of men and women.

Behind the hideous contortions lie the familiar features of paranoid inversion. The torturer sees in his victim the agent of social poison, perhaps even the Enemy of the Human Race. Yet is this not a reflection of his own designation in the eyes of the rest of society, even that which he sabotages his honour to defend? Are not the agonized grimaces on the face of his victim really mirror images of his own hatred of mankind, projections of his inner self-contempt? So it must be also with the Grand Conspiracy in its relations with those institutions whose existence depend upon fighting and rooting it out. For what are these institutions dedicated to the struggle against 'subversion' if not themselves the principal agents of subversion? The Grand Conspiracy is more than the freakish fantasy of deluded inquisitors, soldiers or policemen: it is the scenario according to which inquisitors and police or military terrorists achieve their own subversive aims of subjugating society and destroying the rule of Law in the name of Order. Torture which is invoked to defend the state in effect destroys it. It is the instrumentality by which the real enemies of society, the men in cassocks or jack-boots, attack that invisible solidarity between individuals and groups which is the basis of all social existence, and without which all human beings are reduced to a primal condition of slavery. The vilifying propaganda of these, the real subhumans, which withers and corrupts like poisonous vapours should not delude us. The real devil-worshipper was a Dominican friar, just as the twentieth-century terrorist is usually a man in uniform.

NOTES

NOTES

CHAPTER I   THE ABOLITIONISTS

1   P. Verri, *Osservatzione sulla tortura* (Milan 1803); A. Manzoni, *The Column of Infamy*, tr. K. Foster, with Beccaria, *Of Crimes and Punishments* (Oxford 1964)

2   cited by A. d'Entreves, introduction to Manzoni, *op, cit.*, p. x

3   see also C. Beccaria, *An Essay on Crimes and Punishment* (London 1769, commentary by Voltaire); *ibid. dei delitti e delle pene* (Milan 1961 with letters of Beccaria, Alessandro and Pietro Verri); C. Cantu, *Beccaria et le droit pénal*, tr. Lacointa and Delpech (Paris 1885); M. Maestro, *Voltaire and Beccaria as Reformers of Criminal Law* (New York 1942)

4   Beccaria in Manzoni, *op. cit.*, p. 13

5   *ibid.*, p. 38

6   *ibid.*, p. 85

7   A. d'Entreves, *ibid.*, p. xi

8   *ibid.*, p. 31

9   *ibid.*, p. 33

10 *ibid.*

11 *ibid.*, p. 34

12 *ibid.*

13 *ibid.*, p. 35

14 *ibid.*

15 *ibid.*, p. 32

16 *ibid.*, p. 36

17 Montesquieu, *Esprit des Lois*, VII, 7

18 Voltaire, *Memoires d'Elizabeth Canning* (London 1762), p. 5

19 Voltaire in Beccaria, *op. cit.* (London 1769), pp. 40–1

20 Maestro, *op. cit.*, p. 28

21 Maestro, *op. cit.*, p. 34

22 W. E. H. Lecky, *History of the Rise and Influence of the Spirit of Rationalism in Europe* (London 1913), vol. i, p. 333

23 cited in Manzoni, *op. cit.*, p. 124
24 Bentham, *Works*, ed. Bowring (Edinburgh 1843), vol. i, p. 414
25 Manzoni, *op. cit.*, p. 105
26 *ibid.*
27 Bentham MSS (University College, London), cited in W.L. and P.E.Twining, 'Bentham on Torture', *Northern Ireland Legal Quarterly* (1973), vol. 24, no. 3, pp. 305-56
28 *ibid.*, p. 308
29 *ibid.*, p. 309
30 Bentham, *Works*, vol. i, p. 393
31 Bentham in Twining, *op. cit.*, p. 311
32 *ibid.*, p. 334
33 *ibid.*, p. 336
34 *ibid.*, p. 337
35 *ibid.*, p. 338

CHAPTER 2   TORTURE IN THE ANCIENT WORLD

1 G. Maspero, *Hist. ancienne des peuples de l'orient* (Paris 1875), p. 220
2 M.I.Finley in M.I.Finley (ed.), *Slavery in Classical Antiquity* (Cambridge 1961), p. 60
3 Thucydides, *History*, VII, 86
4 H.R.W.Harrison, *The Law of Athens* (Oxford 1969), vol. ii, pp. 147-50
5 Aristophanes, *The Frogs*, II, 6.v.ff.
6 Aristotle, *Rhetoric*, I, xv, 26
7 Lycurgus, *Against Leocrates*, tr. J. Burtt (Oxford 1954)
8 Antiphon, *On the Choreutes*, tr. K.Maidment (Oxford 1941), 23-5
9 *ibid.*, *On the Murder of Herodes*, 31-2
10 cf. J.W.Headlam, 'Slave torture in Attic law', *Classical Review* (1893), vol. vii, p. 2. For contrary views, see J.Lipsius, *Das Attische Recht* (Leipzig 1905-8), p. 889 n. 91; J.Thomson in *Classical Review*, vol. viii, p. 136
11 Cicero, *De partitionibus oratoriis*, 34; cited in *Encyclopaedia Britannica* (11th ed., 1910), s.v. Torture, n. 14
12 H.C. Lea, *Superstition and Force* (Philadelphia 1892), p. 433
13 Valerius Maximus, III, chs 4, 5, 6
14 Andocides, *On the Mysteries* and *On the Return* (ed. Macdowell, Oxford 1962), p. 175
15 see H. Levy-Bruhl in Finley, *op. cit.*, p. 161
16 Finley, *op. cit.*, p. 55, ff.; see also R. Schlaifer, *ibid.*, p. 110; Levy-Bruhl, *ibid.*, pp. 151-69 passim
17 see P. Garnsey, *Social Status and Legal Privilege in the Roman Empire* (Oxford 1970), pp. 122 ff.; 221 ff.; 280 and passim
18 Digest 48.18.1; 27.8

19 *ibid.*, 48.18
20 *ibid.*, 48.18.1
21 *ibid.*, 24.18.4
22 *ibid.*, 48.18.27.20
23 *ibid.*, 48.18.17
24 *ibid.*, 48.18.5
25 *ibid.*, 48.18.1.5
26 *ibid.*, 48.18.1.19; cf. W.W. Buckland, *The Roman Law of Slavery* (Cambridge 1908), pp. 87–91
27 Digest 48.18.1 ; 23
28 Cicero, *Pro Sulla*, ch. 28
29 Quintilian, *De Institutione Oratoria*, V, 4
30 Digest 48.18.9; Garnsey, *op. cit.*, p. 216
31 *ibid.*, p. 216
32 *ibid.*, pp. 142, 246
33 *ibid.*, p. 110
34 T. Mommsen, *Le Droit Penal Romain*, tr. Duquesne (Paris 1907), vol. i, pp. 233–7
35 see also *Dictionnaire des antiquités grecques et romains*, (ed. Daremberg and Saglio, Paris 1875), s.v. majestas, perduellio
36 Cicero, *In Catilinam* IV, cited by A. Mellor, *La Torture* (Paris 1961), p. 48
37 Suetonius, *Augustus*, ch. xxvii; Tacitus, *Annals*, ii, 30
38 Suetonius, *Tiberius*, ch. lxii
39 *ibid.*, *Caligula*, ch. xxxii
40 *ibid.*, *Claudius*, ch. xxxiv; Cassius Dio 60.15.6; Garnsey, *op. cit.*, pp. 143–4
41 Tacitus, *Annals*, xi, 22; Garnsey, *op. cit.*, p. 145
42 Tacitus, *Annals*, xv, 56
43 *ibid.*, 16, 20; Garnsey, *op. cit.*, p. 145
44 *ibid.*, p. 107
45 Digest 48.18.12; 48..1.1.13; Garnsey, *op. cit.*, p. 215
46 Digest 48.18.1.27.10.1
47 see Daremberg and Saglio, *op. cit.*, s.v. majestas
48 Tacitus, *Annals*, xv, 44
49 Tertullian, *Apologeticus*, ii, 10
50 Mommsen, *op. cit.*, vol. i, pp. 233–7
51 Levy-Bruhl in Finley, *op. cit.*, p. 152
52 see F.H. Cramer, 'The Caesars and the Stars' in *Seminar* (1952), vol. x, p. 24
53 *ibid.*, p. 4
54 Tacitus, *Annals*, xvi, 31 ; Cramer, *op. cit.*, p. 9

55 Cramer, *op. cit.*, p. 53
56 Clyde Pharr, 'The interdiction of magic in Roman Law' in *Transactions of the American Philological Society* (1932), vol. 63, p. 282
57 cited in Pharr, *op. cit.*, p. 283
58 *ibid.*, p. 284
59 *ibid.*, p. 290
60 Emile Durkheim, *The Rules of Sociological Method* (8th ed.), cited in Finley, *op. cit.*, p. 70
61 *ibid.*
62 see chapter 4
63 Finley, *op. cit.*, p. 68
64 F. Douglass, *My Bondage and My Freedom* (New York 1855), pp. 263–4; cited in Finley, *op. cit.*, p. 67
65 Lipsius, *op. cit.*, p. 890 ff.
66 Headlam, *op. cit.*, p. 2
67 cf. Manzoni, *op. cit.*, p. 161
68 Buckland, *op. cit.*, pp. 36, 91
69 see R. Schlaifer in Finley, *op. cit.*, pp. 93–132 passim

CHAPTER 3 THE INQUISITORIAL PROCESS

1 H.C. Lea, *Superstition and Force* (Philadelphia 1898), p. 477
2 Augustine, *City of God*, XIX, vi
3 Lea, *op. cit.*, p. 478
4 cited in C. Cantu, *Beccaria et le droit penal*, tr. Lacointa and Delpech (Paris 1885), p. 35; A. Mellor, *La Torture* (Paris 1961), p. 142
5 Gratian, *Decretum* V, 5, iv; Lea, *op. cit.*, p. 478; Mellor, *op. cit.*, p. 101
6 M. Bloch, *Slavery and Serfdom in the Middle Ages* (Los Angeles 1975), p. 25
7 *ibid.*, pp. 1–31 passim
8 Lea, *op. cit.*, p. 451–3; A. Esmein, *History of Continental Criminal Procedure* (New York 1911), p. 108
9 Lea, *op. cit.*, p. 1–99 passim
10 *ibid.*, pp. 249–428 passim; J.W. Baldwin, 'The intellectual preparation for the canon of 1215 against ordeals' in *Speculum* (Oct. 1961) vol. 36, pp. 613–36
11 C. Pharr, 'The interdiction of magic in Roman Law' in *Transactions of the American Philological Society*, (1932) vol. 63, p. 271
12 Baldwin, *op. cit.*, p. 628; Matt. IV, 7; cf. Deut, VI, 16
13 Baldwin, *op. cit.*, p. 629
14 Lea, *op. cit.*, pp. 279, 304, 312
15 *ibid.*, p. 410; H.C. Lea, *History of the Inquisition of the Middle Ages* (London 1888), vol. i, p. 308
16 Lea, *Superstition and Force*, p. 411

17   *ibid.*
18   Baldwin, *op. cit.*, pp. 631–6 passim
19   *ibid.*
20   Esmein, *op. cit.*, pp. 111, 112
21   see P. Parfouru, *La torture en Bretagne* (Rennes 1896)
22   Esmein, *op. cit.*, p. 78 ff.; Lea, *Inquisition*, vol. i, p. 312
23   *ibid.*, p. 311
24   *Livre de Jostice et de Plet*, XIX, 44.8; cited in Esmein, *op. cit.*, p. 98–9
25   cf. Esmein, *op. cit.*, p. 52
26   W. Ullmann, 'Reflections on Medieval Torture' in *Judicial Review*, 56 (Dec. 1944), no. 3, p. 123 ff.
27   Mellor, *op. cit.*, p. 77
28   Bloch, *op. cit.*, p. 161
29   Esmein, *op. cit.*, p. 110; cf. Tanon, *Histoire des tribunaux de l'inquisition en France* (Paris 1893), p. 363
30   Esmein, *op. cit.*, p. 110
31   Lea, *Superstition and Force*, p. 490
32   *ibid.*
33   J. H. Langbein, *Prosecuting Crime in the Renaissance* (Cambridge, Mass. 1974), pp. 158–9
34   *ibid.*, p. 157
35   *ibid.*, passim
36   E. Schmidt, *Inquisitionsprozess und Rezeption* (Leipzig 1940), p. 32; cited by Langbein, *op. cit.*, p. 149
37   Langbein, *op. cit.*, p. 151
38   G. Dahm, *Untersuchungen zur Verfassungs—und Strafrechtsgesichte der italienischen Stadt im Mittelalter* (Hamburg 1941), pp. 30–56 passim; cited by Langbein, *op. cit.*, p. 151
39   Esmein, *op. cit.*, p. 52
40   cf. *ibid.*, p. 52
41   Lea, *Inquisition*, vol. i, pp. 320–2
42   Eymericus, *Directorium Inquisitorum*, with commentary by Pegna (Rome 1578), p. 313
43   *ibid.*, p. 229
44   J. Damhouder, *Rerum Praxis Criminalium* (Antwerp 1554) chs. 35–9
45   cf. Bentham, *Works*, ed. Bowring (Edinburgh 1843), vol. i, p. 525
46   Damhouder, *op. cit.*, ch. 37
47   *ibid.*
48   *ibid.* ch. 38
49   Lea, *Inquisition*, vol. i, pp. 310, 457
50   Eymericus, *op. cit.*, p. 313
51   *ibid.*, p. 314

52   Damhouder, *op. cit.*, ch. 37

53   P. Grillandus, *De Quaestionibus et tortura*, Zilettus, *Tractatus illustrium &c* (Venice 1584), vol. xii

54   H. de Marsiliis, *Tractatus de Quaestionibus &c* (1524), fol. 5 ff.

55   H. de Marsiliis, Singularia, no. 455 (Venice 1555); cited in Lea, *Superstition and Force*, p. 539

56   J. Grevius, *Tribunal Reformatum* (1767), p. 561 ff.

57   cited in Esmein, *op. cit.*, p. 235

58   *ibid.*, pp. 235–6

59   Muyart de Vouglans, *Institutes de droit criminel* (Paris 1757), p. 403; cited in Esmein, *op. cit.*, pp. 235–6

60   Langbein, *op. cit.*, pp. 160–2

61   *ibid.*, p. 140

62   *ibid.*, pp. 179–80

63   *ibid.*, p. 183

64   *ibid.*, p. 184

65   cited in G. Verdène, *La torture [etc.] dans la justice allemande* (Paris 1906), p. 232

66   H.C. Lea, *History of the Inquisition of Spain* (London 1911), vol. iii, p. 33

67   Damhouder, ch. 37

68   *ibid.*

69   H. de Marsiliis, Tractatus, *loc. cit.*

70   Grillandus, *op. cit.*

71   Grevius, *op. cit.*, p. 561 ff.

72   A. Nicolas, *Dissertation Morale et Juridique sur la torture* (Antwerp 1681), p. 21; cited by Lea, *Superstition and Force*, p. 535

73   A. Macfarlane, *Witchcraft in Tudor and Stuart England* (London 1970), p. 139 ff.

74   Eymericus, *op. cit.*, p. 314

75   Tanon, *op. cit.*, pp. 377–80

76   cf. Bentham, *Works*, vol. i, p. 393

77   Tanon, *op. cit.*, p. 378

78   H. C. Lea, *Materials towards a History of Witchcraft*, edited and arranged by A. C. Howland (Philadelphia 1939), p. 554 ff.

79   Damhouder, *op. cit.*, ch. 38

80   Lea, *Superstition and Force*, p. 549

81   *ibid.*, p. 558

82   Eymericus, *op. cit.*, p. 314

83   Lea, *Superstition and Force*, p. 549

84   *ibid.*, p. 550

85   Esmein, *op. cit.*, pp. 270–1

86   Lea, *Superstition and Force*, p. 520

87 *ibid.*, p. 521
88 Digest 48.18.16.1
89 Esmein, *op. cit.*, p. 137

CHAPTER 4   THE ALBIGENSIAN CRUSADE

1   for the Albigensian war, see H.C. Lea *History of the Inquisition of the Middle Ages* (Longon 1911), vol. ii, pp. 1–110; Z. Oldenbourg, *Massacre at Montsegur* (London 1961)
2   J. Guiraud, *The Medieval Inquisition*, tr. E. C. Messenger (London 1929), p. 29; Lea, *op. cit.*, vol. i, pp. 69–71
3   Guiraud, *op. cit.*, p. 29
4   H. Maisoneuve 'Études sur l'origine de l'inquisition' in *L'Église et l'état au moyen age*, vii (Paris 1960), pp. 129–35
5   Roger of Hovenden, *Chronica* (ed. Stubbs), Rolls series vol. ii, pp. 150–5; cited in Wakefield and Evans, *Heresies of the High Middle Ages* (London and New York 1969), p. 196
6   *ibid.*, pp. 36, 705
7   *ibid.*, p. 197
8   *ibid.*
9   *ibid.*
10 Lea, *op. cit.*, vol. i, p. 124
11 Oldenbourg, *op. cit.*, pp. 96–7
12 Lea, *op. cit.*, vol. i, p. 249; Oldenbourg, *op. cit.*, pp. 95–7
13 Lea, *op. cit.*, vol. i, pp. 256–7
14 Oldenbourg, *op. cit.*, p. 105
15 Lea, *op. cit.*, vol. i, p. 166, ff.; J.H. Mundy, *Liberty and Political Power in Toulouse 1050–1230* (New York 1954), pp. 60, 74
16 Oldenbourg, *op. cit.*, p. 149
17 *ibid.*, pp. 165–9
18 *ibid.*, p. 198
19 Wakefield and Evans, *op. cit.*, p. 38
20 For Cathars and Waldensians generally, see Wakefield and Evans, *op. cit.*; Lea, *op. cit.*, vol. i, pp. 57–125; A.S. Turbeville, *Mediaeval Heresy and the Inquisition* (London 1920) passim
21 S. Runciman, *The Medieval Manichee* (Cambridge 1949), pp. 12–16, 92–4, 118, 171–3; Wakefield and Evans, *op. cit.*, pp. 17–18
22 N.G. Garsoian, *The Paulician Heresy* (New York 1967) passim; Wakefield and Evans, *op. cit.*, p. 13
23 *ibid.*, p. 18
24 *ibid.*, pp. 7, 26
25 *ibid.*, pp. 7, 8
26 Lea, *op. cit.*, vol. i, p. 62

27 Wakefield and Evans, *op. cit.*, p. 25
28 Oldenbourg, *op. cit.*, p. 43
29 For a summary of recent scholarship on Cathar origins, see Wakefield and Evans, *op. cit.*, pp. 17–23.
30 Lea, *op. cit.*, vol. i, p. 79 ff.
31 *ibid.*, p. 81
32 *ibid.*, pp. 411–13
33 *ibid.*, p. 82
34 Wakefield and Evans, *op. cit.*, p. 38
35 J.B. Russell, *Dissent and Reform in the Early Middle Ages* (Berkely and Los Angeles 1965), pp. 220–1
36 Wakefield and Evans, *op. cit.*, p. 38
37 Russell, *op. cit.*, pp. 220–1
38 *ibid.*, p. 213; Wakefield and Evans, p. 46
39 Lea, *op. cit.*, vol. ii, pp. 149–50
40 Wakefield and Evans, *op. cit.*, p. 46
41 Oldenbourg, *op. cit.*, pp. 90–1
42 Wakefield and Evans, pp. 35, 691
43 Wakefield and Evans, *op. cit.*, p. 35; Runciman, *op. cit.*, pp. 147–8
44 Lea, *op. cit.*, vol. iii, pp. 441, 564
45 cf. Oldenbourg, *op. cit.*, p. 43
46 *ibid.*, p. 231
47 *ibid.*, p. 43
48 Wakefield and Evans, p. 649
49 Oldenbourg, *op. cit.*, p. 48
50 Wakefield and Evans, *op. cit.*, p. 45
51 Oldenbourg, *op. cit.*, pp. 269–71
52 *ibid.*, pp. 275–9
53 *ibid.*, p. 288
54 *ibid.*
55 *ibid.*, p. 306; Lea, *op. cit.*, vol. i, pp. 407–9 passim
56 *ibid.*, p. 438
57 *ibid.*, p. 435
58 *ibid.*, p. 436
59 *ibid.*, p. 441
60 see Tanon, *Histoire des tribuneaux de l'inquisition en France* (Paris 1893), pp. 150 ff., 350
61 Lea, *op. cit.*, vol. i, p. 432; Oldenbourg, *op. cit.*, p. 307
62 Lea, *op. cit.*, p. 431
63 *ibid.*, p. 432
64 *ibid.*, p. 433
65 *ibid.*, vol. ii, p. 31

66 Wakefield and Evans, *op. cit.*, p. 721
67 Lea, *op. cit.*, vol. i, p. 431
68 *ibid.*, pp. 415–16, 421
69 *ibid.*, pp. 418–19
70 *ibid.*
71 *ibid.*, p. 453
72 *ibid.*, p. 421 ff.
73 e.g. A. P. Evans, 'Hunting Subversion in the Middle Ages' in *Speculum*, 23 (Jan. 1958), pp. 1–22
74 cited in E. Vacandard, *The Inquisition*, tr. B. L. Conway (New York 1908), p. 150
75 Lea, *op. cit.*, vol. ii, pp. 68, 71–83 passim
76 *ibid.*, p. 59
77 *ibid.*, pp. 59–60
78 *ibid.*, p. 62
79 *ibid.*, p. 69
80 *ibid.*, p. 71 ff.
81 *ibid.*, pp. 80–1
82 *ibid.*, pp. 86–7
83 *ibid.*, pp. 92–4
84 *ibid.*, p. 96
85 *ibid.*, pp. 97, 425, 293; vol. ii, pp. 96, 97

CHAPTER 5   THE PURGE OF THE TEMPLARS

1 H. C. Lea, *A History of the Inquisition of the Middle Ages* (Philadelphia 1888), vol. iii, pp. 238–329; E. Simon, *The Piebald Standard* (London 1959); Norman Cohn, *Europe's Inner Demons* (Sussex 1975), pp. 75–98
2 Lea, *op. cit.*, vol. iii, p. 243
3 *ibid.*, p. 248
4 Cohn, *op. cit.*, p. 81
5 Lea, *op. cit.*, p. 254
6 G. Lizerand, *Le dossier de l'affaire des Templiers* (Paris 1923), p. 223
7 *ibid.*, pp. 28–9
8 R. Oursel, *Le procès des Templiers* (Paris 1955), p. 223
9 Lea, *op. cit.*, vol. iii, p. 255
10 Oursel, *op. cit.*, p. 227
11 Lea, *op. cit.*, vol. iii, p. 255
12 Simon, *op. cit.*, p. 293
13 *ibid.*, p. 48
14 Lea, *op. cit.*, vol. iii, p. 256
15 Simon, *op. cit.*, p. 95

16 Simon, *op. cit.*, p. 291
17 Lizerand, *op. cit.*, pp. 32–3, 24–5
18 *ibid.*
19 *ibid.*, pp. 26–7
20 Cohn, *op. cit.*, p. 90
21 J. Michelet, *Procès des Templiers* (Paris 1841, 1851), vol. ii, p. 315
22 Cohn, *op. cit.*, p. 91
23 Oursel, *op. cit.*, pp. 24–5; Cohn, *op. cit.*, p. 91
24 *ibid.*; H. Finke, *Papsttum und Untergang des Templerordens* (Leipzig 1907), vol. ii, pp. 342–64
25 Oursel, *op. cit.*, pp. 24–5
26 *ibid.*, pp. 28–39 passim
27 *ibid.*, pp. 24–5
28 Michelet, *op. cit.*, vol. ii, pp. 274–5; Lea, *op. cit.*, vol. iii, pp. 266–7; Oursel, *op. cit.*, p. 27
29 see confessions in Oursel, *op. cit.*, pp. 32–4
30 Finke, *op. cit.*, vol. ii, pp. 316–18
31 Oursel, *op. cit.*, p. 32
32 *ibid.*, pp. 28, 33; Michelet, *op. cit.*, vol. ii, p. 278
33 *ibid.*, vol. ii, pp. 363–4; Oursel, p. 35
34 *ibid.*
35 Michelet, *op. cit.*, vol. ii, p. 305; Oursel, *op. cit.*, p. 24
36 Lizerand, p. v
37 Cohn, *op. cit.*, p. 92
38 *ibid.*, pp. 93–4
39 Lizerand, pp. 70–3
40 *ibid.*, pp. 154–7; Michelet, *op. cit.*, vol. i, p. 36; Oursel, *op. cit.*, p. 58
41 *ibid.*
42 Oursel, *op. cit.*, p. 64
43 Cohn, *op. cit.*, p. 94
44 Finke, *op. cit.*, vol. ii, p. 332
45 Oursel, *op. cit.*, pp. 66–71
46 Cohn, *op. cit.*, pp. 15–21 passim
47 *ibid.*, p. 21
48 *ibid.*
49 *ibid.*, p. 22
50 *ibid.*, pp. 29–31
51 see W. Sargant, *Battle of the Mind* (London 1957); J. Vernon, *Inside the Black Room* (Harmondsworth 1964)
52 cf. J.-P. Sartre, 'Une Victoire', in H. Alleg, *The Question* (London 1958), p. 19
53 Lea, *op. cit.*, vol. iii, p. 295

54 Lizerand, *op. cit.*, p. 191n.
55 Cohn, *op. cit.*, p. 97

CHAPTER 6 THE GREAT WITCH-HUNTS

1   Text in *Malleus Maleficarum*, tr. M.Summers (London 1948), p. xix
2   H.Erik Midelfort, *Witch-hunting in South-West Germany 1562–1684* (Stanford 1972), p. 31
3   N.Cohn in Mary Douglas (ed.), *Witchcraft Confessions and Accusations* (London 1970), p. 12
4   H.C.Lea, *Materials towards a History of Witchcraft*, edited and arranged by A.C.Howland (Philadelphia 1939), p. 180
5   *ibid.*
6   H.R.Trevor-Roper, 'The European Witch-Craze' in *Religion, the Reformation and Social Change and other essays* (London 1967), p. 156
7   Lea, *op. cit.*, p. 818
8   *Malleus Maleficarum*, pp. 8, 84–5
9   *ibid.*, p. 99
10 *ibid.*
11 *ibid.*, p. 96
12 *ibid.*, p. 26
13 *ibid.*, p. 169
14 *ibid.*, p. 47
15 *ibid.*, pp. 109, 128
16 *ibid.*, p. 25
17 *ibid.*, p. 212
18 *ibid.*, p. 46
19 Lea, *op. cit.*, p. 260; R.Kieckhefer, *European Witchtrials: their foundation in popular and learned culture 1300–1500* (London 1976), p. 20
20 Lea, *op. cit.*, p. 145
21 *ibid.*, p. 151
22 *ibid.*, p. 289
23 *ibid.*, p. 262
24 *ibid.*, pp. 273–4
25 *ibid.*, p. 275
26 cited in N.Cohn, *Europe's Inner Demons* (Sussex 1975), p. 211
27 Midelfort, *op. cit.*, p. 17
28 Lea, *op. cit.*, p. 341
29 *Malleus Maleficarum*, p. 7
30 *ibid.*, pp. 223–7
31 Lea, *op. cit.*, p. 276
32 *ibid.*, pp. 282–4
33 *ibid.*, p. 229, 349–51, 374, 377

34   Lea, *op. cit.*, p. 395
35   *ibid.*, p. 404
36   cf. Midelfort, *op. cit.*, pp. 14–17 passim
37   Lea, *op. cit.*, pp. 554, 557
38   *ibid.*, pp. 554–72
39   *ibid.*, pp. 604–24
40   *ibid.*, p. 644
41   *ibid.*, pp. 417–23
42   *ibid.*, pp. 430–1
43   Midelfort, *op. cit.*, p. 53
44   *ibid.*, p. 106
45   *ibid.*, pp. 98–108 passim
46   *ibid.*, pp. 98–9
47   *ibid.*, p. 129
48   *ibid.*, p. 130
49   *ibid.*, pp. 126–31
50   Lea, *op. cit.*, pp. 524–5
51   *ibid.*
52   K. Thomas, *Religion and the Decline of Magic* (London 1973), p. 693
53   Midelfort, *op. cit.*, pp. 37, 51
54   Lea, *op. cit.*, pp. 648–70
55   *ibid.*, p. 671
56   *ibid.*, pp. 670–87
57   Midelfort, *op. cit.*, p. 28
58   Lea, *op. cit.*, p. 701
59   *ibid.*, p. 705
60   *ibid.*, p. 706
61   *ibid.*, p. 707
62   *ibid.*, p. 708
63   *ibid.*, p. 710
64   *ibid.*, p. 725
65   see R. H. Bainton, *George Lincoln Burr* (New York 1943)
66   C. L'Estrange Ewen, *Witch Hunting and Witch Trials* (London 1929); *Witchcraft and Demonianism* (London 1933)
67   Margaret Murray, *The Witch-Cult* in Western Europe (Oxford 1921); *The Good of the Witches* (London 1931, 1952)
68   Montague Summers, *The History of Witchcraft and Demonology* (London 1926); *The Geography of Witchcraft* (London 1927)
69   Cohn, *Europe's Inner Demons*, pp. 107–21 passim; cf. Alan Macfarlane in Max Marwick (ed.) *Witchcraft and Sorcery* (London 1967), p. 201
70   M. Summers in Introduction to Nicholas Rémy, *Demonolatry* (London 1930), p. xxvi; cf. Cohn, *Europe's inner Demons*, pp. 120–1

71 Bainton, *op. cit.*, p. 470
72 Thomas, *op. cit.*, p. 525
73 Ewen, *Witch-Hunting and Witch Trials*, p. 60
74 M. Hopkins, *Discovery of Witches* (1647), p. 57 ff.
75 A. Macfarlane in *Witchcraft in Tudor and Stuart England* (London 1970), p. 142
76 Thomas, *op. cit.*, p. 531; Kieckhefer, *op. cit.*, p. 29
77 Ewen, *Witch Hunting and Witch Trials*, p. 31
78 Trevor-Roper, *op. cit.*, p. 162
79 Kieckefer, *op. cit.*, pp. 28–9
80 *ibid.*, pp. 32–3
81 *ibid.*, pp. 88–9; Lea, *Materials*, 238
82 Kieckhefer, p. 22
83 cf. Trevor-Roper, *op. cit.*, p. 113
84 H. C. Lea, *A History of the Inquisition in Spain* (London 1906), vol. iv, pp. 244–5
85 Kieckhefer, *op. cit.*, p. 40
86 *ibid.*, p. 41
87 L. Mair, *Witchcraft* (London 1969), pp. 36–47 passim
88 E. E. Evans-Pritchard, *Witchcraft, Oracles and Magic among the Azande* (Oxford 1937), p. 66
89 *ibid.*
90 Mair, *op. cit.*, pp. 10–13, 202
91 Evans-Pritchard, *op. cit.*, pp. 94–8
92 *ibid.*, p. 119
93 *ibid.*, p. 120
94 Mair, *op. cit.*, pp. 102-3
95 *ibid.*, p. 118; Mary Douglas in *Witchcraft Confessions &c*, p. 159
96 Mair, *op. cit.*, pp. 116–38 passim, 203
97 T. O. Biedelman in J. Middleton and E. H. Winter (eds), *Witchcraft and Sorcery in East Africa* (London 1963), p. 76; Middleton in *ibid.*, p. 271; Mair, *op. cit.*, p. 214
98 cf. Mair, *op. cit.*, pp. 161–3
99 cf. E. H. Winter in Middleton and Winter, *op. cit.*, p. 287
100 M. Douglas in Middleton and Winter, *op. cit.*, pp. 123–41
101 Mair, *op. cit.*, p. 44
102 R. Redfield, cited in Kieckhefer, *op. cit.*, p. 94
103 Mair, *op. cit.*, p. 178
104 Thomas, *op. cit.*, p. 594
105 Macfarlane, *op. cit.*, p. 168
106 Thomas, *op. cit.*, p. 594
107 cf. Mair, *op. cit.*, p. 215

108   Thomas, *op. cit.*, p. 669
109   M.G.Marwick, *Sorcery in its Social Setting* (Manchester 1965), p. 221
110   *ibid.*, 'The Social Context of Witch Beliefs' in *Africa* (1952), xxii, p. 232
111   *ibid.*, 'The Continuance of Witchcraft Beliefs' in P.Smith (ed.), *Africa in Transition* (London 1958), p. 112
112   Redfield in Kieckhefer, *op. cit.*, p. 94
113   see D.Herlihy, 'Mapping Households in Medieval Italy' in *Catholic Historical Review* (1972), lviii, pp. 1–24
114   Thomas, *op. cit.*, p. 670
115   Mair, *op. cit.*, p. 203
116   Evans-Pritchard, *op. cit.*, p. 51
117   Biedelman in Middleton and Winter, *op. cit.*, p. 68
118   J.Buxton in *ibid.*, pp. 104–5
119   R.F.Gray in *ibid.*, pp. 166–7
120   Winter in *ibid.*, p. 283
121   J.R.Crawford, *Witchcraft and Sorcery in Rhodesia* (London 1967), pp. 49–54, 114; cf. Cohn, *Europe's Inner Demons*, pp. 220–1
122   G. Mongrédien, *Mme. de Montespan et l'affaire des poisons* (Paris 1953)
123   Mair, *op. cit.*, p. 102
124   Evans-Pritchard, *op. cit.*, p. 26; Mair, *op. cit.*, p. 140 ff.
125   cf. Crawford, *op. cit.*, pp. 59–65

CHAPTER 7   NEAPOLITAN DUNGEONS AND REVOLUTIONARY BROTHER-HOODS

1   W.E.Gladstone, *Two letters to the Earl of Aberdeen on the State Prosecutions of the Neapolitan Government* (London 1851)
2   G.M.Trevelyan, *Garibaldi and the Thousand* (London 1931), p. 62
3   Gladstone, *Two Letters*, p. 9
4   *ibid.*, p. 18
5   Trevelyan, *Garibaldi and the Thousand*, p. 69
6   W.E.Gladstone, *Examination of the Official Reply of the Neapolitan Government* (London 1852), p. 20
7   *ibid.*, p. 27
8   Trevelyan, *Garibaldi and the Thousand*, p. 58
9   Gladstone, *Two Letters*, p. 29
10   R.T.Shannon, *Gladstone and the Bulgarian Agitation* (London 1963), p. 20
11   G.Raffaele, *Rivelazioni storiche della rivoluzione del 1848* (1860), pp. 274–319
12   *ibid.*, p. 305
13   G.M.Trevelyan, *Garibaldi's Defence of the Roman Republic* (London 1928), p. 55

14 Felice Orsini, *The Austrian Dungeons in Italy*, tr. J.M.White (London 1856), p. 74

15 *ibid.*, p. 14

16 *ibid.*, p. 96

17 *ibid.*, p. 117

18 *ibid.*, pp. 28–33

19 *ibid.*, p. 37

20 M.St J.Packe, *The Bombs of Orsini* (London 1959), p. 221

21 *ibid.*, p. 237 ff.

22 J.Gondon, 'De l'état des choses à Naples et en Italie', *Lettres à George Bower Esq., MP* (London and Paris 1855)

23 *ibid.*, pp. 54–7

24 Anon., *A detailed Exposure of the Apology put forth by the Neapolitan Government in reply to the Charges of Mr Gladstone* (London 1852)

25 *ibid.*

26 For a detailed account of the conspiracy theories of the French Revolution, see J.M.Roberts, *The Mythology of the Secret Societies* (London 1974), pp. 146 ff., 155 ff., 217–21, 228–32, 262–3 and passim

27 *ibid.*, p. 58

28 *ibid.*, p. 98

29 *ibid.*, p. 182

30 *ibid.*, p. 227

31 Augustin de Barruel, *Mémoires pour servir à l'histoire du jacobinism* (London 1797), p. xi, cited by Roberts, p. 204

32 Roberts, *op. cit.*, pp. 199–219

33 Joseph de Maistre, *Oeuvres completes*, VIII, 330–3; Roberts, *op. cit.*, pp. 306, 312

34 *ibid.*, pp. 233–48 passim; on Babeuf, see R.B.Rose in *Encounter* (July 1976), pp. 28–36

35 Roberts, *op. cit.*, pp. 331–3

36 *ibid.*, pp. 339–41

37 *ibid.*, p. 315

38 *ibid.*, pp. 356–7; cf. E.J.Hobsbawm, *Primitive Rebels* (Manchester 1957), pp. 156–62

39 Roberts, *op. cit.*, pp. 346–7

40 Roberts, *op. cit.*, pp. 34–5

41 Roberts, *op. cit.*, p. 299

42 E.L.Eisenstein, *The First Professional Revolutionist: Filippo Michele Buonarotti* (Cambridge, Mass. 1959), p. 48; cited by Roberts, p. 282

43 Hobsbawm, *Primitive Rebels*, p. 169

44 in Victor Schloecher, *Le gouvernement du 2 décembre* (London 1853), p. 2

45 cf. Hobsbawm, *Primitive Rebels*, p. 166. Hobsbawm argues that the

lengthy and elaborate rituals of the Carbonari were 'standing invitations to police infiltration'.

46   George Rudé, *The Crowd in the French Revolution* (Oxford 1959), p. 193
47   Honoré Riouffe, in *Mémoires sur les prisons* (Paris 1823), Vol. i, p. 36
48   V. Mongey, 'Les horreurs des prisons d'Arras', in *ibid*. vol. ii, pp. 336, 347, 355
49   Donald Greer, *The Incidence of Terror during the French Revolution* (Harvard 1935), p. 121
50   Mongey in *Mémoires*, Vol. ii, p. 504
51   Riouffe in *Mémoires*, Vol. i, p. 56
52   Greer, *op. cit.*, p. 74
53   *ibid.*, pp. 117, 120
54   *ibid.*, pp. 76, 77
55   *ibid.*, pp. 33–7
56   *ibid.*, pp. 117, 122
57   *ibid.*, p. 123
58   *ibid.*, p. 121
59   'Tableau historique de la maison lazare', in *Mémoires*, vol. i, pp. 237, 245
60   P. de Polnay, *Napoleon's Secret Police* (London 1970), pp. 8, 38
61   *ibid.*, p. 44
62   *ibid.*, p. 198
63   P. H. Stead, *The Police of Paris* (London 1957), pp. 31, 40, 51, 81, 83
64   A. Mellor, *Je denonce la torture* (Paris 1972), citing G. Lenotre, *Georges Cadoudal* (Paris 1929), p. 193
65   Stead, *op. cit.*, pp. 90, 117
66   *ibid.*, p. 126
67   V. Schloecher, *Le gouvernement du 2 décembre*, p. 11
68   *ibid.*, p. 31
69   *ibid.*, p. 38
70   Stead, p. 135; higher casualty figures are given in P. Lissagaray, *History of the Commune of 1871*, tr. Eleanor Marx Aveling (London 1886), pp. 442, 458
71   Lissagaray, *op. cit.*, p. 411
72   *ibid.*, p. 412
73   C. Gavan Duffy, *Young Ireland* (1880), cited by George Sigerson in *Political prisoners at home and abroad* (London 1890), p. 28
74   Sigerson, *op. cit.*, pp. 52, 56, 57
75   C. Dickens, *American Notes* (London 1842), p. 70
76   Sigerson, *op. cit.*, pp. 157–8
77   see I. Butt, *Ireland's appeal for Amnesty* (1870), p. 70
78   Sigerson, *op. cit.*, p. 62
79   *ibid.*, pp. 152, 160

80 Lissagaray, *op. cit.*, p. 490
81 cf. Hannah Arendt, *The Origins of Totalitarianism* (London 1958), ch. 9; see also alternative title *The Burden of our Time*
82 Gladstone, *Two Letters*, p. 51

CHAPTER 8   THE MADRAS REVELATIONS

1 *Report of the Commissioners for investigating the alleged cases of torture in Madras with correspondence relating thereto* (Fort St George 1855), pp. 3, 5
2 *Hansard*, 11 July 1854, p. 61; *Calcutta Review*, no. 29 (1857), p. 442
3 *The Times*, 11 July 1855
4 Quoted by H.Arendt, *Origins of Totalitarianism*, p. 183
5 *The Times, ibid.*
6 see *Calcutta Review, ibid.*, p. 439 ff.
7 Madras report, para. 4
8 *ibid.*, paras 6, 32
9 *ibid.*, para. 44
10 *ibid.*, paras 64, 65
11 *ibid.*, paras 6, 28
12 *ibid.*, para. 60
13 *ibid.*, para. 61
14 *ibid.*, para. 26
15 *ibid.*, para. 67
16 correspondence to Madras report, p. 4
17 *Calcutta Review, ibid.*, p. 439
18 *ibid.*, p. 455
19 *ibid.*, p. 160
20 N.Chevers M.D., *A manual of medical jurisprudence for India* (Calcutta 1870), p. 547; Panchkouree Khan, *Revelations of an orderly* (Calcutta 1857), p. 11
21 Chevers, *op. cit.*, pp. 528, 549; Madras report, p. 80
22 Panchkouree Khan, *op. cit.*, p. 38
23 Chevers, *op. cit.*, p. 528
24 *ibid.*, p. 529
25 Macaulay, *Critical and Historical Essays* (6th ed. 1849), vol. iii, pp. 219–358
26 Madras report, para. 87, App. C
27 *ibid.*, para. 60, N
28 *ibid.*, pp. 2–33 passim
29 Anon, *Police torture and murder in Bengal* (Calcutta 1861), p. 2 [India Office Library]
30 *Calcutta Review* (1885), vol. 80, p. 83
31 *ibid.*, p. 76

32 *Calcutta Review* (1885), vol. 80, p. 85

33 *ibid.*, p. 131

34 *ibid.*, p. 291

35 Panchkouree Khan, *op. cit.*, p. 43

36 *Calcutta Review*, *ibid.*, pp. 109, 290

37 *ibid.*, pp. 6, 294

38 see J.C.Curry, *The Indian Police* (London 1932), p. 24; J.C.Arthur, *Reminiscences of an Indian Police Officer* (London 1894), pp. 109–11; Ram Gopal, *How India Struggled for Freedom* (London and Bombay 1967), pp. 46, 111, 118; *Report of the Committee Appointed to Investigate Revolutionary Conspiracies in India*, cd 9190 (1918) (Rowlatt report), p. 19; E.Hobsbawm, *Primitive Rebels* (Manchester 1963), pp. 162, 167

39 *Selections from the Records of the Government of the North West Province* (Agra 1856), p. 101

40 See Stephen, *The Indian Evidence Act 1871* (Bombay 1873)

41 *Report of the Indian Police Commission and Resolution of the Government of India*, cd 2478 (London 1905), para. 23

42 *ibid.*, para. 26

43 *ibid.*, para. 12

44 *ibid.*, para. 26

45 *ibid.*, para. 163

46 *ibid.*, para. 32

47 *ibid.* (resolution), paras 7, 9

48 F.C.Mackarness, *Methods of the Indian Police in the Twentieth Century* (1910); Reprinted by the Hindu Ghadr Office (San Francisco 1915), pp. 16–21

49 *ibid.*, p. 15

50 Gopal, *op. cit.*, p. 189

51 Rowlatt report, p. 88

52 Mackarness, *op. cit.*, p. 13

53 East India Police, *Correspondence relating to confessions of persons accused of criminal offences*, cmd 7234 (1914), para. 1

54 *ibid.*, para. 4

55 Gopal, *op. cit.*, p. 133

56 cmd 7234, para. 5

57 *ibid.*

58 *ibid.*

59 *ibid.*, p. 32

60 *ibid.*, p. 19

61 *ibid.*, p. 22

62 *ibid.*

63 *ibid.*

64   *ibid.*, p. 16
65   Gopal, *op. cit.*, p. 133
66   *ibid.*, p. 25
67   Rowlatt report, p. 88
68   *ibid.*, p. 76
69   *ibid.*, pp. 59–64; cf. *report of Committee appointed to investigate the Disturbances in the Punjab*, cmd 681 (1920) (Hunter report), p. 95
70   Hunter report, p. 57
71   cf. Arthur, *op. cit.*, p. 111
72   *report of Indian Police Commission*, cd 2478, para. 21
73   Rowlatt report, p. 44
74   Arthur, *op. cit.*, pp. 109–10
75   Rowlatt report, p. 76
76   *ibid.*, p. 21
77   *ibid.*
78   *ibid.*, p. 57
79   *ibid.*, p. 89
80   *ibid.*, p. 88
81   *ibid.*, p. 90
82   *ibid.*, p. 45
83   Hunter report, p. 60
84   Hunter report, passim
85   cf. Sir Dingle Foot, 'Massacre that started the ending of the Raj', *Observer Magazine* (6 April 1975)
86   Hunter report, para. 43
87   R. E. H. Dyer, *Statement on the Disturbances in the Punjab*, cd 771 (1920), p. 6
88   Hunter report, p. 30
89   *ibid.*, p. 113
90   *ibid.*
91   *ibid.*, p. 116
92   *ibid.*, p. 93
93   *ibid.*
94   *ibid.*
95   *ibid.*, p. 63
96   *ibid.*, pp. 57, 68
97   *ibid.*, p. 88
98   Gopal, p. 314
99   *ibid.*, p. 329
100 *ibid.*, p. 335
101 *ibid.*, p. 333
102 *ibid.*, p. 351
103 *ibid.*, p. 353

104   A.J.P.Taylor, *English History 1914–1945* (Harmondsworth 1970), p. 324
105   Gopal, *op. cit.*, p. 354; L.Hutchinson, *Conspiracy at Meerut* (London 1935)
106   Gopal, *ibid.*
107   Gopal, *op. cit.*, p. 409
108   cited in Gopal, p. 367
109   Gopal, *op. cit.*, p. 431
110   Gopal, p. 436
111   Hutchinson, *op. cit.*, p. 69
112   *The Times* (27 June 1975)
113   *Hindustani Times* (25 April 1977)

CHAPTER 9   STALIN AND THE RUSSIAN DEVILS

1   G.Katkov, *The Trial of Bukharin* (London 1969), p. 88
2   R.Conquest, *The Great Terror* (Harmondsworth 1971), p. 81
    R.Medvedev, *Let History Judge* (London 1976), p. 165
3   (Nickolayevsky) *Letter of an Old Bolshevik: a key to the Moscow Trials* (London 1938), pp. 34–9; A.Orlov, *The Secret History of Stalin's Crimes* (London 1938), pp. 29–30; Conquest, *op. cit.*, p. 77; Medvedev, *op. cit.*, p. 168
4   Conquest, *op. cit.*, p. 80; Medvedev, *op. cit.*, p. 159
5   W.G.Krivitsky, *I was Stalin's Agent* (London 1939), p. 211
6   *Report of the Court Proceedings in the Case of the Anti-Soviet 'Bloc of Rights and Trotskyites'* (Moscow 1938), English ed.; cited as *Bukharin trial*, pp. 375–76
7   (Nikolayevsky), *op. cit.*, p. 43
8   *ibid.*, p. 24–5
9   L.Schapiro, *The Communist Party of the Soviet Union* (London 1963), p. 339
10   (Nikolayevsky), *op. cit.*, p. 8
11   *ibid.*, p. 19; Conquest, *op. cit.*, p. 52 ff.; Medvedev, *op. cit.*, p. 157
12   B.Wolfe, *Kruschev and Stalin's Ghost*, including text of Kruschev's Secret Report to the XXth Congress of the CPSU (London 1957), p. 128
13   Medvedev, *op. cit.*, p. 159
14   (Nikolayevsky), *op. cit.*, p. 39
15   Conquest, *op. cit.*, pp. 83–4
16   *ibid.*, p. 90; Medvedev, *op. cit*, p. 163
17   *Report of Court Proceedings: The Case of the Trotskyite–Zinovievite Centre* (Moscow 1936), English ed.; cited as *Zinoviev trial*
18   Conquest, *op. cit.*, p. 141
19   *ibid.*, pp. 157, 160, 166
20   *ibid.*, p. 147
21   Orlov, *op. cit.*, p. 176
22   Conquest, *op. cit.*, p. 171; Orlov, *op. cit.*, pp. 56–7

23 *Report of the Court Proceedings in the Case of the Anti-Soviet Trotskyite Centre* (Moscow 1937), English ed.; cited as *Pyatakov trial*

24 *Zinoviev trial*, p. 81

25 Conquest, *op. cit.*, p. 233

26 *ibid.*, p. 732

27 A. Solzhenitsyn, *The Gulag Archipelago* (London 1974), vol. i, pp. 374–5

28 *ibid.*, p. 394

29 Conquest, *op. cit.*, p. 225; Medvedev, *op. cit.*, p. 124

30 Medvedev, *op. cit.*, pp. 125–31

31 Conquest, *op. cit.*, pp. 734–6; cf. Solzhenitsyn, *op. cit.*, pp. 376–99

32 *Wrecking Activities at Power Stations in the Soviet Union*, English ed. (Moscow 1933), vol. i, p. 167

33 A. Monkhouse, *Moscow 1911–33 Memoirs* (London 1933), pp. 99–115, 281–325; G. W. Keeton, *The Problem of the Moscow Trial* (London 1933), pp. 1–22

34 *ibid.*, p. 81

35 *ibid.*, p. 56

36 *ibid.*, p. 58

37 *ibid.*, p. 90

38 see also *Arrest of employees of the Metropolitan Vickers Company at Moscow*, cmd 4286; *Further correspondence*, cmd 4290 Conquest, *op. cit.*, pp. 738–40

39 Conquest, *op. cit.*, pp. 258–65; Medvedev, *op. cit.*, pp. 194–5

40 Conquest, *op. cit.*, p. 237

41 *Pyatakov trial*, p. 135

42 Conquest, *op. cit.*, pp. 238–9

43 Orlov, *op. cit.*, p. 119

44 Conquest, *op. cit.*, p. 384

45 *ibid.*, p. 375

46 A. Weissberg, *Conspiracy of Silence* (London 1952), p. 380

47 Conquest, *op. cit.*, p. 380

48 Weissberg, *op. cit.*, p. 311

49 *ibid.*, p. 386

50 F. Beck and W. Godin, *Russian Purge and the Extraction of Confession* (London 1951), p. 47

51 *ibid.*

52 Weissberg, *op. cit.*, pp. 352–5; Conquest, *op. cit.*, p. 419

53 Conquest, *op. cit.*, p. 419

54 cited in Conquest, *op. cit.*, p. 741 ff.

55 cited in *ibid.*, p. 422

56 S. Wolin and R. Slusser, *The Soviet Secret Police* (New York 1957), p. 188; Conquest, *op. cit.*, p. 423

57   E. Lipper, *Eleven Years in Soviet Prison Camps* (London 1951), p. 48; Conquest, *op. cit.*, p. 423

58   E. Ginzberg, *Into the Whirlwind* (Harmondsworth 1968), p. 88

59   A. Koestler, introduction to Weissberg, *op. cit.*, p. x

60   Beck and Godin, *op. cit.*, p. 102

61   *ibid.*

62   *ibid.*, p. 46

63   Koestler, *loc. cit.*

64   Conquest, *op. cit.*, pp. 702–11

65   Ginzburg, *op. cit.*, p. 324

66   Conquest, *op. cit.*, p. 382

67   American Committee for the Defence of Leon Trotsky (Dewey Commission), *Not Guilty* (London and New York 1938); Conquest, *op. cit.*, p. 670

68   *Bukharin trial*, p. 36; Medvedev, *op. cit.*, p. 175

69   *Bukharin trial*, p. 49

70   *ibid.*, pp. 58–9

71   *ibid.*, pp. 157–8; Medevedev, *op. cit.*, p. 175

72   Conquest, *op. cit.*, p. 510

73   Medvedev, *op. cit.*, p. 87

74   Conquest, *op. cit.*, p. 147

75   Orlov, *op. cit.*, p. 133

76   Conquest, *op. cit.*, p. 149

77   *ibid.*, p. 504

78   *ibid.*, p. 169

79   Orlov, *op. cit.*, p. 283

80   *ibid.*, p. 290

81   Conquest, *op. cit.*, p. 340, 580; Medvedev, *op. cit.*, pp. 219, 311

82   Medvedev, *op. cit.*, p. 174

83   *ibid.*, p. 186

84   F. Maclean, *Eastern Approaches* (London 1949), p. 96

85   *Bukharin trial*, p. 379

86   *ibid.*, p. 395

87   *ibid.*, p. 375

88   *Pyatakov trial*, p. 339

89   A. London, *On Trial* (London 1970); E. Loebl, *Sentenced and Tried* (London 1969), passim

90   *Bukharin trial*, pp. 370–1

91   *Bukharin trial*, pp. 102–3

92   Medvedev, *op. cit.*, pp. 202 ff.

93   cf. M. Fainsod, *Smolensk under Soviet Rule* (London 1959), p. 58

94   Schapiro, *op. cit.*, pp. 394–8

95   Fainsod, *op. cit.*, pp. 165–6
96   *ibid.*, pp. 48–9, 151
97   *ibid.*, pp. 135–6
98   *ibid.*, p. 134
99   e.g. V.Kravchenko, *I Chose Justice* (London 1951), p. 96
100 *I Chose Freedom* (London 1950), p. 217
101 *ibid.*, p. 218
102 *ibid.*
103 *ibid.*, p. 231
104 R.Pethybridge, *The Social Prelude to Stalinism* (London 1974), p. 132
105 Schapiro, *op. cit.*, p. 311
106 *ibid.*
107 H.P.Kennard, *The Russian Peasant* (London 1907), p. 60
108 *ibid.*, p. ix
109 *ibid.*, p. 67
110 *ibid.*, p. 69
111 *ibid.*, p. 70
112 *ibid.*, p. 68
113 *ibid.*, pp. 73–4
114 *ibid.*, p. 118
115 P.Bogatuirev, *Actes magiques, rites et croyances en Russie subcarpathique* (Paris 1929), p. 11
116 *ibid.*, p. 14
117 *ibid.*, p. 20
118 cited in Z.Brzezinski, *The Permanent Purge* (Cambridge, Mass. 1956), p. 86
119 Keeton, *op. cit.*, p. 38
120 Conquest, *op. cit.*, pp. 207–8
121 Ginzburg, *op. cit.*, p. 125
122 Kravchenko, *I Chose Justice*, p. 216
123 Fainsod, *op. cit.*, pp. 161–2
124 for Marxism and Soviet Law, see J.Hazard, *Law and Social Change in the USSR* (London 1953); cf. M.Damaska, 'Evidentiary barriers to conviction and two models of criminal procedure' in *University of Pennsylvania Law Review* (Jan 1973), 121, no. 3, pp. 506–89 passim
125 R.Pipes, *Russia under the Old Regime* (London 1974), p. 158
126 Beck and Godin, *op. cit.*, p. 57
127 Medvedev, *op. cit.*, p. 263
128 Conquest, *op. cit.*, p. 102
129 *ibid.*
130 Solzhenitsyn, *op. cit.*, p. 122
131 see G.Popoff, *The Tcheka* (London 1925), p. 289 ff.

132   P.S.Squire, *The Third Department: The Political police under Nicholas I*
      (Cambridge 1968), pp. 1–23
133   see H.C.Lea, *Superstition and Force* (Philadelphia 1892), pp. 578–9
134   R.Hingley, *The Russian Secret Police 1565–1970* (London 1970), p. 54
135   R.Hingley, *Nihilists: Russian Radicals and Revolutionaries in the reign of Alex-
      ander II (1855–81)* (London 1967), p. 103
136   cf. F.M.Dostoyevsky, *Memoirs of the House of the Dead* (London 1911),
      passim
137   for atrocities committed by the White armies, see H.Barbusse, *Les Bour-
      reaux* (Paris 1920); for Bolshevik atrocities, see S.P.Melgounov, *The Red
      Terror in Russia* (London 1925)
138   Melgounov, *op. cit.*, pp. 3–5
139   L.N.Trotsky, *Defence of Terrorism* (London 1935), p. 55 (1st edition,
      published 1921 as *Terrorism and Communism*)
140   quoted by E.H.Carr, *The Bolshevik Revolution* (Harmondsworth 1966),
      vol. i, p. 177
141   *ibid.*, p. 163
142   see chapter 7, p. 181
143   cited in E.H.Carr, *The Soviet impact on the Western World* (London 1946),
      p. 91
144   Pipes, *op. cit.*, p. 233
145   Carr, *Bolshevik Revolution*, vol. i, p. 175
146   *Izvestia*, no. 192 (1918), cited in Popoff, *op. cit.*, p. 233
147   Wolin and Slusser, *op. cit.*, p. 6
148   Melgounov, *op. cit.*, p. 187
149   *ibid.*, p. 39
150   *ibid.*, p. 135
151   *ibid.*, pp. 127–8
152   *ibid.*, pp. 166, 184
153   Carr, *Bolshevik Revolution*, vol. i, p. 174
154   Melgounov, pp. 182–3
155   *ibid.*, pp. 162–3
156   Popoff, *op. cit.*, pp. 68–9
157   *ibid.*, p. 237
158   *ibid.*, p. 244
159   Melgounov, *op. cit.*, p. 147
160   quoted by Melgounov, p. 23
161   *ibid.*, p. 106
162   Solzhenitsyn, *op. cit.*, p. 396
163   *ibid.*, p. 98
164   Medvedev, pp. 111–13; Conquest, pp. 731–2
165   Medvedev, *op. cit.*, pp. 125–31

166   Weissberg, *op. cit.*, pp. 248–9
167   *ibid.*, pp. 243–4
168   *ibid.*, pp. 404–6
169   Beck and Godin, *op. cit.*, p. 188
170   cited by Conquest, *op. cit.*, p. 196
171   Weissberg, *op. cit.*, p. 294
172   Beck and Godin, *op. cit.*, p. 54
173   cf. Brzezhinski, *op. cit.*, p. 131
174   Barrington Moore Jnr, *Terror and Progress USSR* (Cambridge, Mass. 1954), pp. 174–5
175   Z. Stypulowski, *Invitation to Moscow* (London 1951)
176   Lobl, *op. cit.*; London, op. cit., passim
177   Conquest, *op. cit.*, pp. 193, 201
178   see R. J. Lifton, *Thought Reform and the Psychology of Totalism* (London 1961)

EPILOGUE

1   Amnesty International *World Report on Torture* (New York 1976), p. 21
2   see N. Margaree, *Istoria tees Makronisou* (Athens 1966), 2 vols
3   European Commission of Human Rights, *The Greek Case* (Strasbourg 1970)
4   John Calder et al, *Gangrene* (London 1959)
5   Sir William Blackstone, *Commentaries on the Laws of England* (London 1876), vol. iv, pp. 340–2
6   J-P. Sartre, *Une Victoier*, in H. Alleg, *The Question* (London 1958), p. 24
7   *ibid.*, p. 13
8   cf. H. Arendt, *The Origins of Totalitarianism* (London 1958), p. 308 ff.
9   *ibid.*, pp. 185–221 passim
10   H. Rauschning, *Hitler Speaks* (London 1939), pp. 235–6; N. Cohn, *Warrant for Genocide:* The myth of the Jewish world-conspiracy and the Protocols of the Elders of Zion (London 1967), p. 193
11   Arendt, *op. cit.*, pp. 358–60. For an account of the provenance of the *Protocols*, see N. Cohn, *op. cit.*
12   H. C. Lea, *History of the Inquisition in Spain* (London 1906); vol. i, p. 130 ff.
13   *ibid.*; see also C. Roth, *The Spanish Inquisition* (London 1937), passim
14   cf. F. L. Carsten, *The Rise of Fascism* (London 1967), p. 24
15   H. Kraunsnick and M. Brozat, *Anatomy of the SS State* (London 1970), p. 49 ff.
16   see H. Arendt, *Eichmann in Jerusalem* (London 1964), p. 53 ff.
17   International Military Tribunal (Nuremberg 1946), vol. iii, p. 496 ff.
18   *ibid.*, vol. i, p. 233
19   *ibid.*, vol. xxii, p. 537

20 International Military Tribunal (Nuremberg 1946), vol. v, p. 405

21 Arendt, *Origins*, p. 185

22 E. H. Winter in Middleton and Winter, *Witchcraft and Sorcery in East Africa* (London 1963), p. 296

23 cited by R. Hofstadter, *The Paranoid Style in American Politics and other essays* (London 1966), p. 7

24 A. L. Katz, 'A psychoanalytic peek at conspiracy', *Buffalo Law Review*, 20 (1970), pp. 239–51

25 *ibid.*, p. 243; cf. J. Piaget, *The Moral Judgement of the Child* (1965), pp. 61–63

26 cf. Twining on Bentham, *Northern Ireland Legal Quarterly*, (Autumn 1973), vol. 24, no. 3, pp. 346–7

27 Katz, *op. cit.*, p. 43

Index